FALSE IMPRISONMENT

FALSE IMPRISONMENT

Nigel Joseph Ley, Barrister

JORDANS
2001

Published by
Jordan Publishing Limited
21 St Thomas Street
Bristol BS1 6JS

British Library Cataloguing-in-Publication Data
A catalogue record for this book is available from the British Library.

ISBN 0 85308 689 3

Typeset by Mendip Communications Ltd, Frome, Somerset
Printed by MPG Books, Bodmin, Cornwall

PREFACE

The number of people arrested and charged with an indictable offence, rather than merely receiving a summons, increased from 75% in 1992 to 90% in 1996. Against this seemingly inexorable increase must be set out the words of McCardie J in *Heddon v Evans* (1919) 35 TLR at p 643:

> '[The Mutiny Act of 1689] was passed at a time when the rights of personal freedom had been successfully re-asserted in the country. No more cogent weapons for enforcing such rights then existed or can now exist than the writ of *habeas corpus* and the *actions for false imprisonment* and assault.' (Author's emphasis.)

With the above *dicta* of McCardie J in mind, I decided to write a book explaining the citizens' rights of free movement and the limitations placed on exercising them by the power of the police and others to make a summary arrest. What will surprise many citizens is just how many other people besides the constabulary have been invested by Parliament with the authority to apprehend their fellow citizens. Indeed, the reader will discover that he or she is not powerless in the war against crime and can personally take a whole host of suspected offenders into custody and deliver them over to the police or bring them before a magistrate. Most of these powers were put on a statutory footing by the Police and Criminal Evidence Act 1984, the rationale of which was described by Bingham LJ (as he then was) in *R v Lewes Crown Court, ex parte Hill* (1991) 93 Crim App R 60 at 65 as:

> '... seek[ing] to effect a carefully judged balance between these interests [ie the freedom of the individual and the catching of those who engage in crime].'

This book considers and sets out how this balance has been achieved. It also gives guidance as to the remedies available to those who suffer the misfortune of being falsely imprisoned as to the level of compensation they are likely to receive. The amount of damages can be forecast with some accuracy because the Court of Appeal has taken upon itself the task of laying down and enforcing guidelines.

What finally convinced me of the need for such a book were two Court of Appeal cases. First, in *Dodd v Chief Constable of South Wales* (unreported) 3 February 1999, the Court held that the police possessed the necessary suspicion so that the plaintiff had been lawfully arrested for fraudulently using an excise licence – despite the fact that such a crime was not an arrestable offence! Secondly, the comment by Simon Brown LJ in *Burke v Chief Constable of Merseyside* (unreported) 12 January 1999, that it was only after the jury had retired that counsel for the first time raised the fundamental question of whether the misdemeanour for which his client had been apprehended was in fact an arrestable offence.

If this book helps to redress the difficulties apparently encountered by the bar and judiciary, then my purpose will have been fulfilled.

The law is that existing at 1 January 2001 and naturally with references to the Human Rights Act which came into force in October 2000.

NIGEL LEY
Gray's Inn Chambers
Gray's Inn, WC1R 5JA
February 2001

Second floor,

London

WC1R 5JA

England.

CONTENTS

TABLE OF CASES

References are to paragraph numbers.

TABLE OF STATUTES

References are to paragraph numbers.

TABLE OF STATUTORY INSTRUMENTS

References are to paragraph numbers.

TABLE OF OTHER MATERIAL

References are to paragraph numbers.

TABLE OF MILITARY RULES AND REGULATIONS

References are to paragraph numbers.

TABLE OF ABBREVIATIONS

AA 1955	Army Act 1955
AFA 1955/1971	Air Force Act 1955/1971
AFDA 2000	Armed Forces Discipline Act 2000
AHA 1981	Animal Health Act 1981
AIA 1996	Asylum and Immigration Act 1996
AIAA 1993	Asylum and Immigration Appeals Act 1993
ALDA 1979	Alcoholic Liquor Duties Act 1979
BA 1967/1976	Bail Act 1967/1976
CA 1989	Children Act 1989
CA(YP)A 1997	Confiscation of Alcohol (Young Persons) Act 1997
CDA 1998	Crime and Disorder Act 1998
CEMA 1979	Customs and Excise Management Act 1979
CJA 1967/1982/1988/1999	Criminal Justice Act 1967/1982/1988/1999
CJDA 1998	Criminal Justice and Disorder Act 1998
CJ(IC)A 1990	Criminal Justice (International Co-operation) Act 1990
CJPOA 1994	Criminal Justice and Public Order Act 1994
CLA 1967/1977	Criminal Law Act 1967/1977
C(S)A 1997	Crime (Sentences) Act 1997
CYPA 1969	Children and Young Persons Act 1969
DA 1991	Deer Act 1991
DTA 1994	Drug Trafficking Act 1994
EPA 1920	Emergency Powers Act 1920
FA 1968	Firearms Act 1968
FA 1994/1996	Finance Act 1994/1996
F(A)A 1997	Firearms (Amendment) Act 1997
FLA 1996	Family Law Act 1996
F(O)A 1991	Football (Offences) Act 1991
FSA 1989	Football Spectators Act 1989
GA 1831	Game Act 1831
GL(A)A 1960	Game Laws (Amendment) Act 1960
HA 1996	Housing Act 1996
HRA 1998	Human Rights Act 1998
IA 1971	Immigration Act 1971
IAA 1999	Immigration and Asylum Act 1999
LCC(G)A 1894/1900	London County Council (General Powers) Act 1894/1900
MDA 1971	Misuse of Drugs Act 1971
MHA 1983	Mental Health Act 1983
MLA 1892	Military Land Act 1892
MSA 1995	Merchant Shipping Act 1995

NDA 1957	Naval Discipline Act 1957
OPA 1959	Obscene Publications Act 1959
OSA 1920/1959/1989	Official Secrets Act 1920/1959/1989
OWA 1996	Offensive Weapons Act 1996
PA 1952	Prison Act 1952
PAA 1911	Protection of Animals Act 1911
PACE 1984	Police and Criminal Evidence Act 1984
PCA 1953	Prevention of Crimes Act 1953
PCA 1978	Protection of Children Act 1978
PHA 1997	Protection from Harassment Act 1997
PH(CD)A 1984	Public Health (Control of Disease) Act 1984
POA 1936/1986	Public Order Act 1936/1986
PT(TP)A 1989	Prevention of Terrorism (Temporary Provisions) Act 1989 – (this will be repealed by the Terrorism Act 2000 when the latter comes into force in February 2001)
RCCA 1845	Railway Clauses Consolidation Act 1845
RCTA 1888	Railway and Canal Traffic Act 1888
RFA 1996	Reserve Forces Act 1996
RPA 1983	Representation of the People Act 1983
RPA 1984	Repatriation of Prisoners Act 1984
RRA 1871/1889	Regulation of Railways Act 1871/1889
RTA 1972/1988/1991	Road Traffic Act 1972/1988/1991
SA 1887	Sheriffs Act 1887
SE(CA)A 1985	Sporting Events (Control of Alcohol etc) Act 1985
SFFA 1975	Salmon and Freshwater Fisheries Act 1975
SOA 1956	Sexual Offences Act 1956
SOA 1959	Street Offences Act 1959
TA 1870	Tramways Act 1870
TA 1968/1978	Theft Act 1968/1978
TULRCA 1992	Trade Union and Labour Relations Consolidation Act 1992
TWA 1992	Transport and Works Act 1992
VATA 1994	Value Added Tax Act 1994
VFA 1952	Visiting Forces Act 1952
WCA 1981	Wildlife and Countryside Act 1981
the 1987 Regulations	Prosecution of Offenders (Custody Time Limits) Regulations 1987
CCR	County Court Rules 1981
CPR	Civil Procedure Rules 1998
RSC	Rules of the Supreme Court 1965

Chapter 1

HISTORICAL BACKGROUND

1.1 FALSE IMPRISONMENT AS A FORM OF TRESPASS

False imprisonment is both a crime and a tort. In its latter form, it is a species of trespass, which is an actionable civil wrong that developed from the criminal law. Until the Norman Conquest, justice was administered by local courts. The new French rulers extended their power by replacing the old tribunals with their own itinerant judiciary. At first, the jurisdiction of these 'roving' officials was confined to certain types of cases, for example *placita coronae*, but was gradually increased to include the enforcement of the criminal law and the keeping of the Peace, which, with its forfeitures, fines and amercements, was also a profitable way of filling the coffers of the Treasury. At first, the *Pax Regis* covered only certain places at defined times but was extended piecemeal over the years until it covered the whole of the Realm. It was out of breaches of the King's Peace that the law of trespass developed. A useful synopsis is given by FW Maitland in *The Forms of Action at Common Law*[1]:

> 'The new phenomenon appears about the year 1250 and it is an action that might be called an attenuated appeal based on an act of violence. The defendant is charged with a breach of the King's Peace, though with one that does not amount to felony. Remember that throughout the Middle Ages there is no such word as misdemeanour – the crimes which do not amount to felony are trespasses [Lat. *Transgressiones*]. The action of trespass is founded on a breach of the King's Peace:-with force and arms the defendant has assaulted and beaten the plaintiff, broken the plaintiff's close or carried off the plaintiff's goods; he is sued for damages. The plaintiff seeks not violence but compensation but the unsuccessful defendant will also be punished and pretty severely . . . the defendant found guilty of trespass is fined and imprisoned . . . In order to constitute a case for "Trespass *vi et armis*", it was to the last necessary that there should be some wrongful application of physical force to a plaintiff's land or goods or person but a wrongful step on his land, a wrongful touch to his person or chattels was held to be force enough and an adequate breach of the King's Peace. This action then has the future before it.'[2]

> 'From Edward I's day onwards trespass vi et armis is a common action. We may notice three main varieties – unlawful force has been used against the body, the goods, the land of the plaintiff . . . These are the main varieties but the writ can be varied to meet other cases and sometimes states the facts of the particular case pretty fully, eg the defendant has not only assaulted the plaintiff but *has imprisoned him and kept him in prison* so many days. But for a while it seems essential that there should be some unlawful force, however slight, something that can by a stretch of language be called a breach of the peace.'[3] (Author's emphasis.)

---

1   Cambridge University Press.
2   1958 reprint, pp 49–50.
3   Ibid, p 53.

The action was started by a standard writ issued out of the Courts of either King's Bench or Common Pleas. FW Maitland[1] gives an example of such a writ issued by the latter tribunal:

> 'Rex vicecomiti salutem. Si [name of plaintiff] fecerit te securum de clamore suo prosequendo tunc pone per vadium et salvos plegios [name of defendant] quod sit coram justiciaris nostris apud Wesmonasterium [tali die] ostensurus quare vi et armis in ipsum [plaintiff] apud [the location] insultum fecit et ipsum vulneravit imprisonavit et male tractavit et alia enormia ei intulit ad grave damnum ipsius [name of the plaintiff] et contra pacem nostram. Et habeas ibi nomina plegiorum et hoc breve.'

The first recorded case of false imprisonment appears to have occurred some time between 1279 and 1289[2] and arose out of an incident in Lincolnshire that led to Peter of Appleby suing the Lord of Boston Fair (John, Duke of Brittany and Earl of Richmond). It is also interesting to note that it is one of the only two trespass actions published in *Earliest English Law Reports*[3]:

> 'Court of Common Bench
>
> 1278–89.2
>
> Peter of Appelby brought his writ of imprisonment against the bailiff of the Court of Brittany and said that he had wrongfully imprisoned him at Boston fair and had taken goods of his there and carried them off and kept them, viz. a charter and a tally.
>
> *Bereford* made the following answer to the imprisonment. A merchant named S had claimed forty pounds from Peter at Boston fair by deed. Peter had admitted both the deed and the debt. It was therefore adjudged under the law merchant that he be arrested. The law merchant provides that where a merchant claims a debt from another merchant in a fair and it is found that the debt is owed then by judgment of merchants the debt is to be levied from his goods during the fair or goods to the value of the debt (as fairly valued by merchants) are to be delivered to him or he is to find a good surety to pay the debt during the fair. And as he could not do this he was arrested, but without being put in fetters or imprisoned.
>
> *Lowther.* Sir, we tell you that one R de A and another merchant offered to stand surety for the debt and were refused. So we asked for judgment.
>
> *Bereford*: R is a knight of the county and not destrainable under the law merchant. The others offered to stand surety for payment of the debt one year later etc.
>
> *Lowther.* What is your answer to our complaint concerning the taking away of our goods?
>
> *Bereford*: We tell you that some goods of his which were within a day chest that was sealed by himself and six others were held against amercements arising out of this plea as adjudged by the count's court. The amercements of the fair court are part of the profits of the fair which belong to the count.

---

1   1958 reprint, pp 89–90.
2   The exact date of the case is unknown.
3   The Selden Society, 1996, vol II pp 359–60).

Lowther: What warrant do you have for this franchise?

Bereford: The count has sufficient warrant from the King.

Lowther: Sir, we tell you that the jurisdiction of the fair court last only for a specific limited time and that they made the distress after that time. So we ask for judgment.

Bereford: The count's jurisdiction lasts for as long as the fair does.

BROMPTON J: That cannot be, for each fair lasts only for a limited time.

Bereford: It is not our business to argue about the precise limits of the count's jurisdiction. But we tell you that we made the distraint while the jurisdiction was in operation.

BROMPTON J: A good jury will tell us the truth.
So the case went to the jury.'

The background to this case was as follows[1]:

'In an action of trespass brought against the bailiff of the count of Brittany (the earl of Richmond) alleging wrongful imprisonment at Boston fair and the seizure of a charter and tally there, the bailiff justified the imprisonment under the law merchant which allowed such imprisonment where a debtor admitted owing a debt and was unable to pay it, had insufficient goods for it to be levied and could not find sufficient sureties. He also justified the seizure of the charter and tally as within a box which was seized to ensure payment of the amercement adjudged by the fair court. Whether or not the seizure was properly made within the period allowed under the earl's grant of fair jurisdiction was to be a matter for a jury.'

1.2 STATUTORY INNOVATIONS FROM *MAGNA CARTA* TO THE POLICE AND CRIMINAL EVIDENCE ACT 1984

The importance that was attached to the freedom of movement can be seen from *Magna Carta*. Chapter 29 stated:

'Nullus liber homo capitur vel imprisonet ... nisi p legale judiciu piu suo, vel p legem terre.'

By the fourteenth century, false imprisonment was proving a popular action for the following reason.

'Arrests and imprisonments were, of course, enormously frequent during the Middle Ages ... The fact that all these causes of arrest (and more) appear on the plea rolls with such regularity points to the frequency with which suits against public ministers were brought.'[2]

The criminal aspects of the writ of trespass begin to disappear and the payment of a fine (judgment *quod capitur pro fine*) became a mere formality long before

---

1   *Early English Law Reports* (Selden Society, 1996) Vol II, p 391.
2   *Select Cases of Trespass from the King's Courts 1307–1399*, vol 1, pp xxxv–xxxvi, The Selden Society, 1984.

its abolition in 1694 by 5 and 6 Will and Mary c 12. All the technical requirements were swept away by s 3 of the Common Law Procedure Act 1852 whereby no form of action was to be mentioned in a writ, which became a simple writ of summons.

Meanwhile, under the Stuarts, often lip service only was paid to *Magna Carta* so that in 1640 Parliament passed the Habeas Corpus Act whereby it was ordered that, on a complaint being made to the Courts of Common Pleas or King's Bench of an unlawful imprisonment, they were to issue a writ forthwith for the prisoner to be brought before them and to inquire into the lawfulness of the incarceration; and if they were of the opinion that it was contrary to law, they had to order his release.

Originally, the only tribunal of fact in the common law courts was the jury but a relaxation of this rule began towards the end of the nineteenth century and temporary measures virtually stopped its use during the 1939–45 War. Despite the end of hostilities, the jury has not been restored to its previous 'glory' and has now died out in nearly all civil suits. However, because of the importance played by actions of false imprisonment in protecting the liberty of the subject, any party involved in litigation about that tort has an almost automatic right to be tried by 'twelve good men and true'.

Nowadays such actions are almost always brought against the police arising out of an arrest. With the rise in crime, the authority of the constabulary to apprehend suspects has been increased by the legislature. The purpose of the law is:

> 'to balance and maintain the fundamental freedom of the individual, on the one hand, against the public interest of society at large, on the other, of apprehending wrongdoers and suppressing crime',

to quote May J in *Wershof v Commissioner of Police*.[1] The vehicle used to achieve this was the Police and Criminal Evidence Act (PACE) 1984, which is the source of most of the present-day powers of the police. A good insight into that statute was given by Bingham LJ, in *R v Lewes Crown Court, ex parte Hill*[2]:

> 'The Police and Criminal Evidence Act governs a field in which there are two very obvious public interests. There is, first of all, a public interest in the effective investigation and prosecution of crime. Secondly, there is a public interest in protecting the personal and property rights of citizens against infringement and innovation. There is an obvious tension between these two public interests because crime could be most effectively investigated and prosecuted if the personal and property rights of citizens could be freely overridden and the total protection of the personal and property rights of citizens would make investigation and prosecution of many crimes impossible or virtually so.
>
> The 1984 Act seeks to effect a carefully judged balance between these interests and that is why it is a detailed and complex Act.'

---

1   [1978] 3 All ER 540 at 551C.
2   (1991) 93 Crim App R 60 at 65.

1.3   THE PRESENT DAY

PACE 1984 increased the powers of the constabulary to make arrests and both the present Labour and the former Conservative administrations have encouraged the police to use their new powers to the fullest extent. Not to be outdone by the 15% increase (under his predecessor) in the number of adults apprehended rather than summoned for indictable or either way offences, the Rt Hon Jack Straw has given the following advice to the police in Circular 24/98:

> '18. Forces are now advised to summon only in those cases which cannot proceed by way of charge (for example common assault, offensive calls).'

Thus the present Labour government no longer follows the policies advocated by its political predecessor, the Callaghan Administration – the Rt Hon Jeremy Thorpe was never arrested; he merely attended for interview at the police station by appointment and later on received a summons by post to appear at court. Those days are unfortunately long past.

Chapter 2

WHAT AMOUNTS TO AN IMPRISONMENT AND THE *MENS REA* REQUIRED TO BE A TORTFEASOR

2.1 THE REQUISITE RESTRICTION ON THE LIBERTY OF MOVEMENT

An imprisonment is the confinement of a person within a boundary on all sides. In *Simpson v Chief Constable of South Yorkshire*[1], the Court of Appeal approved the description given in Blackstone's *Commentaries*[2]:

> 'Unlawful or false imprisonment consist in such confinement or detention without lawful authority.'

In *R v Bournewood Community and Mental Health NHS Trust, ex parte L*[3], Lord Goff said:

> 'I observe however that ... for the tort of false imprisonment to be committed, there must be *in fact* a complete deprivation of, or restraint upon, the plaintiff's liberty. On this the law is clear. As Aktin LJ said in *Meering v Grahame-White Aviation Co Ltd* (1919) 122 LT 44, 54, "any restraint within defined bounds which is a restraint in fact may be an imprisonment". Furthermore it is well settled that the deprivation of liberty must be actual, rather than potential. Thus in *Syed Mahamad Yusuf-ud-Din v Secretary of State for India in Council* (1903) 19 TLR 496, 497 Lord Macnaghten said that: "Nothing short of actual detention and complete loss of freedom would support an action for false imprisonment".'

In *R v Governor of Brockhill Prison, ex parte Evans*[4], Lord Steyn said:

> 'It is common ground that the tort of false imprisonment involves the infliction of bodily restraint which is not expressly or impliedly authorised by the law. The plaintiff does not have to prove fault on the part of the defendant. It is a tort of strict liability.'

In *R v Francis*[5], the complainant had not been kept in one location but had been forced to drive a car with his captors inside to destinations of their choice and to go to different places. The Court of Appeal rejected the defence argument that because the victim had not been confined to a particular place, there was no false imprisonment. This must be right because at all times his freedom of movement was totally restricted, ie he was not allowed to leave the car.

---

1   [1991] TLR 121.
2   Book III, p 127.
3   [1999] AC 458 at 486C–D.
4   [2000] 3 WLR 843 at 847H.
5   (Unreported) 15 January 1998.

It is not sufficient if there be an unobstructed exit. In *Bird v Jones*[1], the plaintiff had been prevented by the Clerk of the Bridge from using part of the carriage-way on Hammersmith Bridge because seats had been erected thereon to enable people to watch a regatta on the River Thames. The Court of Queen's Bench sitting *in banc* (Lord Denman CJ, dissenting) held that no tort had been committed. In the words of Coleridge J:

> 'And I am of the opinion that there was no imprisonment. To call it so appears to confound partial obstruction and disturbance with total obstruction and deten-tion. A prison may have its boundary large or narrow, visible and tangible, or, though real, still in the conception only; it may be moveable or fixed; but a boundary it must have; and that boundary the party imprisoned must be prevented from passing; he must be prevented from leaving that place within the ambit of which the party imprisoning would confine him, except by prison-breach. Some confusion seems to me to arise from confounding imprisonment of the body with loss of freedom; it is one part of the definition of the freedom to go withersoever one pleases; but imprisonment is something more than the mere loss of this power; ... It includes the notion of restraints within some limits defined by a will or power exterior to our own[2].

> 'If it be said that to hold the present case to amount to an imprisonment would turn every obstruction of a right of way into an imprisonment, the answer is that there must be something like personal menace or force accompanying the act of obstruction, and that, with this, it will amount to imprisonment. I apprehend this is not so. If, in the course of a night, both ends of a street were walled up, and there was no egress from the house but into the street, I should have no difficulty in saying that the inhabitants were thereby imprisoned, but if only one end were walled up ... I should feel equally clear that there was no imprisonment[3].'

That definition was approved by the Privy Council in *Syed Mahamad Yusuf-ud-Din v Secretary of State for India*[4], and has not been altered in modern times. Similar words are still used by the judiciary today to describe its *actus reus*. In *R v Rahman*[5], the Court of Appeal said that it was:

> '[the] restraint of a victim's movements from a particular place. In other words it is an unlawful detention which stops the victim moving away as he would wish to move.'

In *Wright v Wilson*[6], Holt CJ held that there was no false imprisonment if the victim had an unobstructed way out, even though by using that exit he would commit a trespass on somebody else's land. It is submitted that if the only way of escape involved the risk of injury or unreasonable damage to property, it would be another matter. *R v James*[7] held that a victim of an assault was not imprisoned when her fear of moving was simply the by-product of her injuries rather than her assailant's intentional frightening of her in order to detain her.

---

1   (1845) 7 QB (NS) 742.
2   Ibid, at 744.
3   Ibid, at 745–6.
4   (1903) 19 TLR 496.
5   (1985) 81 Cr App R 349 at 353.
6   (1699) 1 Ld Ray, 739.
7   (1997) TLR, October 2.

In *Kuchenmeister v Home Office*[1] immigration officers exercised their power to stipulate in which part of Heathrow Airport the plaintiff (who was German) had to remain, while in transit from Holland to Ireland. (This was a power given to them under art 2(1)(b) of the Aliens Order 1952, SI 1952/160.) The designated location was the immigration hall adjacent to where he had landed and he was not permitted to leave for his embarkation point until it was too late for him to catch his 8.40 pm flight to Dublin. This meant that he had to stay overnight until the next aeroplane took off for that city at 7.45 am the following day. Barry J held that this amounted to the tort of false imprisonment. This was because art 2(1) was intended to enable an eye to be kept on aliens in transit and to prevent them from leaving the airport and staying uninvited in the UK. It did not allow immigration officers to use those powers to prevent a person continuing on to his destination in a foreign country. Thus, having acted outside the powers given to them, the civil servants could not rely upon the Aliens Order 1952 as a defence to an action for trespass.

What has not been decided is whether the area of detention can become so large, that there ceases to be any commission of a tort. Virtually all the cases are concerned with a few acres, for example a prison. The one exception appears to be *Re Mwenya*[2] where the applicant's movement was restricted to some 1,500 square miles in a particular part of his native country of Northern Rhodesia. The Court of Appeal merely decided the action on the grounds that the respondent (the Secretary of State for the Colonies) could not be held responsible for the actions of a colonial government. In theory, the size of the 'prison' is irrelevant. In practice the crucial factor will be where the 'prisoner' can, and cannot, go. Preventing somebody from leaving a defined area, for example Scotland, would probably be a tort, although in view of the size of the area in which the captive could go, any damages would probably be nominal. Restricting a person from entering London would not be considered to be imprisoning him within the rest of the world. The relevant question is whether there is a confinement in a specified location or just a prevention of going to a certain place. The former amounts to tortious conduct, the latter does not. For the view of the European Court of Human Rights as to what is, or is not, incarceration, see **17.2**.

2.2 CONSENT

For there to have been an 'imprisonment', the plaintiff must not, of her own volition, have chosen to remain in a place to which she was in fact free to come and to go as she wished: see *Latter v Braddell*[3] where it was held that a submission through a mistake of law was a voluntary act. Professor Street was of the view that the case was on its facts wrongly decided and can best be understood as the view of the judiciary that, if a servant chooses to inconvenience her mistress by

---

1   [1958] 1 QB 496.
2   [1960] 1 QB 241.
3   (1881) 50 LJ QB 448.

getting pregnant, she has only herself to blame for what has happened; in that case being forced to submit to a medical examination. Although probably not borne out by the facts, the *ratio* of that decision was that where there had been no physical obstructions or obstacles which had to be overcome before an escape could be effected, it was necessary for there to have been some compulsion but that such could be implied by the actions of the tortfeasor and need not have been mentioned explicitly. As Williams J said in *Bird v Jones*[1]:

> 'If the bailiff (as the case is put in Bull NP 62) who has a process against one, says to him, "You are my prisoner, I have a writ against you", upon which he submits, turns back or goes with him, though the bailiff never touched him, yet it is an arrest, because he submitted to the process. So, if a person should direct a constable to take another into custody, and that person should be told by the constable to go with him, and the orders are obeyed, and they walk together in the direction pointed out by the constable, that is, constructively, an imprisonment, though no actual violence is used. In such cases, however, though little may be said, much is meant and perfectly understood. The party addressed in the manner above supposed feels that he has no option, no more power of going in any but the one direction prescribed to him than if the constable or bailiff had actually hold of him: no return or deviation from the course prescribed is open to him. And it is that entire restraint upon the will which I apprehend constitutes the imprisonment ...'

Similar sentiments were expressed by Willes J in *Warner v Riddiford*:

> 'Whilst in the house in a room with the two policemen, he was refused permission to go upstairs; and ultimately he seems to have been allowed to go but accompanied by an officer. I think it impossible that, upon these facts, anyone can doubt that it was meant to be conveyed to the mind of the plaintiff that he should not go out of the presence and control of the police officers. That in my mind clearly amounts to an imprisonment.'[2]

As the case of *Latter v Braddell*, above, illustrates, the judiciary are more reluctant to hold that a person's will has been overpowered and that her actions were not voluntary when the incarceration was alleged to have been done by people who were not officials.

2.3   KNOWLEDGE

However, it follows from the *obiter dicta* of the House of Lords in the Irish appeal of *Murray v Ministry of Defence*[3], that a man can be falsely imprisoned even though he is ignorant of the fact that compulsion would be used, if it became necessary, to compel him to remain where he was. In the words of Lord Griffiths[4]:

> 'If a person is unaware that he has been falsely imprisoned and has suffered no harm, he can normally expect to recover no more than nominal damages, and it is

---

1   (1845) 7 QB (NS) 742 at 748.
2   (1858) 4 CB (NS) 180 at 204.
3   [1988] 2 All ER 521.
4   Ibid, at 529f–g.

tempting to redefine the tort in terms of the present rule in the American Law Institute's Restatement of the Law of Torts [the person is conscious of the confinement or is harmed by it]. On reflection I would not do so. The law attaches supreme importance to the liberty of the subject and if he suffers a wrongful interference with that liberty it should remain an actionable wrong, even without proof of special damage.'

Thus, although an individual has willingly accompanied a constable to the police station in the belief that, should he decline to do so, no further action would be taken by the officer, nevertheless he would now be able to recover damages for his trip to that location, if it should later transpire that, unknown to him at the time, force would have been used to compel him to travel to the station if he had announced that he no longer wished to go there. Indeed, this is more or less what happened in *Meering v Grahame-White Aviation Company*[1], where the plaintiff had voluntarily waited (at his place of work) for the police, unaware that if he had attempted to leave prior to their arrival, he would have been restrained by the security staff. The Court of Appeal held by a majority (Warrington and Atkins LJJ, Duke LJ dissenting) that those facts amounted to the tort of false imprisonment. That case was contrary to the decision in *Herrings v Boyle*[2], where the Court of Exchequer held that knowledge was a *sine qua non* and upheld the nonsuit of the plaintiff. In that case, the headmaster refused to allow the parents of a 10-year-old pupil (the plaintiff in the action) to take him to their residence over Christmas because they had not paid his school fees. To secure his return home, his mother had to obtain a writ of *habeas corpus*, but her son's action for damages failed. There was no evidence that the child knew that he was prohibited from leaving the school. These two conflicting decisions led to a disagreement among academics (accompanied by a number of learned articles as to which of the last two cited cases was correctly decided) which was not finally resolved until the above quoted speech of Lord Griffiths.

2.4 MALFEASANCE OR NONFEASANCE AND CONTRACTUAL OBLIGATIONS

It was laid down by the House of Lords in *Herd v Weardale Steel Coal and Coke Co Ltd*[3] that the imprisonment must be caused by a positive act. In that case, a miner sued his employers. Under his contract, he was working a shift which ended at 4 pm. At 11 am, believing it unsafe to remain underground, he asked to be brought to the surface. The mine owners declined to do this and refused him permission to enter their lift – the only exit – until his shift had ended. (When he had gone into the elevator, the defendants just let it remain where it was.) His claim for false imprisonment failed. Their Lordships held that he had voluntarily gone down and his employers were under no duty to do anything to facilitate his leaving until his contractual hours of employment had terminated. The plaintiff had descended of his own volition and had agreed to work at the

---

1   (1919) 122 LT 44.

2   (1834) 1 Cr M & R 377n.

3   [1915] AC 67.

coal seam until a specified time. It was a case of *volenti non fit injuria*. The Court of Appeal went further and said that even if he had not been brought up at 4 pm, his only remedy would have been an action for breach of contract, not trespass, because his master would not have done any positive act to prevent his servant from leaving the place to which he had willingly gone. In the words of Buckley LJ[1]:

> 'The master has not imprisoned the man. He has not enabled him to get out as under the contract he ought to have done, but he has done no act compelling him to remain there.
>   ... The question is whether the defendants falsely imprisoned the plaintiff. To my mind they did not imprison him, because they did not keep him there; they only abstained from giving him facilities for getting away.'

Thus, the law draws a clear distinction between a positive act and an omission. Only the former can amount to a trespass.

So in *Burns v Johnstone*[2] the Irish Court of Appeal held that it was not trespass for a factory owner to refuse to unlock the gates before the contractual time for the workers to go home, even if one of them wished to leave before then. Holding a person to the agreement into which he has entered cannot amount to a false imprisonment. Thus, in *Robinson v Balmain New Ferry Co Ltd*[3] a passenger had contracted with the owners to enter their wharf and to depart by boat. He then changed his mind and tried to leave the wharf without paying the one penny exit toll charge. He was forcibly prevented from so doing, but the Privy Council held that the defendants were entitled to resist an evasion of their tolls.

In *Toumia v Evans*[4], the Court of Appeal refused to strike out an allegation by a serving prisoner against his warders for trespass, when the latter, during an industrial dispute, had come on duty but had refused to unlock the inmates and allow them out of their cells to be fed, although this was part of their normal duties. Brooke and Clarke LJJ held that it was arguable that those facts did amount to the tort of false imprisonment, and that a final decision on this issue should be left to the trial judge. Indeed, if a person is under a duty to release somebody, then, surely, there is no reason why a deliberate failure to comply with his obligation should not found an action for false imprisonment, just as if he had incarcerated somebody by a positive act rather than by an omission.

It is submitted that such conduct amounted to the positive act of restraining somebody against their will, for example by keeping his or her door locked. In *R v Governor of Brockhill Prison, ex parte Evans (No 2)*[5], the House of Lords accepted without argument that the failure to release a prisoner at the end of her sentence amounted to the tort of false imprisonment – the respondent never suggested otherwise. (The dispute between the parties was whether a mistake of law could amount to a defence – see Chapter 8.) This decision is, of course, distinguishable from *Herd* above, where the only omission was a refusal

---

1   [1913] 3 KB 771 at 789.
2   [1917] 2 IR 137.
3   [1910] AC 295.
4   (1999) TLR, April 1.
5   [2000] 3 WLR 843.

to facilitate the exit of the plaintiff from a location to which he had voluntarily gone; while Ms Evans was at all times being kept in a place against her will.

2.5   A CHANGE IN THE QUALITY OF THE INCARCERATION

In *R v Deputy Governor of Parkhurst Prison, ex parte Hague*[1] it was argued that even though the Home Office was entitled to incarcerate the plaintiff (in that case as a prisoner serving a custodial sentence), nevertheless the quality of his detention could render his captors liable for false imprisonment. That submission was rejected by the House of Lords who approved the dicta of Tudor-Evans J in *Williams v Home Office (No 2)*[2]:

> 'In my judgment, the sentence of the court and section 12(1) [of the Prison Act] always afford a defence to an action of false imprisonment. The sentence justifies the fact of imprisonment and the subsection justifies the confinement of a prisoner in any prison.'

(Section 12(1) of the Prison Act 1952 states that 'a prisoner, whether sentenced to imprisonment or committed to prison on remand or pending trial or otherwise, may be lawfully confined in any prison'.)

In *Ex parte Hague*, above, it was held that no action for false imprisonment would lie against the warders or the Crown no matter how intolerable the conditions were inside the jail. The only remedy would be an action in negligence for breach of the duty of care owed towards the inmates. It would be another matter if the incarceration was not by the prison authorities, for example if some of the convicts had locked up one of their number in a coal shed, then they could be sued in trespass. This latter view found favour with the court in *Toumia v Evans*, above.

2.6   *DE MINIMIS*

In *Christie v Leachinsky*[3], Lord Simonds was of the opinion that if the detention had only been for a minute, it would have been *de minimis* and no action would lie. That *obiter dicta* is at variance with the view expressed in *Bird v Jones*[4] by Paterson J (with whom Coleridge J agreed) that false imprisonment is 'a total restraint on the liberty of the person, *for however short a time*' (author's emphasis). It is submitted that any unlawful restraint should attract an award of compensation; but if it was *de minimis*, then the jury would no doubt only give a nominal sum. In *Frewin v Metropolitan Police Commissioner*[5], the plaintiff had been arrested at his home and taken to the police station where he was

---

1   [1992] 1 AC 58.
2   [1981] 1 All ER 1211 at 1241.
3   [1947] AC 573 at 595.
4   (1845) 7 QB (NS) 742 at 752.
5   (Unreported) 1990.

thereafter lawfully detained for about 14 hours. Popplewell J ruled that because he had not been told the reason why he had been apprehended until his arrival at that location, the plaintiff had been falsely imprisoned in the 20 minutes that it took to get there – for which the jury awarded £1,000 in damages.

2.7 EXCESSIVE DURATION AND TRESPASS *AB INITIO*

If a person is detained for longer than the law allows, he can recover damages for the extra and unlawful imprisonment; see *John Lewis & Co v Tims*[1]. The question of when lawful custody by the police becomes a tort because of its unreasonable duration is discussed at **10.9.3**.

Does this additional incarceration make the whole of the restraint upon one's freedom actionable under the doctrine of trespass *ab initio*? In *Smith v Egginton*[2], the plaintiff was arrested by the Sheriff for contempt of the Chancery Court and was confined in the local jail. Under the legislation then in force, if she was not brought before the Bar of the Court within 30 days, she had to be set free. Neither of those things were done. In law, she was being detained by the prison jailer, who was not the agent of the sheriff, and the latter would have no idea whether or not she was brought up before the Chancery Court. Thus, the Sheriff was held not to be responsible for her false imprisonment. (The jailer would have been liable after the 30 days, if sued; see *Moore v Rose*[3].) The plaintiff had claimed that the sheriff had to compensate her for all her imprisonment because, once part of it became unlawful that made all his actions a trespass from the moment he had arrested her. That was not accepted by the judges. Littledale J said:

> 'The general rule is in the *Six Carpenters' Case* ((1610) 8 Co Rep 146a). Where there is an authority given by law for doing an act, there an abuse may turn the act into a trespass *ab initio*. But the rule does not apply here. The rule is said to rest upon this; that the subsequent illegality shews the party to the trespass to have contemplated an illegality all along, so that the whole becomes a trespass. But here the sheriff could not, from the first, have had in view the detention of the plaintiff after the time should have expired.'[4]

Patterson J concurred:

> 'Then, after a plea in the process, what is the replication? Not that the plaintiff's action is not brought for the act justified in the plea, but that the defendant detained the plaintiff too long. The purpose of this is to show that the defendant is a trespasser *ab initio*. But he clearly is not so. I should say that he is not a trespasser; clearly he is not so *ab initio*. And I doubt very much whether the present action will lie at all; for the rule [about being discharged after 30 days] applies to only two species of contempt. The writ does not show it.'[5]

---

1   [1952] AC 676.
2   (1837) 7 Ad & E 167.
3   (1869) LR 4 QB 492.
4   7 Ad & E 167 at 176.
5   Ibid, at 177.

Thus, the principle of trespass *ab initio* (if still extant) does apply to this tort but, it would seem, only where the same person was responsible for the incarceration both while legal and when it became unlawful. In *Smith v Egginton*, above, the sheriff ceased to be responsible for her detention once he had handed her over to the jailer. Thus, a person who lawfully made a citizen's arrest could not be sued if the policeman to whom he surrendered his prisoner kept that person in custody for longer than was permitted. Also the abuse which nullifies the lawful authority must itself amount to a trespass, though not necessarily of the same species; see *Ward's Case*[1].

The preceding paragraph uses the phrase 'if still extant', as some judges have had doubts about whether it had survived into the twentieth century. Lord Denning MR, in *Chic Fashions Limited v Jones*[2] was of the view that it was no longer part of the common law, but over 10 years later in *Cinnamond v British Airports Authority*[3] he was an enthusiastic supporter of such a principle! The abuse of the original lawful authority must be a positive act and not an omission[4]; see *Blake v Isle of Wight District Council*[5]. Even by the twenty-first century, no member of the judiciary had formally pronounced 'the sentence of death' over the doctrine of trespass *ab initio*, although when it had been raised by counsel it had not been greeted with great enthusiasm. In two cases in the millennium year, a plea of trespass *ab initio* was held not to apply on the facts but the reaction of the judges was the same. In *R v Chesterfield Justices, ex parte Bramley*[6]:

> '... sections 15 and 16 of the [Police and Criminal Evidence Act 1984] were intended to provide a code for the form and execution of search warrants and even if the doctrine of trespass *ab initio* is still alive it could not be prayed in aid to attack an entry of premises to which these sections apply.'

In *Blake v Isle of Wight District Council* (above), Sedley LJ said (at para 28):

> 'If it were not so, the question of trespass *ab initio*, which is canvassed in the local authority's skeleton argument, would arise. While the practical necessity of limiting trespass *ab initio* to acts of misfeasance is evident, the continuing utility of the entire doctrine has been doubted. In the present case there is no need to embark on this issue.'

With due respect to his Lordship, the doctrine does serve a very useful purpose. It acts as a deterrent to prevent the executive from abusing their common law powers which enable them to do what would, when undertaken by others, become acts of trespass. Should servants or officers of the Crown contemplate acting outside the exemption from tortious liability given to them, they are

---

1   (1636) Clay 44.
2   [1968] 2 QB 299 at 313F–G.
3   [1980] 1 WLR 582 at 588.
4   This led to counsel in *Smith v Eggington* (above), to argue that the failure to release a captive whose legal incarceration later became unlawful was a mere omission. The court expressed no view on this topic, but it is submitted that commonsense would suggest otherwise. It was after all the original locking of the gates (a positive act) that caused the physical act of detention.
5   (Unreported) 6 October 2000 (see the quotation below).
6   [2000] QB 576 at 596 (*per* Jowitt J).

likely to desist from so doing by the knowledge they would lose their immunity and all their actions would become tortious, with the result that they would have to pay damages far in excess of what they would have been, if their award had been limited only to what had been done in excess of their lawful authority. In the millennium year, the opportunity for an authoritative ruling by the highest court in the land arose in *R v Governor of Brockhill Prison, ex parte Evans (No 2)*[1] (for the facts, see **8.2** below). However, it was not taken up and no allegation of any trespass *ab initio* was made by the applicant.

2.8 THE MENTAL ELEMENT

The main difference between a civil wrong and a crime is the mental element required[2]. To be liable for a trespass, one must merely voluntarily do the act that constitutes the tort; see *Basely v Clarkson*[3], where the defendant had to pay damages to his neighbour when he mowed part of the latter's lawn, believing it to be his own. As Lord Mansfield CJ said in *Tarlton v Fisher*[4], 'innocence is no excuse'. However, except for a few regulatory offences of strict liability, to be guilty of a crime the accused must have intended all the consequence of his conduct. Thus, in the example given above the *mens rea* for the criminal damage would be: (1) intentionally cutting grass; (2) which he knew belonged to the person next door or was reckless as to whether it did so belong. Whereas in a civil action for that trespass, an innocent intention would be no excuse. This is because:

> '... he that is damaged ought to be compensated. But otherwise it is in criminal cases for there *actus non facit rerum nisi mens sit rea.*'[5]

2.9 CAUSATION

The law must draw the line somewhere as to how far one can ascribe the responsibility for the occurrence of the *actus reus* to the person who is sued because of it. The answer is that liability will only be escaped for a voluntary act if its consequences were an incvitable accident. An example of this is *Stanley v Powell*[6], where the defendant fired at a pheasant and missed, but the bullet ricocheted at a great angle off a tree on to the plaintiff. The action was dismissed as the injury was accidental and there was no negligence in the way the gun had been discharged. In *National Coal Board v Maberley Parker & Co*[7], the Court of Appeal approved the decision in *Weaver v Ward*[8], as correctly setting out the relevant law about causation:

---

1   1 [2000] 3 WLR 843.
2   Chapter 16 of this work is devoted to the criminal aspects of false imprisonment.
3   (1681) 3 Lev 37.
4   (1781) 2 Doug KB 671.
5   *The Case of Thorns* 1466 YB 6 Ed IV, 7 pl 18.
6   [1891] QB 86.
7   [1951] 2 KB 861.
8   (1616) Hob 134.

'No man shall be excused a trespass (for this is the nature of an excuse, and not of a justification, *prout ei bene liculit*) except that it may be judged utterly without his fault.

As if a man by force take my hand and strike you, or if the defendant had said that the plaintiff had ran across his piece when it was discharging or had set forth the case with circumstances so as it appeared to the court that it had been inevitable, and that the defendant had committed no negligence to give occasion to the hurt.'

Chapter 3

DEFENCES

3.1 INTRODUCTION

Lord Hope said in *R v Governor of Brockhill Prison, ex parte Evans (No 2)*[1]:

'The tort of false imprisonment is a tort of strict liability. But the strict theory of civil liability is not inconsistent with the fact that in certain circumstances the harm complained of may have been inflicted justifiably. This is because it is of the essence of the tort of false imprisonment that the imprisonment is without lawful justification. As Sir William Holdsworth, *A History of English Law*, 2nd edn (1937) vol VIII, p 446 puts it:

"A defendant could escape from liability if he could prove that his act was, in the circumstances, permitted by law, either in the public interest, or in the necessary defence of his person or rights of property ..."'

The purpose of this chapter is to consider what justification the law allows for the interference with the free movement of another. They can be classified as follows:

(1) *volenti non fit injuria* (ie the plaintiff was not detained against his will and could have gone elsewhere at any time);
(2) necessity;
(3) duress;
(4) immunity from suit;
(5) confession and avoidance (ie an imprisonment authorised by law – for example, an arrest or detention authorised by statute).

3.2 CONSENT

Consent is usually a good defence to an action for trespass. As to how this general rule applies to that species known as false imprisonment is a topic already considered in Chapter 2.

3.3 NECESSITY

Necessity is an act which was done to prevent death or serious injury, or damage to property and it was reasonable in the circumstances to commit what, but for the necessity, would have been a tort, ie proportionality, to use the language of continental lawyers. It has exculpated those who had detained a mentally ill

---

1   [2000] 3 WLR 843 at 852.

person to prevent him injuring himself or others, see *R v Bournewood Community and Mental Health NHS Trust, ex parte L*[1] and *Scott v Wakem*[2].

3.4   DURESS

An example of duress is where somebody has been ordered at gunpoint to drive the getaway car of a kidnapper and his victim and told that, if he does not do this, he will be shot dead. Whether a threat can absolve liability again comes down to a question of proportionality. In such cases, there are two questions for the jury. The first question is whether the avoidance of the consequences that would otherwise have flowed from the implementation of the threat justified the harm which was caused by the act of trespass; see *R v Martin*[3]. The second question is whether a sober person of reasonable firmness sharing the same characteristics as the defendant would have acted as the latter did; see *R v Bowen*[4]. Also there must have been no opportunity of escaping the consequences of the threat before it could be put into effect.

3.5   IMMUNITY

Legislation has granted certain people immunity from being sued for false imprisonment and this is discussed in Chapter 13.

3.6   LAWFUL ARREST AND DETENTION

These can be categorised as:

(1) a lawful arrest, which consists of the following factors, each of which is discussed in a separate chapter:

    (a)   what constitutes an arrest;

    (b)   what are arrestable offences;

    (c)   when an arrest can be lawfully made by the citizen;

    (d)   the extra privileges of the constabulary to apprehend people;

    (e)   reasonable suspicion – this is usually sufficient, rather than the actual commission of a crime, to justify action by the police; and

    (f)   the reasonableness of the exercise of the power of arrest (just because a right of apprehension exits, its use is discretionary and can be challenged if Wednesbury unreasonable, at any rate if effected by the executive, which includes a constable);

---

1   [1999] AC 458.
2   (1862) 3 F & F 328.
3   [1989] 1 All ER 652.
4   [1996] 2 Cr App R 157.

(2) lawful detention in police custody after the initial apprehension and other powers of restraint vested in the police;

(3) detention pursuant to a lawful order, or sentence imposed, by a court of law; and

(4) detention authorised by an Act of Parliament, for example the Immigration Act 1971 or the Mental Health Act 1983.

3.7 THE DEFINITION OF AN ARREST

The remaining part of this chapter considers what amounts, in law, to an arrest and what is the legal way in which it must be carried out. If the correct procedure is not followed, then the arrest is unlawful:

> 'It is a general rule, which has always been acted on by the courts of England, that if any person procures the imprisonment of another he must take care to do so by steps, all of which are entirely regular, and that if he fails to follow every step in the process with extreme regularity the court will not allow the imprisonment to continue.'[1]

> 'To arrest a person is to deprive him of his liberty by some lawful authority for the purposes of compelling his appearance to answer a criminal charge, or as a method of execution. (1) Arrest on mesne process was to compel the defendant to appear in an action. (2) Arrest on final process was a mode of execution or enforcing judgment by means of the writ of *a capias ad satisfaciendum.*'[2]

In *Mohammed-Holgate v Duke*[3], Lord Diplock said:

> 'First, it should be noted an arrest is a continuing act; it starts with the arrester taking a person into his custody . . . and it continues until the person so restrained is either released from custody or, having been brought before a magistrate, is remanded in custody by the magistrate's judicial act.'

Another description to like effect was given by Avory J in the first edition of *Halsbury's Laws of England*[4]:

> 'The first step in the ordinary course of criminal proceedings is to bring a person charged with a crime before a justice or justices of the peace in order that the charge may be investigated. The attendance of an accused person before justices is secured, either by summons or by arrest, either under or without a warrant.'

Nowadays, an arrest of a person who has not been caught *in flagrante delicto* will usually be made in order to question him under the pressure of hostile surroundings, see *Mohamed-Holgate v Duke*[5].

---

1   Per Brett J in *Dale's Case* (1881) 6 QBD 376 at 461, approved by Kennedy LJ and Blofield J in *R v Governor of Brixton Prison, ex parte Cuoghi* [1998] 1 WLR 1513 at 1522.
2   PG Osborn *A Concise Law Dictionary* (5th edn, 1964) pp 31–32.
3   [1984] AC 437 at 441.
4   Vol 9, p 77, para 102.
5   [1984] AC 437.

3.8   HOW AN ARREST IS BROUGHT ABOUT

In *Spicer v Holt*[1], Viscount Dilhorne quoted with approval the definition in *Halsbury's Laws of England*[2] of what amounts to an arrest:

> 'Arrest consists in the seizure or touching of a person's body with a view to his restraint; words may, however, amount to an arrest if, in the circumstances of the case, they are calculated to bring, and do bring, to a person's notice that he is under compulsion and he thereafter submits to the compulsion.'

In the words of Lord Devlin when he delivered the Privy Council's opinion in *Hussien v Chong Fook Kam*[3]:

> 'An arrest occurs when a police officer states in terms that he is arresting or when he uses force to restrain the individual concerned. It also occurs when by words or conduct he makes it clear that he will, if necessary, use force to prevent the individual from going where he may want to go.'

In *Spicer v Holt*[4], Lord Dilhorne stated:

> 'Whether or not a person has been arrested depends not on the legality of the arrest but on whether he has been deprived of his liberty to go where he pleases.'

It must be made plain to the person that he is under arrest, but no special form of words is required. In *Alderson v Booth*[5], Lord Parker CJ said:

> 'Equally it is clear, as it seems to me, that an arrest is constituted when any form of words is used which in the circumstances of the case were calculated to bring to the defendant's notice, and did bring to the defendant's notice, that he was under compulsion and thereafter he submitted to that compulsion'.

In *R v Inwood*[6], Stevenson LJ said:

> 'No formula will suit every case and it may well be that different procedures might have to be followed with different persons depending on their age, ethnic origin, knowledge of English, intellectual qualities, physical or mental disabilities. There is no magic formula; only the obligation to make it plain to the suspect by what is said and done that he is no longer a free man. However, what we think is clear is that it is a question of fact, not of law, and must be left to the jury to decide whether a person has been arrested or not, at least where there is a real dispute as to the question whether the defendant understood that he was being arrested.'

So, in *R v Brosch*[7], it was held that a lawful arrest had been made by the grabbing of the shoulder, accompanied by the words, 'Stay there!' That had been immediately preceded by the arrester, a manager at a McDonald's takeaway, seeing Brosch with a syringe in one hand and with the other picking up a piece of foil in an ashtray. He then said to him, 'You're on drugs, aren't you?' and asked him to roll up his sleeves.

---

1 [1977] AC 987 at 999G.
2 4th edn, vol 11, para 99 (now 4th edn reissue).
3 [1970] AC 942 at 947A–B.
4 Viscount Dilhorne in *Spicer v Holt* [1977] AC 987 at 1000.
5 [1969] 2 QB 216 at 220–221.
6 [1973] 1 WLR 647 at 652–653.
7 [1988] Crim LR 743.

Also for an arrest (whether lawful or otherwise) to occur, there must be either an act of submission by the person detained or a touching of the man or woman to be apprehended by whoever is making the arrest. This is well illustrated by *Nichols v Bulman*[1]. The defendant opened his front door, but remained in the house. On his doorstep were the police who asked him to take a breath test, but this request was refused. A constable then told him that he was under arrest, so the latter tried to close the door but was prevented by the officer. A scuffle took place with the accused being overpowered inside the premises. It was held that there was no lawful arrest, because such could not be effected merely by words which were not accepted; and that the police had become trespassers once they were inside the house, as the Road Traffic Act 1972 (as amended by the Transport Act 1981, s 25(3) and Sch 8) did not give a right of entry in order to administer a breath test (unless there has been a traffic accident involving personal injury, which was not the case here). That decision was followed in *R v McMillan*[2], where Judge A.A. Edmondson directed an acquittal on an assault charge. The accused had been pursued into the car park of the public house where he lived with his wife who was the innkeeper. (It was then closing time.) He provided a positive breath test. The constable told him that he was under arrest, so he ran into his residence and was followed by the officer. He then attempted to eject this unwelcome visitor by physical force. The judge held that mere words, without any submission thereto, could not amount to an arrest. The police had no right to enter private property and the lawful occupier was entitled, as he did, to use no more force than was necessary to expel a trespasser. In *Russen v Lucas*[3], a sheriff's officer went to a tavern and told Mr Hamer that he wanted him[4]. The latter said, 'Wait outside and I will come to you'. However, he went out by a different door and made good his escape. It was held that there had been no arrest. However, once an arrester touches the person to be apprehended, that contact constitutes an arrest, even if the person to be detained then makes good his escape and ignores the touching, see *Hart v Chief Constable of Kent*[5].

R v Brosch, above, held that PACE 1984 (see below) did not alter the common law rules about what constituted an arrest, but was concerned with whether the arrest was a lawful one.

In the armed forces there are two types of arrest: 'open' and 'closed'. The former is the equivalent of a remand in custody and the latter is the grant of bail; see *R v Officer Commanding Depot Battalion RASC, Colchester, ex parte Elliot*[6].

---

1   [1985] RTR 236.
2   (Unreported) 9 July 1986. (For powers of entry to make an arrest, see **3.11**.)
3   (1824) 1 C & P 153.
4   These words were found to have been understood as being words of arrest.
5   [1983] RTR 484.
6   [1949] 1 All ER 373 at 379, per Lord Goddard CJ.

3.9   SURRENDER TO POLICE BAIL

Under PACE 1984, s 34(7) (as amended by the Criminal Justice and Public Order Act 1994, s 29) a person who, in accordance with his bail, returns to the police station is, on his arrival, deemed to have been arrested for the offence for which he had been granted bail.

3.10   WHO CAN BE ARRESTED?

Apart from the Sovereign, the only other people who are totally immune from arrest are diplomats and members of certain international organisations and their respective households; see Diplomatic Privileges Act 1964, Sch 1, art 29 and Consular Relations Act 1968, Sch 2, para 4. The same privilege is enjoyed by non-British nationals and those who are not permanently resident here and who render assistance pursuant to the Convention on Assistance in the Case of a Nuclear Accident or Radiological Emergency done at Vienna on 26 September 1986; see the Schedule to the Atomic Energy Act 1989. A certificate of the Secretary of State is conclusive proof of any fact therein about a person's status in the United Kingdom (see, for example, s 4 of the 1964 Act).

Members of Parliament are immune from civil process during sittings and 40 days before and afterwards, which, with the frequency that the legislature meets in modern times, means that this freedom from arrest will normally always be extant. This period of 40 days after a sitting still applies to an ex-member who has lost his seat at an election, vide *Re Anglo-French Co-operative Society*[1]. A peer of the Realm (whether or not he has a seat in Parliament) has a similar immunity at all times, see *Couche v Lord Arundel*[2]. This privilege does not extend to criminal charges for which Lords and MPs can be taken into custody just like anybody else, see *Wellesley v Duke of Beaufort*[3]. This same privilege is possessed by 'witnesses going to or coming from courts of justice in obedience to subpoenas, and by solicitors and barristers attending courts to discharge their professional duties', per Brett MR in *Re Freston*[4]. The route taken need not be the quickest; it is sufficient if it was a reasonable way of travelling to court, see *A-G v Leathersellers' Co*[5]. In this context, the word 'court' means those tribunals exercising a judicial, as opposed to an administrative, function, see *Jolly v Hull; Jolley v Jolley*[6] which approved for this purpose the definition given in *Attorney-General v British Broadcasting Corporation*[7]. That case concerned what was a court for the purposes of RSC Ord 52, r 1(2)(a)(iii), ie contempt of which could be punished by the High Court. Lord Scarman said[8]:

---

1   (1880) 14 ChD 533.
2   (1802) 3 East 127.
3   (1831) 2 Russ & M 639.
4   (1883) 11 QBD 545 at 552.
5   (1844) 7 Beav 157.
6   [2000] 2 FLR 69, CA.
7   [1981] AC 303.
8   Ibid, at 359.

I would identify a court in (or "of") law, ie a court of judicature, as a body established by law to exercise, either generally or subject to defined limits, the judicial power of the state. In this context judicial power is to be contrasted with legislative and executive (ie administrative) power. If the body under review is established for a purely legislative or administrative purpose, it is part of the legislative or administrative system of the state, even though it has to perform duties which are judicial in character. Though the ubiquitous presence of the state makes itself felt in all sorts of situations never envisaged when our law was in its formative stage, the judicial power of the state exercised through judges appointed by the state remains an independent, and recognisably separate, function of government. Unless a body exercising judicial functions can be demonstrated to be part of this judicial system, it is not in my judgment a court of law. I would add that the judicial system is not limited to the courts of the civil power. Courts-martial and consistory courts (the latter since 1540) are as truly entrusted with the exercise of the judicial power of the state as are civil courts: *R v Daily Mail, ex parte Farnsworth* [1921] 2 KB 733 and *R v Daily Herald, ex parte Bishop of Norwich* [1932] 2 KB 504.'

In that case, a local valuation court, despite its very name, was held not to be a 'court *of law*'. Lord Edmund-Davies[1] said that the following attributes were not conclusive of whether or not a body fell within that description:

(1) its decisions are final;
(2) it hears witnesses on oaths;
(3) two or more contending parties appear before it and between whom it has to decide;
(4) its rulings affect the rights of the subject;
(5) the presence or absence of an appeal to a court against its findings;
(6) matters are referred to it by another body;
(7) it is called a court;
(8) it sits in public;
(9) its determinations are subject to judicial review by the High Court; and
(10) absolute privilege against an action for defamation protects the participators in its proceedings.

However, *Jolley's Case* held that the privilege attached to the court and not the detained person, so that he could obtain a writ of *habeas corpus* but could not bring an action for damages.

In *R v Gordon*[2], the Court of Appeal doubted if a person once apprehended could be re-arrested before he was released from custody. However, once at a police station, he can now be re-arrested (see PACE 1984, s 31).

3.11   THE LOCATION OF THE ARREST AND SANCTUARY

A power of arrest does not, *ipso facto*, mean that it can be exercised anywhere. There are strict laws governing the entering of private premises without consent. This issue is considered in Chapter 9 at **9.1** *et seq*.

---

1   [1981] AC 303, at 347–8.
2   [1970] RTR 125.

The suggestion in *Comyn's Digest*[1] that a person cannot be apprehended in a court of law was doubted in *Christie v Leachinsky*[2] per Lord Simonds[3] and Lord du Parcq[4], although the latter regarded it as undesirable and thought that, in some circumstances, it might even amount to a contempt of court.

At common law, a person could take sanctuary in a church and, while he was there, he was safe from arrest. However, this immunity was abolished by 21 Jac 1 (Continuance of Acts) (1623–24), s 7.

3.12   INFORMATION TO BE GIVEN ON ARREST

In *Christie v Leachinsky*[5], the House of Lords held that for an arrest to be lawful, the arrester[6] must inform the detained person as soon as possible that he has been arrested and give him details of the offence for which he has been detained, unless those facts were obvious. In the words of Viscount Simon:

> '(1) If a policeman arrests without warrant upon reasonable suspicion of felony, or other crime of a sort which does not require a warrant, he must in ordinary circumstances inform the person arrested of the true ground of the arrest. He is not entitled to keep the reason to himself or to give a reason which is not the true reason. In other words a citizen is entitled to know on what charge or on suspicion of what crime he is seized. (2) If the citizen is not so informed but seized, the policeman, apart from certain exceptions, is liable for false imprisonment. (3) The requirement that the person arrested should be informed of the reason why he is seized naturally does not exist if the circumstances are such that he must know the general nature of the alleged offences for which he is detained. (4) The requirement that he is so informed does not mean that technical or precise language need be used. The matter is a matter of substance and turns on the elementary proposition that in this country a person is, *prima facie*, entitled to his freedom and is only required to submit to restraints on his freedom if he knows in the substance why it is claimed that this restraint should be imposed. (5) The person arrested cannot complain that he has not been supplied with the above information as and when he should be, if he produces the situation which makes it practically impossible to inform him, eg by immediate counter-attack or running away.'[7]
>
> ... This is I think, the fundamental principle, viz, that a man is entitled to know what, in the apt words of Lawrence LJ ([1946] KB 124, 147), are "the facts which are said to constitute a crime on his part".'[8]

Thus, the information required to be imparted must include not just the classification of the crime, but also its date and location, sufficient for the prisoner to know for exactly what transgression his freedom is being denied

---

1   Imprisonment H 5.
2   [1947] AC 573.
3   Ibid, at 595.
4   Ibid, at 603.
5   [1947] AC 573.
6   Or another person; see *Dhasi v Chief Constable of the West Midlands* (2000) TLR, May 9.
7   [1947] AC 573, at 587.
8   Ibid, at 593.

him, unless the arresting officer has not had time to ascertain all these facts; see *R v Telfer*[1]. It was held to be insufficient merely to tell a person that he was being arrested for burglary; he must also be told where and when it occurred. In *Murphy's Case*[2] the plaintiff was arrested in Liverpool and given the reason for his apprehension as 'suspicion of burglary in Newquay'. No further facts were imparted to him during his ensuing 4 hours' incarceration. The reason supplied was held by the Court of Appeal to have been inadequate. He should have been given the date when the burglary occurred, and the address at which it happened or at any rate the type of premises (in that case a hotel). The appeal was not argued on the grounds that this information had to be made known at the time of the initial taking into custody but that it should have been obtained by the police once the plaintiff had arrived at the station (if not before) and told to him. In *Dhesi v Chief Constable of the West Midlands*[3], the plaintiff had taken part in an affray and had run off when the police arrived. He was arrested half-an-hour later with his weapon, a hockey stick, which he had raised in a threatening manner to his pursuers. The Court of Appeal held that merely telling him that he was being arrested for an affray could leave him in no doubt as to exactly why he was being apprehended, in view of his reaction when approached by members of the local constabulary. In *Wilson v Chief Constable of Lancashire*[4], the complainant had his cheque book stolen out of his jacket pocket at a community centre which the plaintiff also attended. On 1 November one of the cheques had been cashed at a bank in Clevelys. The plaintiff was visited by the police and asked about his whereabouts on that day. He denied going into Clevelys, stating that he had been at his girlfriend's home all day, looking after her younger child. He was then apprehended 'under suspicion of theft of cheques'. The Court of Appeal (by a majority) held that there had not been compliance with the requirements of PACE 1984, s 28(3). This was because the fact that the cheques had been stolen from a jacket at the community centre had not been communicated by the arresting officer, nor had the latter 'identified what was alleged to have taken place in Clevelys or a bank there except in so far as the arrest for "theft of cheques" may have done so'. Also, the name or branch of the bank had not been mentioned, and there had been no reference to any encashment of the cheque. The rationale for this was given by Mance LJ[5]:

> 'I would also disagree with the trial judge's evident view that the decision in *Murphy* conflicts with what he called "the real world of policing". On the contrary, it would be unfair if the police could arrest strangers for some unidentified charge of burglary taking place at some unspecified time and place, without indicating either the name or even the nature of the premises or the date, when these facets were known to the police and could have been made available to arresting officers.'

1   [1976] Crim LR 562. It was cited with approval by the Court of Appeal in *Newman v Modern Bookbinders* [2000] 2 All ER 814 at 821.
2   (Unreported) 15 February 1985.
3   (2000) TLR, May 9.
4   *New Law Digest*, 23 November 2000.
5   Ibid, at para 30.

In *R v Kulynycz*[1], it was held that a detainee need only be told the offence for which he was being arrested, and not whether it was 'on suspicion of its commission' or on warrant.

Unless it is obvious, a private citizen must impart the requisite details as soon as practical after he has made an arrest, see *R v Brosch*[2], or in the words of Lord Du Parcq in *Christie v Leachinsky*[3]:

> 'In cases where a statement of the charge at the moment of arrest is, in the circumstances, excused there is still a duty to acquaint him with it at the first reasonable opportunity.'

Exactly how soon after his loss of liberty a suspect must be told the reasons for his incarceration is discussed later on in this chapter[4]. Once a person is told why he is being detained, from thereon his captivity becomes lawful; see *R v Kulynycz*, above, *Lewis v Chief Constable of South Wales*[5] and *DPP v H*[6].

3.13   DETAINEES WHO ARE DEAF OR CANNOT SPEAK ENGLISH

In *John Lewis & Co v Tims*[7], the House of Lords overruled Donovan J and held that no tort had been committed when the plaintiff remained unaware of why she was being detained. This was because she did not hear what was being said solely because she was deaf and this latter fact was not known to the store detective who had apprehended her. In the words of Asquith LJ in the Court of Appeal[8]:

> 'You cannot expect the person arresting to do more than what is reasonable to inform the person arrested of that with which he or she is charged.'

Wheatley v Lodge[9] held that a policeman had complied with his legal duty if he had done all that was reasonably possible in the circumstances, even though the suspect did not understand, for example because he was deaf or did not speak English.

1   [1971] 1 QB 367.
2   [1988] Crim LR 743.
3   [1947] AC 575 at 600.
4   At **3.17**.
5   [1991] 1 All ER 206.
6   (1999) TLR, February 1.
7   [1952] AC 676.
8   [1951] 2 KB 459 at 463.
9   [1971] 1 WLR 29.

3.14   THE CORRECT LEGAL REASON

If the validity of an apprehension is challenged in court, it can only be justified upon the grounds communicated to the prisoner; see *Christie v Leachinsky*[1]. This principle is applied strictly. In *R v Holah*[2], a motorist was told that he was being arrested for failing to provide a specimen, whereas he should have been apprehended for having obtained a positive result on his breath test. He had blown into the breathalyser for less than the 10 seconds specified by the manufacturers, hence the form of words used by the policeman. The driver had, however, managed to turn the crystals green above the line, ie it showed that he had consumed more than the permitted amount of alcohol, and this meant that, on the true construction of the Road Traffic Act 1972, he had satisfactorily taken the test. (Since the amendments made to the law by s 59 of the Transport Act 1982, the same facts nowadays would amount to the crime of failing to take a breath test; see *DPP v Heywood*[3].)

However, if the offence is defined in general terms, which could include more than one crime, that is sufficient. In *Abbassy v Commissioner of Police for the Metropolis*[4], the plaintiff was arrested for the 'unlawful possession' of the car he was driving. The Court of Appeal held that it was for the jury to decide if that was sufficient information, even though such a description covered a number of possible transgressions of the law, for example theft, handling, unauthorised taking contrary to s 12 of the Theft Act 1968, etc. It was open to a jury to find that such a description had conveyed to the plaintiff what was the cause of the apprehension, namely that he had no lawful entitlement to have possession of that car. In the words of Purchas LJ[5]:

> '... it is sufficient that commonplace words be used, the obvious meaning of which informs the person arrested of the offence or type of offences for which he is being arrested.'

It is interesting to note that the same phrase 'unlawful possession' was held in *Christie v Leachinsky*, above, to mean only a contravention of the Liverpool Corporation Act 1921 because this is how people in that city would have interpreted such an expression and would not have considered it to be indicating the crimes of larceny or receiving. In *R v Cooke*[6], the defendant was asked if he had been driving the car which was outside his house and which had been involved in two or three accidents that night; to which question no answer was given. The officer then said that he was arresting him 'on suspicion of impairment. I believe you have been drinking.' The Court of Appeal held that the jury was entitled to find that those words had informed the accused that he was being arrested for driving earlier that night while unfit, contrary to s 4(1) of

---

1   [1947] AC 573.
2   [1973] 1 WLR 127.
3   [1998] RTR 1.
4   [1990] 1 All ER 193.
5   Ibid, at 203.
6   (Unreported) 16 January 1998.

the Road Traffic Act 1988. In *R v Howell*[1], it was held to be sufficient merely to say that the arrest was for 'a breach of the peace', even though it was in fact to prevent one occurring.

In *Abbassy*[2], Purchas LJ (with whom Mustill LJ agreed) depreciated the description by the trial judge (Leonard J) of the common law requirements to give full details of the reason for an arrest as 'a formality'. They also held that unless it was obvious, the constable must make it known that he holds such an office. Viscount Simon, in *Christie v Leachinsky*[3], was also of the opinion that this latter fact was one which had to be communicated to the detained person. In *Edwards v DPP*[4], Evans LJ stated:

> 'It may seem unrealistic that the Court should be concerned after the event with the particular words that were used on the particular occasion. Nevertheless it has to be borne in mind that giving correct information as to the reason for an arrest is a matter of the utmost constitutional significance in a case where a reason can be and is given at the time.'

In *Mullady v DPP*[5] the appellant became agitated, abusive and violent and tried to interpose herself between a constable and the suspect he was lawfully arresting. So another police officer apprehended her for obstruction – which is not an arrestable offence. The High Court resolutely rejected both of the prosecution's submissions that:

(1) on the facts of that case, the arrest for obstruction must necessarily have included an allegation of breach of the peace; and that
(2) this mis-labelling of the offence could not make unlawful an arrest for which a valid reason existed.

Vernon v Lawrence[6] held that any references merely to 'drinking' by a policeman when explaining his reasons to a motorist for making an arrest meant 'drinking alcohol'.

3.15   POSSESSION OF DRUGS

In *Clarke v Chief Constable of North Wales*[7] the claimant was merely told that she was being arrested for possession of drugs. (Only if they are Class A or B is their possession an arrestable offence.) Brooke LJ held there to have been a lawful arrest because[8]:

> 'I am of the clear opinion that Mrs Clarke would have understood perfectly well that the police were arresting her for a serious offence in connection with the

---

1   [1982] QB 416 at 427H–428A.
2   [1990] 1 All ER 193 at 2029.
3   [1947] AC 573 at 586.
4   (1993) 97 Cr App R 301 at 308.
5   (Unreported) 3 July 1995.
6   (1971) 137 JP 867.
7   (Unreported) 5 April 2000.
8   Ibid, at para 54 (Sir Christopher Staughton also concurred with this).

possession of a controlled drug for which they had a power to arrest her. To require a police officer to refer to a Class A drug or a Class B drug because they have no power of arrest in relation to a Class C drug is in my judgment to adopt an over-lawyerly approach and to elevate technical form over real substance. A judge or criminal lawyer may know about the different classification of drugs contained in Schedule 2 of the Misuse of Drugs Act 1971, but the use of this sort of language would leave many citizens none the wiser, and might tend to confuse them unless an even longer explanation is given. Needless to say, if the arrested person then seeks more detailed information about the offence for which he or she is being arrested, the arresting officer must supply it.'

The premise that the police would not detain a suspect for an offence for which they did not possess a summary power of arrest echoes the views expressed in the High Court in *Gage v Jones*[1], where Griffiths LJ (with whom McCollough J agreed) held that there was a presumption that a policeman who had asked a motorist to give a breath test was in uniform because otherwise the whole exercise would be pointless. (The Road Traffic Acts of 1972 and 1988 have only bestowed upon constables in uniform the authority to require a driver to exhale into a breathalyser at the roadside.) The fallacy of this argument was illustrated by *DPP v Harrington*[2] where a plain clothes officer in the Vice Squad made such a request, and arrested the defendant when he refused to await the arrival of a uniformed traffic patrol driver. While in *Clarke*, above, one of the review officers who authorised her continual detention testified that he neither knew nor cared what the drugs were which had caused the plaintiff's arrest, Much more preferable are the views expressed by Sedley LJ in his dissenting judgment[3]:

'There is force in the submission that it would have been easy enough to add to the words "on suspicion of a possession of controlled drugs with intent to supply them", or to say that they included Ecstasy or were Class A. The obvious response, in relation to such an arrest as this, is that it does not really matter: the police would hardly have been mounting such an operation for Class C drugs or against personal users, and the words used were perfectly apt to include an arrestable offence. But suppose the appellant or either of her companions had fought back or tried to escape and people had been hurt; or suppose that they went quietly and later sued for wrongful arrest: everything in either case will turn on the legality of the arrest, and the legality of the arrest would turn on the words used. It is the very fact that not every possession of controlled drugs is an arrestable offence which arguably made some greater specificity, however shortly expressed, essential. Without it, the argument goes, no court could determine whether the arrest was lawful without considering extrinsic evidence of what the ground of arrest actually was (as the judge in this case did), when the whole purpose of the principle now set out in s 28(3) of PACE is to make such enquiry inappropriate. The determination of what was conveyed to the person detained, as opposed to what was in the constable's mind, is a different question: hence the decision in *Abbassy*.

I am also impressed by the consideration that to sanction the words used in the present case in the context in which they were used (which, unlike the situation in *Abbassy*, conveyed no fuller information) as a sufficient compliance with the law

1   [1983] RTR 508.
2   (Unreported) 25 November 1994 (Marlborough Street Magistrates' Court).
3   Ibid, at paras 38 and 39.

may be to invite, in fact to initiate, the erosion of one of our most important historical safeguards of personal liberty. *Christie v Leachinsky* expressly brought the law of arrest into line with the long-standing principle that – in the words of Burrows famous headnote to *Entick v Carrington* (1765) 109 St Tr 1029 – general warrants are illegal. It seems to me at least arguable that to uphold the arrest will mean creating a distinction of law between the unlawful use of general words in *Christie v Leachinsky* (where "unlawful possession" was quite large enough, in non-technical terms, to embrace the arrestable as well as the non-arrestable version of being in possession of stolen goods) and the use of the words, which though not linked to a particular provision, are comparably general and capable of describing both arrestable and non-arrestable offences. Put another way, I do not at present think that an intelligible line can be drawn between where the suspect is told the wrong ground for his arrest and a case where he is not told the right ground for his arrest – and that may be the only real difference between *Christie v Leachinsky* and this case.'

3.16   ADDITIONAL REQUIREMENTS PLACED UPON THE POLICE

Additional formalities must be observed by the constabulary to make their apprehensions legal, ie they must comply with s 28 of PACE 1984. Under that legislation, a police arrest is not lawful unless a prisoner is informed as soon as practical after his detention that (subs (1)) he was under arrest and (subs (3)) the grounds for it; and this still applies even though those facts are obvious; see subss (2) and (4) respectively. Apart from the provisions of subss (2) and (4), PACE 1984 is merely declaratory of the common law. According to *R v Cooke*[1], the likely reason for these extra requirements was:

'... as a result of the international commitments involved in subscription to the European Convention on Human Rights and in particular Article 5.3 of that Convention.'[2]

In *Nicholas v Parsonage*[3], the High Court was of the opinion that when someone was being denied his freedom because one of the general arrest conditions existed in PACE 1984, s 25, that fact need not have been imparted to the detainee, but the latter still had to be told the offence for which he was being arrested and it was not sufficient merely to inform him that he was being apprehended because a specific and named matter mentioned in s 25 had been satisfied. However, although there was no requirement to supply that latter information, it was good practice to do so. That was *obiter* because the prisoner had been made aware of the facts giving rise to the exercise of the constable's powers under s 25. However, that dicta was overruled by the Court of Appeal in *Ghafar v Chief Constable of the West Midlands*[4] which held (in the words of Roch LJ at paras 20 and 21):

---

1   (Unreported) 16 January 1998.
2   See Chapter 17.
3   [1987] RTR 199.
4   (Unreported) 12 May 2000.

'This was a case where two matters had to exist before the officer could exercise a power of arrest: first that a seat belt offence had been committed or the officer reasonably suspected that such an offence had been committed and, secondly, that one of the general arrest conditions existed or appeared to exist. *Both these matters, in my judgment, had to be communicated to the respondent.*' (Author's emphasis)

'... there is no obligation on the arresting officer to refer to the power of arrest as opposed to the matters which have to exist for the officer to exercise that power ... There is no causal link between the offence and the failure to provide a name. They both have to exist if the arrest is to be lawful and both have to be communicated to the person being arrested at the time of the arrest if the arrest is to be lawful ... Neither matter had to be communicated in detail, nor is there any set formula for doing so.'

3.17 AT THE TIME OF THE ARREST

The requisite details must be given, to quote the statute, 'at the time of the arrest'. *Nicholas v Parsonage*[1] held that those words did not just mean 'simultaneously with', but encompassed, 'a short but reasonable period of time around the moment of arrest, both before and, as the statute specifically says, after'. There a cyclist had been riding without touching his handlebars. A constable told him to hold on and repeated that command after it had first been ignored; and on this second occasion the request was complied with by the appellant but he also made an abusive gesture towards the police as they drove away. This prompted PC Parsonage to tell him that his identity and residence were required because he had been riding in a dangerous manner. When those details were not forthcoming, he was made aware of the powers of arrest under s 25 but still this did not evoke any response. Accordingly, he was arrested 'for failing to give his name and address'. The High Court held that the mention of s 25 was not by itself sufficient. However, the police had made known to the appellant the offence about which they were complaining and had made it clear to him that this was the crime for which he was being detained; therefore, the apprehension was lawful.

In *Ghafar v Chief Constable of the West Midlands*[2], Roch LJ (para 20) said:

'[The requisite information must be imparted] at the time of arrest, which includes a short period of time either side of the physical time of arrest.'

How short was not stated but in that case it was a matter of minutes.

The only reason allowed for not complying with subss (1) and (3) of s 28 is that given in subs (5), namely where it had not been practical to do so before their prisoner had managed to escape. In *DPP v Hawkins*[3] (a case of police assault), it was conceded by the respondent that his arrest was initially lawful. The justices had found that not only did his violence prevent him being made aware, prior

---

1   [1987] RTR 199 at 204J–K.
2   (Unreported) 12 May 2000.
3   [1988] 1 WLR 1166.

to his arrival at the police station, of the reason for him being taken there but also that, once he was at that location, he was still not told why. The High Court held[1] that any shortcomings at the police station did not mean that the arresting officers were not acting in the execution of their duty prior to their entering that place. There was a duty to make, and to maintain, the arrest until it became practical to inform their prisoner of why he was being detained; and any failure to do this when it became practical to do so could not have any effect on what had occurred prior to that time, unless specific provision had been made in the Act for this – and it had not been. Thus the High Court was saying that a failure to comply with s 28(3) does not make the arrest unlawful *ab initio*, but only from the time when it became practical to impart the requisite information. However, the actual words of that subsection are:

> '(3) . . . no arrest is lawful unless the person arrested is told the grounds of his arrest at the time of, or as soon as is practical after, the arrest.'

It is submitted that the meaning is clear, namely 'no arrest is lawful, unless'. It is stretching the use of language to give it the meaning ascribed to it by the High Court, which would appear to be that the detention always remains lawful until after the time for giving reasons has passed. It has been suggested[2] that the latter interpretation is required, to obviate the need of a citizen wishing to help a policeman trying to arrest a violent felon from refusing to join in until the criminal has been told the reason for the arrest. Such a citizen, to prevent himself from being sued for trespass, would surely also demand the full details of why the officer was interfering with the liberty of one of Her Majesty's subjects, so that he could judge for himself if those grounds afforded reasonable suspicion. He would definitely act thus if he was aware of the case of *R v Curvan*[3]. There, a constable had apprehended the defendant for what was not (to use modern-day terminology) an arrestable offence. Later his captive escaped, so the officer asked Edward Warby to give chase, which he did. That attempt at recapturing (which led to Warby being stabbed with a knife) was held to be illegal and, thus, no offence of wounding with intent to resist arrest had been committed.

3.18   TRAPS FOR THIEVES WHICH LOCK AUTOMATICALLY

In *Dawes v DPP*[4], the defendant was caught in an automatically locking car, which the police had used as a trap. The High Court held that he had been arrested at the moment when he had become unable to leave the vehicle; and there was a duty to inform him that he was under arrest and the reason why as soon as practical thereafter. That had been done when the police arrived a few minutes later, so the apprehension was lawful. Kennedy LJ said that on

---

1   [1988] 1 WLR at 1170.
2   According to the commentary at [1988] Crim LR 742.
3   (1826) 1 Moody 132.
4   (1997) TLR, March 2.

different facts, the arrest could have been illegal and suggested that a device be fitted inside such a car which would make known to the person locked therein the information required to be given by s 28.

3.19 SUFFICIENCY OF THE EVIDENCE NEEDED TO PROVE THAT THE REQUISITE REASONS WERE GIVEN

In *Bookman v DPP*[1], the accused had escaped from custody. The issue in the case was whether he had been lawfully arrested. In the magistrates' court, a lady had testified that he had stolen her purse, that she had complained to the police and had accompanied them to the defendant's home. Her account amounted to reasonable suspicion. (She had left her handbag very near him in a public house when she went to the toilet. On her return, her purse was missing. When asked about it, he gave evasive answers.) The arresting officers were not called to give evidence, but, in cross-examination, the defendant said that he had been apprehended for theft. The High Court rejected the argument that the justices had erred in holding a lawful arrest. As the appellant's answer showed that he knew why he was being arrested, then the court could assume that he had been told this. It is submitted that just because a person was aware of the reason why he was being incarcerated, this did not *ipso facto* mean that he must have been given that information by his arresters. If a person has committed a burglary, for example, he may well have no doubts about why he is being taken down to the station and then locked in a cell, even if nothing at all is said by the police about their reasons for doing this.

---

1   (Unreported) 13 November 1997.

Chapter 4

SERIOUS AND OTHER ARRESTABLE OFFENCES

4.1 INTRODUCTION

The common law invested every person in England and Wales with a power to arrest, without a warrant, any felon, but this became obsolete with the abolition of felonies by s 1 of the Criminal Law Act 1967. Instead, a new category of criminal activity was created by s 2 of that statute which enabled its perpetrators to be detained without a warrant, and was given the name of 'arrestable offence'. Section 2 was repealed by PACE 1984 which set out an up-to-date list of arrestable offences and has since been amended to include crimes created both before and after it had been placed on the statute book. In s 116, it made certain crimes 'serious' ones, in respect of which the police could, *inter alia*, keep a suspect in custody before charge for longer than the normal 24 hours. The fact that no charge is preferred after an arrest does not of itself make the apprehension unlawful; see *Rigg v Commissioner of Police*[1]. This chapter sets out what are arrestable offences. The question of when a suspect can be detained for them is considered in subsequent chapters (in the case of non-police officers in Chapter 5 and constables in Chapter 6).

4.2 THE DEFINITION OF AN ARRESTABLE OFFENCE

An 'arrestable offence' is defined in PACE 1984, s 24(1) as being one of the following.

(1) An offence for which the sentence is fixed by law. There are three offences which fall into this category:

   (a) treason (Treason Act 1814, s 1 as amended by s 36 of the Crime and Disorder Act 1998);

   (b) piracy which is accompanied immediately before, during, or immediately afterwards by:

   (i) an assault; or
   (ii) any act which endangers life,

   if done with an intent to murder (Piracy Act 1837, ss 1 and 2 as amended by s 36 of the Crime and Disorder Act 1998);

   (c) murder; see the Murder (Abolition of Death Penalty) Act 1965, s 1.

(2) An offence for which a person aged 21 years or over, who has no previous convictions, may be sentenced to 5 years' imprisonment, ignoring any restrictions placed by s 33 of the Magistrates' Courts Act 1980 on the sentence which can be imposed on a summary trial for:

---

1   (Unreported) 25 March 1997, per Ward, LJ.

(a) committing; or
(b) attempting to commit, the offence of criminal damage not exceeding £5,000; or
(c) aiding and abetting; or
(d) counselling or procuring; or
(e) inciting, the offence of committing criminal damage not exceeding £5,000.

A list of the most common offences classified as 'arrestable' by virtue of this subsection is in Appendix 1. (Some of the obscure ones, especially those contained in private acts, have been omitted.)

(3) The offences listed in PACE 1984, s 24(2), which are as follows.

4.2.1 Customs and excise offences: PACE 1984, s 24(2)(a)

These are defined by s 24(2)(a) as offences for which an arrest may be made under any 'Customs and Excise Act'. These in turn are defined by s 1 of the Customs and Excise Management Act 1979 (CEMA 1979) as 'any enactment for the time being in force relating to customs and excise'[1]. The following are the offences and powers of arrest which fall within this definition.

4.2.1.1 *CEMA 1979 (as amended by s 114(1) of PACE 1984)*

SECTION 13

Unlawful assumption of character of customs officer
Section 13 authorises the arrest of any person who falsely assumes the name, designation or character of a Commissioner, or an officer of HM Customs and Excise or a person appointed by the Commissioners:

CEMA 1979, s 13

(1) for the purposes of doing or procuring any act which he could not otherwise have done or procured on his own authority; or
(2) for any other unlawful purpose.

SECTION 15

Bribery and collusion
Section 15 authorises the arrest for an offence contrary to s 15(1) or (2). Under s 15(1), it is an offence for a Commissioner, or an officer of Customs and Exercise, or for any person authorised by the Commissioners to discharge any assigned matter (see below):

CEMA 1979, s 15

---

1   CEMA 1979, s 1(1).

(1) to ask for; or

(2) to receive,

any payment (other than one to which they are lawfully entitled) for (subs (a)) the discharge of their duties or (subs (b)) for:

(i) doing; or

(ii) not doing; or

(iii) for concealing anything in relation to an assigned matter, whereby Her Majesty is, or may be, defrauded, or which is unlawful.

Under s 15(2), it is an offence for anybody to make or to offer any payment or reward, the receipt of which is an offence under s 15(1).

Section 15(1) defines an 'assigned matter' as any matter in relation to which HM Commissioners of Customs and Excise are for the time being required, in pursuance of an enactment, to perform any duties.

SECTION 16

Obstruction of officers

Section 16(3) authorises the arrest for any offence created by s 16(1) as follows:

CEMA 1979, s 16

(1) obstructing, molesting or assaulting:

(a) any person who is duly engaged in his statutory duties, or is exercising his statutory powers, relating to an assigned matter (see s 15(1) above); or

(b) any person assisting him.

Hinchliffe v Sheldon[1] held that 'obstructing' meant anything which made it more difficult for a man or woman to accomplish what they want to do;

(2) doing anything which impedes, or is calculated, to impede the carrying out of any search for anything liable to be forfeited under the customs and excise legislation or the:

(a) detention;

(b) seizure; or

(c) removal of any such thing;

(3) rescuing, damaging or destroying anything liable to forfeiture; or doing anything calculated to prevent the procuring, or giving of, evidence as to whether or not any such thing is liable to forfeiture;

(4) preventing the arrest of somebody by a person duly engaged or acting as aforesaid, or rescuing any person so arrested.

---

1   [1955] 3 All ER 406.

SECTION 24

Movement of goods by pipeline without the Commissioners' approval
Section 24(5) authorises the arrest of a person who:

CEMA 1979, s 24

-   (subs (a)) commits an offence under subss (1) or (2) or who fails to comply with a condition imposed under subs (3) for the import and export by pipeline; or
-   (subs (b)) obtains access to goods in an approved import or export pipeline without the authority of the proper officer or for just and sufficient cause.

Under s 24(1), it is an offence to import or export goods by a pipeline not approved by the Commissioners.

Under s 24(2), it is an offence to move by a pipeline not approved by the Commissioners (for import or export):

(1) imported goods which have not been moved out of charge; or
(2) dutiable goods from a warehouse without the duties having been paid.

SECTION 50(2), (3)

Improper importation of goods
Section 50(2) authorises the arrest of any person who commits an offence under that subsection, ie a person who, either with intent to defraud Her Majesty or to avoid any statutory restriction or prohibition on the import of goods, is concerned in either:

CEMA 1979, s 50(2)

(1) unshipping; or
(2) landing in any port; or
(3) unloading from any aircraft, such goods; or
(4) in the removal of any such goods from:

    (a) any approved wharf;
    (b) examination station;
    (c) transit shed; or
    (d) Customs and Excise station.

Section 50(3) authorises the arrest of anybody who commits an offence under that subsection, ie a person who is concerned in importing any goods contrary to any statutory prohibition or restriction on their import (whether or not the goods are unloaded) with intent to evade the prohibition or restriction.

CEMA 1979, s 50(3)

SECTION 53(8)

Fraudulent shipment for exportation, etc
Section 53(8) authorises the arrest of anybody who, with intent to defraud, is concerned in the export by ship of dutiable or restricted goods or the shipment of such goods as stores, or the

CEMA 1979, s 53(8)

making waterborne of such goods for shipment for exportation, before they have been presented to the proper officer of Customs and Excise.

SECTION 63(5), (6)

Fraudulent loading of ship for exportation, etc

Section 63(6) authorises the arrest of anyone who, contrary to subs (5), with intent to defraud, is concerned in the loading of goods for export, or as stores, on a voyage to an eventual destination to a non-EEC country by a ship before delivering to the proper officer of Customs and Excise: CEMA 1979, s 63(5), (6)

(1) an entry outwards of the ship in such form as the Commissioners might direct;
(2) a certificate from the proper officer of the clearance inwards or coastwise of her last voyage with cargo; and
(3) if the ship has already loaded goods at some other port for exportation or as stores for use aforesaid or has been cleared in ballast from some other port, the clearance outwards from that other port.

SECTION 64(7)

Fraudulent loading of aircraft for exportation, etc

Section 64(7) authorises the arrest of anybody who: CEMA 1979, s 64(7)

(1) with intent to defraud;
(2) is concerned with the loading of any ship or aircraft;
(3) which is going to any place outside the EEC or Isle of Man; and
(4) before application for clearance has been made.

SECTION 68(1), (2)

Knowing exportation in breach of statutory prohibition or restriction

Section 68(2) authorises the arrest of anybody who contrary to subs (1): CEMA 1979, s 68(2)

(1) exports or ships good as stores; or
(2) imports goods for the purpose of exporting or shipping them as stores;
when such is in breach of any statutory prohibition or restriction. A similar power of arrest applies to any agent of such people who is also concerned in such an activity.

SECTION 68A(1)

Fraudulent evasion of agricultural levy

Section 68A(1) authorises the arrest of anybody who is concerned with any fraudulent evasion or attempted evasion of any
agricultural levy chargeable on the export of goods.

CEMA 1979,
s 68A(1) (as
inserted by the
Finance Act
1982, s 11(2))

SECTION 84(2)

Signalling to smugglers

Section 84(2) authorises the arrest of anybody who sends signals
or messages connected with smuggling or intended smuggling:

(1) from any part of the United Kingdom; or
(2) from any ship; or
(3) from any aircraft.

CEMA 1979,
s 84(2) (as
amended by
PACE 1984,
s 114(1))

SECTION 86

Armed or disguised

Section 86 authorises the arrest of anybody who is armed with an
offensive weapon or disguised in any way while being concerned
in the movement, carriage or concealment of any goods which is
either:

(1) contrary to any statutory prohibition or restriction on their
     importation or exportation; or
(2) without having first paid or given security for any duty
     payable on them.

CEMA 1979,
s 86 (as
amended by
PACE 1984,
s 114(1))

SECTION 87

Offering goods for sale as smuggled goods

Section 87 authorises the arrest of anybody who offers for sale, as
having been imported without payment of duty or having been
otherwise illegally imported, any goods, whether or not the
goods were so imported or chargeable with duty.

CEMA 1979,
s 87 (as
amended by
CJA 1982, ss 38,
46, PACE 1984,
s 114(1))

SECTION 100(1)

Unauthorised access to warehouse or warehoused goods

Section 100(1) authorises the arrest of anyone who, without
authority of the proper officer or for just and sufficient cause,
opens the doors or locks of a warehouse (including the Queen's
warehouse) or makes or obtains access thereto or to any goods

CEMA 1979,
s 100(1) (as
amended by
CJA 1982, ss 38,
46)

therein. A warehouse is defined in CEMA 1979, s 1 as meaning a place of security approved by the Commissioners and includes a distiller's warehouse.

SECTION 100(3)

Fraudulent removal etc of goods
Section 100(3) authorises the arrest of anybody who takes, removes, or conceals any goods which are, or should have been, warehoused, if done with intent either to defraud Her Majesty or to evade any statutory prohibition or restriction on the goods.

CEMA 1979, s 100(3)

SECTION 129(3)

Separating denatured goods
Section 129(3) authorises the arrest of anybody who separates goods which have been mixed with other goods and on which less duty has been charged because the mixing has caused the goods to be worth less than the full duty chargeable on them.

CEMA 1979, s 129(3)

SECTION 158(4)

Destruction etc of lock etc
Section 158(4) authorises the arrest of anybody who is a revenue trader or who is required to give security to the Commissioners for any place to be used for the examination of goods or who is a servant of any such person AND who, having provided or maintained a fitting for a lock required by a Customs and Excise officer under s 158(3):

CEMA 1979, s 158(4) (as amended by CJA 1982, ss 38, 46, by PACE 1984, s 114(1))

(1) wilfully destroys, or damages the fitting, or the lock, or the key provided for use with the fitting, or any label or seal placed on such lock; or
(2) improperly obtains access to any place or article secured by such lock; or
(3) has any such fitting, or any article intended to be secured by means thereof, so constructed that this intention is defeated.

SECTION 159(6)

Fraudulent removal of imported goods
Section 159(6) authorises the arrest of anybody who, with intent to defraud Her Majesty of any duty chargeable thereon or to avoid any statutory prohibition or restriction on their importation or exportation, removes any imported goods liable to be examined by an officer of Customs and Excise before they have

CEMA 1979, s 159(6) (as amended by PACE 1984, s 114(1))

been so examined and without the authority of the appropriate officer.

SECTION 167(1)

Making untrue declarations, etc

Section 167(1) authorises the arrest of anybody who, either knowingly or recklessly:

CEMA 1979, s 167(1) (as amended by PACE 1984, s 114(1))

(1) makes, or signs, or causes to be made or signed, or delivers, or causes to be delivered, any type of document; or
(2) gives replies to questions which he is required by statute to answer,

being a document or a statement produced, or made, for any assigned matter[1] which is untrue in any material particular.

SECTION 168(1)

Counterfeiting documents etc

Section 168(1) authorises the arrest of anybody who does any of the acts mentioned in the lettered subsections of s 168(1), viz:

CEMA 1979, s 168(1)

(1) counterfeits, or falsifies, any document which is required by or under a statute relating to an assigned matter[2], above), or which is used in the transaction of any business relating to an assigned matter[3];
(2) knowingly accepts, receives or uses any such document so counterfeited or falsified;
(3) alters any such document after it has been officially issued; or
(4) counterfeits any seal, signature, initials or other mark of, or used by, any officer of Customs and Excise for the verification of such a document or for the security of goods or for any other purpose relating to an assigned matter.

SECTION 170(1)

Section 170(1) authorises the arrest of anybody who, with intent to defraud Her Majesty of any duty chargeable thereon or to avoid any statutory prohibition or restriction on their importation or exportation:

CEMA 1979, s 170(1)

(a) knowingly acquires possession of goods which:

(i) have been unlawfully removed from a warehouse; or
(ii) are chargeable with a duty which has not been paid; or
(iii) are subject to any statutory prohibition or restriction on their importation; or

---

1 For the definition, see 'section 15' at **4.2.1**.
2 Ibid.
3 Ibid.

(b) is in any way knowingly concerned in:

  (i)   carrying; or
  (ii) removing; or
  (iii) depositing; or
  (iv) harbouring; or
  (v)   keeping; or
  (vi) concealing; or
  (vii) in any manner dealing with any such goods.

SECTION 170(2)

Fraudulent evasion of duty etc
Section 170(2) authorises the arrest of anybody who, in relation to any goods, is knowingly concerned in any fraudulent evasion or attempt at evasion of:

CEMA 1979, s 170(2)

(a) any duty chargeable thereon; or
(b) any statutory prohibition or restriction in respect of the goods; or
(c) any of the provisions of the Customs and Excise Acts applicable to the goods.

4.2.1.2 *Alcoholic Liquor Duties Act 1979 ('ALDA 1979')*

SECTION 17(1)

Unauthorised removal of spirits from distillery etc
Section 17(1) authorises the arrest of any person who:

ALDA 1979, s 17(1)

(a) without the consent of the proper officer of Customs and Excise, conceals in, or removes from a, distillery (see below), any wort (ie alcohol which is unfermented or in the process of fermentation), wash (ie fermented liquor), low wines (see below), feints (see below) or spirits; or
(b) knowingly buys or receives any wort, wash, low wines, feints or spirits, so removed or concealed; or
(c) knowingly buys or receives or has in his possession spirits which have been removed from a place where they ought to have been charged with duty before that duty had been paid or secured – the spirits not having been condemned, or deemed to have been condemned, as forfeited.

Section 4(1) states that 'distillery' means 'premises where spirits are manufactured, whether by distillation of a fermented liquor or by any other process'. The Spirits Regulations 1951, SI 1951/ 2229 define 'low wines' as 'spirits of a first extraction [ie distillation] conveyed into a low wine receiver'; and 'feints' as 'spirits conveyed into a receiver', or in simple English 'impure spirits'.

SECTION 25(1), (3)

Being on premises on which spirits are being unlawfully manufactured
Section 25(3) authorises the arrest of any person who is found on
any premises on which spirits are being unlawfully manufactured
or on which a 'still' is being unlawfully used for rectifying or
compounding spirits. The doing of any those acts is an offence
under subs (1).

ALDA 1979,
s 25(1), (3)

4.2.1.3   Value Added Tax Act 1994 ('VATA 1994')
Section 1 defines value added tax as a tax on the 'supply of goods
or services'. As it is a duty charged on the supply of goods, it
comes within the definition of 'excise'[1] and any offence for which
this Act gives a power of apprehension is *ipso facto* an arrestable
offence.

VATA 1994, s 1

SECTION 72

Various offences
Section 72(9) authorises the arrest for any of the offences
contained in s 72, as follows:

VATA 1994,
s 72

–   s 72 (1): knowingly concerned in, or the taking of steps with
    a view to, the fraudulent evasion of value added tax by
    anybody, including (subs (2)) the claiming of a refund;
–   s 72(3)(a): with intent to deceive, furnish or use any
    document for the purposes of that Act which is false in a
    material particular (including securing a machine to
    respond to the document as if it were a true document, see
    s 72(6)); or (b) when furnishing any information for the
    purposes of the Act, making any statement which is known
    to be false in any material particular or recklessly making a
    statement which is false in a material particular.

4.2.1.4   Finance Act 1994 ('FA 1994')

SCHEDULE 7, PARAS 4, 9

Fraud offences
Schedule 7 concerns insurance premium tax. As that tax is
chargeable *ad valorem* on a service, it is most likely to come under
the same category as a tax on the sale of goods and, therefore, is
an excise duty. Paragraph 4(6) authorises the arrest for any fraud
offence; which is defined in para 4(7) as any offence under
para 9(1) to (5), viz:

FA 1994, Sch 7,
paras 4, 9

---

1   See *Oxford Dictionary of Current English* (Oxford University Press).

- para 9(1)(a) makes it an offence for a registered person to be concerned in, or to take steps with a view to, the fraudulent evasion of insurance premium tax by any registered person or body, which, under subpara (2), includes the obtaining of a repayment;
- para 9(1)(b) makes it an offence for a non-registered person to do any of the acts described in para 9(1)(a), above;
- para 9(3) makes it an offence for anybody with intent to deceive, or to secure that a machine will respond to the document as if it were a true document, to do any of the following acts:

  (a) to produce, or to furnish, or to send, or to cause to be sent, any document for the purposes of the insurance premium tax which is false in a material particular; or
  (b) otherwise make use of such a document for those purposes;

- para 9(4) makes it an offence, when furnishing any information for the purposes of the insurance premium tax, to make any statement which is known to be false in any material particular or recklessly to make any statement which is false in any material particular;
- para 9(5) makes a person guilty of an offence if his conduct during any specified period must have involved the commission of any offence under any of the preceding parts of para 9.

4.2.1.5 Finance Act 1996 ('FA 1996')

SCHEDULE 5, PARAS 6, 15

Fraud offences
Schedule 5 concerns land fill tax. It is submitted that the reasons for regarding land fill tax as an excise duty apply to insurance premium tax (see above). Paragraph 6(1) authorises the arrest for any fraud offence, which is defined in para 6(2) as any offence under para 15(1) to (5), viz:

FA 1996, Sch 5, paras 6, 15

- para 15(1)(a) makes it an offence for a registered person to be concerned in, or to take steps with a view to the fraudulent evasion of land fill tax by any registered person or body, which, under para 15(2), includes the obtaining of a repayment;
- para 15(1)(b) makes it an offence for a non-registered person to do any of the acts described in para 15(1)(a), above;
- para 15(3) makes it an offence for anybody to do any of the following acts:

(a) to produce, or to furnish, or to send, or to cause to be sent, any document for the purposes of the land fill tax which is false in a material particular; or

(b) otherwise makes use of such a document for those purposes,

and in either case did so with intent to deceive, or to secure that a machine will respond to a document as if it were a true document;

– para 15(4) makes it an offence, when furnishing any information for the purposes of the land fill tax, to make any statement which is known to be false in any material particular or recklessly to make any statement which is false in any material particular;

– para 15(5) makes a person is guilty of an offence if his conduct during any specified period must have involved the commission of any offence under any of the preceding parts of para 15.

4.2.2 Certain offences under the Official Secrets Act 1920 ('OSA 1920'): PACE 1994, s 24(2)(b) (as amended by the Official Secrets Act 1989 ('OSA 1989') s 11(1))

These are offences under OSA 1920 for which the maximum sentence is less than 5 years in prison. OSA 1920

4.2.3 Certain offences under OSA 1989: PACE 1984, s 24(2)(bb) (inserted by OSA 1989, s 11(1))

These are offences under any provision of OSA 1989 (except under s 8(1), (4) or (5)) for which the maximum sentence is less than 5 years in prison. OSA 1989

4.2.4 Offences under the Sexual Offences Act 1956 ('SOA 1956'), ss 22 (causing prostitution of women), s 23 (procuration of girl under 21): PACE 1984, s 24(2)(c) (as amended by the Sexual Offences Act 1985, s 5(3))

Section 22 prescribes the procuring of a woman to become, anywhere in the world, a common prostitute, or procuring her to leave the United Kingdom with intent that she become an inmate of, or that she frequent, a brothel. SOA 1956, ss 22 and 23

Section 23 prohibits the procuring of a girl under the age of 21 years to have sexual intercourse anywhere in the world with another person.

4.2.5 Offences under the Theft Act 1968 ('TA 1968'), ss 12(1) (taking motor vehicle etc without authority etc), 25(1) (going equipped for stealing etc): PACE 1984, s 24(2)(d)

Section 12(1) prohibits the taking of a conveyance, except (s 12(5)) a pedal cycle, without the consent of the owner or other lawful authority; or, knowing that one has been so taken, allowing oneself to be carried in it. It is a defence under s 12(6) to believe that one would have had the owner's authority if he had known of the taking. *Whittaker v Campbell*[1] held that the owner's consent was not vitiated even if obtained by fraud.

TA 1968, s 12

Section 25(1) prohibits anybody, when they are not at their place of abode, from having with them any article for use in the course of, or in connection with:

TA 1968, s 25

(1) any burglary;
(2) theft; or
(3) cheating (under s 25(4)); or
(4) obtaining property by deception; or
(5) taking a conveyance without lawful authority.

4.2.6 Any offence under the Football (Offences) Act 1991 ('F(O)A 1991'): PACE 1984, s 24(2)(e) (inserted by F(O)A 1991, s 5(3), Sch)

Offences under F(O)A 1991 comprise the commission of any of the following acts from up to 2 hours before the start of, until 1 hour after, a football match designated by the Secretary of State:

F(O)A 1991
ss 2–4

(1) without lawful authority or reasonable excuse, throwing anything at, or towards, the playing area or where spectators or other persons may be present (contrary to s 2);
(2) the chanting (ie repeating and utterings in concert with another) of an indecent or racialist nature – which is defined in s 3(2)(b) as 'threatening, abusive or insulting to a person by reason of his colour, race, nationality (including citizenship) or ethnic origin' (contrary to s 3); or.
(3) without lawful authority or reasonable excuse, going on to the playing area or land adjacent to it where spectators are not generally admitted (contrary to s 4).

---

1   [1983] 3 All ER 582.

4.2.7 An offence under the Obscene Publications Act 1959 ('OPA 1959'), s 2 (publication of obscene matter): PACE 1984, s 24(2)(f) (inserted by the Criminal Justice and Public Order Act 1994 (CJPOA 1994), s 85(1)

Section 2 makes it an offence to publish for gain or have with one for gain (of oneself or another person) an obscene article, ie (s 1(1)), an article which tends to deprave and corrupt those who, in all the circumstances, are likely to read, to see, or to hear it.

OPA 1959, s 2

Publication includes transmitting any data which is stored electronically; see s 1(3)(b) as inserted by CJPOA 1994, s 168(1), Sch 9, para 3. It is a defence under s 2(5) for a person to show that he had not examined the article and had no reasonable cause to suspect that its publication would constitute an offence.

4.2.8 An offence under the Protection of Children Act 1978 ('PCA 1978') s 1 (indecent photographs etc of children): PACE 1984, s 24(2)(g) (inserted by CJPOA 1994, s 85(2))

The offences created by PCA 1978, s 1(1) are:

PCA 1978, ss 1–7

(1) subs (a): taking, or permitting to take, any indecent photograph or pseudo-photograph of a child;
(2) subs (b): distributing or showing any indecent photograph or pseudo-photograph of a child to another person (see *R v T*)[1];
(3) subs (c): possessing any indecent photograph or pseudo-photograph of a child, with a view to it being distributed or shown by himself or others; or
(4) subs (d): publishing, or causing to be published, any advertisement likely to be understood as meaning that the advertiser distributes or shows indecent photographs or pseudo-photographs of a child.

A photograph includes a copy or negative thereof, a film, a video recording and any image stored on a computer which can be reproduced as a photograph, see s 7(2), (4) and (5). To be guilty, the accused must know that the image is stored on his computer, see *Atkins v DPP*[2].

In *G v DPP*[3], it was held that in this statute the word 'photograph' was used only in the singular and, therefore, did not include two photographs stuck together. However if they were then copied while still attached to each other, the resulting picture would be a

---

1   [1999] Crim LR 749.
2   [2000] 2 All ER 425.
3   *New Law Digest*, 8 March 2000.

'pseudo-photograph'. The latter is defined in s 7(7) 'as an image which appears to be a photograph'.

A child is somebody who is under the age of 16 years, see s 7(6); and if the impression is given that the picture is of a child, then the latter shall be deemed to be such, irrespective of his or her actual age, see s 7(8). It is not a defence that the accused did not know the person photographed was indeed a child, see *R v Land*[1].

Under s 1(4)(a), it is a defence to have a legitimate reason for doing any of the above mentioned things; and, under s 1(4)(b), not to have seen the photograph or pseudo-photograph and not to have known, nor had cause to suspect, that it was indecent.

4.2.9   An offence under CJPOA 1994, s 166 (sale of tickets by unauthorised persons): PACE 1984, s 24(2)(h) (inserted by CJPOA 1994, s 166(4))

Section 166 makes it an offence to sell, offer, or expose for sale, a ticket or purported ticket for a football match designated by the Secretary of State under s 1(1) of F(O)A 1991, (see above), without the written permission of the home club or organisers of the match; such sale, offer or exposure being either in a public place or, if in the course of a trade or business, at any place.

CJPOA 1994, s 166, F(O)A 1991, s 1(1)

4.2.10   An offence under the Public Order Act 1986 ('POA 1986') s 19 (publishing etc material intended or likely to stir up racial hatred): PACE 1984, s 24(2)(i) (inserted by CJPOA 1994, s 155)

Section 19 makes it an offence to publish or distribute to the public, or a section of the public, written material which is threatening, abusive or insulting with intent to stir up racial hatred, or where it is likely to stir up racial hatred – which is defined in s 17 as hatred against a group of persons in Great Britain defined by reference to colour, race, nationality, citizenship or ethnic or national origins. Written material is defined in s 29 as including 'any sign or other representation'.

POA 1986, ss 17, 19, 29

---

1   *New Law Digest*, 10 October 1997.

4.2.11 An offence under CJPOA 1994, s 167 (touting for hire car services): PACE 1984, s 24(2)(j) (inserted by CJPOA 1994, s 167(7))

Section 167 makes it an offence to solicit, in a public place, persons to hire vehicles in order to carry them as passengers, other than licensed taxis and omnibuses whose owners have an operator's licence.

CJPOA 1994, s 167

4.2.12 An offence under the Prevention of Crime Act 1953 ('PCA 1953'), s 1(1) (carrying offensive weapons without reasonable authority or excuse): PACE 1984, s 24(2)(k) (inserted by the Offensive Weapons Act 1996 ('OWA 1996'), s 1(1))

Section 1(1) makes it an offence, unless there is reasonable excuse or lawful authority, to have in a public place any offensive weapon, which (by s 1(4) as amended by POA 1986, s 40(2) and Sch 2, para 2) means any article made or adapted to cause personal injury, or intended by its possessor to be used (by himself or somebody else) for that purpose.

PCA 1953, s 1 (as amended by POA 1986, s 40(2), Sch 2, para 2)

4.2.13 An offence under the Criminal Justice Act 1988 ('CJA 1988'), s 139(1) (having article with blade or point in public place): PACE 1984, s 24(2)(l) (inserted by OWA 1996, s 1(1))

Section 139(1) makes it an offence to have in a public place any article which has a blade or is sharply pointed, except a folding pocket knife with a blade not exceeding 3 inches, unless there is lawful authority or good reason to do so, which includes (s 139(5)) having the article for use at work, for religious reasons or as part of any national costume. For an article to be within the definition of 'folding pocket knife', its blade must not be capable of being locked in the open position and must be able to be folded immediately at all times; see *R v Deegan*[1].

CJA 1988, s 139

4.2.14 An offence under CJA 1988, s 139A(1), (2) (having article with blade or point etc on school premises): PACE 1984, s 24(2)(m) (inserted by OWA 1996, s 1(1))

It is an offence under subss (1) and (2) of s 139A to have any of the following chattels on school premises, without lawful authority or good reason which includes (subs (4)) having the article for use at work, for religious reasons or as part of any national costume:

CJA 1988, s 139A

---

1   [1998] 2 Cr App R 121.

(1) subs (1): any article which has a blade or is sharply pointed, except a folding pocket knife with a blade not exceeding 3 inches; see *R v Deegan*, above;

(2) subs (2): any offensive weapon (as defined is s 1(4) of the PCA 1953, see above).

School premises are defined in s 139(6) as being land used for the purposes of a school except land occupied solely as a dwelling by a person employed at the school.

4.2.15　An offence under the Protection from Harassment Act 1997 ('PHA 1997') s 2 (harassment): PACE 1984, s 24(2)(n) (inserted by PHA 1997, s 2(3))

Section 2(3) makes it an offence for a person unreasonably to pursue a course of conduct which amounts to the harassment of another AND which he knows, or ought to known, amounted to such harassment (s 1(1)). Under s 1(2), a person ought to know that his conduct would amount to harassment if a reasonable person with the same knowledge as himself would think that the conduct complained of did amount to such harassment. Under s 1(3), it is a defence if the actions of the accused were done in order to prevent or to detect crime, or were necessary to comply with any statute or rule of law.

PHA 1997, ss 1, 2

4.2.16　An offence under CJPOA 1994, s 60(8)(b) (failing to comply with requirement to remove mask etc): PACE 1984, s 24(2)(o) (inserted by CDA 1998, s 27(1))

It is an offence under subs 60(8)(b) to fail to remove any item pursuant to a direction given under subs (4A). Under s 60, a police superintendent or officer of higher rank, who reasonably believes:

CJPOA 1994, s 60, PACE 1984, s 1(9)

(1) that incidents involving serious violence might take place; and that

(2) it would be expedient to prevent such an incident by taking the following action,

may authorise constables in uniform to stop and to search pedestrians, vehicles or their occupants for offensive weapons (as defined in PACE 1984, s 1(9)) or for dangerous instruments, which are defined in s 60(11) as 'instruments which have a blade or are sharply pointed'. When exercising that power under s 60, a constable may – by virtue of s 60(4A) – require a person to remove any item which the policeman reasonably believes that person is wearing wholly or mainly for the purposes of concealing his identity, and failure to remove the said item is an offence contrary to s 60(8)(b).

4.2.17 An offence under CDA 1998, s 32(1) (racially aggravated harassment): PACE 1984, s 24(2)(p) (inserted by CDA 1998, s 32(2)) (not in force at time of writing)

An offence under s 32(1) of CDA 1998 consists of committing an offence under PHA 1997, either against s 2 (harassment see **4.2.15**) or contrary to s 4 (putting people in fear of violence AND in either case it was racially aggravated).

CDA 1998, s 32(1), PACE 1984, s 24(2)(p)

4.2.18 An offence under FSA 1989, s 16(4) (failing to comply with reporting duty imposed by a restriction order): PACE 1984, s 24(2)(q) (inserted by s 84(2) of the Crime and Disorder Act 1998)

Under s 15 *et seq* of FSA 1989, a court, on a conviction for an offence under Sch 1 to that Act, can make an order that the person found guilty does report to the police when designated football matches are taking place.

FSA 1989, s 16(4), PACE 1984, s 24(2)(q)

4.2.19 An offence under POA 1986, s 32(3) (entering premises in breach of a domestic football banning order): PACE 1984, s 24(2)(r) (inserted by s 8(3) of the Football (Offences and Disorder) Act 1999)

Section 30 of POA 1986 allows a court to ban from attending football matches anyone who has been convicted of having committed at a football match an offence contrary to ss 1 or 1A of the Sporting Events (Control of Alcohol etc) Act 1985 (see **6.7.3**) which involved violence or a threat of violence to persons or property.

POA 1986, s 32(3), PACE 1984, s 24(2)(r)

4.2.20 Inchoate offences

PACE 1984, s 24(2) also makes it an arrestable offence:

PACE 1984, s 24(2)

(1) to attempt to commit (see also **5.5.2.8**);
(2) to aid and to abet;
(3) to counsel or to procure; or
(4) to incite any of the above offences, except an attempt to commit an offence under TA 1968, s 12(1); see CJA 1988, s 170(11), Sch 15, paras 97 and 98.

4.3 SERIOUS ARRESTABLE OFFENCES

These are set out in the amended s 116 of PACE 1984:

PACE 1984, s 116

(1) under s 116(2)(a):

(a) treason,
(b) murder,
(c) manslaughter,
(d) rape,
(e) kidnapping,
(f) incest with a girl under the age of 13,
(g) buggery with a person under the age of 16,
(h) indecent assault which constitutes an act of gross indecency;

(2) under s 116(2)(b): any of the offences set out in the amended Part 2 of Sch 5:

(a) causing an explosion likely to endanger life or property (Explosive Substances Act 1883, s 2)
(b) intercourse with a girl under the age of 13 years (SOA 1956, s 69)
(c) possession of a firearm with intent to injure (Firearms Act 1968, s 16)
(d) use of firearms, or imitation ones, to resist an arrest (Firearms Act 1968, s 17)
(e) carrying firearms with criminal intent (Firearms Act 1968, s 18)
(f) hostage taking (Taking of Hostages Act 1982, s 1)
(g) hi-jacking (Aviation Security Act 1983, s 1)
(h) death by dangerous driving (Road Traffic Act 1988 (RTA 1988), s 1)
(i) causing death by the careless or inconsiderate driving of a mechanically propelled vehicle on a road or other public place:

   (i)   while unfit through drink or drugs; or
   (ii) after having consumed alcohol above the prescribed limit; or
   (iii) after having failed, without reasonable excuse, to provide a specimen for analysis within 18 hours of the fatal accident (RTA 1988, s 3A (as inserted by RTA 1991, s 3)) – this was made a serious arrestable offence by RTA 1991, Sch 4, para 39,

(j) torture (CJA 1988, s 134, inserted by s 170(1), Sch 15, paras 97 and 102 of that Act),
(k) endangering safety at aerodromes (Aviation and Maritime Security Act 1990, s 1, inserted by s 53, Sch 3, para 8 of that Act),
(l) hi-jacking of ships (Aviation and Maritime Security Act 1990, s 9, inserted by s 53, Sch 3, para 8 of that Act),
(m) seizing or exercising control of fixed platforms (Aviation and Maritime Security Act 1990, s 10, inserted by s 53, Sch 3, para 8 of that Act),
(n) hi-jacking of Channel Tunnel systems (Channel Tunnel Act (Security) Order 1994, SI 1994/570, art 4, inserted by art 38, Sch 3, para 4),
(o) seizing or exercising control of the tunnel system (Channel Tunnel Act (Security) Order 1994, SI 1994/570, art 5, inserted by art 38, Sch 3, para 4),
(p) indecent photographs and pseudo-photographs of children (PCA 1978, s 1, inserted by CJPOA 1994, s 85(1)),
(q) publication of obscene matter (Obscene Publications Act 1959, s 2, inserted by the CJPOA 1994, s 85(3));

(3) under s 116(2)(c): any offence set out in s1(3)(a)–(f) of the Drug Trafficking Act 1994 (DTA 1994):

    (a) producing, supplying and possessing with intent to supply, controlled drugs (ss 4(2) or (3) or 5(3) of the Misuse of Drugs Act 1971 (MDA 1971),

    (b) assisting in, or inducing, the commission outside of the United Kingdom of an offence under MDA 1971, which is punishable under a corresponding law (s 20 of MDA 1971),

    (c) an offence in connection with a prohibition or restriction on a drug imposed by s 3 of MDA 1971 (ss 50(2), 50(3), 68(2), or 170 of CEMA 1979) (see above).

    (d) the manufacture or supply of substances specified in Sch 2 to the Criminal Justice (International Co-operation) Act 1990 (CJ(IC)A 1990) (s 12 of CJ(IC)A 1990),

    (e) using ships for illicit traffic in controlled drugs (s 19 of CJ(IC)A 1990),

    (f) concealing, transferring, acquiring, possessing or using the proceeds of drug trafficking; or failing to disclose one's knowledge or suspicion of drug money laundering when the knowledge or suspicion was acquired in the course of one's trade, profession, business or employment (ss 49, 50 and 51 of DTA 1994). Drug trafficking was defined in s 1(1) of DTA 1994 as the illegal production, or supply, or transporting, or storing, or importing, or exporting, or manufacturing, of a controlled drug, ie a substance specified in Sch 2 to MDA 1971);

(4) under s 116(3): any arrestable offence if any of the consequences set out in the lettered paragraphs of subs (6) are caused by it, or were intended, or were likely to be caused by it, namely:

    (a) serious harm to the security of the state or to public order,

    (b) serious interference with the administration of justice or with the investigation of any offence,

    (c) the death of any person,

    (d) serious injury, which includes any disease or any impairment of any person's physical or mental condition (subs (8)),

    (e) substantial financial gain to any person,

    (f) serious financial loss to any person – 'serious' means to the person who suffered it (subs (7)); and

(5) under s 116(4): an arrestable offence which consists of making a threat, if the carrying out of that threat would lead to any of the consequences specified in subs (6) (see above).

Chapter 5

THE CITIZEN'S POWER OF ARREST WITHOUT A WARRANT

5.1 INTRODUCTION

The law has always bestowed upon the general public the right to make arrests for certain types of misconduct and has also given greater powers to certain sections thereof, and especially to police officers. This chapter sets out the offences for which a citizen's arrest can be made.

Reasonable suspicion is normally sufficient to make an arrest, even though the actual words of the legislation merely give a power to detain somebody who has been caught *in flagrante delicto*, or, to use the statutory language, 'is committing the offence'; see *Wills v Bowley*[1]. Subsequent chapters look at the extra privileges granted to constables and other specifically defined categories of the populace.

5.1.1 The general rule: crimes triable within the jurisdiction

Save as provided by s 137 of CJPOA 1994 (see Chapter 6), all powers of summary arrest in England and Wales apply only to crimes which can be tried in those countries. The nationality of the suspect is irrelevant.

5.1.2 Statutory exceptions: crimes committed outside the jurisdiction

The general rule is that only offences committed in England and Wales are justiciable therein; see *R v Harden*[2]. In a few cases, Parliament has made certain actions undertaken abroad by British subjects triable in the United Kingdom as if such conduct had been perpetrated therein. These extra-territorial offences are as follows.

5.1.2.1 High treason and terrorism
(1) **Treason Act 1351, s 1** – high treason can be committed anywhere in the world;
Terrorism Act 2000 – terrorism committed anywhere in the world.

5.1.2.2 Offences at sea or by seamen
(2) **Offences at Sea Act 1799, s 1** – extending the jurisdiction of an English court to try any offence perpetrated on the high seas outside of any other nation's territorial waters;

---

1   [1983] AC 57.
2   [1963] 1 QB 8.

(3) **Merchant Shipping Act 1995, s 282** – an offence committed anywhere by the crew of a British-registered vessel.

5.1.2.3   *Offences committed whilst in the service of Her Majesty*
(4) **Criminal Jurisdiction Act 1802, s 1** – a person who commits any offence whilst abroad in the service of Her Majesty can be tried for that conduct in the United Kingdom.

5.1.2.4   *Homicide*
(5) **Offences Against the Person Act 1861** – a subject of Her Majesty may be tried in an English court for any murder or manslaughter (s 9) (s 57) committed abroad; and, under s 4, it is illegal, within the jurisdiction:

(a) to solicit;
(b) to encourage;
(c) to persuade;
(d) to endeavour to persuade a person

to commit a murder anywhere in the world.

5.1.2.5   *Bigamy*
(6) **Offences Against the Person Act 1861** – a subject of Her Majesty may be tried in an English court for bigamy committed abroad.

5.1.2.6   *Offences against Protected Persons*
(7) **International Protected Persons Act 1978, s 1 and the United Nations Personnel Act 1997, s 2** – give the English courts jurisdiction over anybody who commits, anywhere in the world, the misdemeanours specified in those statutes against Heads of State, diplomats and their families, and similar people. These are as follows and include attempting, counselling, procuring, or aiding and abetting their commission:

–   murder,
–   manslaughter,
–   rape,
–   assault occasioning actual bodily harm,
–   kidnapping,
–   abduction, save for an offence under s 1(1) of the Child Abduction Act 1984 (ibid s 11(3)),
–   false imprisonment,
–   criminal damage,
–   causing an explosion likely to endanger life or property,
–   the following offences under the Offences Against the Person Act 1861:

    shooting or attempting to shoot, or wounding, with intent to do grievous bodily harm or to resist apprehension (s 18),
    inflicting bodily injury with or without a weapon (s 20),
    attempting to choke in order to commit or assist in the committing of any indictable offence (s 21),

using chloroform etc to commit or assist in the committing of any indictable offence (s 22),

maliciously administering poison etc so as to endanger life or inflict grievous bodily harm (s 23),

maliciously administering poison etc with intent to injure, aggrieve or annoy any other person (s 24),

causing bodily injury by gunpowder (s 28),

causing gunpowder to explode, or sending to any person an explosive substance, or throwing corrosive fluid on a person, with intent to do grievous bodily harm (s 29),

placing gunpowder near a building etc with intent to do grievous bodily harm (s 30).

5.1.2.7 *Offences in relation to nuclear material*

(8) **Nuclear Material (Offences) Act 1983** bestows upon the English courts jurisdiction over anybody who, *by means of, or in relation to, nuclear material,* commits (s 1); or holds or deals with in the intention that he or another do commit (s 2(2)); or threatens to commit (s 2(3)), any of the following offences:

– murder,
– manslaughter,
– assault to injure,
– shooting or attempting to shoot, or wounding, with intent to do grievous bodily harm or to resist apprehension (s 18 of the Offences Against the Person Act 1861),
– inflicting bodily injury with or without a weapon (s 20 of the Offences Against the Person Act 1861),
– theft,
– embezzlement,
– robbery,
– assault with intent to rob,
– burglary,
– aggravated burglary,
– fraud,
– obtaining by deception,
– blackmail.

5.1.2.8 *Causing nuclear explosions*

(9) **Nuclear Explosions (Prohibition and Inspections) Act 1998** – it is an offence to cause nuclear explosions anywhere.

5.1.2.9 *Sexual offences*

(10) **Sexual Offenders (Conspiracy and Incitement Act) 1996, s 2** makes triable in England and Wales the incitement therein of the commission anywhere in the world of a listed sexual offence (ie the same offences as are covered

by the Sexual Offenders Act 1997, below). (NB Section 1 of the 1996 Act was repealed and replaced by the Criminal Justice (Terrorism and Conspiracy) Act 1998.)

(11) **Sexual Offenders Act 1997, s 7(1)** – it is an offence for a British citizen or UK resident to commit, to attempt to commit, to council or to procure abroad any of the following crimes under SOA 1956, provided that they are also illegal in the country where they occur:

    (i)   raping a girl under the age of 16 years (s 1),
    (ii) intercourse with a girl under the age of 13 years (s 5),
    (iii) intercourse with a girl aged 13–16 years (s 6),
    (iv) buggery with a boy or girl under the age of 16 years (s 12),
    (v) indecently assaulting a girl under the age of 16 years (s 14),
    (vi) indecently assaulting a boy under the age of 16 years (s 15),
    (vii) assault with intent to bugger a boy or girl under the age of 16 years (s 16).

The same also applies to:

(1) indecent conduct towards a young child, contrary to the Indecency with Children Act 1960, s 1;
(2) taking etc indecent photographs of children, contrary to the Protection of Children Act 1978.

5.1.2.10 Perjury

Perjury Act 1911, s 8 makes triable in England and Wales any offence against that statute – which includes knowingly making false statements in those countries for use in judicial proceedings abroad and vice-versa.

5.1.2.11 Conspiracy

Criminal Law Act 1977, s 1A(1–5) (as amended by the Criminal Justice (Terrorism and Conspiracy) Act 1998, ss 5–8) makes triable in this country a conspiracy, where the agreement is to commit a crime abroad (which is also punishable under the laws of this country); and the conspirator had, in England or Wales, entered into the pact, or done an overt act in pursuance thereof.

5.1.2.12 War crimes and landmines

War Crimes Act 1991, s 1 makes justiciable in this country acts:

(1) which were undertaken by a person who was a British citizen or resident on or after 8 March 1900; and
(2) which were contrary to the laws and customs of war; and
(3) which were done in Germany or in a place under German occupation; and
(4) which happened between 1 September 1939 and 5 June 1945.

Landmines Act 1998, s 3 makes punishable in this country the possession, manufacture, or use, etc of landmines anywhere in the world.

5.1.2.13   Fraud

Criminal Justice Act 1993, s 1 et seq (brought into force on 1 June 1999 by SI 1189/1999) makes certain frauds committed abroad an offence in England and Wales if overt acts in pursuance of the dishonest conduct are perpetrated in those latter countries.

5.1.2.14   Offences on aircraft

Civil Aviation Act 1982, s 92(1) makes all offences committed on British aeroplanes (other than military ones) while in flight triable in England and Wales.

Aviation Security Act 1982, s 1 makes an aeroplane hijacking wherever it occurs an offence triable in this country.

5.2   PROSECUTIONS WHICH CAN BE BROUGHT ONLY BY THE LAW OFFICERS OR THE DIRECTOR OF PUBLIC PROSECUTIONS OR OTHER NOMINATED PEOPLE

Prosecution for certain crimes can be brought only with the *fiat* of a law officer or certain other people. That restriction does not prevent a warrant being issued, or the apprehension of a suspect prior to the necessary consent being granted; see s 25 of the Prosecution of Offences Act 1985; nor does it prevent him from being remanded in custody after his arrest. The same applies to making arrests for offences, the prosecution of which can only be instituted by HM Commissioners of Customs and Excise; see CJA 1988, s 93F (as inserted by CJA 1993, s 35 and DTA 1994, s 60(5)).

5.3   PUBLIC PLACE

A number of activities become unlawful only if carried out in a 'public place'. Thus, it is necessary to consider the meaning of those words, which is basically a location to which the members of the public are admitted (whether on payment or otherwise). The leading case is *Cutter v Eagle Star; Clarke v Kato*[1], where the House of Lords approved the definition given by Lord Sands in *Harrison v Hill*[2].

> 'Any [place] may be regarded as [public] to which the public have access [or] upon which members of the public are to be found who have not obtained access either by overcoming a physical obstruction or in defiance of a prohibition express or implied.
>
> I think that when the statute speaks of "the public" in this connection, what is meant is the public generally, and not the special class of members of the public who have occasion for business or social purposes to go to the farmhouse or to any

---

1   [1998] 4 All ER 417 at 420.
2   1932 SC(J) 13 at 17.

part of the farm itself; were it otherwise, the definition might just as well have included all private roads as well as public highways.'

Thus, in *Deacon v AT (A Minor)*[1], it was held that an access road to a council estate was not a road within the meaning of the RTA without evidence that it was frequented by the public at large. It was not sufficient that it was frequented by estate residents and their guests. The High Court also held that there must be some evidence of tolerance by the owner to the public at large using the access road. However, in *DPP v Vivier*[2], the private grounds of a caravan club were held to be a public place as membership was automatically granted to anybody who was prepared to pay the subscription and abide by the rules. In *Harwell v DPP*[3], a car park of a community centre was found not to be a public place because a prospective member had to be proposed and seconded and his election was not a formality. In *DPP v Greenwood*[4], a hospital car park which was restricted to, and only used by, people on hospital business, including those visiting patients, was held to be open to the public because of the large numbers of people using it. In *DPP v Cargo Handling Ltd*[5], it was held that, although the airport roads at Heathrow had signs saying 'not open to the public', they were in law 'public places' as they were used by millions of people every year. The number of people who used them made them, as a matter of law, 'public'. A place can be 'public' at one time and 'private' at another time, for example the grounds of a public house in which parking is only permitted during opening hours (see *Sandy v Martin*[6]) or a field where point-to-point races are held a few times a year (see *R v Collinson*[7]).

5.4   COMMON LAW POWERS

The only common law powers of arrest without a warrant to survive until the present day are:

(1) to apprehend traitors;
(2) to prevent a breach of the peace; and
(3) to arrest a person who is unlawfully at large.

5.4.1   Treason

At common law, there was a right, if not a duty, to arrest a person committing high treason in one's presence and also a power to apprehend a person reasonably suspected of a treasonable act that had actually been committed[8]. It

1   [1976] RTR 244.
2   [1991] 4 All ER 18.
3   [1993] Crim LR 621.
4   (Unreported) 12 February 1997.
5   [1992] RTR 318.
6   [1974] RTR 263.
7   (1931) 23 Cr App R 49.
8   See Hawkins *Pleas of the Crown* (8th edn, 1824), vol iv, p 174, s 3 and Stephen *Commentary on the Law of England* (21st edn, 1950), vol iv, p 223.

is also a statutory arrestable offence as the penalty is fixed by law, ie life imprisonment (see Treason Act 1814, s 1 as amended by the Crime and Disorder Act 1998, s 36). At the request of a petition by the House of Commons, the Sovereign laid down in the Treason Act 1351 what acts amounted to treachery. It has been amended a number of times with the result that any of the following conduct now constitutes the *actus reus* of High Treason:

(1) compassing or imagining the death of:

    (a) the King, or

    (b) the Queen, or

    (c) His Majesty's heir;

(2) violating:

    (a) the Queen, or

    (b) the King's eldest unmarried daughter, or

    (c) the wife of the heir to the throne;

(3) levying war against the King in his realm;

(4) giving aid and support to the King's enemies, both within and without the realm; and

(5) killing the Chancellor, Treasurer or His Majesty's justices of the superior courts but in latter case only while sitting on the Bench or on circuit.

The Treason Act 1795 made the following High Treason: compassing, imagining, inventing, devising or intending:

(1) the death; or

(2) the destruction; or

(3) any bodily harm tending to death or destruction; or

(4) the maiming; or

(5) the wounding; or

(6) the imprisonment; or

(7) the restraint,

of His Majesty, his heirs and successors.

R v Sindercome[1] stated that the Treason Act 1795 was declamatory of the common law. By the Treason Acts of 1695, s 5 and 1795, there is a 3-year limitation period in which a person must be committed for trial for treason or misprision of treason committed in England or Wales, save (s 6) for designing, endeavouring or attempting the assassination of the King.

5.4.2   Breach of the peace

5.4.2.1   *Definition*

Every person is under a duty to preserve the peace; see *The Charge to the Bristol Grand Jury*[2]. In *Albert v Lavin*[3], Lord Diplock stated:

---

1   (1657) 5 St Tr 842.

2   (1832) 5 C and P 259.

3   [1982] AC 546 at 565.

'It is: that every citizen in whose presence a breach of the peace is being, or reasonably appears about to be, committed has the right to take reasonable steps to make the person who is breaking or threatening to break the peace refrain from doing so; and those reasonable steps in appropriate cases include detaining him against his will. At common law this is not only the right of every citizen, it is also his duty, although, except in the case of a citizen who is a constable, it is a duty of imperfect obligation.'

A 'breach of the peace' and the power of arrest associated with it were described thus by the Court of Appeal in *R v Howell*[1]:

'We hold that there is power of arrest for breach of the peace where: (1) a breach of the peace is committed in the presence of the person making the arrest or (2) the arrestor reasonably believes that such a breach will be committed in the immediate future by the person arrested although he has not yet committed any breach or (3) where a breach has been committed and it is reasonably believed that a renewal is threatened.'[2]

In *Laine v Chief Constable of Cambridge*[3] the Court of Appeal held that (3) also applied where it was reasonably believed that a breach had already actually occurred. The judges in *R v Howell*[4] went on to say:

'We are emboldened to say that there is a breach of the peace whenever harm is actually done or is likely to be done to a person or in his presence to his property or a person is in fear of being harmed through an assault, an affray, a riot, unlawful assembly or other disturbance.'

5.4.2.2   When an arrest can be made
R v Howell, above, also laid down when a person could be detained:

'It is for this breach of the peace when done in his presence or the reasonable apprehension of it taking place that a constable, or anyone else, may arrest an offender without warrant.'[5]

In *G v Chief Superintendent of Police at Stroud*[6], it was held that where there had been no actual breach of the *Pax Reginae*, at common law the arrester had to believe, on reasonable grounds, that his prisoner was about to commit an actual breach of the peace and not merely that he was going to provoke somebody else into so doing. This aspect was touched upon in *Foulkes v Chief Constable of Merseyside*[7], but note the use of the word 'may' (rather than 'does') by Beldam LJ[8]:

'In the circumstances of this case, although I am prepared to hold that a constable may exceptionally have power to arrest a person whose behaviour is lawful but provocative, it is a power which ought to be exercised by him only in the clearest of

---

1   [1982] QB 416.
2   Ibid, at 426C.
3   (Unreported) 14 October 1999.
4   [1982] QB 416 at 427E.
5   Ibid, at 427F.
6   (1988) 86 Crim App R 92.
7   [1998] 3 All ER 705.
8   Ibid, at 711b.

circumstances and when he is satisfied on reasonable grounds that a breach of the peace is imminent.'

That quotation was cited with approval by a differently constituted appellate court in *R v Ramsell*[1]. There is no case on exactly how long constitutes 'imminent'. It is submitted that it must be measured in minutes rather than hours. In *Ramsell*, above, the court was of the view that this word meant more than just 'there and then'. In that case, the defendant had engaged in a violent altercation with her neighbour in the latter's garden, so the police went to her house. She told them to leave, stating that she would 'sort it out'. Her arrest was ruled to be lawful. On what she had told the local constabulary, they could reasonably conclude that a breach of the *Pax Reginae* was *about to take place*. The limits of those italicised words were not discussed. What is the position if, for example, the police learn that a person is going to London the next day to visit his estranged spouse – a visit which, if past experience is anything to go by, is likely to lead to violence? It is submitted that the legal answer would be for the local beat officer to go round to the wife's address just before the arrival of her husband in order to warn him off, failing which an arrest could be executed, as by then a disturbance would be imminent. Whether such a course of action would be practical, bearing in mind the constraints on police manpower, is another matter, but, as the authorities stand, until he is approaching his spouse's residence, the constabulary would not be able to restrain him from travelling to his intended destination (save by verbal persuasion).

In *Beatty v Gillbanks*[2] and *R v City of Londonderry Justices, ex parte Orr*[3], it was held that a person can be held responsible for a breach of the peace only if the latter would have been the natural outcome of his conduct; and that unlawfulness was not a natural consequence of a legitimate act. It would be another matter if the language used was of a deliberately inflammatory nature which was clearly going to stir up violence in the audience (as appears to have been the case in *Duncan v Jones*[4]); likewise if the words to be uttered were so insulting that it would manifestly inflame the audience to break the peace. At the end of the day, the distinction would appear to be between, on the one hand, acting in a way which the judiciary consider reasonable in which case any violence could not be laid at the actor's door and, on the other hand, conduct or words which were an abuse of the right to freedom of speech in that they went beyond the mere expression of an opinion and were clearly so outrageous as would incite violence in the audience. At the end of the day, it will all depend on the political climate existing at the relevant time.

In *Foulkes v Chief Constable of Merseyside*, above, the police were called by the plaintiff and found him sitting on his front doorstep. He was very nervous and jittery and not completely coherent. He clearly had a nervous disposition, his hands were shaking but otherwise he seemed calm. The plaintiff related to PC McNamara that he had had disagreements with his children and they had

---

1   (Unreported) 25 May 1999.
2   (1882) 9 QBD 308.
3   (1891) LR 28 IR 440.
4   [1936] 1 KB 219.

locked him out when he went to telephone the police. PC Mackay went inside the house and was there for several minutes with the front door closed. While that officer was speaking to the people therein, the plaintiff gave PC McNamara an account of the incident earlier that morning, telling him that the local constabulary had attended and that in general terms the nature of the argument was over the children playing loud music. PC Mackay returned and said that his wife and offspring did not want him to re-enter the premises. The policeman was of the view that if the plaintiff went inside there would be arguments, which could well lead to violence. He suggested to Mr Foulkes that he should go and have a cup of tea or visit a relative until tempers had cooled. The plaintiff's response was to keep repeating, 'It's my house. I called you. I want to go back inside the house'.

As he refused to depart, PC McNamara arrested him for breach of the peace. The Court of Appeal held that Mr Foulkes had done nothing wrong and it was not reasonable to suspect that he would cause an imminent breach of the peace. Likewise, in *Redmond-Bate v DPP*[1], a Christian fundamentalist had preached to the public from the steps of Wakefield Cathedral. The High Court cited and followed the decision in *Beatty v Gillbanks*, above, holding that it had been unreasonable for the arrester to have suspected him of conduct likely to cause a breach of the peace. Provided he did not use provocative language, he was acting perfectly lawfully, even if other people might unreasonably have reacted with violence because of what he was saying (although here there was no such evidence of this). This principle was applied in *Bibby v Chief Constable of Essex*[2], where it was held to have been unlawful for a constable to have arrested a bailiff who was in the process of levying execution on a debtor's chattels. The officer was quite right to have feared an imminent breach of the peace, but the cause of it would not have been the claimant lawfully going about his duty but the debtor in resisting the legal seizing of his goods.

In *Timothy v Simpson*[3], it was held that both people involved in a fight could be arrested for breach of the peace, even though it could not be said who was the aggressor. In *Porter v Metropolitan Police Commissioner*[4], the claimant refused to leave an electricity board showroom. The police were called. She resisted being evicted and was arrested for breach of the peace. The court held that merely refusing to leave was not a breach of the peace, but if any resistance at all was made to the attempts to remove her from the premises (ie if she did not remain totally passive), then there was always the danger that the situation could escalate into violence, so that the police were entitled to arrest her to prevent a breach of the *Pax Reginae*.

In *Steel et al v United Kingdom*[5], the European Court of Human Rights held that an arrest to prevent a breach of the peace did not violate the Convention. The

1   [1999] Crim LR 998.
2   (2000) 164 JP 297.
3   (1835) 1 CM & R 757.
4   *New Law Digest*, 20 October 1999.
5   (1998) 28 EHRR 603.

latter prevented 'arbitrariness'. A breach of the peace was well defined; its limits were known.

5.4.3 A person unlawfully at large

In the past, the right to recapture somebody who was unlawfully at large probably depended on whether his incarceration was for a felony or for a misdeamour, but that difference disappeared with the abolition of those categorisations of transgressions in 1967. However, it was always a crime to escape from lawful custody (see *R v Frascati*[1]), which, being a contravention of the common law, carries a maximum penalty of life imprisonment and is, accordingly, an arrestable offence, enabling a citizen's arrest to be made.

5.5 STATUTORY POWERS

5.5.1 Nineteenth-century statutes

5.5.1.1 *Unlawful Drilling Act 1819*[2]
Section 2 authorises any person acting in aid of, or in the assistance of, a constable or justice of the peace to arrest any person present at, or aiding, or assisting, or abetting, a meeting or assembly held for military drilling or training without the authority of a Secretary of State[3].

5.5.1.2 *Vagrancy Act 1824*
Section 6 authorises anybody to apprehend and to hand over to a justice of the peace or a constable any person whom he finds offending against that Act, namely:

(1) those begging or gathering alms in a public place, or procuring, or encouraging children to do so (contrary to s 3); and
(2) rogues or vagabonds, who are defined in s 4 as:

   (a) people who live rough without proper accommodation and are unable to give a good account of themselves,
   (b) those who indecently expose themselves (ie their penis[4]) in front of a female (whether in public or on private property[5]),
   (c) those who use false pretences to obtain charity, and
   (d) those who are found in a dwelling house, or warehouse, or coach house or stable or outhouse or in any enclosed yard, garden or area for any unlawful (ie illegal) purpose; see *Hayes v Stevenson*[6]. In *Talbot v*

---

1   (1981) 73 Cr App R 28.
2   As amended by the Statute Law Reform Act 1888 and the Courts Act 1971, s 56(4) and Sch 11, Part IV.
3   Statutes always merely say 'Secretary of State', they never specify which, so in law any Secretary of State can give the necessary authorisation.
4   See *Evans v Ewels* [1972] 2 All ER 22.
5   See *Ford v Falcone* [1971] 2 All ER 1138.
6   (1860) 3 LT 296.

DPP[1], it was held that the word 'area' was to be construed *eius generis* with the two preceding words. In *Knott v Blackburn*[2], it was held that 'yard' meant a small yard akin to a garden in size and not, for example, a railway goods yard.

5.5.1.3   Licensing Act 1872

Section 12 gives to the public at large a power to arrest any person who is drunk on any highway or other public place while he is in charge thereon of any:

(1) carriage;
(2) horse;
(3) cattle (which includes pigs and sheep)[3]; or
(4) steam engine.

A carriage includes a motor vehicle (see RTA 1988, s 191) and a bicycle whether ridden or pushed[4]. Section 12 also gives a power to arrest anyone who has in his possession, while drunk, a loaded firearm, which includes an air-gun[5]. *Neale v RMJE (A Minor)*[6] held that this section applied only to those under the influence of alcohol and not to a glue sniffer.

5.5.1.4   Public Stores Act 1875

Section 12(1) empowers the public at large to arrest anyone who is, or whom they with reasonable cause suspect to be, in the act of committing or attempting to commit an offence contrary to s 5 or s 8 of the statute. Section 5 makes it an offence to destroy or obliterate any mark on property belonging to Her Majesty's government with intent to conceal the ownership of the said chattels. Section 8 makes it illegal, without written permission from a public department, or from some person authorised by a public department in that behalf (proof of which permission shall lie on the party accused), to gather or search for stores, or to creep, sweep, or dredge in the sea or any tidal water, within one hundred yards from any vessel belonging to Her Majesty or in Her Majesty's service, or from any mooring place or anchoring place appropriated to such vessels, or from any moorings belonging to Her Majesty, or from any of Her Majesty's wharves, or dock, victualling or steam factory yards, or within one thousand yards from any battery or fort used for the practice of artillery either by the Royal Artillery or by ... volunteer artillery, or in or on any part of the spaces or distances, whether covered with water or not, from time to time marked out as ranges for artillery practice for the use of Her Majesty's ships, or marked out and appropriated for ranges under the provisions of the Artillery Ranges Act 1862.

---

1   [2000] 1 WLR 1102.
2   [1944] 1 All ER 116.
3   See *Child v Hearn* (1874) LR 9 Exch 176.
4   See *Corkery v Carpenter* [1951] 1 KB 102.
5   See *Seamark v Prouse* [1980] 3 All ER 26.
6   (1984) 80 Cr App R 21.

5.5.2 Twentieth-century pre-PACE statutes

5.5.2.1 *Visiting Forces Act 1952*

Section 13 extends the powers of arrest without warrant contained in s 186 of the Army Act 1955 (see below) to the apprehension of deserters and those absent without leave from visiting forces. This power of arrest can be exercised only on the express invitation of the appropriate authority which is defined in s 17(3) as such authority as may be appointed for that purpose by the government of the country whence the visiting forces have come.

5.5.2.2 *Army Act 1955*

Where no constable is available, s 186(2) authorises anybody to arrest, without warrant, any regular soldier whom he has cause to suspect to be a deserter, or to be absent without leave. The detainee must be taken before a magistrates' court as soon as reasonably possible (s 186(4)). The actual power of arrest is vested in 'any officer, warrant officer, non-commissioned officer or soldier of the regular army or any other person'. Does the *eius generis* rule apply to the meaning of 'any other person'? If it did, then the only people who would fall into that category are officers and other ranks serving in the air and naval forces. If that was the intention of Parliament, it could just as well have said so instead of using the phraseology it did. Thus, it is submitted that the *eius generis* rule should not be adopted when construing s 186.

5.5.2.3 *Air Force Act 1955*

Where no policeman is available, s 186(2) empowers any person to arrest without warrant any regular member of the Royal Air Force whom he has cause to suspect to be either a deserter or absent without leave; and his captive must be taken before a magistrates' court as soon as is practicable (s 186(4)).

The courts might apply the *eius generis* rule to the meaning of 'any other person' and hold that those words were referring only to officers etc of the other armed services, but if that were the case, the phrase 'any other person' is unfortunate (see the commentary on s 186 of the Army Act 1955, above).

5.5.2.4 *Sexual Offences Act 1956*[1]

Section 41 empowers 'anyone' summarily to apprehend a man 'found committing an offence under section 32' of SOA 1956, namely persistently soliciting or importuning in a public place for immoral purposes. The last two words in this context relate solely to sexual mores (see *Crook v Edmondson*[2]) although that conduct need not be illegal (see *R v Ford*[3]). For a discussion on the meaning of other words used in s 35, see the commentary on s 1 of the Street Offences Act 1959 in Chapter 6. Although the statute gives a power to arrest a male 'committing the offence', in accordance with *Wills v Bowley*[4] a reasonable

---

1   As amended by CJA 1967, s 10(2) and Sch 3, Part III.
2   [1966] 2 QB 81.
3   [1977] 1 All ER 1129.
4   [1983] AC 57. See also **5.1**.

suspicion that somebody was in the act of perpetrating this crime will be sufficient.

What is more curious is that para 9 of Sch 6 to PACE 1984 restricts the power of the police to make an arrest under s 41 of SOA 1956, so that they can only exercise it if one of the general arrest conditions (see **6.8** *et seq*) also applies. Thus, for example, any citizen, except a police officer, can arrest a man who is kerb-crawling, whereas a constable can only do the same if he did not happen to know, and was unable to discover, the name and address of the offender. This distinction may be due to the fact that a person is more likely to give his personal details to an officer of the law, rather than somebody whom he may well regard as an interfering busybody.

5.5.2.5   Naval Discipline Act 1957
Where no constable is available, s 105(2) empowers any officer or rating subject to the Act or any other person to arrest without warrant any regular naval officer or rating whom he suspects was a deserter or was absent without leave; and the arrested person must be taken before a magistrates' court as soon as is practicable (s 105(4)).

As to the meaning of 'any other person', see the Army Act 1955 and the Air Force Act 1955, above.

5.5.2.6   Criminal Justice Act 1967
Section 91 allows a citizen to arrest anybody who, whilst drunk, is guilty of disorderly behaviour in a public place. *Neale v RMJE (A Minor)*[1] held that this section applied only to those under the influence of alcohol. Despite the statute using the present tense, in *Fay v DPP*[2] it was held that the *actus reus* need neither be occurring at the time of the apprehension nor need the arrester have witnessed personally the criminal activity. The rationale of the High Court in so holding was given by Sullivan J:

> 'No doubt it was not intended that the power conferred by section 91(1) should be exercised many hours or days after the event. Some degree of immediacy is required. But a police constable who sees someone engaged in such behaviour may, for some reason, be prevented from making an arrest immediately. The offender, for example, may flee. When the officer or his colleagues finally catches him, the offender may well have ceased to be disorderly. I do not see why, in those circumstances, the officers cannot affect an arrest under section 91(1).
>
> If a member of the public complains to the police that a person has been behaving in a drunk and disorderly manner, but the complainant is too old or infirm and unable or unwilling to make the arrest himself, then are the police to be powerless to take any action unless and until they themselves witness behaviour that is drunk and disorderly? In my view, the answer to that question, as a matter of common sense, must be "No".'

---

1   (1984) 80 Cr App R 21.
2   (Unreported) 7 April 1998.

5.5.2.7 *Theft Act 1978*

Section 3(3) empowers the citizen to arrest anybody who is, or whom he with reasonable cause suspects to be, committing or attempting to commit an offence under s 3(1) of the Act – namely making off without paying a lawful debt with intent to avoid payment, when the debt is payable on the spot for goods supplied or services rendered. 'Payable on the spot', as defined in s 3(2), also includes a payment due at the time of the collection of goods on which work has been done or services provided.

This power of arrest only arises while a person is actually in the process of 'making off' without paying. The question is when does a person cease to have 'made off'? How far must he have travelled before the offence ceases to be in the process of 'being committed' and instead becomes 'already perpetrated'? In no reported case has s 3(3) been relied upon as a defence to a trespass action. A somewhat similar question has arisen in cases involving PACE 1984, s 24(4) (see below), but there the test is different. 'Making off' clearly involves some form of continuous activity. The Minister of State at the Home Office told the Lords in Committee[1], that this power of arrest was to enable store keepers etc to detain those who made off without paying because if such 'bilkers' were not apprehended on the spot, there would probably be no means of tracing them subsequently and, therefore, they would get away scot free. Accordingly, applying a purposeful approach to s 3(3) of TA 1978, an arrester ought to be able to detain anybody if he more or less immediately follows them on their departure from the place where the payment ought to have been made and is able to catch them up either before, or more or less immediately upon, their arrival at home or another location where they intend to stay for some time (eg a cafe to have a cup of tea). Although unlikely, there is always a possibility that a court in a 'law and order' mood could hold that until a person had got to his residence or other place where he was staying for the night he was still in the process of making off without payment.

5.5.2.8 *Criminal Attempts Act 1981*

Section 2(2)(e) makes an attempt to commit an indictable offence subject to the same powers of arrest as the full offence, which, if such did exist, would normally be 'on reasonable suspicion'. The *actus reus* is (s 1) conduct which is more than merely preparatory to its commission, while the *mens rea* is a desire to commit the full offence and recklessness is not sufficient, see *R v Pearman*[2]. Thus the question arises of whether it is reasonable to suspect somebody merely because the natural consequence of his actions would, if uninterrupted, have been a crime. It is submitted that the answer is 'yes'. Such would be reasonable because it is impossible to know what is in somebody else's mind; and if foresight of the latter was a requirement, then hardly anybody would ever be arrested for attempting a transgression of the law.

---

1   *Hansard* HL 31 January 1978, vol 380, cols 707–710.
2   [1985] RTR 39.

5.5.3 PACE 1984

Under s 24, anybody may arrest without warrant a person:

–   s 24(4): who is, or whom he has reasonable grounds to suspect (see below)
    to be, committing an arrestable offence (see Chapter 4).
–   s 24(5): who is, or whom he reasonable suspects to be guilty of that offence,
    provided that the arrestable offence has actually been perpetrated by
    somebody.

Section 24(4) merely re-enacted word-for-word s 2(2) of the Criminal Law Act
1967 (CLA 1967). In *Wills v Bowley*[1], the majority agreed with the *obiter dicta* of
Lord Bridge[2] that s 2(2) of that statute allowed a person to make an arrest even
though no crime had actually been committed:

> 'But a new provision is found in section 2(2) [of CLA 1967] ...
>
> But I thought it right to draw attention to it as it affords a good example of a
> modern statute, using language with the precision one expects, expressly
> recognising the futility of giving to anybody the power to arrest a person caught in
> the act of committing an offence, or appearing to do so, if the legality of the arrest
> depends on whether the person arrested turns out later to have been in fact
> committing an offence or not. That, at all events seems to me to be the rationale
> which underlies section 2(2) of the Criminal Law Act 1967.'

That decision was not cited in *R v Self*[3], which latter case found to the contrary
and therefore must be regarded as having been decided *per incuriam*. However,
s 24(4) does give rise (especially in theft cases) to the problem of when is a
crime being 'committed' as against 'having been committed'. In *R v Hale*[4], the
accused burgled a house and on his way out with his ill-gotten gains he assaulted
the occupier. His defence to a robbery charge was that he had already stolen
the jewellery before he had tied up his victim. The Court of Appeal upheld the
conviction, stating:

> '[An appropriation] is conduct which usurps the rights of an owner. To say that the
> conduct is over and done with as soon as he lays hands upon the property, or when
> he first manifests an intention to deal with it as his, is contrary to common sense
> and to the natural meaning of words.
>
> However, the act of appropriation does not suddenly cease. It is a continuous act
> and it is a matter for the jury to decide whether or not the act of appropriation has
> finished.'

In *Davidson v Chief Constable of North Wales*[5], the plaintiff had been apprehended
(to quote the arrester's own words) 'for shoplifting'. He had gone straight from
Woolworths (the *locus in quo*) to a cafe across the road, where he was detained
while drinking coffee – by which time the offence had already been committed,
according to Staughton LJ. In *Stanley v Benning*[6], the plaintiff was seen to pick

1   [1983] AC 57.
2   Ibid, at 104C/D.
3   [1992] 3 All ER 476.
4   (1978) 68 Cr App R 415.
5   [1994] 2 All ER 597.
6   (Unreported) 4 July 1998.

up two pairs of trousers from the rack and take them into the store's changing room. He emerged carrying only one pair which he replaced whence he had taken it. He was challenged by the manager, but ran off. He was pursued and was apprehended 10 yards from the shop. He was wearing two pairs of trousers, the outer one concealing the other pair which he had taken off the rack. The Court of Appeal said that it was a question for the jury as to whether he was still in the course of theft. They said that any other answer but 'yes' would have been contrary to common sense. In the words of Scott V-C:

> 'It seems to me thoroughly artificial to treat the conduct of Mr Stanley in entering the shop, selecting the trousers, going into the cubicle, putting on a pair of the shop's trousers underneath his own, tucking the ends into his socks to avoid them being apparent, endeavouring to walk out from the shop with the concealed pair of trousers, being half apprehended while so doing, seeking to evade apprehension and being apprehended 10 yards from the shop entrance to a continuous process of criminal intent, as susceptible of being split into two sections, one of which involved the commission of the crime of theft and the other of which involved acts done after the commission of the crime. Section 24(4) was intended to confer powers of arrest on individuals in whose presence an offence is committed. How could a shop owner or the owner of domestic premises possibly undertake with any sort of safety a citizen's arrest of a miscreant whom they found making off from their premises, be it shop or home, with their property in his pocket if the lawfulness of the arrest was going to depend, first, on a fine legal analysis of the point in the course of the miscreant's unlawful conduct at which the theft had been completed, perhaps the time at which the watch had been put into the pocket or, as in this case, the trousers put on in the cubicle. There will always be the possibility that at trial some state of mind of the apparent miscreant, which they would have no possible means of knowing or detecting in advance, would lead to an acquittal.'

However, the lords justices in that case also held that the offence had already been completed when the arrest was made in *R v Self*, above. There the plaintiff was seen by a shop assistant picking up a bar of chocolate from the counter, putting it in his pocket and leaving the department store without paying for it. He was followed into the street and was seen to take the chocolate out of his pocket and throw it under a car. He was then approached by a store detective and apprehended. The lords justices in *Stanley*, above, also said that the test to be applied in s 24(4) was not the same as in a criminal trial for theft on the issue of when an appropriation had taken place.

A far less strict approach was taken in *Dhesi v Chief Constable of the West Midlands*[1]. There the police had arrived at an affray, shortly after which the claimant ran away, carrying a hockey stick. Officers went looking for those involved. Half-an-hour later they came across the plaintiff who was hiding in some overgrown bushes on wasteland. He had with him his weapon from the affray (a hockey stick), which he raised in a threatening manner when PC Brown approached him. The Court of Appeal held:

> 'Even if there was such an opportunity [to arrest him before he got to the park] – and there is no finding by the Recorder to that effect – it is obvious that the two brothers made off before they could be arrested and with a view to avoiding arrest.

---

1   (2000) TLR, May 9.

> In my judgment, the recorder was perfectly entitled to regard the whole matter as one continuing affray. I would reject that ground of appeal.'

That decision is explicable on the basis that the threatening of the police officers with the same weapons as used half-an-hour earlier made the whole affair one incident. Thus the case is different from that of a shoplifter, the latter is not likely to attempt to steal anything from the store detective when he comes to arrest him!

Thus, until very recently, it would appear that a crime was no longer considered to be in the process of 'being committed' once the perpetrator had left the building where the *actus reus* had occurred together with its curtilage, and had become engaged in an activity unconnected with his transgression and his getaway. Thus, because Constable Self had already divested himself of the proceeds of his alleged theft and as Mr Davidson was sitting down partaking of refreshments in a cafe, they could not be arrested under s 24(4) because by that time their conduct and actions were unconnected with any criminal activity. Mr Stanley was in a different position, because he was being followed in hot pursuit with his booty deliberately concealed about his person. Unfortunately for Mr Dhesi, a more liberal approach appears to have been taken by the judiciary in his case. He had stopped being violent and had left the *locus in quo*, yet he was held still to have been committing an affray. The rationale would appear to be that so long as he was making his getaway he was deemed to be still perpetrating his offence. That is, of course, contrary to *R v Self*, above, as it was interpreted in *Stanley v Benning*, above. The only difference between the cases of *Self* and *Dhesi* is that, in the former, the proceeds of the theft had been thrown away, whereas in the latter, the claimant still had his hockey stick – surely a somewhat artificial distinction. No doubt the real reason for giving judgment for the defendant in the latter case was that if the violence had stopped once the police arrived, then they would have been powerless to detain any of those involved in the incident. That overlooks the general arrest conditions which authorise the incarceration of those whose identity is unknown or where it is necessary to protect life and property. Thus, those whose names could not be ascertained or who were thought to be likely to re-start their violent conduct could always be apprehended under PACE 1984, s 25 (see Chapter 6).

In *R v Monville*[1], two men heard the alarm of a friend's car go off and, on approaching the vehicle, they saw that its window had been broken and the defendant was leaning into the car. On being asked what he was up to, he ran off. Chase was given and, on being caught, he punched one of his pursuers, but was detained until the police arrived. He was indicted and was found guilty of assault with intent to avoid arrest contrary to s 38 of the Offences Against the Person Act 1861, but he was acquitted of attempting to steal from the car. In seeking to uphold the conviction, the prosecution argued that the arrest was justified under PACE 1984, s 24(4), to which the Court of Appeal merely remarked that 'that may be so'. However, the court went on to state that clearly the arrestable offence of malicious damage to the vehicle had been committed and it had been reasonable to suspect the defendant of that crime, so that his

---

1   (Unreported) 15 December 1997.

apprehension was lawful under s 24(5). The judgment does not record what offence, if any, the accused had been given as the justification for his apprehension. As the arresters were not constables, they had probably said nothing, which did not matter as the reasons would have been obvious – at any rate, the Court of Appeal must have thought so.

5.5.4 Twentieth-century post-PACE statutes

5.5.4.1 *Criminal Attempts Act 1981*
Section 2(2)(c) grants the same power of arrest in relation to an offence of 'attempt' under s 1 as applies to the substantive offence which the criminal has attempted to perpetrate.

5.5.4.2 *Reserve Forces Act 1996*
Where no constable is available, s 100 and Sch 2, para 2(2) empower any person to arrest without warrant anybody whom he has reasonable cause to believe is a reservist who is a deserter or is absent without leave; and the prisoner must be taken before a magistrates' court as soon as is practicable (para 2(4)). In this context, a reservist means a member of the Royal Fleet Reserve, the Royal Naval Reserve, the Royal Marine Reserve, the Army Reserve, the Territorial Army, the Air Force Reserve and the Royal Auxiliary Air Force, who is liable to recall; see ss 1 and 68.

5.6 CONCLUSIONS

Thus, it will be seen that Parliament has entrusted the citizenry at large with a power of summary arrest for a great number of offences, including every one for which a convict can be sentenced to 5 years' or more imprisonment.

Chapter 6

THE POWERS OF ARREST OF A CONSTABLE WITHOUT A WARRANT AND POWERS OF DETENTION FALLING SHORT OF AN ARREST

6.1   INTRODUCTION

The common law and Parliament have sought to keep the balance between the need for the police to arrest those who commit crimes and the right of the individual not to have his freedom curtailed unnecessarily. This has led to the giving of extra powers to constables, but has always been hedged around with safeguards. This is well summed up by Watson B in *Hogg v Ward* (an action for false imprisonment)[1]:

> 'I have attentively considered whether the charge in this case was reasonable, because it is of the utmost importance that the police throughout the country should be supported in the execution of their duty, – indeed it is absolutely essential for the prevention of crime; on the other hand, it is equally important that persons should not be arrested and brought before magistrates upon frivolous or untenable charges.'

6.2   CONSTABLES – WHO THEY ARE – AND THEIR TERRITORIAL JURISDICTION

Although there is no case on it, as a matter of common sense, 'constable' must mean anybody who has been sworn in as such in England and Wales, irrespective of his actual position in the police hierarchy. It would be illogical if on promotion to sergeant a person's powers of arrest were limited to those of any ordinary citizen. This is borne out by the Police Act 1996. Section 39 states that every member of an English or Welsh police force and every special constable shall, on appointment, be attested as a constable and s 30(1) enacts that a member of a county constabulary or of the Metropolitan or City of London police forces shall have all the powers and privileges of a constable throughout England and Wales. A special constable can exercise all the powers of a policeman within the boundaries of both his own force and of those which are contiguous to it; see s 30(2). (A City of London Special has the same territorial jurisdiction as his brother officer in the Metropolis.) The Channel Tunnel Act 1987 extended a constable's jurisdiction to include the Channel Tunnel and a tunnel control area in France.

The territorial jurisdiction of 'private' police forces is governed by statute. For example, constables who are appointed by the chancellor or vice-chancellor or

---

1   (1858) 4 H and N 417 at 423.

a pro- or deputy vice-chancellor of Oxford or Cambridge can exercise their jurisdiction within 4 miles of their university precincts; see the University Act 1825, s 1.

6.3 IRISH, SCOTTISH, CHANNEL ISLAND AND FOREIGN CONSTABLES

If Northern Irish and Scottish policemen are seconded to forces in England and Wales, then by s 98 of the Police Act 1996 they are invested with all the powers of the constables with whom they are serving. The authority invested in the constabulary by the Prisons Act 1952 can also be exercised in England and Wales by a police officer from Scotland, Northern Ireland, Jersey or Guernsey; see para 17(2) of Part 3 of Sch 1 to the Crime (Sentences) Act 1997.

Under s 137 of CJPOA 1994 a Northern Irish or Scottish constable may arrest a person in England and Wales for an alleged offence committed in their own country if the suspect could legitimately have been detained under the laws existing in the jurisdiction where the crime was perpetrated. Once apprehended, the prisoner must be taken back to that country.

The Channel Tunnel Act 1987 gives French policemen power to exercise their jurisdiction inside the Channel Tunnel and a tunnel control area in this country.

6.4 CONSTABLES IN UNIFORM

Parliament has sometimes bestowed a power of arrest only on 'constables in uniform'. In *Wallwork v Giles*[1], it was held that those words did not require the officer to be in full uniform, for example he need not be wearing his helmet. The object of the legislation in prescribing that a policeman must be dressed in a certain way was to ensure that the constable would be easily recognisable as such. In *Taylor v Baldwin*[2], a constable was held to be 'in uniform' when wearing a civilian (and not a regulation) raincoat. A court may infer from the circumstances that the policeman is wearing uniform: for example in *Cooper v Rowlands*[3] a motor patrol officer, and in *Richards v West*[4] a special constable were presumed to have been in uniform because the justices knew that those people (patrol officers and specials) never wore civilian clothing when on duty. The court in *Gage v Jones*[5] was even prepared to hold that there was a presumption that a policeman who told a motorist to blow into a breathalyser was in uniform because only such an officer would make that requirement, as

---

1   (1969) 114 SJ 36.
2   [1976] RTR 265.
3   [1971] RTR 291.
4   [1980] RTR 215.
5   [1983] RTR 508.

otherwise it would be a pointless exercise (see RTA 1988, s 6). This has not proved to be the author's experience. In *DPP v Harrington*[1], a motorist was requested by plain clothes vice squad officers to take a breath test and when he attempted to depart before one of their uniformed colleagues had arrived with the necessary apparatus, he was detained (needless to say, unlawfully) under s 6 of RTA 1988 (see Chapter 7).

6.5   COMMON LAW POWERS

With the abolition of felonies in 1967, the constabulary no longer possess any common law powers beyond those bestowed upon the citizenry at large, except possibly in one case. In *Wershof v Commissioner of Police*[2], May J held that a police officer can make an arrest without warrant for an offence which is neither an arrestable one nor one for which a power of apprehension has been given by statute, but where, in connection therewith, a breach of the peace has been committed or is reasonably apprehended. In that case, a police sergeant was being obstructed and believed that if he tried to continue going about his duty, the plaintiff would use force to try to prevent him from so doing. Therefore, he arrested him for obstructing a constable. The judge held the defendant liable in damages but solely on the basis that it was not a reasonable belief that the plaintiff (who was a solicitor) would act violently. Apart from offences of obstruction and assault, it is difficult to see how the commission of any other non-arrestable crime would involve, or be likely to cause, a breach of the peace. The Court of Appeal in *Sutton v Commissioner of the Metropolitan Police*[3] treated *Wershof*, above, as correctly decided, and counsel did not argue to the contrary.

6.6   ABOLITION OF PRE-1984 STATUTORY POWERS OF ARREST

PACE 1984, s 26 abolished all the police's statutory rights of summary arrest, both for 'an offence' and 'otherwise than for an offence', as existed prior to 31 October 1984, except those contained in certain specifically named Acts of Parliament and which are set out in Sch 2 to PACE 1984 (see below). However, the offence of drunk and disorderly contained in CJA 1967, s 91[4] was not mentioned in that Schedule nor was it included in Sch 7, which contained details of which statutes the Act was repealing. So the question arose as to whether the power of arrest in CJA 1967 had survived s 26 of PACE 1984. In *DPP v Kitching*[5], Parker LJ stated:

> 'It is further pointed out by [Prosecuting Counsel] that the repeal schedule (Sch 7) contains no repeal of s 91(1) of the 1967 Act [CJA 1967].

---

1   (Unreported) 25 November 1994, Marlborough Street Magistrates' Court.
2   [1978] 3 All ER 540 at 550D.
3   (Unreported) 29 July 1998.
4   See **5.6.2.6**.
5   [1989] 154 JP 293 at 297A/B.

In my judgment, therefore, it is plain that s 26 of the 1984 Act does not repeal the constable's power of arrest under s 91(1) of the 1967 Act [CJA 1967].'

It is submitted that the word 'therefore' used by Parker LJ was referring not to the previous sentence in his judgment, but to the fact that PACE 1984 amended CJA 1967, s 91 by authorising places other than a police station to which a constable could take a person detained under that section. That provision would be nonsense if the power of arrest had ceased to exist. PACE 1984, s 26 does not say it repeals the statutory provisions in Sch 7; it says the opposite, namely that it does not affect the Acts specified in Sch 2. Therefore, Sch 7 must be regarded as merely setting out for guidance some of the legislation repealed, but it cannot be considered to be an exhaustive list because it omits a number of powers of arrest (eg Public Stores Act 1875, s 6; London County Council (General Powers) Act 1894, s 7 etc).

However, s 26 did not in any way limit the power of arrest invested in the citizenry at large – included amongst whom are the men and women who serve in the police force. Thus, the latter can still make a citizen's arrest. As the Court of Appeal held in *Gapper v Chief Constable of Avon and Somerset Constabulary*[1] per Swinton Thomas J:

> 'In my judgment s 26 [of PACE 1984] bites on those Acts [which give a power of arrest to a constable] and not an Act such as the Vagrancy Act 1824 which conferred a general power of arrest. If it were otherwise, then the absurd position would arise that a citizen would be entitled to arrest a person under the provision of s 6 of the Vagrancy Act 1824 whereas a constable would not.'

That must clearly be right, as it could never have been the intention of the legislature, *sub silentio*, to remove from those sworn in as constables a weapon in the war against crime which it had left in the possession of all those who did not wear a blue uniform, especially as the statute was introduced by a Conservative Government. Also if Parliament had intended this result, it would surely have said so, as it did in relation to the power of arrest under s 41 of SOA 1956[2] (see PACE 1984, s 119(1) and Sch 6, para 9).

Section 26 appears also to abolish the power of arrest for an attempt given by the Criminal Attempts Act 1981, s 2(2)(e) which made an attempt to commit an indictable offence subject to the same powers of arrest as the full offence. Thus, unless there is a specific power of arrest given by a post-PACE statute, a person cannot be taken into custody merely for attempting to commit an offence which does not fall within the classification of an 'arrestable offence'. The power to detain for attempting to commit a misdemeanour of the latter description (other than one under the Theft Act 1968, s 12(1)) is given by PACE 1984, s 24(3)(b).

---

1   [2000] QB 29 at 31H.
2   See **5.5.2.4**.

6.7 PRESENT DAY POWERS OF ARREST

6.7.1 Arrestable offences

PACE 1984, s 24 empowers a constable to arrest without warrant:

(1) where he has reasonable grounds to suspect that an arrestable offence (see Chapter 4) has been committed and that the person to be arrested is guilty of that offence subs (6);

(2) anybody who is about to commit an arrestable offence subs (7)(a); and

(3) anybody whom he has reasonable grounds to suspect of being about to commit an arrestable offence subs (7)(b).

In *Smitten v Smith (Chief Constable of Wiltshire)*[1] the Court of Appeal (per Mann LJ) held that subs (6) had three components:

> '... firstly suspicion, secondly reasonable grounds for suspicion and, thirdly, the decision to act upon the suspicion and to arrest.
>
> I have no doubt that an executive decision to arrest is a decision which is subject to the *Wednesbury*[2] principles.'

6.7.2 Breach of police bail

Section 46A (inserted by s 29 of CJPOA 1994) authorises a constable to arrest without warrant a person who, having been released on police bail to attend at a police station, fails to do so at the appointed time and place. A person so arrested shall be taken as soon as practicable to the station at which he was due to attend.

6.7.3 Statutory powers of summary arrest not repealed by PACE 1984

PACE 1984, Sch 2 set out the Acts in which the power of arrest was not repealed by s 26. That Schedule has been amended both by the deletion of repealed statutes and by the insertion of other Acts, which had been omitted from PACE 1984 as originally enacted. Also certain pre-PACE legislation (since the coming into force of that statute) has been amended by having a power of arrest inserted into it. At the date of writing the summary powers of arrest in the following pre-1984 legislation remain extant.

---

1   (Unreported) 27 February 1991.

2   See *Associated Provincial Picture Houses Ltd v Wednesbury Corp* [1948] 1 KB 223. See **9.4** below.

6.7.3.1   Game Act 1831

SECTION 31A

Trespassers in daytime in search of game
Section 31A bestows upon constables the same power of arrest as
is given to landowners by s 37 (see **12.7**).

Game Act
1831, s 31A (as
inserted by
PACE 1984,
s 119(1), Sch 6
Pt I)

6.7.3.2   Military Land Act 1892 ('MLA 1892')

SECTION 17(2)

Trespass on military land
Section 17(2) empowers a constable (or an officer authorised by
the by-laws) to arrest a person who is trespassing contrary to a
prohibition in the by-laws on *land appropriated for military use.* The
words in italics refer to the purpose behind the appropriation
and not what use is actually made of it. So in one case 70% of the
land was farmed but the MLA 1892 was still held to apply to that
location, see *DPP v John; DPP v Lee*[1]. Land includes any right of
firing or any other easement over land; see s 23. Under s 14(1),
such by-laws cannot take away or prejudice any rights of
commons.

MLA 1892,
s 17(2) (as
amended by
CJA 1982,
s 39(3), Sch 3)

6.7.3.3   Protection of Animals Act 1911 ('PAA 1911')

SECTION 12(1)

Cruelty to animals
Section 12(1) empowers a constable to arrest anybody whom he
has reasonable cause to believe was guilty of an offence under
that Act which is punishable by imprisonment without an option
of a fine, ie an offence of cruelty to *domestic* or *captive* animals
which is defined as doing, or causing, or procuring, any of the
activities set out in the lettered subsections of s 1(1), viz:

PAA 1911,
ss 1(2), (3),
12(1), 1(1),
15(1)(a)

(a)   cruelly beating, or kicking, or ill-treating, or over-loading or
       terrifying any animal; or procuring, or causing, the com-
       mission of any act which causes unnecessary suffering;
(b)   conveying or carrying an animal in such a way as to cause it
       unnecessary suffering;
(c)   being concerned in the fighting or baiting of any animal; or

---

1   [1999] 1 WLR 1883.

(1) keeping or
(2) using, or
(3) being concerned in, or
(4) assisting in, the management of any premises or place used wholly or partly for purposes of fighting or baiting any animal; subs (c) also makes it an offence (for which a summary arrest can be made) to receive money for the admission of any person to such premises or place.

For there to be an offence, both the animals fighting must be domestic or captive; see s 15(1) and *DPP v Barry*[1];

(d) administering, without reasonable cause or excuse, any poisonous or injurious drug or substance to any animal;
(e) subjecting an animal to undergo any operation which is performed without due care or humanity;
(f) (as inserted by s 1 of the Protection against Cruel Tethering Act 1988) tethering any horse or ass or mule so as to cause that animal unnecessary suffering.

Section 15(1)(a) defines 'animal' as any domestic or captive animal. The offence of cruelty to animals is committed if there is, as a matter of fact, cruelty even if there was no intention to cause such; see *Duncan v Pope*[2]. Section 1(2) makes an owner also guilty of cruelty if he has failed to exercise reasonable care and supervision to protect his animals from suffering cruelty but that is not an arrestable offence as he must be given the option of a fine if convicted of that offence. Under subs (3), no offence is committed under the Act for anything done:

(i) under the Animals (Scientific Procedures) Act 1986,
(ii) killing for food, unless accompanied by the infliction of unnecessary suffering,
(iii) the actual hunting or coursing of any captive animal, unless either the animal is released in an injured, mutilated or exhausted condition, or if it is hunted or coursed within an enclosed space from which it has no reasonable chance of escape; see the Protection of Animals Act (1911) (Amendment) Act 1921, s 1.

6.7.3.4   *Emergency Powers Act 1920 ('EPA 1920')*

SECTION 2

State of emergency
Section 2 empowers The Queen, in Council, to make regulations to deal with a state of emergency declared by Her Majesty when it appears to Her Majesty that events have or will

EPA 1920, s 2

---

1   [1989] Crim LR 648.
2   (1899) 80 LT 120.

occur which will interfere with the supply and distribution of food, water, fuel or light or with the means of locomotion such as to deprive the community, or any substantial proportion thereof, of the essentials of life. It is submitted that those regulations can provide for a power of arrest without a warrant.

6.7.3.5 Public Order Act 1936 ('POA 1936')

SECTION 7(3)

Wearing of political uniform
Section 7(3) empowers a constable to arrest anyone whom he reasonably suspects to be committing an offence under s 1 of that Act, namely the wearing, in any public place or at any public meeting, of a uniform which signifies an association with any political organisation or with the promotion of any political office. The High Court in *O'Moran v DPP; Whelan v DPP*[1] (per Lord Widgery CJ) held that 'uniform' was any clothing worn 'to indicate association with a political body'; in that case it was a black beret.

POA 1936, ss 17(3), 9 (as amended by CJA 1972, s 33)

Section 9 defines a 'public place' as including 'any highway, any other premises or place to which at the material time the public have or are permitted to have access, whether on payment or otherwise'. For a more detailed discussion of that phrase, see **5.3**.

6.7.3.6 Prison Act 1952 ('PA 1952')

SECTION 49

Absconders
Section 49 empowers a constable to arrest and to return to his lawful place of custody anybody who is unlawfully at large from a prison, detention centre, a young offenders' institution, or a remand centre – which is situated anywhere in the United Kingdom or the Channel Islands; see para 17(1) of Part 3 of the First Schedule to the Crime (Sentences) Act 1997. This power of arrest extends to the recapture of an escapee from custody imposed under the Extradition Act 1989; see s 17(2).

PA 1952, s 49 (as amended by CJA 1967, s 103(2), Sch 7 and CJA 1982, s 77, Sch 14, para 8(a))

---

1   [1975] QB 864.

6.7.3.7   Visiting Forces Act 1952 ('VFA 1952')

SECTION 13

Deserters etc from visiting forces

Section 13 invests a constable with the same powers of arrest without warrant over deserters and those absent without leave from visiting forces as he has over those who have similarly absconded from Her Majesty's land forces pursuant to s 186 of the Army Act 1955 (see below). This power of arrest can be exercised only on the express invitation of the appropriate authority which is defined in s 17(3) as such authority as may be appointed for that purpose by the government of the country whence the visiting forces have come.

VFA 1952, s 13 (as amended by Revision of the Army and Air Force Acts (Transitional Provision) Act 1955, ss 3, 5(2), Sch 2, para 17(1), Sch 4)

6.7.3.8   Army Act 1955 ('AA 1955')

SECTION 186(1)

Deserters from Army

Section 186(1) empowers a constable to arrest without warrant any person whom he reasonably suspects to be a regular soldier (of any rank) who has deserted, or is absent without leave. The arrested person must be taken before a magistrates' court as soon as practicable (s 186(4)).

AA 1955, s 186(1)

SECTION 190B

Absconders from army custody

Section 190B empowers a constable to arrest without warrant a person unlawfully at large from the custody imposed on him pursuant to Part II of AA 1955 and may take him to his lawful place of detention. It should be noted that, unlike s 186(1), the person must actually be at large and not merely suspected of being so.

AA 1955, s 190B (as inserted by Armed Forces Act 1971, s 44(2))

6.7.3.9   Air Force Act 1955 ('AFA 1955')

SECTION 186(1)

Deserters etc from RAF

Section 186(1) empowers a constable to arrest without warrant any person whom he reasonably suspects to be a regular member of the Royal Air Force who has deserted, or is absent without leave; and the arrested person must be taken before a magistrates' court as soon as is practicable (s 186(4)).

AFA 1955, s 186(1)

SECTION 190B

Absconders from RAF custody
Section 190B empowers a constable to arrest without warrant a
person unlawfully at large from the custody imposed on him
pursuant to Part II of AFA 1955 and may take him to his lawful
place of detention. It should be noted that, unlike s 186(1), the
person must actually be at large and not merely suspected of
being so.

AFA 1955,
s 190B (as
inserted by
AFA 1971,
s 44(2)

6.7.3.10   Naval Discipline Act 1957 ('NDA 1957')

SECTION 104

Absconders from naval custody
Empowers a constable to arrest without warrant a person
unlawfully at large from the custody imposed on him pursuant to
Part II of NDA 1957 and may take him to his lawful place of
detention.

NDA 1957,
s 104

SECTION 105

Deserters etc from Royal Navy
Empowers a constable to arrest any person whom he has
reasonable cause to suspect of being a regular naval officer or
rating who has deserted, or is absent without leave. The arrested
person must be taken before a magistrates' court as soon as is
practicable (s 105(4)).

NDA 1957,
s 105

6.7.3.11   Street Offences Act 1959 ('SOA 1959')

SECTION 1(3)

Prostitution etc
Section 1(3) empowers a constable to arrest without warrant any
woman (see *DPP v Bull*[1]) whom he finds in a street or public
place and whom he suspects with reasonable cause to be a
common prostitute loitering or soliciting for the purposes of
prostitution.

SOA 1959,
s 1(3)

R v De Munck[2] defined a common prostitute as somebody who
regularly offers her body for lewdness (which need not include
sexual intercourse) for payment.

---

1   [1995] QB 88.
2   [1918] 1 KB 635.

Horton v Mead[1] held that soliciting can consist of deeds alone, without words and need never have reached the attention of the person at whom it was aimed. It must involve the physical presence of the prostitute; see *Burge v DPP*[2]. In *Behrendt v Burridge*[3], it was held that sitting on a stool in a window under a light could amount to soliciting.

There are no reported English cases on the meaning of 'loiter' but in Scotland the Lord Justice Clerk held that it meant lingering and did not cover the slowing down of a motor vehicle on one particular occasion; see *Williamson v Wright*[4].

6.7.3.12   Firearms Act 1968 ('FA 1968')

SECTION 50(2)

Firearms offences
Section 50(2) bestows upon a constable a summary power of arrest of anybody whom he has reasonable cause to suspect to be committing any of the following offences under the 1968 Act:

FA 1968, s 50(2) (power of arrest inserted into PACE 1984, Sch 2 by F(A)A 1997, Sch 2, para 9)

–   s 5(5): the non-compliance with conditions of the Defence Council for possessing one of the following prohibited weapons:

(1)   automatic weapons,
(2)   semi-automatic and pump action rifles other than those firing .22 rim fire cartridges,
(3)   semi-automatic and pump action smooth-bore short guns other than those firing .22 rim fire cartridges and either with a barrel of at least 24 inches or are 40 inches or over in total length,
(4)   smooth bore revolvers unless they either fire .22 rim fire cartridges or are muzzle loading,
(5)   rocket launchers and mortars, other than those designed for line throwing, pyrotechnic purposes or as signalling apparatus,
(6)   any weapon which discharges any noxious liquid or gas, and
(7)   any bullet which is designed to contain any such liquid or gas or which is a dumdum (ie splinters on penetrating its target);

–   s 5(6): the non-compliance within 21 days of a requirement by the Defence Council to surrender an authority for a prohibited weapon;

---

1   [1913] 1 KB 154.
2   [1962] 1 All ER 666.
3   [1976] 3 All ER 285.
4   [1924] SC(J) 57.

- s 20(2): having a firearm or imitation firearm while trespassing on any land (as opposed to a building);
- s 21(4): contravention of s 24, which prohibits certain convicted criminals from possessing firearms and ammunition;
  in the case of those who have been sentenced to a custodial
  sentence of 3 years or more, they are banned for life and
  those who have been sentenced to between 3 months and 3
  years in custody are banned for 3 years; and
- s 47(2): failing to obey a request by a constable to hand to
  him any firearm or ammunition – such a request may be
  made either in a public place or, indeed, anywhere else, but
  in the latter case only if the constable reasonably suspects
  that an offence under one of the following sections of the
  Act is being committed or is about to be committed: s 18
  (having (subs (1)) a firearm or (subs (2)) an imitation
  firearm, with intent to commit a crime, or to avoid arrest) or
  s 20 (trespassing with a firearm or imitation firearm).

6.7.3.13   *Children and Young Persons Act 1969 ('CYPA 1969')*

SECTION 32(1A)

Absconders from local authority accommodation

Section 32(1A) empowers a constable to arrest without warrant
any child or young person (ie under 16 years old) who has
escaped from local authority accommodation in Great Britain in
which:

(1) he has been ordered to reside by a court under s 12AA of the
    CYPA 1969; or
(2) he is being held pending his appearance in court after being
    arrested on a warrant under s 16 of the CYPA 1969; or
(3) he has been remanded (otherwise than on bail) by a court
    before which he has been charged or convicted of a criminal
    offence, pursuant to s 23(1).

CYPA 1969, s 32(1A) (power of arrest, as inserted into PACE 1984, Sch 2 by CA 1989, s 108, Sch 13, para 55)

This power of arrest is extended by s 32(1) to children and young
persons who have run away from similar places in Northern
Ireland. Anybody arrested pursuant to s 32 shall be returned to
the place whence he came. The costs of so doing must be paid for
by those who were responsible for looking after the escapee prior
to his absconding.

SECTION 23

Breaking conditions of remand

Section 23A authorises a constable to arrest, without a warrant, a person who has been remanded or committed to the care of a local authority with conditions attached under s 23(7) to (10) and whom he has reasonable grounds to suspect of being in breach of one of those conditions. The detained person must as soon as is practicable, and in any event within 24 hours (not counting Christmas Day, Good Friday or a Sunday), be brought before a justice of the peace for the petty sessional division in which he was arrested, unless he was apprehended within 24 hours of the time fixed for his court appearance, in which case he must be brought, within the same time-limits, before the court before which he is due to appear.

CYPA 1969, s 23A (power of arrest, as inserted into PACE 1984, Sch 2 by CJPOA 1994, s 23)

6.7.3.14 *Immigration Act 1971 ('IA 1971')*

SECTION 28A

Immigration offences

Section 28A(1) (as inserted by the Immigration and Asylum Act 1999, s 128, on 14 February 2000 by the Immigration and Asylum Act 1999 (Commencement No 2 and Transitional Provisions) Order 2000, SI 2000/168) empowers a constable to arrest without warrant anyone who has, or whom he reasonably suspects to have, committed, or to have attempted to commit, an offence which is either contrary to s 24A (seeking or obtaining leave to enter the UK by deception, or to avoid or postpone deportation by deception) or is contrary to any of the lettered subsections (except (d)) of s 24(1), namely:

IA 1971, s 28A (as inserted by IAA 1999, s 128)

(a) knowingly to have entered the United Kingdom in breach of a deportation order or without leave required by that Act. (Leave is usually required by an alien other than an Irish citizen or a visitor from an EEC country (and his or her family) intending to work here.);

(b) if having limited leave to enter or to remain, knowingly to have remained after the expiry of the leave or in breach of a condition of the leave (this is a continuing offence s 24(1A));

(c) having entered lawfully without leave under s 8(1), to have remained beyond the time allowed by that section. Section 8(1) allows a member of the crew of a ship or aeroplane to enter without leave if, under his engagement, he has to depart as a crew member (although not necessarily on the same vessel on which he arrived) within one week of his arrival; and, of course, he must leave within those seven days;

(d) without reasonable excuse to have failed to observe any restriction imposed on him as to: (i) residence; (ii) employment; (iii) occupation; or (iv) reporting to the police or an immigration officer;

(e) to have disembarked in the UK from a ship or aircraft on which he is being deported from this country; and

(f) to have disembarked in contravention of a restriction imposed by an Order in Council.

SCHEDULE 2, PARA 17(1)

Persons liable to be detained

Paragraph 17(1) of Sch 2 empowers a constable to arrest without warrant a person liable to be detained under any of the numbered subparagraphs of para 16 of that Schedule, namely:

IA 1971, Sch 2, para 17(1)

(a) a person required to submit to an examination on his arrival by an immigration officer (he may be detained until that examination);

(b) a person who has been refused entry or is an illegal immigrant (he can be detained until he is deported);

(c) a person refused permission to land (he shall be detained by the captain of the ship or aeroplane on which he arrived if the captain is ordered to do so by an immigration officer);

(d) a person who is being deported from this country.

A person arrested under this section can be detained at any place ordered by the Secretary of State (see para 18(1)).

SCHEDULE 2, PARA 24

Persons released on bail

Paragraph 24 of Sch 2 empowers a constable to arrest without warrant a person who has been released on bail by an immigration officer or adjudicator and is under a duty to surrender to an immigration officer, if (subs (a)) the constable has reasonable cause to believe that the person is not likely to surrender or is likely to breach any other of his bail conditions, or if the constable has reasonable cause to suspect that he is breaking or has broken a bail condition, or (subs (b)) a surety has notified the police in writing that he wishes to be released from his recognisance because the person on bail is unlikely to surrender.

IA 1971, Sch 2, paras 24, 33

Paragraph 33 gives to a constable in relation to those granted bail pending appeal the same powers of arrest as he has under IA 1971, Sch 2, para 24.

SCHEDULE 3, PARA 7

Persons subject to restrictions

Paragraph 7 of Sch 3 empowers a constable to arrest without warrant any person who is subject to restrictions imposed by a court pending deportation, if (subpara (a)) the constable reasonably suspects that the person is contravening, or has contravened, any of those restrictions; or (subpara (b)) the constable has reasonable grounds for believing that the person is likely to contravene them. A person arrested under para 7 must as soon as is practicable, and, in any event, within 24 hours (not counting Christmas Day, Good Friday or a Sunday), be brought before a justice of the peace for the petty sessional division in which he was arrested; see BA 1976, below.

IA 1971, Sch 3, para 7

6.7.3.15   Bail Act 1976 ('BA 1976')

SECTION 7(3)

Persons unlikely to surrender to bail

Section 7(3) empowers a constable to arrest without warrant a person who has been released on bail in criminal proceedings and is under a duty to surrender into the custody of a court, if the constable has reasonable cause to believe that the person is (subs (a)) not likely to surrender or is (subs (b)) likely to breach his bail conditions or the constable has reasonable grounds for suspecting that he has already done so, or (subs (c)) if a surety has told the police in writing that he wishes to be released from his recognisance because the person on bail is unlikely to surrender. Under subsection (4), an arrested person must as soon as practicable, and in any event within 24 hours (not counting Christmas Day, Good Friday or a Sunday), be brought before a justice of the peace for the petty sessional division in which he was arrested, unless he was arrested within 24 hours of the time fixed for his surrender, in which case he must be brought before the court where he was under the obligation to surrender himself. If he does not actually appear in front of a justice within that time, he must be released. Delivery to the court cells is not a sufficient compliance with that requirement; see *R v Governor of Glen Parva Young Offenders Institute, ex parte G (A Minor)*[1]. There, the applicant was taken into custody at 1.28 pm, transported to court and placed in its cells at 12.05 pm the next day. However, he was not brought up before the Bench until 3.30 pm. The High Court held that this was too late and the magistrates had no power to deal with the breach of bail by remanding him in custody.

BA 1976, s 7(3)

---

1   [1998] QB 877.

In *R v Middlesex Guildhall Crown Court ex parte Okoli*[1], it was held that when an oral notice of appeal against a decision to grant bail has been given, the appeal hearing has to commence within 48 hours of that day, and not the time of the notice.

6.7.3.16　Criminal Law Act 1977 ('CLA 1977')

SECTION 6(6)

Using threatening or violent behaviour in order to enter premises
Section 6(6) empowers a constable in uniform to arrest a person who is, or whom the officer has reasonable cause to suspect to be, committing an offence against s 6(1) – namely threatening or using violence to secure entry on to premises where he knows that there is a person on the premises who is opposed to his entry. The only defence is that he is, or is acting on behalf of, the displaced residential occupier of those premises. CLA 1977,
s 6(6)

SECTION 7(6)

Trespassers
Section 7(6) empowers a constable in uniform to arrest a person committing an offence against s 7(1), which makes it illegal to enter upon premises as, and to remain as, a trespasser and to refuse to leave when requested to do so by, or on behalf of, a displaced or intending residential occupier. The latter is either: CLA 1977,
s 7(6)

- s 7(2)): a person who has an estate of fee simple, or a term of not less than 21 years still to run, which he acquired as a purchaser for money or money's worth, and he requires the premises for his own occupation as his residence but is prevented from so occupying it by the trespasser; and he or the person acting on his behalf has a statement containing the above facts which has been witnessed by a commissioner for oaths or a justice of the peace; or
- s 7(4)): a person who has been authorised by a housing authority or housing association to occupy the premises as his residence, but is prevented by the trespasser from so doing and that he or the person acting on his behalf has a certificate from his landlord stating that they are a body to which s 7(4) applies and that the person named in the certificate has their authority to occupy the premises named in the certificate as his residence.

1　(2000) TLR, August 2.

SECTION 8(4)

Trespassers carrying weapons
Section 8(4) authorises a constable to arrest without a warrant any person committing an offence against s 8(1) of CLA 1977, ie a person who enters as, and remains as, a trespasser on any premises and, without any lawful authority or reasonable excuse, has with him any weapon of offence; which is defined by s 8(2) as any article made, or adapted, or intended to be used, for causing personal injury or for incapacitating a person. _{CLA 1977, s 8(4)}

SECTION 9(7)

Trespassers upon premises of foreign missions etc
Section 9(7) empowers a constable without warrant to arrest anybody committing an offence against s 9(1) of the CLA 1977 (as amended by s 7 of the Diplomatic and Consular Premises Act 1987), ie a person who is a trespasser (having entered as such) on any of the premises listed in the following lettered paragraphs of s 9(2): _{CLA 1977, s 9(7)}

(a) a diplomatic mission within the meaning of Art 1(i) of the Vienna Convention on Diplomatic Regulations 1961 as applied in the United Kingdom by s 1 of and Sch 2 to the Diplomatic Privileges Act 1964;
(aa) a closed diplomatic mission as defined by Art 45 of the 1961 Vienna Convention;
(b) consular premises within the meaning of para 1(j) of Art 1 of the Vienna Convention on Consular Regulations 1963 as applied in the United Kingdom by s 1 of and Sch 2 to the Consular Relations Act 1968;
(bb) a closed consular post as defined in Art 27 of the 1963 Vienna Convention;
(c) any other premises of an organisation or body entitled to inviolability; and
(d) the private residence of a diplomatic agent or of anybody who is entitled 'to inviolability of residence'.

SECTION 10(5)

Obstruction etc of court officer
Section 10(5) authorises a constable to arrest a person who commits an offence contrary to s 10(1) of CLA 1977; namely a person who resists or intentionally obstructs any sheriff, under-sheriff, deputy sheriff, bailiff, sheriff's officer, or any officer of the County Court (as defined in s 147(1) of the County Courts Act 1984) when they are engaged in executing any court warrant for the recovery, or delivery up, of the possession of any premises _{CLA 1977, s 10(5)}

by a person (other than a tenant holding over after the termination of his tenancy) who entered into possession without the licence or consent of the person claiming to be entitled to possession or of any predecessor of such a person.

Under s 147 of the County Courts Act 1984 (as amended by s 111 of the Courts and Legal Services Act 1990), 'officer' in relation to a court means any district judge or any deputy or assistant district judge of that court, and any clerk, bailiff, usher or messenger in the service of that court'.

6.7.3.17   Animal Health Act 1981 ('AHA 1981')

SECTION 61(1)

Rabies

Section 61(1) empowers a constable to arrest without a warrant any person whom he reasonably suspects of committing or having committed any of the offences listed in the following lettered subsections of s 61(2): *(AHA 1981, s 61(1))*

(a) the landing or attempted landing of any animal in contravention of an order made under the Act and expressed to be for the purpose of preventing the introduction of rabies into Great Britain;
(b) the failure by the person having the charge or control of any vessel or boat to discharge any obligation imposed upon him in that capacity by such an order; and
(c) the movement, in contravention of an order under ss 17 or 23 of AHA 1981, of any animal into, or within, or out of, any place or area declared to be infected with rabies.

(Sections 17 and 23 empower the Minister of Agriculture Fisheries and Food to make orders as he thinks fit to prevent the spread of animal diseases.)

6.7.3.18   Representation of the People Act 1983 ('RPA 1983')

SCHEDULE 1, PARA 36

Personation

Schedule 1, para 36 authorises the presiding officer to order a constable to arrest, before he leaves the polling station, a person who applies or has applied for a ballot paper if the candidate or his election or polling agent has declared that he has reasonable cause to believe that this person was guilty of the offence of personation and has undertaken to substantiate that charge in a *(RPA 1983, Sch 1, para 36 (power of arrest, as inserted into PACE 1984, Sch 2 by RPA 1985, s 25(1)))* court of law. 'Personation' means assuming the identity of an elector. Schedule 1 applies to elections in both the Westminster and European Parliaments – in the latter case by virtue of the amended European Parliamentary Elections Regulations 1986, SI 1986/2209.

6.7.3.19   Mental Health Act 1983 ('MHA 1983')

SECTION 18

Patients absent without leave
Section 18 empowers a constable to arrest without warrant anybody who is detained under MHA 1983 and who is absent without leave from the hospital where he is detained or, having been granted leave with a condition of residence, lives elsewhere.

MHA 1983, s 18

SECTION 35(10)

Absconding while on remand for medical reports
Section 35(10) empowers a constable to arrest without warrant a person who has been remanded by a court to a hospital for medical reports and who absents himself from the hospital or who absconds whilst being conveyed to or from those premises. A person arrested under s 35(10) must be brought before the court which remanded him as soon as possible.

MHA 1983, s 35(10)

SECTION 36(8)

Absconding while on remand for treatment
Section 36(8) empowers a constable to arrest without warrant a person who has been remanded by a court to a hospital for treatment pending sentence and who absents himself from hospital or who absconds whilst being conveyed to or from that institution. A person arrested under s 36(8) must be brought before the court which remanded him as soon as possible.

MHA 1983, s 36(8)

SECTION 38(7)

Absconding from detention under interim hospital order
Section 38(7) empowers a constable to arrest without warrant a convicted prisoner who has been remanded by a Crown Court under an interim hospital order pending sentence and who absents himself from hospital or who absconds whilst being conveyed to or from the hospital. A person arrested under s 38(7) must be brought before the court which remanded him as soon as possible.

MHA 1983, s 38(7)

SECTION 136(1)

Persons in need of immediate care or control

Section 136(1) enacts a power of detention in the following   MHA 1983,
circumstances. If a constable finds in a place (to which the public   s 136(1)
has access) a male or female who appears to be suffering from a
mental disorder and to be in need of immediate care or control,
the officer, if he thinks it necessary, may remove that person to a
place of safety, which is defined in s 135(6) as: (i) residential
accommodation under Part III of the National Assistance Act
1948; or (ii) a hospital as defined by the MHA 1983; (iii) a police
station; (iv) a mental nursing home or residential home for
mentally disordered persons; or (v) any other suitable place
where the occupier is willing temporarily to receive the patient
(the Roman numerals are those of the author).

SECTION 138

Retaking of patients escaping from custody

Section 138 empowers a constable to take a person detained   MHA 1983,
under MHA 1983 (other than by order of a court) back to the   s 138
place from which he is unlawfully at large provided that his
escape, if from a hospital, was not more than 6 months earlier or,
if from a place of safety, was not more than 72 hours earlier.

6.7.3.20   Repatriation of Prisoners Act 1984 ('RPA 1984')

SECTION 5(5)

Retaking escaped prisoners

Section 5(5) empowers a constable to arrest and to return to the   RPA 1984,
place from which he is unlawfully at large any escaped prisoner   s 5(5)
who, by virtue of RPA 1984, is serving in the United Kingdom a
custodial sentence passed by a court in another country.

6.7.4   Legislation passed since PACE 1984

6.7.4.1   Sporting Events (Control of Alcohol etc) Act 1985 ('SE(CA)A 1985')

SECTION 7(2)

Offences involving alcohol etc at designated sporting events

Section 7(2) empowers a constable both to search and to arrest a   SE(CA)A 1985,
person whom he has reasonable grounds to suspect to be   s 7(2)

committing or to have committed an offence under SE(CA)A 1985 (see below). Those offences are all concerned with a sporting event designated by the Secretary of State under s 9, but cannot apply to such an event where there is no entry fee for competitors and spectators. A designated sporting event lasts from 2 hours before its advertised starting time until 1 hour after it has finished.

SECTION 1

Alcohol on coaches and trains travelling to and from designated sporting events
Section 1 prohibits the carriage of intoxicating liquor on a train or public service vehicle which is being used principally to take passengers to or from a designated sporting event; and makes it an offence:

SE(CA)A 1985, s 1

(a) in the case of a public service vehicle, for the operator or the servant or agent of the operator; and
(b) in the case of a hired vehicle, for the hirer or the servant or agent of the hirer

to knowingly cause or permit the carriage of intoxicating liquor in such circumstances.

SECTION 1A

Alcohol on certain other vehicles
Section 1A applies to a motor vehicle which is not a public service vehicle but which is adapted to carry more than eight passengers and is being used principally to take two or more passengers to or from a designated sporting event. It makes it an offence for the following people knowingly to cause or to permit intoxicated liquor to be carried on such a vehicle:

SE(CA)A 1985, s 1A (as inserted by POA 1986, s 40(1) and Sch 1, Part II, paras 1 and 2)

(a) the driver;
(b) the vehicle's keeper, or that person's servant or agent;
(c) a person to whom the vehicle was made available by its keeper; and
(d) the servant or agent of the person to whom the vehicle was made available.

SECTION 2(1)

Alcohol etc at sports grounds
Section 2(1) makes it an offence, during the period of a designated sporting event, for a person either:

SE(CA)A 1985, s 2(1)

(a) to be inside a designated sports ground from which the event may be directly viewed; or
(b) to attempt to enter a designated sporting ground;

AND to have with him:

(i)   intoxicating liquor; or

(ii) (subs (3)) an article capable of causing injury by striking which (unless it is for holding medicine) is a bottle or other portable container (or part thereof) and which, when empty, is either discarded or returned to, or left for recovery by, its supplier.

SECTION 2(2)

Persons drunk at sports grounds

Section 2(2) makes it an offence to be drunk during the period of a designated sporting event when either inside or attempting to enter a designated sports ground.

SE(CA)A 1985, s 2(2)

SECTION 2A

Fireworks etc at sports grounds

Section 2A makes it an offence, during the period of a designated sporting event, for a person either:

(a)   to be inside a designated sports ground from which the event may be directly viewed; or

(b)   to attempt to enter a designated sporting ground;

SE(CA)A 1984, s 2A (as inserted by POA 1986, s 40(1) and Sch 1, Part I, paras 1 and 3)

AND to have with him, without lawful authority, any article or substance, the main purpose of which is the emission of a flare for the purposes of illumination or signalling (as opposed to igniting or heating) or the emission of smoke or a visible gas.

Section 2A also applies to fireworks (subs (4)), but not to matches, cigarette lighters or heaters (subs (3)).

SECTION 3

Licensing offences

Section 3 makes it an offence for the people named in s 3(10), when inside either licensed premises or a registered club situated in a designated sports area, to sell during a designated sporting event intoxicating liquor in breach of either the conditions imposed by their licence or of an order made by a police officer pursuant to s 3(7). The people named in s 3(10) are the licensee, an officer of the club, and a person who knows or has reasonable cause to believe that the sale is in contravention of s 3. Section 3(7) allows a police officer not below the rank of inspector to vary or cancel a justices' licence if it is in the interests of orderly conduct or of public safety AND if it is impractical to apply to a magistrates' court for the variation or cancellation.

SE(CA)A 1985, s 3

SECTION 5B

Occasional licences

Section 5B states that an occasional licence which would authorise the sale of intoxicating liquor in a designated sports area shall not authorise such sale during a designated sporting event; and (subs (2)) makes it an offence for the occasional

SE(CA)A 1985, s 5B (as inserted by POA 1986, s 40(1) and Sch 1

licensee to sell, and (subs (3)) for any person to consume, alcohol in breach of s 5B.

SECTION 5C

Clubs

Section 5C enacts that s 39(3), (4) and (5) of the Licensing Act 1964 shall not apply to the sale of alcohol during a designated sporting event by a registered club situated in a designated sports area. Instead, s 5C(3) makes it an offence to supply or to authorise the sale of alcohol in breach of s 5C(2), ie at any place within the grounds of the location where the sporting event is being held, except at the registered premises. Section 5C(4) makes it an offence to obtain or to consume alcohol in breach of s 5C(2). Section 5C(5) makes every officer of the club guilty of an offence if any alcohol is kept by the club for consumption in breach of s 5C(2).

SE(CA)A 1985, s 5C (as inserted by POA 1986, s 40(1) and Sch 1)

SECTION 5D

Non-retail sales

Section 5D makes it an offence for any person either (subs (2)) to sell, or to authorise the sale of, or (subs (3)) for any person to obtain or to consume, any alcohol during a designated sporting event at a designated sports ground, unless it is 'sold by retail'.

SE(CA)A 1985, s 5D (as inserted by POA 1986, s 40(1) and Sch 1)

SECTION 6

Failure to close bars

Section 6 makes it an offence for any person during a designated sporting event at a designated sports ground to fail to comply with a requirement by the police to close a bar if its continued opening is detrimental to the orderly conduct or safety of spectators at the event. It is a defence that a person took all reasonable steps to comply with the requirement.

SE(CA)A 1985, s 6

It should be noted that under s 6 the *mens rea* for an offence under ss 3, 4 and 5 is either that the *actus reus* is done intentionally or that the person is aware that his conduct etc might amount to the *actus*; and that a person who has taken drink or drugs (save for medical purposes) is deemed to have known of such things as he would have been aware had he not taken the drink or the drugs (as the case might be).

6.7.4.2   Public Order Act 1986 ('POA 1986')

SECTION 3(6)

Affray
Section 3(6) empowers a constable to arrest without a warrant anyone whom he reasonably suspects to be committing an affray, whether in a public or private place (s 3(5)). An affray is defined in s 3(1) as using or threatening unlawful violence to another, where that conduct would cause a person of reasonable firmness present at the scene to fear for his safety. Under s 3(2) where more than one person is involved, it is their joint conduct which must be considered. Under s 3(3), words alone cannot constitute an affray.

POA 1986,
s 3(6)

SECTION 4(3)

Provocation of violence
Section 4(3) empowers a constable to arrest without a warrant anyone whom he reasonably suspects to be committing an offence under s 4(1), namely:

POA 1986,
s 4(3)

(a) using towards another person threatening, abusive or insulting words or behaviour; or
(b) distributing or displaying to another person any writing, sign or other visible representation which is threatening, abusive or insulting,

and in either case, that is done with intent:

(1) to cause that person to believe that immediate unlawful violence will be used against him or another by any person;
(2) to provoke the immediate use of unlawful violence by that person or another;
(3) whereby that person is likely to believe that such violence will be used; or
(4) it is likely that such violence will be provoked.

The offence may be committed anywhere except where all the people concerned are inside a (but not necessarily the same) dwelling.

SECTION 4A(4)

Intentional harassment, etc

Section 4A(4) empowers a constable to arrest without a warrant anyone whom he reasonably suspects to be committing an offence under s 4A(1), namely if a person, with intent to cause a person harassment or distress:

POA 1986, s 4A(4) (inserted by CJPOA 1994, s 154)

(a) using threatening, abusive or insulting words or behaviour or disorderly behaviour; or

(b) displaying any writing, sign or other visible representation, which is threatening, abusive or insulting,

thereby causes that or another person harassment, distress or alarm.

The offence may be committed anywhere, except where all people concerned are inside a (but not necessarily the same) dwelling (s 4A(2)). Under s 4A(3), it is a defence if a person proves that:

(a) he had no reason to believe that his conduct etc would be heard or seen by a person outside a dwelling; or

(b) it was reasonable.

SECTION 5(4)

Offensive conduct

Section 5(4) empowers a constable to arrest without a warrant anyone who engages in offensive conduct which that constable or another officer has *told him to stop* AND who then engages in what the officer reasonably suspects to be further (but not necessarily the same type of) offensive conduct immediately or shortly after the warning. The above words in italics were held by the High Court to mean any language whereby it was made clear that the conduct had to stop, for example being told to apologise for it (see *Groom v DPP*[1]). Offensive conduct means an offence under s 5, which in subs (1) makes it illegal:

POA 1986, s 5(4)

(a) to use threatening, abusive or insulting words or behaviour or disorderly behaviour, or conduct; or

(b) to display any writing, sign or other visible representation which is threatening, abusive or insulting;

AND that is done within the hearing or sight of a person likely to be caused harassment, alarm or distress thereby – if there is nobody else present, this can include police officers, if they

---

1   [1991] Crim LR 713.

personally were likely to feel harassed, alarmed or distressed (see *DPP v Orum*[1]).

Under s 5(2), the offence may be committed anywhere except where all people concerned are inside a (but not necessarily the same) dwelling. Under s 5(3), it is a defence if a person proves that:

(a) he had no reason to believe that there was any person in sight or hearing who would be caused harassment, alarm or distress; or

(b) that he was inside a dwelling and had no reason to believe that there was any person outside a dwelling house who would be caused harassment, alarm or distress; or

(c) that his conduct was reasonable.

The Public Order (Amendment) Act 1996, s 1 amended POA 1986, s 5 so that the arrest can be made by any police officer and not (as was formerly the case) only by the actual officer who had given the instruction to stop the offensive etc conduct.

SECTION 12(7)

Conditions on public processions

Section 12(7) authorises a constable in uniform to arrest without a warrant anybody he reasonably suspects to be committing an offence under s 12(4), (5) and (6), namely:

POA 1986,
s 12(7)

–   subs (4): makes it an offence for a person to organise a public procession and knowingly to fail to comply with any conditions imposed by the police under s 12(1), ie as appear necessary for public safety. The condition, called a 'direction', can be given either in advance in writing by the Chief Constable (or in London the Commissioner) or at the scene orally by the most senior office present. It is a defence to prove that the failure to comply was due to circumstances beyond the control of the person charged;

–   subs (5): makes it an offence to take part in a public procession and knowingly to fail to comply with any condition imposed by the police under s 12(1) (see s 12(4), above). The same defence applies as for a s 12(4) offence; and

–   subs (6): makes it an offence to incite the commission of an offence under s 12(5).

---

1   [1989] 1 WLR 88.

SECTION 13(10)

Prohibition of public processions

Section 13(10) authorises a constable in uniform to arrest without a warrant anybody whom he reasonably suspects to be committing an offence under s 13(7), (8) and (9). Sections 13(1) and (3) empowers a local council in the provinces or the Commissioner of Police in London to prohibit public processions (with the consent of the Secretary of State) in a designated area for a period not exceeding 3 months:

POA 1986, s 13(10)

- subs (7): makes it an offence to organise a public procession which is known to be prohibited under s 13;
- subs (8): makes it an offence to take part in a public procession which it is known to be prohibited under s 13; and
- subs (9): makes it an offence to incite the commission of an offence under s 13(8).

SECTION 14(7)

Conditions on public assemblies

Section 14(7) authorises a constable in uniform to arrest without a warrant anybody he reasonably suspects to be committing an offence under s 14(4), (5) and (6), namely:

POA 1986, s 14(7)

- subs (4): makes it an offence for a person to organise a public assembly and knowingly to fail to comply with any conditions (see s 12, above) imposed by the police under s 14(1), ie a condition which appears necessary for public safety (it is a defence to prove that the failure to comply was due to circumstances beyond the control of the person charged);
- subs (5): makes it an offence to take part in a public assembly and knowingly to fail to comply with any conditions imposed by the police under s 14(1) (see s 14(4), above). The same defence applies as for a s 14(4) offence; and
- subs (6): makes it an offence to incite the commission of an offence under s 14(5).

SECTION 14B(4)

Trespassory assemblies

Section 14B(4) authorises a constable in uniform to arrest without a warrant anybody he reasonably suspects to be committing an offence under s 14B:

POA 1986,
s 14B(4)
(inserted by
CJPOA 1994,
s 70)

- subs (1): makes it an offence to organise a trespassory assembly which is known to be prohibited under s 14A (see above);
- subs (2): makes it an offence to take part in a trespassory assembly which is known to be prohibited under s 14A (see above); and
- subs (3): makes it an offence to incite the commission of an offence under s 14B(2).

Section 14A empowers a local council in the provinces or the Commissioner of Police in London to prohibit public assemblies (with the consent of the Secretary of State) on land to which the public has no right of access or only a limited right of access and where such a gathering would exceed such right of access as the public have, either at common law or by statute or by permission.

In *DPP v Jones et al*[1], it was held that no offence under s 14B was committed merely by people exercising their lawful right of peaceful assembly on the highway which did not cause any actual obstruction thereof. As they were doing what they were entitled to do legitimately, they were not trespassers and, therefore, the condition precedent for being in breach of an order under s 14A did not exist.

SECTION 14C(4)

Proceeding to trespassory assemblies

Section 14C(4) authorises a constable in uniform to arrest without a warrant anybody he reasonably suspects to be committing an offence under s 14C(1), namely the refusal to obey a direction by a constable to stop and to proceed in the opposite direction of an assembly banned under s 14A, when that direction has been made to a person whom the constable reasonably believes to be on his way to such an assembly and the direction has been made within the area to which the order applies.

POA 1986,
s 14C(4)
(inserted by
CJPOA 1994,
s 71)

---

1   [1999] 2 AC 240.

SECTION 18(3)

Threatening etc words, behaviour etc likely to stir up racial hatred
Section 18(3) authorises a constable in uniform to arrest without a warrant anybody he reasonably suspects to be committing an offence under s 18, namely using threatening, abusive or insulting words or behaviour, or displaying any written material:

POA 1986, s 18(3)

(a) with intent to stir up racial hatred, or if
(b) having regard to all the circumstances, racial hatred is likely to be stirred up thereby.

The offence may be committed anywhere except where all people concerned are inside a (but not necessarily the same) dwelling.

Under s 18(6), it is a defence if all of the following 3 conditions are satisfied:

(a) there was no intention to stir up racial hatred;
(b) the words, conduct or writing were not intended to be threatening, abusive or insulting; and
(c) there was no awareness that they might be such.

6.7.4.3   Road Traffic Act 1988 ('RTA 1988')
This is dealt with in a separate chapter (Chapter 7) in view of the many judicial decisions on its correct interpretation, most of which have almost certainly been brought about by the fact that some drivers 'take the view that it is more convenient to rely on being defended by a sufficiently ingenious lawyer than to take care never to drive with more than the permitted proportion of alcohol', to quote the words of Lord Diplock in *Walker v Lovell*[1].

RTA 1998

6.7.4.4   Football Spectators Act 1989 ('FSA 1989')

SECTION 2(4)

Unauthorised attendance at designated football matches
Section 2(4) authorises a constable to arrest without warrant anybody whom he reasonably suspects of having committed an offence under s 2(1), namely a person, not being an authorised spectator, who goes to watch, at the football ground, a match designated by the Secretary of State and is at the ground during the period of 2 hours until 1 hour after the match has been played. Authorised spectator means that he is either (s 1(5)) a member of a national football scheme or (s 1(6)) has been

FSA 1989, s 2(4)

---

1   [1975] 1 All ER 107 at 111.

admitted to the ground in accordance with the conditions laid down by the Secretary of State.

SECTION 21A

Under s 21A (as inserted by para 4 of Sch 1 to the Football (Disorder) Act 2000), a constable in uniform may arrest a person if: (1) he has reasonable grounds for suspecting that he has engaged in violence anywhere in the United Kingdom; and (2) he reasonably believes that a banning order would help to prevent disorder at a regulated football match. A person so apprehended may be detained for up to 4 hours (or 6 hours on the authority of an officer of the rank of inspector or above) while the officer decides whether or not to issue his prisoner with a notice under s 21B, namely to appear before justices to show cause why a football banning order should not be made.

FSA 1989, s 21A

Under s 21B(5) (as inserted by para 4 of Sch 1 to the Football (Disorder) Act 2000), a constable may arrest a person if he has reasonable grounds to believe that this was necessary in order to secure compliance with the notice referred to above.

6.7.4.5   *Prevention of Terrorism (Temporary Provisions) Act 1989 ('PT (TP)A 1989')*

SECTION 14

Terrorist offences

Section 14 authorises a constable to arrest without a warrant anybody he reasonably suspects:

PT(TP)A[1] 1989, s 14

(a) to be guilty of an offence under ss 2, 8, 9, 10 and 11 (by virtue of the length of the imprisonment which can be imposed for their commission, they are also all arrestable offences);

(b) to be a person who is or has been concerned in the commission, preparation, or instigation of acts of terrorism, except those acts which are solely concerned with the affairs of the United Kingdom other than Northern Ireland; or

(c) to be a person in Great Britain who has been excluded therefrom by an exclusion order.

By s 14(5) a person apprehended under s 14 can only be incarcerated for 48 hours, unless extended by the Secretary of State for up to a maximum of 5 days. This power of arrest is without prejudice to any other power of arrest (s 14(7)).

---

1   At the time of writing, it is still in force by virtue of the Prevention of Terrorism (Temporary Provisions) Act 1989 (Continuance) Order 1999, SI 1999/906 but will cease to have effect when Sch 16 to the Terrorism Act 2000 comes into force.

6.7.4.6   Criminal Justice (International Co-operation) Act 1990 ('CJ(IC)A 1990')

SCHEDULE 3, PARA 4(a)

Drugs offences aboard British ships
Schedule 3, para 4(a) empowers a police officer to arrest without   CJ(IC)A 1990,
Sch 3, para 4(a)
warrant anybody he reasonably suspects to be guilty of an offence
under ss 18 and 19 of the Act, namely (s 18) committing on board
a British ship anywhere in the world any act which would be a
drug trafficking offence, if done on land in the United Kingdom;
and (s 19) having on board a British ship anywhere in the world a
controlled drug, or being knowingly concerned in the carrying
or concealing of a controlled drug on the ship, WITH the
knowledge that, or having reasonable grounds to suspect that,
the drug is intended to be imported, or has been exported,
contrary to s 3(1) of the Misuse of Drugs Act 1971 or the law of
any other State. Section 3(1) prohibits the importation or
exportation of the chemicals listed in Sch 2 to that Act, which is
periodically updated.

6.7.4.7   Transport and Works Act 1992 ('TWA 1992')

Offences by certain transport employees
The powers of arrest created by this legislation extend to only   TWA 1992
part of the population, namely those whom, for want of a better
expression, can best be described as 'relevant transport
employees'; or, to use the statutory definition, those people who
work on a transport system (in one of the capacities set out
below) and the system is used, or is intended to be used, wholly or
partly for the carriage of members of the public and is either:

(1) a railway; or
(2) a tramway; or
(3) any other transport system which uses another mode of
     guided transport and is so designated by an order of the
     Secretary of State. 'Guided transport' is defined in s 67(1) as
     'transport by vehicles guided by means external to the
     vehicles (whether or not the vehicles are also operated in
     some other way)'; and 'vehicle' includes a 'mobile traction
     unit'.

To date, only one relevant statutory instrument has been passed
by Parliament, namely the Transport (Guidance Systems)
Order[1], which made the following modes of conveyance subject
to the provisions of TWA 1992:

---

1   SI 1992/2044.

(1) the magnetic levitation system between Birmingham International Airport and its railway station operated by Birmingham International Airport plc (at the time of going to press, this transport system was not in use due to technical problems);

(2) the monorail operated by Von Roll Transport Systems UK Limited in the West Midlands, between Boulevard and Waterfront East Stations;

(3) the two track-based systems with side guidance operated at Gatwick Airport by Gatwick Airport Limited, between:
    (a) the South and North Terminals; and
    (b) South Terminal and South Terminal satellite/pier 3; and

(4) the track-based systems with side guidance operated at Stansted Airport by Stansted Airport Limited, between the Airport Terminals and satellite 1.

The relevant transport employees are (s 27(1)) those who work:

(1) as drivers;
(2) as guards;
(3) as conductors;
(4) as signalmen;
(5) in any other capacity in which they can control or affect the movement of a vehicle;
(6) in a maintenance capacity;
(7) as a supervisor of, or
(8) look-out for persons working in a maintenance capacity, which is defined in s 27(3) as involving the:

> 'maintenance, repair or alteration of –
>   (a) the permanent way or the means of guiding or supporting vehicles,
>   (b) signals or any other means of controlling the movement of vehicles, or
>   (c) any means of supplying electricity to vehicles or to the means of guiding or supporting vehicles,
> or involves coupling or uncoupling vehicles or checking that they are working properly before they are used on any occasion.'

SECTION 27(1), 30(1)

Working while unfit to carry out duties through drink and drugs

Section 30 enacts the various powers of arrest. Section 30(1) empowers a constable to arrest without warrant a 'relevant transport employee' if he has reasonable cause to suspect that that such a person is or has been committing an offence under s 27(1), namely working whilst unfit to carry out his duties

TWA 1992, ss 27(1), 30(1)

through drink or drugs. 'Unfitness' is defined in s 27(4) as meaning that the ability to carry out one's work is impaired for the time being.

SECTIONS 29, 30(2)

Breath tests

Section 30(2) authorises a constable to arrest a relevant transport employee without a warrant (provided he is not 'at a hospital as a patient' (see Chapter 7) if:

TWA 1992,
ss 29, 30(2), 31

(a) as a result of a breath test under s 29 (see below), he has reasonable cause to suspect that the proportion of alcohol in that person's breath or blood exceeds the prescribed limit; or

(b) that person has failed to provide a specimen of breath for a breath test when required to do so in pursuance of s 29 (see below), and the constable has reasonable cause to suspect that he has alcohol in his body.

The statute defines 'breath test', 'fail' and 'prescribed limit' in exactly the same words as RTA 1988 (see Chapter 7).

Section 29(1) allows a constable in uniform (see above) to administer a breath test on a person at or near (see Chapter 7) the place where the requirement is made, if he has cause to suspect that the person:

(a) is a relevant transport employee working on a transport system with alcohol in his body; or

(b) is a relevant transport employee who has been working on a transport system with alcohol in his body and still has alcohol in his body.

Under s 29(2), where an accident or dangerous incident occurs on a transport system, a constable in uniform may require a person at or near the place where the requirement is made or at a police station to provide a specimen of breath for a breath test, if he has reasonable cause to suspect that at the time of the accident or incident that person was working on the transport system as a relevant transport employee and that any act or omission of that person whilst he was so working may have been a cause of the accident or incident. Section 29(3) defines 'dangerous incident' as 'an incident which in the constable's opinion involved a danger of death or personal injury'.

6.7.4.8   *Trade Union and Labour Relations Consolidation Act 1992* *('TULRCA 1992')*

SECTION 241

Intimidation etc

Section 241(3) empowers a constable to arrest anyone whom he has reasonable cause to suspect of committing an offence under s 241, namely a person who wrongfully and without legal authority:

TULRCA 1992, *s 241*

(a) uses violence to intimidate, or intimidates, another person, his wife or children, or injures his property;
(b) persistently follows that other person about from place to place;
(c) hides any tools, clothes or other property owned, or used by that other person, or deprives him of, or hinders him in, the use thereof;
(d) watches or besets the house or other place where that other person resides, works, carries on business or happens to be, or the approach to any such house or place; or
(e) follows that person with two or more people in a disorderly manner in or though any street or road.

AND when the above acts are done in order to compel that other person either:

(1) to abstain from doing any act which he is legally entitled to do; or
(2) to do any act that he is legally entitled to abstain from doing.

6.7.4.9   *Asylum and Immigration Appeals Act 1993 ('AIAA 1993')*[1]

SECTION 3(5)

Fingerprinting claimants for asylum

Section 3(5) allows a constable to arrest a claimant for asylum who fails to attend at the time and date appointed for his fingerprinting under s 3. He may be taken to a place where his fingerprints may be conveniently taken and, once that has been done, he is entitled to be released.

AIAA 1993, *s 3(5)*

---

1   AIAA 1993, s 3(5) will be repealed when the relevant part of Sch 16 to IAA 1999 is brought into force.

6.7.4.10   *Criminal Justice and Public Order Act 1994 ('CJPOA 1994')*

SECTION 61

Collective trespass etc
Section 61(5) empowers a constable in uniform to arrest without warrant a person whom he reasonably suspects of committing an offence under s 61, namely a person who:

CJPOA 1994, s 61(5)

(1) refuses to obey an order given under s 61(1) to leave the land on which he is believed to be trespassing with at least one other and when any of them is suspected of committing criminal damage or has used threatening, abusive or insulting behaviour towards the occupier, his family, servants or agents; or
(2) having left, returns as a trespasser within 3 months of the order to leave.

Land does not include buildings other than agricultural buildings or scheduled monuments, nor does it include a highway save for a footway, bridleway or a cycle track (s 61(9)(a), (b)). Before giving an order pursuant to s 61(1), it is arguable that the officer must take into account considerations of 'common humanity', per Collins J in *R v West London Magistrates' Court, ex parte Small*[1]. These are the matters referred to in Home Office Circular no 45/1994, 'as the personal circumstances of the trespassers, for example the presence of elderly persons, invalids, pregnant women, children and other persons whose well-being may be jeopardised by a precipitate move'.

SECTION 63

Attending or preparing for a rave
Section 63(8) empowers a constable in uniform to arrest without warrant any person whom he reasonably suspects of committing an offence under s 63, namely a person who refuses to obey a direction under s 63(1) to leave a gathering on land in the open air of 100 or more persons where amplified music is played at night and which, by its loudness and duration, is likely to cause serious distress to the local inhabitants; or having left, re-enters the land within 7 days of being ordered to leave. The direction can be given where two or more people are preparing for such a gathering or 10 or more people are either waiting for the gathering to begin or are attending the gathering once it has begun. Section 63 does not apply where an entertainment licence has been granted.

CJPOA 1994, s 63(8)

---

1   (Unreported) 27 August 1998.

SECTION 65

Proceeding to a rave

Section 65(5) authorises a constable in uniform to arrest without a warrant anybody he reasonably suspects to be committing an offence under s 65(1), namely the refusal to obey a direction by a constable to proceed in the opposite direction of a gathering to which s 63 (see above) applies, when that request has been made to a person whom the constable reasonably believes to be on his way to such a gathering. The direction can only be given within 5 miles of the boundary of the site of the meeting.

CJPOA 1994,
s 65(5)

SECTION 68

Aggravated trespass

Section 68(4) empowers a constable in uniform to arrest without warrant any person whom the constable reasonably suspects is committing an offence of aggravated trespass. That is defined in s 68(1) as trespassing on open land in order either; (a) to deter by intimidation; (b) to obstruct; or (c) to disrupt, any lawful activity which people are engaging in, or are about to engage in, in the open air on land where the trespasser is or on adjoining land. The disruption or obstruction must be by an act which is separate and distinct from the actual entry; see *DPP v Barnard[1]*.

CJPOA 1994,
s 68(4)

SECTION 69

Failing to leave land etc

Section 69(5) empowers a constable in uniform to arrest without warrant a person whom he reasonably suspects of committing an offence under s 69, namely by either refusing to leave the land as soon as is practicable after having been ordered under s 69(1) to leave because he is reasonably suspected of committing, or of intending to commit, an aggravated trespass contrary to s 68(1) (see above); or having left, by returning as a trespasser within the next 3 months.

CJPOA 1994,
s 69(5)

SECTION 76

Trespassing during currency of interim possession order

A constable in uniform may arrest without warrant any person who is, or whom the constable reasonably suspects to be, guilty of an offence under s 76, namely remaining as a trespasser on premises for more than 24 hours after the service, or affixing to the premises, of an interim possession order; or having left, he returns or attempts to return as a trespasser within 12 months of

CJPOA 1994,
s 76(7)

---

1   [1999] TLR 754.

the service or affixing of the order. Trespass means 'trespassing against the occupier'; see s 61(9)(a). Premises mean buildings and land adjacent thereto; see s 76(8) and CLA 1977, s 12.

6.7.4.11 Family Law Act 1996 ('FLA 1996')

SECTION 47(6)

Breach of non-molestation order to which power of arrest attached
Section 47 authorises a constable to arrest, without warrant, a person whom he has reasonable cause to suspect to be in breach of an occupation or non-molestation order to which the court has attached a power of arrest. A person so arrested must be brought before the court which granted the order within 24 hours of his apprehension, not counting Christmas Day, Easter Day or any Sunday (s 47(7)). The court can further remand such an arrested person either in custody or on bail (s 47(10)).

FLA 1996,
s 47(6)

6.7.4.12 Housing Act 1996 ('HA 1996')

SECTION 155

Anti-social behaviour by council tenants in breach of injunction
Section 155 authorises a constable to arrest, without warrant, a person whom he has reasonable cause to suspect to be in breach of an injunction granted to a local authority to prevent anti-social behaviour in its council houses (or flats) and to which, under ss 152(6) or 153, a power of arrest has been attached. A person so arrested must be brought before the court which granted the injunction within 24 hours of his apprehension, not counting Christmas Day, Easter Day or any Sunday. The court can further remand such an arrested person either in custody or on bail (Sch 15).

HA 1996, s 155

6.7.4.13 Reserve Forces Act 1996 ('RFA 1996')

SECTION 100, SCH 2, PARA 2(1)

Reservist absent without leave
Schedule 2, para 2(1) empowers a constable to arrest without warrant anybody whom he has reasonable cause to believe is a reservist in the armed forces who has deserted or was absent without leave; and the arrested person must be taken before a magistrates' court as soon as is practicable (para 2(4)).

RFA 1996, s 100
and Sch 2,
para 2(1)

6.7.4.14 Consumption of Alcohol (Young Persons) Act 1997 ('CA(YP)A 1997')

SECTION 1

Alcohol and young persons
Section 1(5) empowers a constable to arrest without warrant any person who fails to comply with a requirement under s 1(1). That entitles a policeman to require a person to surrender anything in his possession which is, or which the officer reasonably suspects to be, intoxicating liquor, if the officer reasonably suspects that the person has alcohol in his possession and is either in a public place other than licensed premises or is a trespasser on private premises AND the officer also suspects that the person: CA(YP)A 1997, s 1(5)

(1) is under the age of 18 years; or
(2) intends that somebody under the age of 18 years will consume that alcohol either in a public place other than licensed premises or on private premises where he will be a trespasser; or
(3) is with, or has recently been with, a person under the age of 18 years who is drinking, or has recently consumed, intoxicating liquor, either in a public place other than licensed premises or on private premises where he was a trespasser.

6.7.4.15 Crime (Sentences) Act 1997 ('C(S)A 1997')

SECTIONS 17, 18(1)

Failing to comply with release supervision order
Section 18(1) authorises a constable to arrest without warrant anyone he reasonably suspects to be committing an offence under s 17, namely a person in respect of whom there is a release supervision order in force and who fails, without reasonable excuse, to comply with any of its conditions. C(S)A 1997, s 18(1)

6.7.4.16 Immigration and Asylum Act 1999 ('IAA 1999')

SECTIONS 44, 50(1) (at the time of writing not yet in force)

Breach of bail condition
Section 50(1) empowers a constable to arrest without warrant anyone he reasonably believes to have broken, or to be likely to break a condition of bail imposed under s 44. The detained IAA 1999, s 50(1)

person must be brought, within 24 hours, before the person or tribunal before whom he was under to duty to surrender as a condition of his bail.

SECTION 142(3) (at time of writing not yet in force)

Failure to attend for fingerprinting
Section 142(3) empowers a constable to arrest any of the following people, viz: (1) a person who has failed to produce a passport on arrival which would prove his identity or nationality; (2) a person refused entry who has been granted temporary admittance; (3) any person who has been refused entry or against whom a notice of intention to make a deportation order has been issued *and* who is appealing against the same; (4) an asylum seeker; or (5) a dependant of any of the above WHO has failed to attend at the date and time appointed for his fingerprinting under s 141(1). Those apprehended under s 142(3) may be taken to a place where fingerprints can be conveniently taken and once that has been done they are entitled to be released.

IAA 1999, s 142(3)

6.7.4.17 *Terrorism Act 2000 (yet to be brought into force, anticipated to be in February 2001)*

SECTION 41

Terrorists
Under the Terrorism Act 2000, s 41(1), a constable may arrest without warrant a person whom he reasonably suspects to be a terrorist – who is defined in s 40(1) as:

Terrorism Act 2000

(a) having committed one of the following offences contrary to the sections set out below of the Terrorism Act 2000, namely:

    (i) membership of a proscribed organisation (s 11);
    (ii) inviting or canvassing support for a proscribed organisation (s 12);
    (iii) involved in fundraising to support terrorism (s 15);
    (iv) possessing property or money to be used for the purposes of terrorism (s 16);
    (v) fund raising for the purposes of terrorism (s 17);
    (vi) money laundering for the purposes of terrorism (s 18);
    (vii) weapon training (s 54);
    (viii) directing a terrorist organisation (s 56);
    (ix) committing an offence abroad contrary to ss 11–18 above,

OR

(b) been concerned in the commission, preparation or instigation of acts of terrorism, which are defined in s 1 as: (1)
   serious violence; or (2) serious damage to property; or (3)
   endangering life; or (4) serious risk to the health and safety
   of the public; or (5) serious interference or disruption to an
   electronic system

AND which conduct is designed to influence the government or
to influence public opinion or for political, religious or ideologi-
cal purposes.

SCHEDULE 7

Detaining for questioning
Under Sch 7, a constable can detain, for questioning, a person at   Terrorism Act
a port or airport whom he believes is there for the purpose of   2000
embarking on, or disembarking from, a journey into or out of
Great Britain. His captive can be kept at any place designated by
the Secretary of State (Sch 8, para 1(1)). The incarceration
cannot exceed 9 hours from the beginning of the interrogation
(Sch 7, para 6(4)). Because of the conditions prevailing, this
power would not contravene the European Convention of
Human Rights insofar as the interview was held for the purpose
of obtaining information about terrorism in Ireland[1] and no
doubt elsewhere. However, if the Schedule was used for other
purposes unconnected with terrorism then there would also
most certainly be a breach of the Convention because of the
arbitrary power of detention without the requirements of any
reasonable suspicion of any wrongdoing[2].

6.8   THE GENERAL ARREST CONDITIONS – THEIR DEFINITION

Under PACE 1984, s 25(1) and (2), if a constable has reasonable grounds to
suspect somebody (the 'relevant person') of:

(1) committing;
(2) attempting to commit;
(3) having committed;
(4) having attempted to commit, any offence;

then, if any of the general arrest conditions are satisfied, the constable may
arrest without a warrant the relevant person.

The first set of general arrest conditions are that it appears to the constable to
be impractical or inappropriate to serve a summons for one of the reasons set

---

1   See *Ireland v UK* (1978) 2 EHRR 25.
2   See *Fox et al v UK* (1990) 13 EHRR 157.

out in the lettered subsections of s 25(3), as explained by s 25(4) and (5), namely:

(a) the arresting officer does not know and cannot readily ascertain the name of the relevant person;

(b) the arresting officer has reasonable grounds for believing that the name given is in fact not the 'real name' of the relevant person; or

(c) the relevant person has failed to furnish a satisfactory address for service or the arresting officer has reasonable grounds for doubting whether the address given is a satisfactory address for service.

Under s 25(4), an address is satisfactory for service if (under subs 4(a)) it appears to the constable that the relevant person will be at it for sufficiently long so that a summons can be served upon him there; or (under subs 4(b)) some other person specified by the relevant person will accept service on his behalf at that address. *DPP v McCarthy*[1] (a case under RTA 1988, s 170(2)) held that providing the address of one's solicitors complied with the requirement to provide an address.

The second and alternative set of general arrest conditions (which are set out in s 25(3)(d)) are that the arresting officer has reasonable grounds for believing that the arrest was necessary to prevent the relevant person from:

(i) causing physical injury to himself or any other person;

(ii) suffering physical injury;

(iii) causing loss or damage to property;

(iv) committing an offence against public decency but only (s 25(5)) if persons going about their normal business cannot reasonably be expected to avoid the relevant person; or

(v) causing an unlawful obstruction of the highway.

Until recently, the accepted view was that anything other than passing and re-passing amounted to an illegal obstruction, but the wind of change has even blown through the judges' corridor in the Law Courts, and 'in the context of the criminal offence of obstruction, lawful excuse is naturally seen in terms of offending and not in terms of civil trespass' (per Collins J in *DPP v Jones*[2]). Thus, nowadays, provided that nobody is actually obstructed, the criterion is reasonableness. In the words of Glidewell LJ in *Hirst v Chief Constable of West Yorkshire*[3]:

'... have the prosecution proved in such cases that the defendant was obstructing the highway without lawful excuse? That is a question to be answered by deciding whether the activity in which the defendant was engaged was or was not a reasonable user of the highway. I emphasise that for there to be a lawful excuse for what would otherwise be an obstruction of the highway, the activity in which the person causing the obstruction is engaged must itself be inherently lawful. If it is not, the question whether it is reasonable does not arise.'

---

1   [1999] RTR 323.

2   [1997] 2 All ER 119 at 126J (overruled, on other grounds, on appeal [1999] AC 240).

3   (1986) 85 Cr App R 143 at 150.

That view was followed by the majority of the House of Lords in *DPP v Jones (Margaret) et al*[1], which held that people were entitled to use the highway for a peaceful purpose provided such a purpose was reasonable, and that this did not constitute a public or private nuisance if it did not unreasonably impede the public's right of passage. There it was held to be no offence to be part of a 21-strong meeting on the verge of the A344, adjacent to Stonehenge and, accordingly, their convictions for trespassory assembly contrary to the Public Order Act 1986 were quashed.

6.9 COMMENTARY

Edwards v DPP[2] and *Houghton v Chief Constable of Greater Manchester*[3] both held that if an officer did not ask a person for his identity and address, then it could not be said that the officer was not satisfied as to the name and address of that person. To the same effect is *Dunbell v Roberts*[4]. In *Nicholas v Parsonage*[5], it was held that if such a question was put and the information required was not supplied, then a constable was entitled to rely on s 25(3) to effect an arrest. In *Ghafar v Chief Constable of the West Midlands*[6], PC Wilkes stopped the plaintiff's car and asked him his name and address which he declined to give. He was told that he was driving without a seat-belt which was an offence and was then asked if he had any driving documents or anything else to prove his identity, to which the answer was 'no'. The officer then told the plaintiff that he was under arrest until he could verify his name. The court of Appeal held that on those facts the condition in s 25(3)(a) was fulfilled. The Court rejected the argument that as there was no obligation on the plaintiff to give his name and address when first asked, the police could not rely on that as a ground for detaining him. Roch LJ said (para 15):

> 'It must be open to the police officer, in deciding whether it appears to him that the name of a person who has committed an offence which is not an arrestable offence can or cannot be readily ascertained, to take account of the demeanour and response of that person from the moment that the officer first has conversation with him.'

It is submitted that this approach to s 25 is an attack on the freedom of the individual. Why should it be held against a person that he has exercised his right of silence until he is told that he is suspected of committing an offence? Only at that time should his failure to supply details of who he is and where he lives give rise to a general arrest condition. However, it is accepted that *Ghafar* was correctly decided because, as a driver, the plaintiff was under an obligation under RTA 1988, s 165 to give the information requested by the police and this breach of that legal duty did give rise to the fulfilment of the condition in PACE

---

1   [1999] AC 240.
2   (1993) 97 Cr App R 301.
3   (1986) TLR, July 24.
4   [1944] 1 All ER 326.
5   [1987] RTR 199.
6   (Unreported) 12 May 2000.

1984, s 25(3)(a). (This was not a reason given by the Court of Appeal in their judgment.) It was said in *G v DPP*[1] that the reasonable suspicion that a general arrest condition existed must be based on matters special to the detainee and not just generally. In that case, the High Court held the apprehension to be illegal when the only grounds given for doubting that the prisoner had given his genuine name and address was the officer's experience that suspects usually gave false details about themselves.

According to *Edwards v DPP*[2], the two-stage process referred to in *Castorina v Chief Constable of Surrey*[3] applied to s 25, ie did the officer have the relevant condition in his mind at the time and, if so, was that condition fulfilled?

6.10   RESTRICTION OF THE EXERCISE OF THE POWER OF ARREST

PACE 1984, ss 41(9), 42(11) and 43(19) state that when a person has been set free by the police, he cannot be arrested again, without a warrant, for the same offence for which he had been kept in custody, unless either new evidence, justifying that course of action, had come to light after his release or the arrest is under s 46A of that Act (ie breach of a bail condition).

6.11   THE CODES OF PRACTICE

Under PACE 1984, s 66(b), the Secretary of State is under a mandatory duty to issue a Code of Practice for the police about 'the detention of persons'. However, under s 67(10), no civil or criminal liability shall result solely from breaches of the Code. *Prima facie* it would appear therefore that the Code would play no part in the law of false imprisonment. However, in *Ahmed v Chief Constable of the West Midlands Police Force*,[4] Judge LJ said:

> 'Section 67(10) provides restrictions on the use to which breaches of the Code may be deployed in civil proceedings but it is plain that such breaches may be relied upon in relation to claims for false imprisonment and malicious prosecution.'

His Lordship did not elaborate on the above, save that at the very beginning of his judgment he made the following remarks about the Code:

> 'In the result it is unnecessary to decide these interesting questions which must await another opportunity for decision in the light of detailed analysis of the relevant principles.'

In view of s 67(10), it would appear that a breach of the Codes of Practice would not *ipso facto* amount to the tort of false imprisonment, but when such a tort had been committed, then in assessing quantum, a jury would be entitled to take

---

1   [1989] Crim LR 150.
2   (1993) 97 Cr App R 301.
3   (1988) 138 NLJ (R) 180.
4   (Unreported) 28 July 1998.

such breaches into account, especially when deciding whether or not the plaintiff should recover exemplary damages.

6.11.1   Detain for questioning

In *Bentley v Brundzinski*[1], the High Court held that when a constable wished to detain for questioning, short of an arrest, a citizen who did not wish to remain and who had attempted to walk away, then the firm but not hostile placing of the officer's hand upon that person's shoulder with the intention of stopping him might be unlawful so as to amount to false imprisonment. Whether such was the case was not a question of law, but a question of fact depending on the circumstances which preceded it and on the degree of force used. (In that it was held not to amount to the tort of trespass.) This is because the law presumes that everybody consents to the normal bodily contact inherent in everyday life, for example, tapping a person on his back to attract his attention. In *Kenlin v Gardiner*[2], two detectives noticed some school boys visiting a number of houses. On being asked what they were doing, one of the juveniles appeared to be about to make off, so one of the constables seized his left arm. The High Court held that taking hold of an arm was illegal as the police had no power to detain for questioning. The difference between these two cases is that in the former the touching was merely to attract attention, while in the latter it was in order to stop him going any further.

In *Moberly v Allsop*[3], the magistrate had found the following facts:

> '(i) The appellant by failing to produce a ticket on request or at all had *prima facie* committed an offence under s 5(1) of the Regulations of Railway Act 1889. The respondent was trying to investigate this and was entitled to use reasonable force to stop her for the purpose of questioning her. The respondent's conduct so far as this part of the incident was concerned could not amount to an assault.'

Brooke J (with whom Woolf LJ agreed) commented as follows on that passage in the case:

> 'I add, in parenthesis, that at one of the earlier hearings Glidewell LJ expressed a view in support of that finding and I respectfully agree with his statement.'

Kenlin, above, was not cited in *Moberly v Allsop* and, at first sight, the above views expressed by Brooke J and Glidewell LJ appear to be contrary to it. However, those latter judges may have meant that because there was a power to apprehend under the Regulations of Railways Act 1889, but only if the name and address of the prisoner was unknown, then by implication there was a right to detain a person in order to ask him his name and address. However, it is submitted, that unless implicitly authorised by statute, there is no legal authority to detain for questioning and, therefore, in that regard CLA 1967, s 3 (reasonable force allowed to be used to make an arrest) can have no relevance whatsoever.

---

1   (1982) 75 Cr App R 217.
2   [1967] 2 QB 510.
3   (1991) 156 JP 514 at 516.

6.12 OTHER STATUTORY POWERS OF DETENTION

The police have been given by statute the power to detain people for specific purposes, (eg while they administer a breath test pursuant to the Transport and Works Act 1992, s 29(1), see **6.7.4.8**). That could take quite some time, depending on how long the constable had to wait until his brother officer arrived with the necessary equipment. In relation to a similar power under the now reapealed Road Traffic Act 1972, Lord Diplock said in *Morris v Beadmore*[1]:

> '... the driver [is] required, uneer threat of forcible detention in the event of non-compliance, to do the physical act of blowing into a breathalyser against his will; to be detained by force or the threat of force at the place where the constable requires the breath test to be taken until the test has been completed – which in some circumstances may take a considerable time; and to be compelled by force or threat of it to go to a police station to take a breath test if the constable feels fit. I have used the word "detained" rather than "arrested" because the power which section 8 confers upon a constable to restrain the liberty of movement of a person required by him to take a breath test, particularly where the requirement is under subsection (2), is of a wholly different legal nature from the arrest of a suspected offender effected by a constable under powers conferred upon him at common law or under section 2 of the Criminal Law Act 1967.'

A number of statutes authorise the constabulary to search people. In order to exercise that power, the police obviously need to have the legal right to restrain the suspect from going off and thus frustrating their attempts to see what is in his possession. This was recognised by the High Court in *Collins v Wilcock*[2] where Goff LJ said:

> 'A police officer may subject another to restraint when he lawfully exercises his powers of arrest; and he has other statutory powers, for example, his power to stop and search and detain persons under s 66 of the Metropolitan Police Act, with which we are not concerned.'

An example of such powers are those in PACE 1984, s 1(2)(a) which gives a constable the right to stop and to search those people on whose person he has reasonable grounds to believe that he will find: (1) stolen articles; (2) prohibited articles; or (3) any article the possession of which contravenes s 139 of the CJA 1988 (ie an article which is sharply pointed or has a blade, except a folding pocket knife with a blade not exceeding 3 inches). A prohibited article is defined in s 1(7) as:

(a) an offensive weapon,
(b) an article made or
(c) adapted for use in, or
(d) possessed for use by anybody for the purposes of:
    (1) a burglary,
    (2) theft,
    (3) an offence under s 12 of TA 1968 (unlawfully taking a vehicle) or

---

1   [1981] AC 446 at 454H–455A.
2   [1984] 3 All ER 375 at 379.

(4) a crime against s 15 of TA 1968 of dishonestly obtaining possession of property by deception with intent to deprive the owner permanently thereof.

This power of search can be exercised anywhere where a section of the public is admitted and in any place where people go, except a dwelling house.

Apart from PACE 1984, s 1, the other most widely used powers of stop and search are:

- PACE 1984, s 4, which allows the use of road blocks to try to catch perpetrators of serious arrestable offences;
- PACE 1984, s 6, which authorises constables employed by statutory undertakers to stop, detain, and search any vehicle in their employers' good area;
- Misuse of Drugs Act 1971, s 23(2), which empowers a constable to search anybody he reasonably believes to be in unlawful possession of a controlled drug and to detain him for that reason; and
- PT(TP)A 1989 (as amended by CJPOA 1994, s 81(2)), which authorises a constable in uniform to stop and search vehicles if an officer, not below the rank of assistant chief constable, thinks that it is expedient to do so in order to prevent acts of terrorism.

As well as the above, a number of other statutes have invested policemen with similar powers. Some examples are set out below.

- Crossbows Act 1987, s 4(2) allows a constable to detain a person while carrying out a search under s 4(1), ie for a crossbow with a drawn weight of 1.4 kilograms or over (s 5).

- Badgers Act 1992, s 11, enables a constable to stop and to search a person if he reasonably suspects him of having committed an offence under that Act and that there was evidence of that offence on his person or in his vehicle. The Badgers Act 1992 makes the following conduct unlawful, save to the extent that such is permitted by the Act:

  (i)   killing, injuring or taking a badger, or attempting to do so (s 1);
  (ii)   cruelty to a badger (s 2);
  (iii) interfering with a badger sett (s 3);
  (iv)   selling, or having possession of, or control of, a live badger (s 4); and
  (v)   marking or ringing a badger (s 5).

- CJPOA 1994, s 60 authorises a constable in uniform to stop and to search people and vehicles if an officer not below the rank of superintendent believes it to be expedient to do so in order to prevent incidents of serious violence taking place.
- PT(TP)A 1989, Sch 2, para 8(6) states that a person detained under that Schedule may be taken in the custody of a constable to a place where he is required to be under that Act or where his attendance is necessary for

making arrangements for him to enter another country. On a day to be appointed, the above provisions will be repealed and re-enacted by Sch 5 to the Terrorism Act 2000 which allows those entering or leaving the UK to be detained for questioning.

Chapter 7

THE ROAD TRAFFIC ACT 1988[1]

7.1 INTRODUCTION

In addition to the arrestable offences in s 1 (death by dangerous driving), s 3A (causing death by careless driving when under the influence of drink or drugs) and s 22A (causing danger to road users), ss 4(6), 6(5) and 103(3) of RTA 1988 also confer on the police a power of summary apprehension of delinquent motorists. As a mistake of law can never be a defence to an action of false imprisonment (see Chapter 8), it is important to know the judicial definition of certain common words used in the 1988 Act; and this will be considered first, followed by a discussion on each individual power of arrest. Although RTA 1988 does not apply to people in private places, various statutes have extended its provisions to encompass those on such property, for example the British Transport Act 1961, the Dover Harbour Act 1964, the Port of London Act 1968, the Airports Act 1986 and the Channel Tunnel Act 1987.

7.2 DRIVING

There is no statutory definition. The leading case is *R v MacDonagh*[2] (a case on driving while disqualified), where Lord Widgery CJ stated[3]:

> 'The Act does not define the word "drive" and in its simplest meaning we think that it refers to a person using the driver's controls for the purpose of directing the movement of the vehicle. It matters not that the vehicle is not moving under its own power, or is being driven by the force of gravity, or even that it is being pushed by other well-wishers. The essence of driving is the use of the driver's controls in order to direct the movement, however movement is produced.
>
> There are an infinite number of ways in which a person may control the movement of a motor vehicle, apart from the orthodox one of sitting in the driving seat and using the engine for propulsion. He may be coasting down a hill with the gears in neutral and the engine switched off; he may be steering a vehicle which is being towed by another. As has already been pointed out, he may be sitting in the driving seat whilst others push, or half sitting in the driving seat but keeping one foot on the road in order to induce the car to move. Finally, as in the present case, he may be standing in the road and himself pushing the car with or without using the steering wheel to direct it. Although the word "drive" must be given a wide meaning, the courts must be alert to see that the net is not thrown so widely that it includes activities which cannot be said to be driving a motor vehicle in any ordinary use of that word in the English language. Unless this is done, absurdity

---

1   As amended by the RTA 1992.
2   [1974] QB 448.
3   Ibid, at 451.

may result by requiring the obtaining of a driving licence and third party insurance in circumstances which cannot have been contemplated by Parliament.'

In other words, a driver is a person controlling the movement of the vehicle, provided a layman would also call him 'a driver.' Accordingly, in this case, the court held that the ordinary meaning of the word 'drive' did not extend to include the activity of the defendant who was not in the motor car but was merely pushing it with his two feet on the ground and was making no use of the controls apart from an occasional adjustment of the steering wheel. The Lord Chief Justice went on to give examples[1] of people driving by reference to previous decisions, for example *Saycell v Bool*[2], where the owner of a lorry which had run out of petrol released the hand-brake and, while sitting in the driving seat, steered the vehicle down an incline for a distance of 100 yards.

In *R v Roberts*[3], the Court of Criminal Appeal declined to say that the appellant was 'driving' when he had maliciously released the hand-brake of a vehicle and then let it run down a hill unattended. Lord Parker CJ said[4]:

'... on the authorities, a man cannot be said to be a driver unless he is in the driving seat or in control of the steering wheel and also has something to do with the propulsion ... There are no cases, so far as this court knows, where a man has been held to be guilty of taking and driving away if, although he has something to do with the movement and the propulsion, he is not driving in any ordinary sense of the word.'

In *Burgoyne v Phillips*[5], a man sat in the driver's seat after letting the car roll forward, but was unable to steer it as he did not have the keys to the combined ignition and steering lock. He was held to have been 'driving' because he was in control of the car whilst it was moving. On the other hand, in *Leach v DPP*[6], it was held that a person was not 'driving' just because, while sitting in the driving seat of a stationary car, he had switched the ignition on and placed his hands on the steering wheel. It was stated that a *sine qua non* of 'driving' is that movement is brought to the vehicle. So in *Rowan v Chief Constable of Merseyside*[7] the High Court upheld the conviction of the appellant who had knelt on the driving seat, released the hand-brake and thereafter attempted to stop the movement of the vehicle. Watkins LJ said it had to be shown that the defendant had brought movement to the vehicle and had endeavoured to control it once it was in motion. Nolan J said that if the defendant had been in the vehicle trying to control it, then there was material on which a court could find that he had been driving it. In *McKoen v Ellis*[8], the High Court held that it was a matter of fact and degree as to whether or not a person was driving. In that case, the court upheld the conviction of the appellant who had been wearing a motorcyclist's clothing and a crash helmet and, while standing with his legs astride a motorcycle, had,

---

1   [1974] QB 448, at 452.
2   [1948] 2 All ER 83.
3   [1965] 1 QB 85.
4   Ibid, at 88.
5   [1983] RTR 49.
6   [1993] RTR 161.
7   (1985) TLR, December 10.
8   [1986] RTR 26.

for an unspecified distance, been controlling the movement and direction of the motorcycle by pushing and steering it while the ignition was on and its lights were illuminated. That decision was followed in two similar cases where moped riders were held to be 'driving' when they sat astride their vehicles and propelled them with their feet; see *Gunnel v DPP*[1] (where the engine would not start because of a faulty spark plug) and *Selby v DPP*[2]. In the latter case, Henry LJ said that as a person sitting astride a pedal-cycle and propelling it with his feet would be considered to be driving it, it would be strange if the same did not apply to a bicycle merely because it was motor-assisted.

In *Blayney v Knight*[3], the High Court upheld the acquittal for both: (1) driving; and (2) being in charge. In that case, a taxi driver had alighted from his cab to go to where he believed his fare was waiting. He left his engine running and his door open. Two men sat in the back of the taxi. The defendant, seeing his friends in the rear of the vehicle and wishing to talk to them, went and sat in the driver's seat. The cabby returned and tried to eject him. In the course of this struggle, the accused's foot accidentally operated the accelerator pedal, thus moving the cab forward and injuring the driver. The High Court held that although he had put the hackney carriage into motion, he had not intended to do so and had made no attempt to control that movement, for example by steering.

It should always be remembered that the activity complained of must come within the usual meaning of the word 'driving.' Therefore, in *Jones v Pratt*[4], it was held that the actions of a passenger who suddenly grabbed the steering wheel and put the car in a field did not fall into that category. That decision was followed by the acquittal of the front-seat passenger in the similar case of *DPP v Hastings*[5], where the latter had momentarily seized the wheel of the car to steer it towards a pedestrian in order to scare him. The High Court held that this amounted to an interference with the driving rather an act of driving. However, it is possible in law for two people to be driving the same vehicle at once; see *Longman v Valentine*[6], where there was a man in the passenger seat, with one hand on the brake and the other on the steering wheel and who could switch the ignition on and off while a lady sat next to him, controlling the foot brake and accelerator pedal. Thus, as the first-mentioned gentleman was able to start, stop and steer the car, the High Court held that, in law, both he and the person in the driver's seat were driving the car at the same time. That case was distinguished in *Evans v Walkden*[7]. There the driver did not possess a licence, but the defendant was merely next to him, ready to take control of the car if need be. The difference between these two appeals is that for a second occupant to be jointly driving, he must have his hands on the instruments of control and it is not sufficient merely to sit there, ready to take command if an

1   [1994] RTR 151.
2   [1994] RTR 157.
3   (1975) 60 Cr App R 269.
4   [1983] RTR 54.
5   [1993] RTR 205.
6   [1952] 2 All ER 803.
7   [1956] 1 WLR 1019.

emergency should arise. In *Tyler v Whatmore*[1], a young woman in the front passenger seat of a moving car steered it, with both hands on the wheel. She was sitting beside a man in the driving seat, whose view of the road ahead was obstructed as she leant across him, and he was not holding the steering wheel; the hand-brake was below her and within her reach and she was in a position to operate the ignition. The justices were of opinion that, although she had nothing to do with the car's motion, nevertheless she (as steersman) and the man operating the gears and foot controls were together engaged in driving the car in pursuance of an agreement. The High Court held that every case had to be decided on its own facts. The law did not require that, for a person to be driving, she had to be not merely steering but also controlling the propulsion of the vehicle in some way – those tasks could be divided between them and each person involved would be 'a driver'.

7.3   STEERING A VEHICLE

The interpretation section of RTA 1988 (s 192(2)) states that (except for the purpose of s 1) 'where a separate person acts as a steersman of a motor vehicle' that person 'as well as any other person engaged in the driving of the vehicle' is the driver and that the word ' "drive" is to be interpreted accordingly'. In *Whitfield v DPP*[2], the appellant had sat in the driver's seat of a vehicle, the engine of which could not be started and the foot brake had no fluid, so it was inoperative. It was being towed by a bar which was rigid but the attachments at either end were not, so that the appellant had a (albeit limited) degree of control regarding steering. Accordingly, the High Court held that he had been driving. To the same effect is *R v Challinor*[3], where the accused was found to have been driving when he sat behind the wheel of a vehicle being towed by means of a rope.

7.4   STILL DRIVING

According to the Lord Chief Justice in *DPP v James and Chorley*[4], those cases were merely concerned with whether a person had ever driven; and whether or not he was still driving was governed by the test propounded in *Edkins v Knowles*[5]:

> '(1) The vehicle does not have to be in motion; there will always be a brief interval of time after the vehicle has been brought to rest and before the motorist has completed those operations necessarily connected with driving, such as applying the hand brake, switching off the ignition and securing the vehicle, during which he must still be considered to be driving.

---

1   [1976] RTR 83.
2   (Unreported) 13 November 1997.
3   (1985) 80 Cr App R 253.
4   (Unreported) 2 February 1997.
5   [1973] QB 748 at 756F–757B.

(2) When a motorist stops before he has completed his journey he may still be driving; an obvious example is when he is halted at traffic lights. Each case will depend on its own facts, but generally the following questions will be relevant: (a) What was the purpose of the stop? If it is connected with the driving, and not for some purpose unconnected with the driving, the facts may justify a finding that the driving is continuing although the vehicle is stationary. (b) How long was he stopped? The longer he is stopped the more difficult it becomes to regard him as still driving. (c) Did he get out of the vehicle? If he remains in the vehicle, it is some, though not a conclusive, indication that he is still driving.

(3) If a motorist is stopped by a constable in uniform who immediately forms the suspicion that the motorist has alcohol in his body, the motorist should be regarded as still driving at the moment when the suspicion is formed; but if an appreciable time elapses before the constable's suspicion is aroused it will be a question of fact and degree whether the motorist is still to be considered as driving at that time.

(4) When a motorist has arrived at the end of his journey then subject to the brief interval referred to in (1) above he can no longer be regarded as driving.

(5) When a motorist has been effectively prevented or persuaded from driving, he can no longer be considered to be driving.'

That was a prosecution under RTA 1972, where a policeman could only demand a breath test from a person who was 'still driving'. That requirement of 'still driving' was removed by the Transport Act 1981, s 25(3). According to Lord Bridge, that later statute:

'... rendered obsolete the nice distinctions drawn by the courts to determine whether a person who was no longer at the wheel of a vehicle could or could not still be regarded as driving it.'[1]

Hence, the absence of dissent by the High Court in *Leach v DPP*[2] to the justices having held that the answer to the question of whether or not a person was 'driving' had to be determined by the test laid down in *R v McDonagh*. However, *Leach* was concerned with excess alcohol offences, unlike *DPP v James and Chorley*, above, which were about driving while disqualified, ie an offence where a person can only be arrested while he is actually driving. If the cases subsequent to the Transport Act 1981 had released this, it is a moot point whether they would still have considered that the 1981 legislation had by implication altered the definition of 'driving'.

7.5 DEATH BY DANGEROUS DRIVING: SECTION 1[3]

Section 1 concerns death by dangerous driving.

It is an arrestable offence to kill somebody by driving a mechanically propelled vehicle on a road or other public place (see Chapter 4) by dangerous driving, which is defined in s 2A(1) as when:

---

1   *Fox v Chief Constable of Gwent* [1986] AC 281 at 297A/B.
2   [1993] RTR 161.
3   As amended by RTA 1991, s 1.

'(a) the way he drives falls far below what would be expected of a competent driver; and

(b) it would be obvious to a competent and careful driver that driving in that way would be dangerous.'

The word 'dangerous' is defined in s 2A(3) as a risk of injury to the person or of serious damage to property.

It is also (s 2A(2)) dangerous driving if the condition of the vehicle made it obvious to a competent and careful driver that it was dangerous to drive it. This is an absolute offence; see *R v Loukes*[1], no *mens rea* is required.

7.6   CAUSING DEATH BY DRIVING CARELESSLY ETC: SECTION 3A

Section 3A concerns causing death by driving a mechanically propelled motor vehicle on a road or other public place: (1) carelessly; or (2) without reasonable consideration for other road users when: (a) the driver was unfit to drive through drink or drugs; (b) the proportion of alcohol in the driver's breath, blood or urine exceeded the prescribed limit; or (c) the driver failed to provide, without reasonable excuse, a specimen of breath, blood or urine within 18 hours of the driving, having been requested so to do.

The definition speaks for itself. Carelessness merely means driving in a way in which a reasonable and competent driver would not; see *McCrone v Riding*[2]. As to the facts that make up (a), (b) or (c), insofar as they are relevant to making an arrest, they are dealt with in the commentary on ss 4 and 6 of the Act.

7.7   DRIVING WHILST UNFIT: SECTION 4

Section 4 – drive or be in charge whilst unfit.

Section 4(6) empowers a constable to arrest without warrant a person whom he has reasonable cause to suspect is, or has been committing, an offence under s 4, namely driving, attempting to drive, or being in charge of a mechanically propelled vehicle on a road or other public place (see Chapter 4) whilst unfit to drive through drink or drugs. 'Unfit' is defined in s 4(5) as occurring when one's 'ability to drive properly is for the time being impaired'.

This offence can be committed not only by driving, but also by being 'in charge' – the definitive definition of which was given by Taylor J in *DPP v Watkins*[3]:

'Broadly there are two distinct classes of case. (1) If the defendant is the owner or lawful possessor of the vehicle or has recently driven it, he will have been in charge

---

1   [1996] RTR 164.
2   [1938] 1 All ER 157.
3   [1989] 1 All ER 1126 at 1132–1133.

of it, and the question for the court will be whether he is still in charge or whether he has relinquished his charge. That is the class of case to which the *Haines v Roberts*[1] rule was directed. Usually such a defendant will be *prima facie* in charge unless he has put the vehicle in somebody else's charge. However, he would not be so if in all the circumstances he has ceased to be in actual control and there is no realistic possibility of his resuming actual control while unfit, eg if he is at home in bed for the night, if he is a great distance from the car or if it is taken by another. (2) If the defendant is not the owner, the lawful possessor or the recent driver, but is sitting in the vehicle or is otherwise involved with it, the question for the court is, as here, whether he has assumed being in charge of it. In this class of case the defendant will be in charge if, whilst unfit, he is voluntarily in *de facto* control of the vehicle or if, in the circumstances, including his position, his intentions and his actions, he may be expected imminently to assume control. Usually this will involve his having gained entry to the car and evinced an intention to take control of it. But gaining entry may not be necessary if he has manifested the intention in some other way, eg by stealing the keys of a car in circumstances which show he means presently to drive it.

The circumstances to be taken into account will vary infinitely, but the following will be relevant: (i) whether he is in the vehicle, or how far he is from it; (ii) what he is doing at the relevant time; (iii) whether he is in possession of a key that fits the ignition; (iv) whether there is evidence of an intention to take or assert control of the car by driving or otherwise; (v) whether any other person is in, at or near the vehicle and, if so, the like particulars in respect of that person.'

By virtue of s 192A (as inserted by the TWA 1992, s 39), s 4 does not apply to the driver of a vehicle which is subject to ss 27–30 in Part II of the TWA 1992 (see Chapter 6, above).

7.8 ATTEMPTS TO DRIVE

The powers of arrest under s 4 (see **7.7** above and s 6 (see **7.12** below) can also be executed on those who attempt to drive.

7.8.1 The *actus reus*

By the Criminal Attempts Act 1981, s 3(3) the *actus reus* is an 'act which is more than merely preparatory to the commission of that offence'. It is submitted that generally speaking an attempt to drive will occur only in one of two situations, either:

(1) when a person is either pushing a two-wheeled vehicle or driving a four-wheeled one, in both cases towards a public place with intent to continue driving thereon; or

(2) sitting in the driver's seat and doing some act more than merely preparatory to bringing motion to the wheels.

Thus, in *Shaw v Knill*[2], it was held that a motorist who had pushed his motorcycle 6 yards toward the entrance of the road where he intended to drive it was

---

1   [1953] 1 WLR 309.
2   [1974] RTR 142.

guilty of attempting to drive while disqualified. In *Harman v Wardrop*[1], it was held that merely asking for the car keys could not amount to an attempt to drive. In *May v DPP*[2], the appellant was sitting in the driver's seat of his stationary car with three passengers, one sitting next to him and the other two in the rear seat. The ignition key was turned to the auxiliary position in order to turn on the electrical system. His electronically operated window was open. He was asked by the police if he had just arrived or was just going and he replied the latter. Lord Bingham CJ, without deciding the matter, was inclined to the view that those facts amounted to an attempt to drive by Mr May.

7.8.2   The *mens rea*

In *R v Pearman*[3], it was held that the *mens rea* was a desire to commit the full offence. In the case of drinking and driving offences, the accused probably thought that he was fit to drive or did not appreciate that his blood alcohol level exceeded the permitted limit. This presents no difficulty when administering the breathalyser as the constable merely has to suspect the motorist of having alcohol in his body (or of having committed a moving traffic offence). Different considerations will arise when considering an arrest under s 4(6) for attempting to drive while unfit through drink or drugs. This is because motorists often think that they are able to drive properly when they are not. (No doubt this is because alcohol has affected their powers of perception.) Thus the problem occurs of whether it is reasonable to suspect a person of attempting to drive while unfit where he or she almost certainly does not desire to commit the full offence, so there can be no transgression of s 4(2) because of the lack of the necessary intent. However, because the judiciary wish to prevent people driving when unfit to do so, the courts will almost certainly hold that if a motorist's condition is such that he cannot exercise proper control over his vehicle, then it is reasonable to suspect that, by attempting to drive, it is indeed his intention to contravene s 4(1), so that he can be summarily arrested under s 4(6).

7.8.3   Impossibility

Under the Criminal Attempts Act 1981, s 3(3), it is no defence that the full offence which was intended was in fact impossible to commit.

7.9   DRUGS

'Drug' is defined in RTA 1988, s 11(2) as including 'any intoxicant other than alcohol' but no definition of 'drink' is given in the statute. In *Bradford v Wilson*[4], the High Court stated that 'a drug' was any substance taken by a person which affected the control of the human mind and which was neither a beverage

---

1   [1971] RTR 127.
2   [2000] RTR 7.
3   [1985] RTR 35.
4   (1984) 78 Cr App R 77.

nor taken as food; and upheld the conviction under s 4 of a glue sniffer who had inhaled toluene.

7.10 BREATHALYSER OFFENCES: SECTION 6

Section 6 concerns the breathalyser. It does not apply to drivers of vehicles subject to TWA 1992, ss 27–30 (see RTA 1988, s 192A (as amended by TWA 1992, s 39)).

7.10.1 The power of arrest

Section 6(5) empowers a constable in uniform to arrest without a warrant:

(a) any person whom, as a result of a lawful breath test[1], the officer has reasonable cause to suspect has a proportion of alcohol in his blood which exceeds the prescribed limit, which is laid down in s 11(2)(b) as being 80 milligrammes of alcohol per 100 millilitres of blood; or

(b) any person who has failed to take a breath test which has been lawfully required and whom the officer has reasonable cause to suspect has alcohol in his body.

'Fail' includes a refusal; see RTA 1988, s 11(2). A failure is defined in s 11(3), which was interpreted in *DPP v Heywood*[2] to mean that a person had not provided sufficient breath, in the correct manner, to enable the breathalyser to give an accurate result, whether it be negative or positive (to use the terminology of the police to indicate blood alcohol levels that are respectively below and above the prescribed limit of 80 milligrammes). A 'failure' entitles the police to make an arrest even if there is a very good reason for it, for example physical inability to provide sufficient breath, as happened in *R v Kelly*[3], where the defendant had a permanent tracheotomy and his apprehension was held to be perfectly legal.

7.10.2 When an arrest cannot be made

Section 6(5) specifically states that neither power of arrest conferred by that subsection can be executed upon a person 'while he is at a hospital as a patient'.

A hospital is defined in s 11(2) as 'an institute which provides medical or surgical treatment for in-patients or out-patients'.

The statute does not attempt to offer any definition of the word 'patient'. In *R v Crowley*[4], it was held that once a person had arrived at a hospital, he became a patient even though his treatment had not commenced; but did not come within that category merely whilst *en route* to such an institution, so he can be breathalysed in the ambulance whilst travelling there (see *Hollingsworth v*

---

1   See **7.12.3**.
2   [1998] RTR 1.
3   [1972] RTR 447.
4   [1977] RTR 153.

Howard[1]). In *Attorney-General's Reference (No 1 of 1976)*[2] the Court of Appeal held that 'a patient at a hospital' was a person who was physically present in that location for the purpose of obtaining treatment and that encompassed anywhere within its curtilage. The court went on to state that a person would cease to be a patient once he had received all the treatment for which he had visited the hospital and had started to leave for home. Therefore, if a doctor were to tell him to sit down for 30 minutes before he left, he would still remain a patient for this half hour. In that case, the court upheld the validity of a breath test on somebody who was in the car park on his departure from the hospital. In *Askew v DPP*[3], the defendant was found not to be a patient when he was arrested as he was leaving the hospital foyer immediately after having been discharged, even though he was re-admitted the next day. In giving his judgment, Watkins LJ said[4] that the expression 'patient at a hospital' should be given 'a wide interpretation.' His Lordship went on to give guidance[5] on how a court should answer the question of whether or not a person had ceased to be a patient:

> 'In any event, I think it is in essence a question of fact for the jury in the particular circumstances to conclude whether or not a person is a patient at a hospital when spoken to for the purpose of requesting that he take a breath test. The common-sense approach to that problem obviously will involve ascertaining among other things whether or not a person has had treatment at the hospital, whether the treatment has come to an end, whether the doctor in charge of the treatment has informed the police that the treatment has come to an end, or a nurse has said so, as the case may be, and whether that fact having been ascertained the patient has begun at least to prepare himself for making his way out of hospital. It does not seem to me that justices need be influenced in their conclusion by the fact that a person has not actually left the precincts of a hospital when a request by a police officer is made to him to provide a specimen of breath.'

The last part of the penultimate sentence must be interpreted in the light of the fact that Watkins LJ approved the decision of the High Court of Justiciary in *Watt v MacNeil*[6], where it was held that a person whose treatment had concluded but who was sitting on a trolley naked from the waist upwards was still a patient. Accordingly, it is submitted that a person remains a patient until he has dressed himself and is ready to leave the hospital; or to use the picturesque words of the Sheriff of Aberdeen[7]:

> 'He was not miraculously transformed into a creature of some other nature at the moment when the last bandage was secured or the last X-ray photograph taken.'

7.10.3   The lawfulness of the breath test

Under s 6, the power of arrest naturally only arises if the request for the breath test was in accordance with the statutory provisions. In order to induce

---

1   [1974] RTR 58.
2   [1977] 1 WLR 646.
3   [1988] RTR 303.
4   Ibid, at 308.
5   Ibid.
6   [1988] RTR 310.
7   Ibid, at 312.

Parliament to make it compulsory for motorists to undergo what was then thought to be a gross indignity, the then Minister for Transport (The Rt Hon Barbara Castle) inserted into her Road Safety Bill a number of restrictions on the powers of the constabulary to breathalyse drivers, most of which are still continued in RTA 1988. Section 6(1) of RTA 1988 empowers a constable in uniform (see Chapter 4) to require a breath test if he has reasonable cause to suspect:

(a) that a person driving, attempting to drive or in charge of a motor vehicle on a road or other public place has alcohol in his body or has committed a traffic offence (see (c), below), whilst the vehicle was in motion;
(b) that a person has been driving, attempting to drive or has been in charge of a motor vehicle on a road or other public place with alcohol in his body and that he still has the alcohol in him; or
(c) that a person has been driving, attempting to drive or has been in charge of a motor vehicle on a road or other public place and has committed, whilst the vehicle was in motion, one of the following crimes:

(1) any offence under RTA 1988, except under those contrary to ss 123–142 inclusive (ie Part V, which deals with 'Driving Instruction' for learner drivers);
(2) any offence under the Road Traffic Regulation Act 1984;
(3) any offence under the Road Traffic Offenders Act 1988, other than one in Part III (ie non-payment of a fixed penalty);
(4) any offence under Part II of the Public Passenger Vehicles Act 1981; or
(5) any offence created by any regulation made under one of the above-mentioned statutes; see *Rathbone v Bundock*[1].

Section 6(2) empowers a constable (whether or not he is in uniform) to require a breath test from a person whom he believes to have been driving, attempting to drive or in charge of a motor vehicle, the presence of which had caused an accident on a road or other public place. Section 6(2) requires a belief in the existence of certain facts, unlike s 6(1) where suspicion is sufficient. It was held in *Siddiqui v Swain*[2] and *DPP v Godwin*[3] that the mere fact that an officer had required a breath test was no evidence that he had possessed the necessary suspicion enabling him to make the request, which fact must be proved to the criminal standard in a prosecution. Also, in *R v Vardy*[4], it was held that for a motorist to be breathalysed under s 6(2), there had actually to have been an accident.

1   [1962] 2 QB 260.
2   [1979] RTR 454.
3   [1991] RTR 303.
4   [1978] RTR 202.

7.11   COMMENTARY ON SECTION 6: ELEMENTS OF BREATHALYSER OFFENCES

This part considers the construction applied to the following phrases:

(i)   REQUIRE;
(ii) BREATH TEST; and
(iii) MOTOR VEHICLE.

The meaning of other words used in s 6 have already been discussed elsewhere in this book.

7.11.1   Require

In *R v O'Boyle*[1], it was held that any form of words may be used by the police to signify their wish that the motorist undergo a breath test, so long as the actual language employed would be reasonably understood to mean just that. *R v Nicholls*[2] held that a valid request had been made if the constable reasonably believed that the requirement had been heard by the defendant, even if in fact he had neither heard nor understood it. The contrary decision was reached in *Chief Constable of Avon and Somerset v Singh*[3].

In *R v Burdekin*[4], it was held that a policeman could justify administering a breath test on any of the facts known to him at the time of the requirement, whether or not they were the reasons that had actually caused him to require the test. In *McKenna v Smith*[5], it was held that when requesting a breath test, no reason need be proffered to the motorist. In *Atkinson v Walker*[6], it was held that even if the constable gave a wrong reason for requiring a test, that did not invalidate the requirement, provided facts actually existed which entitled the officer to breathalyse the driver. Whether these cases were rightly decided is a moot point since the House of Lords' decisions in *DPP v Warren*[7] and *DPP v Jackson*[8], where it was held that a person must be told why the police were requiring a specimen of body fluid for analysis rather than one of breath. The reason for this, according to Buxton J in *R v Burton-upon-Trent Justices, ex parte Woolley*[9] was because the driver 'might wish to contradict the constable on a factual point; or at least be properly informed for the purposes of future legal proceedings'. The same rationale would apply for making it compulsory for an officer demanding a breath specimen at the roadside to give his reasons for so doing.

---

1   [1973] RTR 445.
2   [1972] 1 WLR 502.
3   [1988] RTR 107.
4   [1976] RTR 27.
5   [1976] Crim LR 256.
6   [1976] RTR 117.
7   [1993] AC 319.
8   [1999] 1 AC 406.
9   [1995] RTR 139 at 150F.

7.11.2   A breath test

7.11.2.1   *Definition*

A breath test is defined in s 11(2) of RTA 1988 as:

> 'A preliminary test for the purpose of obtaining, by means of a device of a type approved by the Secretary of State, an indication whether the proportion of alcohol in a person's breath or blood is likely to exceed the prescribed limit.'

7.11.2.2   *Approved devices*

The following devices have to date been approved by the Home Secretary:

(1) the DRAEGER ALCOTEST 80 (by Breath Test Device (Approval) (No 1) Order 1968);

(2) the DRAEGER ALCOTEST 80A (by Breath Test Device (Approval) (No 1) Order 1975);

(3) the LION ALCOLYSER (by Breath Test Device (Approval) (No 1) Order 1979);

(4) the LION ALCOLMETER (by Breath Test Device (Approval) (No 2) Order 1979);

(5) the DRAEGER ALERT (by Breath Test Device (Approval) (No 1) Order 1980);

(6) the LION ALCOLMETER S-L2A (by Breath Test Device (Approval) Order 1987);

(7) the DRAEGER ALCOTEST 7410 (by Breath Test Device (Approval) Order 1993); and

(8) the LION ALCOLMETER SL-400 (UK) (INDICATING DISPLAY FORM) (by the Breath Test Device Approval (No 2) Order 1993).

The House of Lords held in *DPP v Jones*[1] that a malfunction in an individual device did not cause that machine to lose its seal of approval. Their Lordships stated in *DPP v Carey*[2] that a breathalyser was not an approved device unless it had been assembled in accordance with its manufacturer's instructions.

7.11.2.3   *Their modus operandi*

The manufacturer's instructions for all breathalysers are that the person to be tested should not have drunk alcohol or used a mouthwash within the previous 20 minutes. This is to allow any mouth alcohol to evaporate so that it cannot be blown into the device and give a falsely high reading; see *Walker v Lovell*[3]. (Also a person should not smoke within the previous 5 minutes, but this is because the smoke will damage the instrument, rather than cause a false reading.) In *DPP v Carey*, above, the House of Lords held that provided the constable had acted *bona fide*, it did not matter that he had not followed the manufacturer's instructions; and that he was under no duty to inquire when the motorist had last consumed an alcoholic drink or had smoked. That decision, on this latter

---

1   [1997] 1 WLR 295.
2   [1970] AC 1072.
3   [1975] RTR 377.

point, was followed in *DPP v Kay*[1]. In *Darnell v Portal*[2], it was held that if the constable did not know that these prescribed activities had occurred within the relevant time, then he need not wait before administering the test. However, in *Attorney-General's Reference (No 2 of 1974)*[3], it was held that the officer must follow the instructions applicable to the facts known to him and it was no excuse that he was unaware of those instructions. He must act *bona fide*, but cannot be said to have done so if, on the facts known to him, he, through ignorance, did not do what the manufacturer said he should do. In that case, the officer saw the defendant smoking immediately before the test. He did not realise that he had to wait, with the result that the breath test was held not to be a valid one. Also, if the police have reason to suspect that smoking or drinking has occurred within the prescribed time, there will not be a valid breath test if they do not adhere to the requisite time-limits; see *Webber v Carey*, above. In *Attorney-General's Reference (No 1 of 1978)*[4], it was held that even if the officer had been told that the last drink was within the previous 20 minutes, if he *bona fide* disbelieved that information, the test could be administered forthwith.

7.11.3   Motor vehicle

RTA 1988, s 185(1) defines a 'motor vehicle' as 'a mechanically propelled vehicle intended or adapted for use on roads'. 'Mechanically propelled' covers any transmission of power from the engine to the wheels by mechanical means and the source of that power is irrelevant as it clearly includes those which are electrically propelled. If this were not so, there would have been no need for s 193 to have exempted tram drivers from being subject to s 4(1). In *Floyd v Bush*[5], a cycle fitted with an auxiliary motor was held to remain a motor vehicle even when it was only being propelled by its pedals.

The problem with s 185 has been the meaning of 'intended or adapted for use on a road'. Lord Parker CJ in *Burns v Currell*[6] said:

> 'I think that the expression "intended", to take that word first, does not mean "intended by the user of the vehicle either at the moment of the alleged offence or for the future". I do not think it means the intention of the manufacturer or the wholesaler or the retailer ... but I prefer to make the test whether a reasonable person looking at the vehicle would say that one of its users would be a road user.
>   In deciding that question the reasonable man would not, as I conceive, have to envisage what some man losing his senses would do with a vehicle; nor an isolated user or a user in an emergency. The real question is: is some general use on the roads contemplated as one of the uses?'

In that case, a go-kart being driven on the highway was held not to be a motor vehicle. In *Percy v Smith*[7] the High Court upheld the justices' decision that a

---

1   [1998] RTR 248.
2   [1972] RTR 483.
3   [1975] RTR 142.
4   [1978] RTR 377.
5   [1953] 1 WLR 242.
6   [1963] 2 QB 433 at 440.
7   [1986] RTR 252.

fork-lift truck was intended for use on the roads. In *Chief Constable of Avon and Somerset Constabulary v Fleming*[1], Glidewell LJ stated:

'In my view once a vehicle has been manufactured as one which is intended or adapted for use on a road, it would require very substantial, indeed dramatic, alteration if it could be said no longer to be a "motor vehicle".'

His Lordship was of the opinion that a motorcycle remained a motor vehicle even though its registration plate, reflectors, lights and speedometer had been removed so as to adapt it for scrambling. Glidewell LJ made it clear that at the end of the day it was solely a question for the tribunal of fact.

In *Nichol v Leach*[2] the accused bought himself a Mini motor car as scrap. He rebuilt it for autocross racing, never intending it to run on a road under its own power. (The prosecution related to an incident when it was being towed.) The High Court held that a Mini was intended to be driven on a road and remained a motor vehicle irrespective of the intention of its present owner.

In *Smart v Allan*[3] a car had been purchased for £2. It had been towed from the scrap yard and had been left in the street outside its owner's house. The engine did not work and was very rusty. It had no gearbox or battery and had one tyre missing. The cost of making the conveyance roadworthy was far in excess of what its value would be if it were ever repaired. On that basis, the High Court held that as the car had no reasonable prospects of ever being driven again, it was not a mechanically propelled vehicle. The *ratio decidendi* of that case is that a conveyance ceases to be 'mechanically propelled' only if there is no realistic likelihood of it being made roadworthy, either because it was impossible to do so, or because the cost of so doing would be out of all proportion to its value once it was capable of being driven. In *Newberry v Simmonds*[4], Widgery J said[5] that a car did not cease to be a mechanically propelled vehicle upon the mere removal of its engine, if the evidence admitted the possibility that the motive power might be restored.

In *R v Tahsin*[6], it was held that a moped was designed to be used on the roads and did not cease to be a motor vehicle because some temporary mechanical fault prevented the vehicle from being driven. In this case, the defendant had been pedalling his moped because he had been unable to start it due to some fault in the engine. That case must be distinguished from *Lawrence v Howlett*[7], where the defendant was riding his pedal cycle. It had previously had an engine connected to it so that it was power-assisted but, at the relevant time, the engine had been disconnected from the wheels. That conveyance was found to be a pedal cycle so long as it was not capable of being powered by its own motor. The court emphasised the dual propulsion of the vehicle, and that only one of those

---

1   [1987] 1 All ER 318 at 322.
2   [1972] RTR 476.
3   [1963] 1 QB 291.
4   [1961] QB 345.
5   Ibid, at 350.
6   [1970] RTR 88.
7   [1952] 2 All ER 74.

systems was available for use at the relevant time. In *DPP v Saddington*[1], it was held that the test was whether 'a reasonable person would say that one of the uses of the [vehicle] would be use on a road'. The fact that the manufacturers had recommended against such a use was not conclusive. Accordingly, a 'go-ped' was held to be a 'motor vehicle'.

According to s 188 of RTA 1988, a hover vehicle is a 'motor vehicle', irrespective of whether or not it was intended or adapted for use on the roads. The definition in RTA 1988 was specifically made subject to s 20 of the Chronically Sick and Disabled Persons Act 1970, which provides that an invalid carriage is not to be regarded as a motor vehicle. Under s 189 of RTA 1988, a lawn mower and an electrically assisted pedal cycle are not motor vehicles for the purposes of that Act. In addition, by s 192A of the same statute, a tram-car is not within the provisions of, *inter alia,* of RTA 1988, ss 4 and 6. (Section 192A was inserted by s 39 of the Transport and Works Act 1992.)

7.12   DANGER TO OTHER ROAD USERS: SECTION 22A

Section 22A concerns causing danger to other road users.

According to s 22A(1), a person is guilty of this offence if, intentionally and without lawful authority or reasonable excuse, and in such circumstances which it would be obvious to any reasonable person that to do so would be dangerous, he does any of the following acts:

(a)   causes anything to be done on or over a road;
(b)   interferes with a motor vehicle, trailer or cycle; or
(c)   interferes (directly or indirectly) with traffic equipment (ie subs (3) anything lawfully placed on a road by a highway authority). (By subs (5) road does not include a footpath, or bridleway.)

'Dangerous' is defined in s 22A(2) as a risk of injury to any person while on or near a road, or as a risk of serious damage to property on or near a road and which would be seen as such by a reasonable person with the knowledge of the facts which were known or ought to have been known to the offender.

7.13   DRIVING WHILST DISQUALIFIED: SECTION 103

Section 103 concerns driving whilst disqualified.

Section 103(3) empowers a constable to arrest without warrant anybody actually driving (see above) a motor vehicle (see above) on a road (see below) whom he has reasonable cause to suspect of being disqualified from holding or obtaining a driving licence. In *DPP v James and Chorley*[2], it was held that the arrest must be made while the suspect was actually 'driving', within the

---

1   [2000] TLR 678.
2   (Unreported) 2 February 1997.

definition given to that word in *Edkins v Knowles*[1]. In *DPP v Swan*[2], it was held that mere suspicion that the detained person was driving at the time of arrest was not sufficient – he had actually to be driving.

Unlike the other contraventions of RTA 1988 discussed above, the activity prescribed by s 103 must take place on a road. That word is defined in s 192(1), as amended by RTA 1991, as being:

'Any highway and any other road to which the public has access, and includes bridges over which a road passes.'

At common law, a highway is a path dedicated to the public over which all its members have the right to pass and repass at any time of the day and night; see *Ex parte Lewis*[3], per Willis J. In *Oxford v Austin*[4] the court stated that one must first find a road and then ask if it is open to the public. The court in *Clarke v Catto, Cutter v Eagle Star Insurance Co*[5] approved the definition of a 'road' given by the Scottish judge Lord Sands in *Harrison v Hill*[6]:

'Any road may be regarded as a road to which the public have access *upon which members of the public are to be found* who have not obtained access either by overcoming a physical obstruction or in defiance of a prohibition express or implied.' (Author's emphasis.)

In *Catto*, Lord Clyde, with whom all their Lordships agreed, stated[7]:

'It should always be possible to ascertain the sides of a road or have them ascertained. Its location should be identifiable as a route or way ... It may be continuous, like a circular route or it may come to a termination, as in the case of a cul-de-sac.

... Essentially a road serves as a means of access. It leads from one place to another and constitutes a route whereby travellers may move conveniently between the places to and from which it leads. It is thus a definable way intended to enable those who pass over it to reach a destination.

... A hard shoulder might be seen to form part of a road. A more delicate question might arise with regard to a lay-by, but where it was designed to serve only as a temporary stopping place incidental to the function of the road it might be correct to treat it as part of a road.'

In *Catto*, it was held that a car park was not a 'road' and 'a car might be driven across it but that was only incidental to its function of parking'[8]. A road must be a right of way open to all the public and not just a limited section, for example the inhabitants of a parish (see *Poole v Huskinson*[9]). In *Randall v Motor Insurer's Bureau*[10], a vehicle was held to be on a road when it was partly on a road and partly on private land.

---

1   [1973] QB 784.
2   (Unreported) 30 July 1999.
3   (1888) 21 QB 191 at 197.
4   [1981] RTR 416.
5   [1998] 4 All ER 417 at 422 (HL).
6   (1931) 132 SC(J) 13 at 17.
7   [1998] 4 All ER 417 at 422j *et seq.*
8   Ibid.
9   (1843) 11 M & W 827.
10   [1969] 1 All ER 21.

7.14   SUMMARY

There is a power of arrest, without a warrant, of those suspected of an offence under RTA 1988, ss 1, 3A, 4, 22A and 103. However, it is the exercise of the summary power of apprehending drivers under s 6 (those who have been consuming alcoholic beverages) which occupies by far the largest part of the law reports on false imprisonment. This was because the Road Safety Act 1967 made a lawful arrest a condition precedent to the taking of a blood or urine specimen; see *Scott v Baker*[1]. That requirement was removed in 1983 by the Transport Act 1981. The coming into force in 1986 of s 78 of PACE 1984 gave the court the power to refuse to admit any evidence of what had occurred at a police station if the presence of the accused at that location was solely due to an unlawful arrest; see *DPP v Godwin*[2]. It was only during the interregnum between those two statutes that magistrates were not concerned with the finer points of the law of false imprisonment!

---

1   [1969] 1 QB 659.
2   [1991] RTR 303.

Chapter 8

REASONABLE SUSPICION AND BELIEF

8.1 INTRODUCTION

'Reasonable suspicion was the source from which a constable's power of summary arrest flows.'[1]

'It is in the public interest that felons should be caught and punished. At common law a person who acts honestly and reasonably in taking steps to serve this public interest commits no actionable wrong. What is honesty in this connection does not change; what is reasonable changes as society and the organisation for the enforcement of the criminal law evolves. What was reasonable in connection with arrest and detention in the days of the parish constable, the stocks and lock-up, and the justice sitting in his own justice room before there was an organised police force, prison system or courts of summary jurisdiction is not the same as what is reasonable today. Eighteenth- and early nineteenth-century authorities are illustrative of what was reasonable in the social conditions then existing. They lay down no detailed rules of law as to what is reasonable conduct in the very different social conditions of today'.[2]

This chapter discusses what the judiciary have considered to be, and not to be, 'reasonable suspicion'. Often that will flow from 'information received' and about which the police wish to say nothing in order to protect the anonymity of their source. How far they are entitled to do this is discussed at **15.6.2**.

8.2 MISTAKES OF LAW AND FACT

All powers of arrest by a constable without a warrant can be exercised not just when a crime has been perpetrated by the detainee, but merely where the police officer has reasonable cause to suspect, or (for a few offences) to believe, that his prisoner was guilty of that offence, even though in fact no such transgression of the law had been committed by anybody at all. The test of reasonableness is judged objectively, but on the facts known to the arrester at the time of the apprehension. An arrester is deemed to know the correct legal position and errors of law can never justify depriving a person of his liberty. As Lord Diplock said in *Walker v Lovell*[3]:

'[An arrester] is protected if he has made an honest and reasonable mistake of fact. He is unprotected if he has made a mistake of law, *however excusable* the mistake might seem to be.' (Author's emphasis.)

---

1   Per Bingham LJ in *Chapman v DPP* (1988) 89 Cr App R 190 at 197.
2   Per Diplock LJ in *Dallison v Caffery* [1965] 1 QB 348 at 370.
3   [1975] 1 WLR 1141 at 1151E/F.

Although not cited, its principle was followed in *R v Governor of Brockhill Prison, ex parte Evans (No 2)*[1], where the House of Lords held that the defendant had to pay damages for having kept a convicted prisoner in jail for too long. This occurred because he had calculated her remission by the law as it was then understood in accordance with *R v Governor of Blundeston Prison, ex parte Gaffney*[2]. That case had held erroneously that an inmate was only entitled to remission from his longest sentence for the time he had spent on remand and not off his total sentence. However, that decision was later held to have been wrongly decided when Miss Evans applied for and obtained her freedom by a writ of *habeas corpus*; see *Ex parte Evans (No 1)*[3]. The result of the last case meant that the governor had kept his prisoner incarcerated for 59 days longer than he ought to have done. Judge LJ stated[4]:

> '. . . a significant extension of the law, reducing the protection currently provided by the tort of false imprisonment, would be required [to allow a defence of reasonableness based on an error of law]. That step cannot be taken in this court.'

Ignorantia facti excusat, ignorantia iuris non excusat is an old established rule of the common law (see *Mildmay*[5]). It is applied every day to those who sit in the dock of a criminal court and there can be no reason for exempting police officers or other governmental officials from its scope.

In considering whether a mistake of law has been made, it must be remembered that 'the common law is deemed always to have been as the subsequent court decides – that is of course not withstanding that there has been a prior court decision to the contrary effect which was overruled' – to quote the words of Collins J at first instance in *Ex parte Evans*[6], a view which was approved of in the Court of Appeal, even in the dissenting judgment of Roch LJ[7]:

> 'The fiction, well established in our law, is that when a court interprets a section in an Act of Parliament it is presumed that that section has had that meaning since its commencement date.'

8.3   SUBORDINATE LEGISLATION AND DIRECTIVES OF THE EUROPEAN UNION

The legality of subordinate legislation can be challenged in a criminal case and its invalidity will be a good defence to the charge; see *Boddington v British Transport Police*[8]. The same principle is applied in *habeas corpus* applications, for

---

1   [2000] 3 WLR 843.
2   [1982] 1 WLR 696.
3   [1997] QB 443.
4   [1999] QB 1043 at 1078E (ie the Court of Appeal judgment).
5   (1584) 1 Co Rep 175a at 177b.
6   (Unreported) 10 June 1997.
7   [1999] QB 1043 at 1065F.
8   [1999] 2 AC 143.

example *Eshugbayi Eleko v Officer Administering the Government of Nigeria*[1], where one of the issues was the validity of an ordinance of a colonial government. The respondent argued that such an Order of the Governor was to be treated as a decision of a court of competent jurisdiction with the result that the Privy Council had no jurisdiction to investigate its lawfulness. That submission was wholly rejected[2]:

> 'Their Lordships are satisfied that the opinion which has prevailed that the courts cannot investigate the whole of the necessary conditions is erroneous. The Governor acting under the Ordinance acts solely under executive powers, and in no sense as a court. As the executive he could only act in pursuance of the powers given to him by law. In accordance with British jurisprudence no member of the executive can interfere with the liberty or property of a British subject except on the condition that he can support the legality of his action before a court of justice. And it is the tradition of British justice that judges should not shrink from deciding such issues in the face of the executive.'

However in the two recent cases of *Percy v Hall*[3] and in *R v Governor of Brockhill Prison, ex parte Evans (No 2)*, above, the Court of Appeal held *obiter* that in an action for false imprisonment a plaintiff could not challenge the validity of a by-law relied upon by the defendant as a lawful justification for the detention; and a subsequent declaration of it being *ultra vires* did not make illegal prior acts done in reliance upon it. A contrary view was expressed by Lord Irvine of Lairg LC in *Boddington v British Transport Police*[4], but Lords Slynn and Brown-Wilkinson expressly reserved their opinion on the matter. To quote the latter[5]:

> 'But I am far from satisfied that an *ultra vires* act is incapable of having any legal consequence during the period between the doing of that act and the recognition of its invalidity . . .'

As public funds pay the damages awarded against police officers and civil servants who in the course of their employment falsely imprison people, why should their detainees not recover damages when they lose their liberty through central or local government having enacted *ultra vires* legislation? Although said about prison governors who miscalculate an inmate's remission, the words of Lord Woolf MR in *Evans* are most apt[6]:

> 'Up to this case the consequence of a change in the law has been that the State in positions such as this has had to bear the cost. It is by no means clear to me that this is not the just result, where, albeit because of a mistaken view of the law based on decisions of the courts, individuals have been deprived of their liberty.'

In *Shingara v Secretary of State for the Home Department*[7] the Court of Appeal held that a Direction given by the Secretary of State refusing a French citizen entry to

---

1   [1931] AC 662.
2   Ibid, at 670.
3   [1997] QB 924.
4   [1999] 2 AC 143.
5   Ibid, at 164B.
6   [1999] QB 1043 at 1059A.
7   [1999] Imm AR 257.

the United Kingdom (on the grounds that it was contrary to the public interest) remained valid until quashed by a court of law even if it was contrary to Art 9 of EC Directive 64/221; and, accordingly, the detention by an immigration officer was lawful and did not amount to a trespass.

In the latest case to date, *R v Governor of Brockhill Prison, ex parte Evans (No 2)*[1], the House of Lords deliberately refrained from saying anything on this topic, stating that they would wait until faced with an appeal that directly raised this issue.

8.4 SUSPICION

In *Smitten v Smith (Chief Constable of Wiltshire)*[2], Mann LJ (with whom Butler-Sloss LJ agreed) gave the following definition of 'suspicion':

'[It] is a state of mind and not ascertainable as a matter of fact.'

To the same effect and using very similar language were the views of the Court of Appeal in *Holtham v Metropolitan Police Commissioner*[3]:

'Suspicion was a state of conjecture or surmise where proof was lacking. It was nothing more and was not to be confused with the provision of evidence.'

In *Hussien v Chong Fook Kam*[4] the Privy Council advised Her Majesty that:

'Suspicion in its ordinary meaning is a state of conjecture or surmise where proof is lacking: "I suspect but I cannot prove." Suspicion starts at or near the starting-point of an investigation and of which the obtaining of *prima facie* proof is the end.

. . .

Their Lordships have not found any English authority in which reasonable suspicion has been equated with *prima facie* proof.[5]

. . .

There is another distinction between reasonable suspicion and *prima facie* proof. *Prima facie* proof consists of admissible evidence. Suspicion can take into account matters that could not be put in evidence at all. There is a discussion about the relevance of previous convictions in the judgment of Lord Wright in *McArdle v Egan* (1934) 150 LJ 412. Suspicion can take into account also matters which, though admissible, could not form part of a *prima facie* case.'[6]

In *Dumbell v Roberts*[7], Scott LJ said:

'The protection of the public is safeguarded by the requirement, alike of the common law and, so far as I know, of all statutes, that the constable shall before arresting satisfy himself that there do in fact exist reasonable grounds for suspicion

---

1   [2000] 3 WLR 843.
2   (Unreported) 27 February 1991.
3   (1987) TLR, 28 November.
4   [1970] AC 942 at 948.
5   Ibid, at 948.
6   Ibid, at 949.
7   [1944] 1 All ER 326 at 329.

of guilt. That requirement is very limited. The police are not called upon before acting to have anything like a *prima facie* case for conviction ...

In *Sanders v DPP*[1] the court disapproved of the distinction drawn by prosecuting counsel between 'suspecting that an offence had been committed' and 'suspecting that it might have been committed', because suspicion was merely conjecture and not certainty.

In *Dallison v Caffery*[2], Diplock LJ recognised that:

> 'What is reasonable conduct on the part of a police officer in this respect may not be the same as what would be reasonable conduct on the part of a private arrester.'

In *Fox et al v UK*[3] the European Court of Human Rights expressed similar sentiments to those of the English judiciary quoted above:

> '... [h]aving a "reasonable suspicion" presupposes the existence of facts or information which would satisfy an objective observer that the person concerned may have committed the offence.'

8.5 WHOSE SUSPICION?

In *O'Hara v Chief Constable of the Royal Ulster Constabulary*[4] the House of Lords held that the requisite suspicion could be based on information received, provided that such did indeed amount to reasonable suspicion. Thus, their Lordships appeared to be advocating the proposition that if, for example, a detective sergeant was ordered by his inspector to arrest somebody for, say, theft, that would not be sufficient; he must also know the facts which led his superior to suspect that the person to be detained was a thief and must himself have judged those facts to have afforded reasonable suspicion. In *Jones v Chief Constable of Bedfordshire*[5] the Court of Appeal held that the suspicion must be that of the actual arrester. However, in *Clarke v Chief Constable of North Wales*[6], Sedley LJ said:

> '[The law does] not extend, and does not need to extend, to requiring each constable involved in an arrest and search operation to make an independent evaluation for the grounds of the suspicion. Nothing in *O'Hara* suggests otherwise.'

A similar approach had been taken in *Martin v Chief Constable of Nottinghamshire*[7] where it was held that the lawfulness of an apprehension had to be judged by the knowledge of the officer who had initiated the arrest and not by what was or was not known to those who had physically carried out the detention.

---

1   [1988] Crim LR 605.
2   [1965] 1 QB 348 at 371.
3   (1990) 13 EHRR 157 at para 32.
4   [1997] AC 286.
5   *New Law Digest*, 2 August 1999 (at para 23 of the transcript).
6   (Unreported) 5 April 2000.
7   (Unreported) 29 October 1999.

In *O'Hara*, above, no evidence was given as to why the plaintiff was suspected of murder, while in *Martin*, above, there was before the judge the oral testimony of the initiator as to what his suspicions were. In *Clarke*, above, the actual arrester had attended a briefing beforehand and was merely told that information (which subsequently turned out be totally false) had been received that Mr and Mrs Clarke were supplying drugs to a doorman of a club in Wrexham. The Court of Appeal held that the reasonableness of the arrest had to be judged by the knowledge (as to the reliability of the informer(s)) possessed by the officer who had given the briefing and not by what was known to the policewoman who had actually detained the plaintiff. She could rely upon what she had been told by another officer, otherwise 'policing would be a practical impossibility' (to quote Sedley LJ), if each individual officer involved in a search and arrest operation had to make an independent evaluation of the suspicion so as to be in a position to judge if it was reasonable to rely upon it.

At first sight, *Martin* and *Clarke* appear contrary to *Kerr v DPP*[1]. There, a constable was held not to have been acting in the execution of his duty when he had restrained a woman who was being taken into custody by a colleague because the arrest by the latter was unlawful. Thus, his mistaken belief was not sufficient and the mere fact that a person was being detained by a brother officer did not amount to a reasonable suspicion that there were grounds which justified that incarceration; and this even applied in a situation where there was no time to ask questions and immediate action was required. Trying to reconcile the authorities is not altogether easy, but it would appear that those who physically carry out the arrest are liable in tort if they do not have 'reasonable cause to suspect' their prisoner of having committed an offence; but so far as they are concerned, those words mean very little. It is sufficient if they are asked to detain somebody and told that is because of information received, without being given any further details. A much stricter test will be applied to those who give the orders (see below).

In *Hough v Chief Constable of Leicester*[2] a car was stopped on the M1 because its windscreen was damaged. Its registration number was then checked on the police national computer and the result showed that its keeper had a marker against his name, ie a warning that he might be armed. As a result, the driver and his passenger (the claimant) were arrested for unlawful possession of a firearm. A search of the vehicle and its occupants revealed nothing illegal or suspicious and therefore the latter two gentlemen were released. The claimant, having been refused legal aid, did not oppose the appeal against the judgment he had obtained at first instance in a false imprisonment action. Simon Brown LJ and Lonemore J held that in accordance with *O'Hara*, above, the lawfulness of the apprehension had to be judged by the knowledge of the actual arrester. What he had learnt from the police computer made his suspicion reasonable. However, the appellate court also went on to say that if there was no urgency, then other enquiries might be called for before it could be said to have been reasonable to have based one's suspicions solely on the computer entry. They

---

1   [1995] Crim LR 395.
2   (2001) *New Law Digest*, 16 January.

also stated *obiter* that even though the detainee did not have an action in trespass, he might, depending on the facts, be able to sue, in negligence, the person responsible for making the entry on the computer.

In *Siddiqui v Swain*[1], it was held that not only must the facts known to the arrester have amounted to reasonable suspicion when judged objectively but he, himself, must also have actually suspected his prisoner to be guilty of the offence for which he had been detained.

8.6 THE REASONABLE AND UNREASONABLE SUSPICION OF THE INITIATOR OF THE ARREST

An honest belief in certain facts does not, *ipso facto*, mean that there were also reasonable grounds to suspect the existence of those facts; *Glinski v McIver*[2] and *Tucker v Metropolitan Police Commissioner*[3]. Hereafter are set out examples of what has been held to amount to reasonable suspicion, but as Watson B said in *Hogg v Ward*[4]:

'Now every case must be governed by its own circumstances, and the charge must be reasonable as regards the subject matter and the person making it.'

The Baron went on to give an example of what he meant:

'If an idiot made a charge a constable ought not to take the person so charged into custody.'

In *Sanders v DPP*, above, it was held that to arrest for theft, the suspicion must amount to more than a remote possibility, but in that case this was so when:

(1) the police saw a lorry displaying neither a rear number plate nor an excise licence,
(2) on being stopped, the driver gave an ambivalent answer when asked if he owned the vehicle, and
(3) the driver then started the engine and appeared to be putting the vehicle into gear as if to drive away.

In *Wilding v Chief Constable of Lancashire*[5] the plaintiff did not on appeal challenge Judge Townsend's ruling that the following amounted to reasonable suspicion that she was responsible for the burglary of, *inter alia*, a television and high fidelity equipment from her former boyfriend while he was away:

(1) she had telephoned the victim from public call boxes on two occasions to find out if he had already gone to Ireland;

---

1   [1979] RTR 454.
2   [1962] AC 942.
3   *New Law Digest*, 17 November 1995.
4   (1858) 4 H and N 417 at 423.
5   (Unreported) 22 May 1995.

(2) the day before he returned and discovered the crime, on a nearby estate a man called Turner had been offering a TV set and a stereogram for sale; and

(3) when the police went to the home of the plaintiff's sister, they found Turner on the premises.

In *Dumbell v Roberts*[1] the police saw the plaintiff on his cycle with a large bag attached to its handle bars. He was stopped and the bag was found to contain about 14 lb of soap flakes. Under wartime rationing, he was only entitled to have 3 oz. He said that he had got it from a friend who worked at a garage, but he could not give his name or address. He took the police back to the garage, but on approaching those premises he said that his friend was not on duty. Thereupon, he was arrested. The Court of Appeal held that that those facts did not amount to a reasonable suspicion that the plaintiff was guilty of either larceny or receiving. This being wartime, the most likely explanation for the soap flakes was the black market.

In *Hussien v Chong Fook Kam*[2], a piece of timber fell off the back of a lorry which did not stop. The wood hit the windscreen of a passing car, fatally injuring one of its occupants. The Privy Council held that, on those facts, it was not reasonable to assume that the lorry had been driven dangerously. From the circumstances known to the police, there was nothing to suggest that a normal inspection of the load would have disclosed that one of many timbers was insecure or that the driver had been aware of the accident. Since *Hussien*, above, the judiciary appear to have become much more liberal in their views of what amounts to 'reasonable suspicion'. In *Mulvaney v Chief Constable of Cheshire*[3], two helmeted motor cyclists committed a robbery. Through an anonymous tip-off, one of those conveyances was found, together with two helmets, in a lock-up garage owned by an old lady. She was very unforthcoming when visited by the police and merely told them to see her neighbour, ie the plaintiff. His dimensions were consistent with eye witness accounts of one of the criminals. That was held sufficient to justify his arrest for the robbery. In *Ward v Chief Constable of Avon and Somerset*[4], a large quantity of Easter eggs had been stolen in looting following a riot. At the plaintiff's house the police found 13 Easter eggs which appeared never to have had price labels on them and the sum of money she said she had paid for them was 'too cheap'. The Court of Appeal held that those facts were 'thin' but were sufficient to justify reasonable suspicion.

In *Castorina v Chief Constable of Surrey*[5] the police considered a burglary of a company to be 'an inside and amateur job'. The thief had tried to force a cabinet which contained embarrassing information about the firm rather than stealing more valuable property nearby. The constable suspected that the person responsible had to be somebody who wanted documents to cause trouble. They were told by a Miss Wilton that nobody had any malevolence

1   [1944] 1 All ER 326.
2   [1970] AC 942.
3   (Unreported) 3 March 1990.
4   (1986) TLR, June 26.
5   (1988) NLJ (R) 180.

against her employers except the middle-aged Ms Castorina who had been dismissed after an argument; but she was sure that this woman was not responsible for the burglary. Before making their arrest, the police checked their records and the plaintiff was shown to have no previous convictions. Those facts were held sufficient to justify the apprehension.

In *Black v DPP*[1], the appellant arrived when the police were searching his brother's home for drugs. The High Court said that it was normal for a person to visit his sibling while carrying a bag. Therefore, there were no reasonable grounds to suspect him of having come round to buy drugs or of having any in his possession.

8.7 THE MOST RECENT AUTHORITIES – POST-1998

In *Dodd v Chief Constable of South Wales*[2] the Court of Appeal held that seeing a tax disc with a registration number different from the car on which it was displayed *ipso facto* amounted to reasonable suspicion that the owner was guilty of fraudulently using an excise licence. In *Parker v Chief Constable of Hampshire*[3] the police were keeping watch on certain premises when a car pulled up outside it with two males inside. Enquiries with another force established that the vehicle was connected with two men, A and H, who were wanted for firearms offences. The next day the car returned to the same position and a constable positively identified its sole occupant as A. He followed the vehicle, but lost sight of it. He later saw the car, but by then A was no longer in it. The new driver picked up another male en route and, when he finished his journey, he and his passenger were arrested. The constable thought that one of them might be H. It turned out that neither of them had any connection with the original offence and, indeed, one of then instituted legal proceedings for false imprisonment. The Court of Appeal held that there was direct positive evidence of A which demonstrated a continuing link between the car and the suspect which continued into the afternoon. The police would have been open to criticism had they proceeded on the basis that A's link to the car had been severed, especially as when followed by the police, he had disposed rapidly of any interest in it (ie he had alighted from the car and given the key to somebody else who then drove it). Although A was absent, the constable thought that the claimant might be H. Their Lordships also held that although this state of mind reflected a degree of uncertainty, nevertheless it was sufficient to amount to what was described by Lord Devlin (in *Hussien v Chong Fook Kam*[4]) as 'a state of conjecture or surmise'. Accordingly, the arrest did not amount to a tort. It is submitted that this decision virtually removes the safeguards contained in the word 'reasonable' and that the trial judge was right rather than the appellate court which reversed his decision on the lawfulness of what had occurred.

---

1   (Unreported) 11 May 1995.
2   (Unreported) 3 February 1999.
3   *New Law Digest*, 25 June 1999.
4   [1970] AC at 948.

In *Samuels v Metropolitan Police Commissioner*[1] a constable saw the plaintiff, on a hot day, walking slowly in a high-risk burglary area and with his hands in his pockets. The latter seemed to be looking at some houses on the left-hand side of the road and then he looked over his shoulder at the officer. The Court of Appeal held that this did not amount to reasonable suspicion of possessing a prohibited article (ie an implement for use in house-breaking).

In *Martin v Chief Constable of Nottinghamshire*[2], the claimant had sold his car, but retained the legal title because the contract contained a retention of ownership clause and he had not been paid. The vehicle had been resold and had ended up in the possession of a Mr Wheelhouse, who refused to return it to its rightful owner but instead advertised it for sale. The claimant replied using a false name and, pretending to be a prospective purchaser, went to look at the car. Using his spare set of keys, he drove off while its present possessor was otherwise engaged. An hour and 20 minutes later, while en route to his home in the south of England, the claimant telephoned his local constabulary and told them what he had done. Later that evening, Constable Swetthenham from Nottingham telephoned the police at Chorsham and asked them to recover the car from the claimant and stated that if the latter did not co-operate he was to be arrested for its theft – which is in fact what happened. The detention was held to be lawful because there was reasonable suspicion that the claimant had acted dishonestly, in that he had:

(1) given a false name and address when he went to see Mr Wheelhouse;
(2) driven off when the latter had gone to check up on his address;
(3) not informed the police of what he had done until an hour and 20 minutes after the automobile had been reported stolen; and
(4) refused to reveal the vehicle's location when visited by Sgt Brammer of the Wiltshire Constabulary.

8.8 GIVING MISLEADING INFORMATION TO THE POLICE

In *Hussien v Chong Fook Kam*, above, the police had reasonable suspicion that both plaintiffs were in the lorry at the relevant time and that one of them had been the driver; but there was nothing to suspect them of knowing about the plank falling off the lorry. However, when interviewed, both of them had denied being at the *locus in quo*. The Privy Council held that once they had given what appeared to be a false alibi, the police had the necessary suspicion to detain them on a charge of death by dangerous driving. Thus, lies can give rise to a reasonable suspicion. So in *Holtham v Metropolitan Police Commissioner*[3], the police suspected the plaintiff's son of a murder in London and the theft of electrical equipment from the deceased. On their way to visit his parents in the country, the detectives spoke to their neighbours and were told that, on a date

---

1   *New Law Digest*, 4 March 1999.
2   (Unreported) 29 October 1999.
3   (1987) TLR, 28 November.

after the commission of the crimes then being investigated, the son had visited his mother and father and had unloaded a van containing speakers and similar chattels. The latter denied that, stating that their son had not visited them since the homicide. Those matters (coupled with the fact that their loft was very clean and the police visit was known of in advance) were held sufficient to justify the father's apprehension for an offence under s 4(1) of CLA 1967 of impeding a prosecution (ie by disposing of the property stolen by his progeny before it could be found).

8.9   BEING UNCO-OPERATIVE WITH THE POLICE

In *Smitten v Smith (Chief Constable of Wiltshire)*[1], it was held that a refusal to supply one's fingerprints for an elimination test could not *ipso facto* amount to reasonable suspicion, but did so in that case when linked to the following facts:

(1)   the plaintiff had occupied the premises for part of the time in which the break-in to the electricity meter might have occurred (the exact date was unknown);
(2)   the fingerprint found on the meter was not that of the outgoing tenant;
(3)   moving into a new home was an expensive time; and
(4)   such thefts were usually an inside job, and not that of a burglar.

The exercise of one's lawful right to decline to answer police questions cannot of itself give rise to a reasonable suspicion of wrongdoing. In *Samuels v Metropolitan Police Commissioner*[2], the plaintiff was approached by an officer and asked where he was going, to which he replied:

'It's a free country. I can go where I like.'

A constable then seized him in order to search him and when he resisted, he was arrested for assault. The Court of Appeal upheld his claim for false imprisonment. There were no grounds for suspecting him of any offence before he was stopped and the invoking of his privilege to the right of silence could not convert an unreasonable suspicion into a reasonable one.

8.10   THE RELEVANCE OF PREVIOUS CONVICTIONS

Lord Wright in *McArdle v Egan*[3] said that previous convictions could be taken into account with other matters in deciding whether it was reasonable to suspect somebody of having committed a crime; but if they were the only thing that pointed the finger of suspicion at somebody, then that was not sufficient grounds for making an arrest. Nor can convictions which have been quashed

---

1   (Unreported) 27 February 1991.
2   *New Law Digest*, 4 March 1999.
3   (1934) 150 LJ 412.

on appeal be taken into account. According to the Court of Appeal in *Martin v Chief Constable of Avon and Somerset*[1], they are an irrelevant consideration.

8.11   INFORMATION RECEIVED AND INFORMERS

In *James v Chief Constable of South Wales*[2], it was held that suspicion could be based solely on what an arrester was told by somebody else, depending on what was already known about the latter. In that case the informant had no convictions and on previous occasions what he had said had proved to be true. He had told Sgt Rogers that jewellery stolen in a recent break-in was going to be sold from the home of the plaintiff, a 17-year-old girl who lived with one of the burglars. Inside her house was a large dog and by the bed there was a pick-axe handle, in both cases for use if the premises were raided for drugs. A search warrant was obtained and the facts about the dog turned out to be correct and the boyfriend who was in bed did indeed make a grab for a pick-axe handle which was next to him. On those facts, the Court of Appeal held that the arrest of the plaintiff for handling was justified, even though no stolen property was found. The information had come from somebody who in the past had proved to be reliable and had been found to be correct about the precautions taken to prevent a police search.

8.12   CONFLICTING EVIDENCE

In *Jones v Chief Constable of Bedfordshire*[3], two elderly ladies were mugged within a few streets of each other and gave differing descriptions of their assailant. Two constables caught a fleeting glimpse of the first robber, one of whom, a special, had seen his face. Three hours later the plaintiff was stopped and searched by the same officers, because he fitted the description of the attacker. Nothing was found on him. They consulted their superior, Inspector Turner, and one of them said she identified the man. Those three officers then located the plaintiff, arrested him and went to his flat, but nothing incriminating was discovered. He was released without charge. Subsequently, he sued for trespass (both to the person and to land and for false imprisonment). The Court of Appeal upheld the trial judge's dismissal of the action. It held that a reasonable suspicion based on the description did not cease to be reasonable simply because another witness had given an inconsistent description, nor merely because it was based on a fleeting glance.

---

1   (Unreported) 29 October 1997.
2   (Unreported) 16 April 1991.
3   *New Law Digest*, 2 August 1999.

8.13   THE NEED TO MAKE FURTHER INQUIRIES

In *Herniman v Smith*[1], Lord Atkin said of a defendant in a malicious prosecution case:

> 'His duty [is] not to ascertain whether there is a defence but whether there is reasonable and probable cause for a prosecution.'

That same principle has been applied to the question of what further inquiries a constable has to make once he is possessed of a reasonable suspicion. In *Mulvaney v Chief Constable of Cheshire*[2], it was held that an arrester was under no obligation to ask his captive any questions. Whereas Purchas LJ said in *Castorina v Chief Constable of Surrey*[3]:

> 'There is ample authority for the proposition that courses of inquiry which may or may not be taken before arrest are not relevant to the consideration whether on the information available to him he has reasonable cause for suspicion. Of course, failure to follow an obvious course in exceptional circumstances may well be grounds for attacking the executive exercise of that power [of arrest] under *Wednesbury* principles.'[4]

The last comment is presumably based on the judgment of Scott LJ in *Dumbell v Roberts*[5], where the plaintiff told the police that he had obtained the relevant chattels (the cause of his arrest) from a person in the garage, outside of which he and the police were standing. As that explanation could have been checked through an independent person forthwith without any detour by merely going into those premises, the failure to do so made the detention unlawful. In the words of the Lord Justice[6]:

> 'The duty of making such inquiry as the circumstances of the case ought to indicate to a sensible man is, without difficulty, presently practicable, does rest upon [the arrester]; for to shut your eyes to the obvious is not to act reasonably. In the present case ... they failed to make such enquiry from the plaintiff himself or those at the garage as would entitle them to think that they had reasonable grounds for suspicion either under section 507 [of the Liverpool Corporation Act 1921] or at common law.
>
> ... where there is no danger of the person ... attempting to escape, they should make all present practical inquiries from persons present or immediately assessible who are likely to be able to answer their inquiries forthwith. I am not suggesting a duty on the police to try to prove innocence; that is not their function; but they should act on the assumption that that their *prima facie* suspicion may be ill-founded. That duty attaches particularly where slight delay does not matter because there is no probability, in the circumstances of the arrest, of the suspected person running away. The duty attaches, I think, simply because of the double-sided interest of the public in the liberty of the individual as well as the detection of crime.'

---

1   [1938] AC 305 at 319.
2   (Unreported) 3 March 1990.
3   (1988) NLJ (R) 180.
4   See Chapter 9.
5   [1944] 1 All ER 326.
6   Ibid, at p 329A/B.

Scott LJ treated the failure to make inquiries as tainting the suspicion so that it could not be considered reasonable. Nowadays the judges view it in a different light, not as affecting the quality of the suspicion but (in an appropriate case) as making the exercise of the power of arrest *Wednesbury* unreasonable. By referring to 'exceptional circumstances' in his *dicta* in the *Castorina* case, above, Purchas LJ clearly did not approve of *Dumbell v Roberts*. As a matter of strict jurisprudence, the two cases are compatible, because in the latter case it was *Wednesbury* unreasonable not to have checked out the plaintiff's explanation which could have been done more or less instantaneously. Any duty that a constable may have had to make further inquiries has now for all practical purposes been abrogated as a result of the decision in *Lyons v Chief Constable of West Yorkshire*[1]. A lady's handbag was snatched and the victim claimed to have recognised the plaintiff (whom she knew) as her assailant. The police went to his house to arrest him, but he was not there. On being asked by his mother, they said they had come to see her son about an incident in Batley at lunchtime that day. One of the people present (Mr Inensou) said that the plaintiff could not have been involved as he had been working with him and others all day in Leeds. No further inquiries were made of him or of anybody else. The police just returned later on and detained the plaintiff. The officer said that he had arrested him as he wanted to interview him as soon as possible before he had a chance to concoct an alibi and dispose of evidence, for example his clothes. In his experience, it was quite common for a third party to volunteer an untrue alibi. In this case, he had a written statement positively identifying his suspect. Hutchinson LJ said:

> 'It is easy to envisage circumstances which may militate against exercising a power of arrest. Ordinarily those circumstances will be extraneous to the question of reasonable suspicion; for example that the suspect has the sole care of young children. I would not go as far as to say that the strength or weakness of the evidence justifying reasonable suspicion can never be a material factor at this stage but in most cases it will not be so, and will be material only to the question whether the condition precedent to the exercise of the discretion existed. Certainly in this case what Mr Inensou said had no relevance to the question of discretion.'

In *MacCarrick v Oxford*[2] the Merseyside Police circulated a list of people who were disqualified from driving, but did not give any details of those whose bans had been suspended pending appeal. The plaintiff fell into the latter category. Whilst driving back to his house late at night, he was stopped by a constable because his name was on the list. He said that at home he had a letter from the Crown Court showing his entitlement to drive. The officer would only make a check with his station by radio and was not prepared to go to the plaintiff's residence. The Court of Appeal held the apprehension to be lawful[3]:

> '... but there is no obligation on a police officer when he is told by a person whom he is arresting that he has certain evidence at home, to take him there in order to obtain it.'

---

1   (Unreported) 24 April 1997.
2   [1988] RTR 117.
3   [1988] RTR 117 at 122A.

The last word so far is that of Brooke and Beldam LJJ in *Cooke v Chief Constable of Leicestershire Constabulary*[1], although it is not clear in exactly what context it was said as it is not apparent what more the plaintiff was averring that Constable Box should have done:

> 'The fact that DC Box might have made additional enquiries is as irrelevant as proof of facts he did not know, but which he might have discovered if he had made further enquiries.'

8.14   THE RESULTS OBTAINED FROM FURTHER INQUIRIES

If inquiries are made or information is volunteered by a detainee, then the arrester must take them into account when considering whether or not reasonable cause exists; see *Hogg v Ward*[2]. A good example of this is *Banjo v Chief Constable of Greater Manchester*[3], where the discovery of a cheque book may well have amounted to reasonable suspicion of it being stolen, but that was dispelled by the explanation given by its possessor. The facts were that the plaintiff had stayed overnight in a northern city. The presence of his vehicle in the hotel car park was reported to the local constabulary. They established that it was registered to a Mr Singh and that inside it was a cheque book in the name of a Miss Herbert. However, there were also a cheque book and papers in the name of the plaintiff. According to the latter, on being seen by the police, he gave them his name, told them that he was on business and was engaged to Miss Herbert, into whose bank account he frequently paid money. He had her cheque book so that he could use the deposit slips therein; and he showed the police his own one, the stubs of which gave details of the payments made to his fiancée. He was then arrested for theft. The Court of Appeal held that, on those facts, the police could not reasonably have suspected him of theft and that the trial judge had erred in law in ruling to the contrary.

8.15   ASSAULT CASES

In *Clarke v DPP*[4] the police arrived on the scene and saw a woman and a man. The lady said that the male had punched her. She was holding her stomach and appeared to be in pain. The defendant admitted that he had hit her. He was arrested for 'assault'. He resisted and was charged with assaulting a policeman in the execution of his duty. His acquittal was ordered by the High Court because on the evidence the justices could not have been sure that the officer did not intend to arrest for common assault, which is not an arrestable offence. (The DPP did not seek to rely on s 25 of PACE 1984.) Likewise the decision in

---

1   (Unreported) 10 May 1999.
2   (1858) 4 H & N 417.
3   (Unreported) 24 July 1997.
4   (Unreported) 13 November 1997.

Chapman v DPP[1], where a constable had received a message that a brother officer had been assaulted by five youths who had run away. The constable's arrest of those young men was held to be unlawful. This was because he had not been given details of any injury caused by the attack and, therefore, he could not have any reasonable grounds for suspecting the arrestable offence of assault occasioning actual bodily harm. In the words of Bingham LJ[2]:

> 'It is not of course to be expected that a police constable in the heat of an emergency, or while in pursuit of a suspected criminal, should have in mind specific statutory provisions, or that he should mentally identify specific offences with technicality or precision. He must, in my judgment, reasonably suspect the existence of facts amounting to an arrestable offence of a type which he has in mind. Unless he can do that he cannot comply with section 28(3) of the Act by informing the suspect of grounds which justify the arrest.'

8.16 DRUNKEN DRIVERS

8.16.1 Introduction

In *R v Fardy*[3] the Court of Appeal held that it was not easy to give an answer to the question of how far bad driving, which was possible from all motorists, drunk or sober, could support a reasonable suspicion that one of them had consumed alcohol.

8.16.2 Suspicion of driving

In *Baker v Oxford*[4] a car was involved in an accident and two men alighted from it and ran away. A constable carried out a computer check and ascertained that the defendant was the registered keeper of the vehicle and arrested him. The High Court held that the appearance of Mr Baker's name on the register at the Driving Licence and Vehicle Registration Centre was, in the civil courts, *prima facie* evidence of him having been the driver; and, accordingly, that fact also made it reasonable for the officer to have believed that the accused had been driving. However, the presumption that a vehicle was being driven by its keeper is not sufficient in a criminal case to obtain a conviction without any other evidence; see *Holt v Secretary of State*[5]. It is submitted that being the keeper may well give rise to a reasonable suspicion that this latter person was driving but it is not sufficient to amount to a 'belief' in that fact, as this word has a much stronger meaning attached to it; see Nolan J in *Johnson v Whitehouse*[6].

---

1   (1988) 89 Crim App R 190.
2   Ibid, at 197.
3   [1973] RTR 268.
4   [1980] RTR 315.
5   (Unreported) 3 May 2000.
6   [1984] RTR 38 at 47; see also **8.17**.

In *Browne-Scott*[1], Lord Marnoch held[2] that it was no longer reasonable to suspect the registered keeper of being the driver as 'very often nowadays vehicles are driven by persons other than their registered keepers'. This observation was made in order to help the police to overcome objections based on the European Convention on Human Rights to the use of answers made in reply to a request for information pursuant to RTA 1988, s 172, ie in order to discover who was driving at a particular time and place. If that is the only way to give s 172 its teeth back again, then the English judiciary will almost certainly prefer the *dicta* of Lord Marnoch to that of their brethren in *Baker v Oxford*[3]. This proposition is based on the following *volte face* by the English judiciary in the following circumstances. In *R v Courtie*[4], the highest court in the land unanimously agreed with Lord Diplock that it was beyond argument that where the legislature had enacted that the maximum sentence for a crime depended on the existence of certain aggravating features, then Parliament had created separate offences; and which one had been committed would depend on whether or not these facts had been present at the time of its commission. However, that correct approach would have led to the acquittal of nearly all those who had refused to provide specimens of a body fluid for analysis. (This was because prosecutors had overlooked the opinion of Lord Diplock.) So, in *Butterworth v DPP*[5] a differently constituted appellate committee of the House of Lords stated that the views of Lord Diplock referred to above were not of universal application. Their rationale was no doubt the same as that expressed by Lord Goddard CJ when rejecting a learned argument put forward by a member of the author's circuit who in turn became a High Court judge:

> 'We are not here to listen to academic law. We are not a moot. Our job is to lock up the guilty and that's what your client is!'[6]

8.16.3 Reasonable suspicion of alcohol consumption

In the following cases, it was held that the police suspicion of drinking was well founded. In *R v McGall*[7] the police followed the defendant's car late at night. He was driving slowly in the outside lane with his offside indicator flashing. He came to a road junction, but continued straight across it. The police signalled to him to show that his indicator was on, so he turned it off. However, a little later he switched it on again, although there was no turn-off in the immediate vicinity. In *Pamplin v Fraser (No 1)*[8] a motorist had driven at an excessive speed, and, on approaching a give way line at a roundabout, the front end of his vehicle dipped drastically but he did not stop. Instead, he went across the give way line and turned left. In *Everitt v Trevorrow*[9] the accused had exceeded the 30

---

1   [2000] SLT 379.
2   Ibid, at 308.
3   [1980] RTR 315.
4   [1984] AC 463.
5   [1995] 1 AC 381.
6   *Ex relatio* Mr Assistant Registrar Kratz, who was sitting in court on that case.
7   [1974] RTR 216.
8   [1981] RTR 494.
9   [1972] Crim LR 566.

miles per hour speed limit and, after rounding a bend, had driven for 100 yards on the wrong side of the road without causing inconvenience to other traffic.

In *Clark v Price*[1], it was held that it was correct to have suspected the defendant of having consumed alcohol when, on being followed by the police, he stopped his car on a bend, blocking half the road. He alighted and ran off, leaving his jacket and ignition key in the car. On returning, he told a policeman that the car was his. In *Vernon v Lawrence*[2], it was held that an affirmative answer to the question of whether or not one had been drinking (without qualifying it with the word 'alcohol'), was sufficient to raise the necessary suspicion of having consumed liquor.

In R *v Fardy*[3] the defendant, at 3.30 am, had driven out of a minor road and stopped 2 ft into the major road, causing an approaching police car to brake hard in order to avoid a collision. The court upheld the jury's conviction on the grounds that the manner of his driving could have given rise to a reasonable suspicion of the accused having consumed alcohol; the basis for this being that the driving would have caused an accident but for an emergency stop by another motorist. The jury, and the police, were entitled to conclude that a sober driver would have seen the approaching car and stopped inside the minor road. Therefore the error made by the accused, coupled with the time when it occurred, gave rise to the suspicion that he had been drinking.

8.16.4   No reasonable suspicion of alcohol consumption

A contrary view to *Fardy* was taken in *Mulcaster v Wheatstone*[4], where it was held not to be a reasonable suspicion of drinking that a driver had pulled away from a stop sign and then suddenly braked to avoid a collision with two cars on the major road. It is submitted that this is a correct decision as the failure to see these automobiles could easily have been due to a momentary inadvertence totally unconnected with the consumption of alcohol. In *Williams v Jones*[5], at 3.30 am a motorist had done a U-turn when starting off, switched on his right-hand indicator to show that he intended to take the second of two left-hand exits off a roundabout and had exceeded the speed limit by 8 miles per hour. Browne J said that if that had been done on a busy road in the rush hour, it might have been another matter. In *Griffiths v Willett*[6] a blood-splattered van was found in a ditch. Caufield J stated that there could have been many reasons why the vehicle ended up where it did.

In *Clements v Dams*[7] the constables based their grounds for a breath test on suspicion of the accused having been involved in an accident, but they also said in evidence that they thought that there had been signs of alcohol on the driver's breath but had not really considered the matter. The High Court held

1   (1984) 148 JP 55.
2   (1972) 137 JP 867.
3   [1973] RTR 268.
4   [1980] RTR 190.
5   [1972] RTR 5.
6   [1979] RTR 195.
7   [1978] RTR 206.

that the latter did not amount to reasonable suspicion of the driver having drunk alcohol. If the officers had been questioned further about the matter, they may well in fact have had the necessary suspicion but that was not disclosed on the evidence before the justices.

8.16.5 Observed coming out of licensed premises

In *R v Furness*[1] the defendant was seen by a policeman outside a public house, staggering and smelling of drink. Half an hour later the same officer saw him drive out of the car park of that inn. Those facts were held to amount to reasonable suspicion that the defendant had alcohol in his body. However, the court deprecated the idea of police officers lying in wait outside licensed premises at closing time in order to stop, at random, departing motorists. No case has decided the question of whether it would be reasonable to suspect a driver of having consumed alcohol merely because he was driving out of an inn's car park when there is no knowledge of what kind of beverage (if any) he had been imbibing. It is submitted that the answer is 'no', for two reasons: first, the decision in *Monaghan v Corbett*[2], where a policeman went round to the defendant's home and breathalysed him at 2.30 pm on a Sunday afternoon. It was held that it was not reasonable to have suspected the motorist, at the time of the test, of having alcohol in his body merely because the officer:

(1) on the previous day, had smelled that substance on his breath; and
(2) had been told by neighbours that he invariably frequented a public house at Sunday lunchtime and that they had seen the defendant drive off at lunchtime that day.

In the words of the High Court:

> 'It would be a very dangerous extension of the law to permit reasonable suspicion to be founded on facts wholly unconnected with the driving of a motor vehicle at the time to which the suspicion related.'

Secondly, as was said by Viscount Dilhorne in *Spicer v Holt*[3]:

> 'It is a matter of common knowledge of which one can in my view properly take judicial notice, that at the time when the creation of the new offence was under consideration, there was great concern about the possibility of random tests and the possible harassment of motorists with the result that Parliament required certain conditions to be complied with for an analysis to be admissible.'

In *R v Aust*[4], it was held not to have been reasonable to have suspected the accused of having consumed alcohol merely because he had been seen in the 'parking lot of a tavern' walking towards his car, which he entered and started to drive away. Porter J said that the officer had merely assumed, without any foundation, that the defendant had come from the bar rather than 'a room at the hotel'. It is submitted that even if there were no sleeping accommodation at

---

1   [1974] Crim LR 759.
2   (1983) 147 JP 545.
3   [1977] AC 987 at 996F/G.
4   (1988) 15 MVR (2nd) 304 (Alberta Provincial Court).

the inn, and the driver had been seen coming out of the bar, that does not mean he must have been consuming alcohol; he could just as well have been having a meal or been drinking soft drinks, and so to suspect him of more, in the eyes of the law, would not be justified. This is (as Porter J recognised) because it would be allowing random breath tests, which the legislature would have specifically sanctioned, if such a thing were wanted.

8.16.6   Suspicion of unfitness to drive

In *Joiner v DPP*[1], it was held that the facts set out below amounted to a reasonable suspicion of driving whilst unfit. As the police followed the defendant's car, he accelerated and overtook another vehicle. He switched his lights off and turned into another street. The police took another route to head him off. The next they saw of him was when his vehicle mounted the kerb and parked on the verge. He got out of his automobile and ran into a nearby garden. He smelled strongly of intoxicants and, on being asked what he was doing, he replied:

> 'Well, you've got to try, haven't you.'

8.16.7   Suspicion of being involved in an accident causing injury

In *Fox v Chief Constable of Gwent*[2], it was held that merely because a car had been involved in an accident, that did not give rise to a reasonable suspicion that somebody had been injured, and the appeal to the House of Lords[3] was determined on that factual basis.

8.17   BELIEF

In *Johnson v Whitehouse*[4], it was held that the constable had not merely to suspect, but actually to believe in, the existence of certain facts to justify a breath test under what is now RTA 1988, s 6(2). Nolan J stated:

> '... the submission which she makes to the court now as to the importance of the distinction between the word "suspect" and the word "believe". I should make it clear for my part that the greater force of the word "believe" is an essential part of the law and that the requirement for a breath test under section 7(2) can only be justified if there are reasonable grounds for believing – in the full sense of that word – that the person concerned was the driver of the vehicle.'

The difference between suspicion and belief is well illustrated in the case of *Bunyard v Haynes*[5]. In that case, a car owner heard a crash whilst in his living room and went outside. He saw that his vehicle had been damaged by another

---

1   [1997] RTR 387.
2   [1984] RTR 402.
3   [1986] AC 281.
4   [1984] RTR 38 at 47.
5   [1985] RTR 348.

automobile. His neighbour was also present and said that the other car was his
and it must have been stolen. The magistrates were of the opinion that those
facts gave rise to a reasonable suspicion that the neighbour had in fact being
driving his own car at the time of the accident but did not justify a belief in that
fact. The words 'to believe' have been interpreted to mean both 'belief based
on facts which are reasonably believed to exist' (see *Liversidge v Anderson*[1]) and
as meaning that the facts on which the belief is based must actually exist (see
Nakkuda Ali v M F de S Jayaratne[2]). As the police on many occasions rely on
'tip-offs', especially for breathalysing a driver who fails to stop after an accident,
the former depiction is most likely what Parliament intended.

8.18   CONCLUSION

Virtually all powers of arrest without warrant bestowed upon the constabulary
can be exercised not on certainty, but merely on reasonable suspicion based on
the facts as the arrester perceives them to be at the time of the apprehension;
although occasionally a higher standard is required, namely a belief in certain
facts. It is submitted that 'suspicion' simply means that the arrester thinks that
the suspect may have committed the offence but is by no means certain,
whereas 'belief' means 'thinking that the man was probably guilty' (to use the
definition of Lord Bridge in *Wills v Bowley*[3]). Thus, a constable can arrest on
suspicion a number of people, any one of whom might have committed the
crime, although only one of them could actually be guilty; see *Pearson v
Metropolitan Police Commissioner*[4]. If an arrest is unlawful because the requisite
suspicion is lacking, nevertheless it will *ipso facto* become legal once the police
have acquired sufficient knowledge for their suspicions to be considered
reasonable; see *Hussien v Chong Fook Kam*[5], where the plaintiffs were arrested at
9 am and taken before the magistrate the next day. The police only acquired
reasonable suspicion at 6 pm, when they were given a false alibi. The Federal
Court of Malaya held all the incarceration to be unlawful but, on appeal, the
Privy Council held that only the first 9 hours were unlawful, ie until the
reasonable suspicion arose.

---

1   [1942] AC 206.
2   [1951] AC 66.
3   [1983] AC 57 at 103F.
4   [1988] RTR 276.
5   [1970] AC 942.

Chapter 9

OTHER GROUNDS THAT RENDER AN ARREST UNLAWFUL

9.1 TRESPASS TO LAND

All common law rights of entry possessed by the police (except to deal with or to prevent a breach of the peace) were abolished by PACE 1984, s 17(5). In *Finnigan v Sandiford; Clowser v Chaplin*[1] the House of Lords held that where a statute conferred a right of arrest without a warrant, but did not also contain a specific power to go into private premises for that very purpose, then it was rarely, if ever, possible to imply into the wording of the Act the power to enter without permission. This was because Parliament was not to be considered to have authorised inroads into the rights of the individual other than those which it had expressly enacted. Their Lordships further held that if those making the arrest were trespassers, then the apprehension was unlawful and the detention remained tortious throughout its duration. However, if the prisoner had himself been a trespasser, then he cannot rely upon the police being in the same position. Thus, jumping over the nearest hedge into somebody else's garden as was attempted in *R v Burdekin*[2] does not provide a means of escape from capture.

Thus, it is necessary to ascertain if the arrester had a right of entry when considering the lawfulness of his actions. Everybody has an implied permission to enter the curtilage of private premises and to knock at the door of a house (see *R v Allen*[3]), but not to enter inside a dwelling (see *Fox v Chief Constable of Gwent*[4]). A person may lawfully make an arrest while legally present upon any property so long as he does this before he has been ordered to leave (*Faulkner v Willets*[5]). On being told to depart, he must do so forthwith (see *R v Allen*, above). Merely telling the police to 'F— off' may not amount to a withdrawal of their implied licence to enter. In *Gilham v Breidenbach*[6] the High Court upheld the decision of the magistrates that those words were mere vulgar abuse. It is submitted that much more preferable, and in accordance with common sense, is the decision of Judge AA Edmondson at Carlisle Crown Court in the case of *R v McMillan*[7]. The judge was clearly of the view that words like 'F— off' uttered by a driver to policemen who wished to breathalyse him manifestly meant that the local constabulary should forthwith depart from the motorist's property and leave him alone. The High Court has held that the

---

1   [1981] 2 All ER 267.
2   [1976] RTR 27.
3   [1981] RTR 410.
4   [1986] AC 281.
5   [1982] RTR 159.
6   [1982] RTR 328.
7   (Unreported) 9 July 1986.

following facts did not amount to the withdrawal of the general implied licence which allowed anyone to enter the curtilage of a person's home, namely when pursued by the police, the mere act of a freeholder of driving into his own backyard, winding up the windows of his automobile and locking himself in his vehicle while officers on the outside attempted to open its doors. That situation occurred in *Pamplin v Fraser (No 1)*[1], where the accused was duly convicted of failing to provide a breath test. As the landowner's actions in that case did not amount to the revocation of the consent which he had impliedly granted to the police to go into the grounds of his residence, it would appear that only express words can withdraw that permission. To prevent intrusions of this nature, some members of the judiciary have made useful suggestions that notices should be erected saying, for example, 'Police keep out', (the idea of Donaldson LJ in *Lambert v Roberts*[2]) or more politely 'No admittance to police officers', ie proposal of Diplock LJ in *Robson v Hallett*[3], where he also stated that once the officers were told to leave they must do so forthwith. PACE 1984, s 17(5) has not affected the doctrine of an implied licence as that is in theory not a right given by law but revocable permission granted by the owners of premises.

Consent can also be inferred from conduct. In *Faulkner v Willets*[4], a constable knocked at the defendant's front door which was opened by his wife who then walked back inside her home. She was followed by the officer, who was at no time requested to leave. The High Court held that this amounted to an implied invitation to enter. The rights of co-owners over their property are concurrent, so that when one joint tenant invites a person inside the property, the other cannot revoke that licence (see *R v Thornley*[5] and *Clarke v DPP*[6]). A freeholder has no power to grant or to revoke a licence to enter premises which he has demised to a tenant (see *Preston Borough Council v Fairclough*[7]).

A number of statutes have authorised arrestors to enter private premises without the permission of the owner or occupier. Some of these Acts are set out below. The most important one is PACE 1984, s 17, which allows entry for the purposes of, inter alia, apprehending for an arrestable offence.

---

1   [1981] RTR 494.
2   [1981] 2 All ER 15 at 19.
3   [1967] 2 QB 939 at 954B.
4   [1982] RTR 159.
5   (1981) 72 Cr App R 302.
6   (Unreported) 30 April 1996.
7   (1982) TLR, December 15.

9.2   STATUTORY RIGHTS TO ENTER

Game Laws (Amendment) Act 1960 ('GL(A)A 1960')

SECTION 2

Poaching   *Authority*
Section 2 authorises a constable to enter upon land in order to   GL(A)A 1960,
arrest somebody who he reasonably suspects to be poaching   s 2 (as
contrary to ss 1 and 9 of the Night Poaching Act 1828 or s 30 of   amended by
                                                              PACE 1984,
the Game Act 1831. (Such an arrest can only be made if one of   s 118 and Sch 6,
the general arrest conditions apply.) Section 2 does not apply to   Part I)
land occupied by the Secretaries of State for Defence or the
Environment, Transport and the Regions, the UK Atomic Energy
Authority, the service authority of a visiting force and any
organisation designated under the International Headquarters
and Defence Organisations Act 1964.

Wildlife and Countryside Act 1981 ('WCA 1981'); PACE 1984

WCA 1981, s 19; PACE 1984, s 24

Offences against wildlife, etc
If a constable has reasonable cause to suspect an offence under   WCA 1981, s 19
Part I of WCA 1981 has been committed, he is empowered to
enter any private property, except a dwelling house, for the
purpose of effecting an arrest under the powers granted to him
by s 24 of PACE 1984. The reader is also referred to the
commentary on the Deer Act 1991 (DA 1991), below.

Animal Health Act 1981 ('AHA 1981')

SECTIONS 61, 62(1)

Rabies
Section 62(1) gives a power of entry and search in relation to any   AHA 1981,
vessel, boat, aircraft or vehicle of any other description in order   s 62(1)
to make an arrest under s 61 (see Chapter 6).

PACE 1984

SECTION 17

Various offences
Section 17(1) empowers a constable without a warrant to enter   PACE 1984,
uninvited and to search premises if (s 17(2)(a)) he has reason-   s 17(1)
able grounds for believing that on those premises is a person

whom he is seeking for any of the purposes set out in the
following lettered subparagraphs of s 17(1):

(a) the execution of: (1) a warrant of arrest in criminal proceed-
     ings; or (2) a warrant of commitment issued under s 76 of
     the Magistrates' Courts Act 1980 for failure to pay 'any sum
     adjudged to be paid on conviction', which (s 150(3))
     includes costs, damages and compensation;
(b) the apprehension for 'an arrestable offence' (see Chapter
     6);
(c) to effect an arrest for any of the offences set out below (full
     particulars of the constituents of which are set out in
     Chapter 6):

     (i)   an offence under s 1 of POA 1936,
     (ii) an offence contrary to CJA 1977, ss 6, 7, 8 or 10,
     (iii) (inserted by POA 1986, s 40(2) and (3) and Sch 2,
           para 7 and Sch 3) an offence under s 4 of POA 1986,
     (iv) (inserted by CJPOA 1994, s 168(2)(b) and Sch 10,
           para 53) an offence under s 76 of CJPOA 1994, and
     (v)   (inserted by C(S)A 1997, s 18(3)) an offence under s 17,
           namely a person in respect of whom there is a release
           supervision order in force and who fails, without
           reasonable excuse, to comply with any of its conditions;

(ca) (inserted by the Prisoners (Return to Custody) Act 1994,
     s 21) to make an arrest pursuant to s 32(1A) of CYPA 1969;
(cb) (inserted by the Prisoners (Return to Custody) Act 1994,
     s 21) to recapture any person who is or is deemed to be
     unlawfully at large while liable to be detained:

     (i)   in a prison, remand centre, young offenders' institute
           or secure training centre, or
     (ii) in such place and on such conditions as the Secretary of
           State may direct pursuant to s 53 of CYPA 1933 (ie the
           sentence which can be passed on anybody under 18
           years of age, who has been convicted on indictment of
           murder, manslaughter or of any offence for which an
           adult could be sentenced to 14 or more years in prison);
           and

(d) the recapturing of a person who is unlawfully at large and
     who is being pursued. This power of entry applies only
     where there is a chase during which the constable follows
     the pursued person on to the premises; see *D'Souza v DPP*[1].

---

1   [1992] 1 WLR 1073.

Road Traffic Act 1988 ('RTA 1988')

SECTIONS 4, 6

Alcohol etc related offences

Gives a right of entry to effect an arrest under s 4(6) (suspicion of
driving or being in charge of a mechanically propelled vehicle
when unfit though drinks or drugs). Section 6(6) gives a similar
power when effecting an arrest under s 6(5) (failing to take, or
giving a positive reading on, a breath test), but only if there has
actually been an accident due to the presence of a motor vehicle
on a road or other public place, which the constable reasonably
suspects has caused injury to somebody other than the person to
be breathalysed.

RTA 1988,
ss 4(7), 6(6)

Deer Act 1991 ('DA 1991'), PACE 1984

DA 1991, s 12(2)(b); PACE s 25

Deer-related offences

Section 12(2)(b) allows a constable to enter premises without
permission when effecting an arrest by virtue of PACE 1984,
s 25 of a person suspected of committing a crime prohibited by
DA 1991. What happens if, on entering the land, the officer
realises that he knows the identity of the poacher, so that he
cannot make an arrest in reliance on his powers under s 25? In
that case, can the owner of the land bring a civil action for
trespass against the chief constable? This is an interesting
question, but one which is unlikely ever to arise in practice,
because no estate owner would want the fear of being sued to
hinder the police in their apprehension of those who go around
shooting other people's game.

DA 1991,
s 12(2)(b)

Transport and Works Act 1992 ('TWA 1992')

SECTIONS 27, 30

Offences involving drink and drugs

Section 30(3) gives a right of entry to effect an arrest under
s 30(1) [1]. Section 30(4) gives a similar power to make an arrest
in relation to an offence under s 30(2), but only where there has
actually been an accident, which the constable reasonably
suspects has caused a death, or an injury to somebody other than
the person to be breathalysed.

TWA 1992,
s 30(3)

---

1   See Chapter 6, above.

9.3   TRESPASS TO THE PERSON

The amount of violence tolerated by the law is governed by s 3 of CLA 1967, which abolished the common law rules and instead enacted that:

'3(1) A person may use such force as is reasonable in the circumstances in the prevention of crime or in effecting or assisting in the lawful arrest of offenders or suspected offenders or of persons unlawfully at large.'

Viscount Dilhorne commented on s 3 in *Farrell v Secretary of State for Defence*[1]:

'Section 3(1) would provide no defence to soldier "X" in respect of a claim in the planning of the operation. It can only provide a defence for those who used force and if the force the four soldiers used was reasonable in the circumstances in which they used it, the defects, if there were any, in the planning of the operation would not deprive them of that defence and render the force used unreasonable.'

In *Pollard v Chief Constable of West Yorkshire*[2] the Court of Appeal held that it was reasonable to use a police dog to arrest drunken and noisy vandals, even though they had only broken a streetlight worth £18.62. Their Lordships also approved the *dictum* of Lane J in *Reed v Wastie*[3]:

'One does not use jeweller's scales to measure reasonable force.'

In *Pollard*, above, the police dog had been sent after the plaintiff and would not have bitten him if he had not tried to make his escape, after being warned that the dog was going to be released. That decision was cited in *Coles v Chief Constable of South Yorkshire*[4], where a differently constituted court held the opposite, on the facts of that case. There the dog was ordered straightaway to bite the plaintiff. Also the latter was suspected of the offence of having been carried on a stolen or unlawfully taken motor bicycle. He was later seen in a scrap yard. It was held to be unreasonable to have used a dog when the suspect was well known to the police who knew where they could find him. There was no suggestion of him committing any further offence and the crime of which he was suspected was a comparatively minor one. The court said that if he had been going to commit other misdemeanours, it would have been another matter and the use of force would have been lawful. It might also have been justified if it was only thought that the offender could not be traced; but those were not the facts of that case.

Also, PACE 1984, s 117 authorises a constable to use reasonable force, if necessary, when exercising any of the powers given to him by that statute, which, of course, would include making an arrest pursuant to ss 24 and 25 of that Act.

---

1   [1980] 1 WLR 172 at 179.
2   [1999] PIQR P219.
3   [1972] Crim LR 221.
4   (Unreported) 12 October 1998.

In *Glowacki v Long and the Chief Constable of Lincolnshire*[1], the Court of Appeal left open the questions of whether the words 'reasonable force' in CLA 1967, s 3 were to be construed objectively or subjectively. According to Ward LJ:

> 'Finally we observe that in paragraph 20.8 of the Law Commission Consultation Paper No 122, *Legislating the Criminal Code, Offences Against the Person and General Principles*, the Law Commission in proposing an amendment to the criminal law, said:
>
>> "But the clause will be concerned with criminal liability only; civil liability will continue to be governed by the objective test now contained in the Criminal Law Act 1967, which permits only such force as is reasonable in the actual circumstances in the prevention of crime or in effecting an arrest."
>
> No reason is given for that conclusion but it may well stem from the language of section 3 which on its face is wholly objective.
>
> It is not necessary for me to resolve this question.'

Nor can any guidance be gained from the criminal context. This is because in relation to the equivalent of s 3 in Northern Ireland, Viscount Dilhorne in *Farrell v Secretary of State for Defence*[2] thought it was to be judged objectively; whereas Lord Diplock appeared to take the opposite view in *Attorney-General for Northern Ireland's Reference (No 1 of 1975)*[3].

The Court of Appeal in *Plange v Chief Constable of South Humberside*[4] and *Hill v Chief Constable of South Yorkshire*[5] left open the question of whether the use of more force than was reasonable to effect an arrest would *ipso facto* make the apprehension illegal. However in *Simpson v Chief Constable of South Yorkshire*[6] Fox LJ said:

> 'The first of those allegations is in effect an assertion of the use of undue force in effecting an arrest, making the arrest itself unlawful . No authority was cited for such a proposition. Nor would it be a sensible state of the law. The circumstances of many arrests are such that errors of judgment may be made. It the arrest is justified in law, such errors in the mode of conducting it, though they may be the basis for other remedies, do not seem be a good basis for invalidating the arrest itself which is necessarily in the public interest ... Blackstone himself makes no suggestion that undue force will nullify an arrest.
>
> It is to be observed that the Act contains no provision that the use of greater force than is necessary will invalidate an arrest.
>
> In the circumstances I see no real basis for a plea of false imprisonment by virtue of the use of undue force in the making of the arrest.'

That decision overlooks the doctrine of trespass *ab initio*, of which no mention was made by any of the three judges. It is submitted that as one species of trespass (ie onto land) has the effect of making an otherwise lawful arrest illegal

---

1   (Unreported) 18 June 1998.
2   [1980] 1 WLR 172 at 178/9.
3   [1977] AC 105, 137.
4   (1992) 156 LG Rev 1024.
5   (1991) 135 SJ 383.
6   Reported very briefly at (1991) TLR, March 7.

(see *Finnigan v Sandiford; Clowser v Chaplin*[1]) there is no good reason why the same principle should not apply to any other species of the *genus* trespass. If the assault only occurred at the police station after the initial apprehension, it might well depend on who was responsible for it. If it is one of the arresters, that would make the imprisonment unlawful (assuming the doctrine of trespass *ab initio* – see Chapter 2 – to be still extant). This is because he has abused the power given to him by law, which is presumed to have been his intention all along. If the violence was perpetrated by somebody other than those involved in the initial apprehension, it would most likely be considered a *novus actus interveniens* and, accordingly, would not affect the legitimacy of the detention.

9.3.1   Finding of facts as to the cause of the injury

In *Pearl v Commissioner of Police*[2], Nourse LJ granted the plaintiff leave to appeal out of time. He had alleged that excessive force had been used to arrest him. The trial judge found that the plaintiff's injuries were as a result of his own violence in resisting a lawful arrest. Because the judge had not listed each injury individually and had not given his reasons for saying why it was caused by the lawful application of force, leave to appeal was granted. Nourse LJ said it was 'not so much a question of the seriousness of the injuries as the places on the plaintiff's body that they occurred'. In *Clewley v Chief Constable of the West Midlands Police*[3] the Court of Appeal refused to interfere with the decision of the trial judge as to whose account he believed of how the plaintiff suffered his injuries while being arrested. In that case, the medical reports were not inconsistent with the police account of what had occurred.

9.4   *WEDNESBURY* UNREASONABLENESS

In *Associated Provincial Picture Houses Ltd v Wednesbury Corporation*[4] the Court of Appeal held that it could interfere with the findings of a decision-making body if:

(1) the tribunal appealed against had taken into account irrelevant matters; or
(2) omitted to consider all the material factors; or
(3) in the court's opinion, the decision was one that no reasonable body could have reached (in other words, it was perverse and irrational, ie *Wednesbury* unreasonable).

In *Hussien v Chong Fook Kam*[5] the Privy Council delivered the following advice to Her Majesty:

'To give a power of arrest on reasonable suspicion does not mean that it is always or even ordinarily to be exercised. It means that there is an executive discretion. In

---

1   [1981] 2 All ER 267.
2   (Unreported) 19 November 1998.
3   (Unreported) 19 October 1998.
4   [1948] 1 KB 223.
5   [1970] AC 942 at 948.

the exercise of it many factors have to be considered besides the strength of the case. The possibility of escape, the prevention of further crime and the obstruction of the police inquiries are examples of those factors with which all judges who have to grant or refuse bail are familiar.'

In *Mohammed-Holgate v Duke*[1], Lord Diplock said that the making of an arrest was an executive decision, expressly conferred by statute on a public officer. Accordingly, its exercise must conform with *Wednesbury* principles of reasonableness. That unfortunately gives little protection to the public as the facts of this case demonstrate. The police had reasonable grounds for suspecting the plaintiff of theft based on identification, but were aware that such was not sufficient to obtain a conviction. They hoped to be able to obtain extra evidence by questioning her and considered that she was more likely to confess if that took place in the atmosphere of a police station rather than in her own home. The trial judge considered this reason for making an arrest to be *Wednesbury* unreasonable. He was overruled on appeal. The House of Lords held that an interrogation to confirm or to dispel suspicions of guilt was a perfectly proper reason for apprehending somebody; and there was nothing *ultra vires* about wishing to carry it out in a police station because that was more likely to produce results.

In *R v Moore*[2], two constables saw the appellant run off from his car, so they approached the vehicle and removed its rotor arm, thus making it immobile. When he came back and entered his car, he fell asleep. While in that state, the officers returned and arrested him for being in charge while unfit. The Court of Appeal held his apprehension to be lawful and rejected the suggestion that the police had no power to arrest him because they were fully aware that he had the statutory defence of there being no possibility of him driving while unfit. (This was because of the missing the rotor arm[3].) The court said that the police did not have to consider what possible defences a suspect might have before detaining him. It is submitted that this decision should no longer be regarded as correct in view of the later case of *Plange v Chief Constable of South Humberside*[4] where Parker LJ said that as a result of the decision in *Mohammed-Holgate v Duke*, above, once the defendant had established that the condition precedent existed for depriving the plaintiff of his liberty (ie reasonable suspicion of an arrestable offence), it was for the plaintiff to show that one of the *Wednesbury* principles of unreasonableness had invalidated the legality of the apprehension. In that case, the complainant had withdrawn his allegation of assault against the plaintiff. As that was known to the arresting officer, he therefore was also aware that no prosecution would be brought, and accordingly his arrest was held to be unlawful. It is submitted that, by analogy, it would be unreasonable for a constable to detain somebody whom he knew had not

---

1   [1984] AC 437 at 443B.
2   [1975] RTR 285.
3   This missing rotor arm could be considered to be damage to the car because it made the vehicle less useful (*Morphitis v Salmon* [1990] Crim LR 48), in which case the justices are entitled to ignore this when trying an allegation of being in charge; see RTA 1988, ss 4(4) and 5(3). However, this was not a point argued on appeal.
4   (1992) TLR, March 23.

perpetrated the offence for which he was being apprehended. Once an arrester has reasonable suspicion, his failure to carry out further inquiries, prior to the apprehension, which would have shown his suspicion to be unfounded, can only give rise to an action for false imprisonment if the failure was *Wednesbury* unreasonable. This topic is discussed at **8.13**.

Even if the only ground for alleging false imprisonment is that the actual decision to make an arrest was *Wednesbury* unreasonable, the correct method for obtaining redress is an action for trespass, not judicial review, because what is being alleged is an infringement of the private right not to be incarcerated; see *R v Chief Constable for Warwickshire, ex parte F*[1].

9.5 HOLDING CHARGES

In *R v Chalkey, R v Jeffries*[2] the appellants had been arrested on minor fraud charges. However the reason for their apprehension was in no way related to these credit card matters. Its sole purpose was to keep them out of the way while the police broke into their premises and installed hidden listening devices. The Court of Appeal held that provided the facts justified[3] keeping the suspects in custody for the actual crimes for which they were being detained (which was the case here), then it was lawful so to do and the fact that it was done to further an investigation into more serious offences was irrelevant.

---

1   [1998] 1 All ER 65.
2   [1998] QB 848.
3   See **10.3**.

Chapter 10

LAWFUL DETENTION AFTER THE INITIAL ARREST

10.1   INTRODUCTION

What has to be done with a person who has been lawfully taken into custody depends on by whom he has been arrested and why. Some statutes, when conferring a power of detention, lay down special rules about what is to happen, for example PA 1952. Those procedures are set out in this book when discussing that specific power of arrest. This chapter looks at the existing common law rules and PACE 1984, which applies to the apprehension of any person for an offence, which includes (s 34(6)) an arrest under s 6(5)(a) of RTA 1988 for having provided a positive roadside breath test and (s 34(7)) the surrender by a person to his police bail at the station. (Section 34(7) was added by the Criminal Justice and Public Order Act 1994, s 29(1) and (3).)

10.2   PRIOR TO THE ARRIVAL AT A POLICE STATION

At common law, a person who executes an arrest has to hand his prisoner over to a constable or to bring him before a magistrate as soon as is reasonably possible. He is not allowed to detain the suspect while he seeks to obtain further evidence; see *John Lewis & Co v Tims*[1]. In that case, the plaintiff had been detained by a store detective for theft. Under the shop's regulations, only the managing director or the general manager could authorise a prosecution, so the detective took the plaintiff to the general manager and told him what had occurred, after which the police were called. This caused about 30 minutes' delay in the contacting of the constabulary. The House of Lords held that there had been no undue dilatoriness and (as the apprehension had been lawful) gave judgment for the defendant. It was perfectly reasonable for a shop to give a free hand to its store detectives in the making of arrests and to leave the question of prosecuting to a more senior official.

Under PACE 1984, s 30, unless already in a police station, a person who is apprehended by a constable (or having been arrested by a civilian, is taken into custody by a police officer) must be taken to the station as soon as possible, although (s 30(10)) this can be delayed if the detainee's presence is required elsewhere 'to carry out such investigations as it is reasonable to carry out immediately'. That does not entitle the police to ask questions beyond what is necessary for the investigation being immediately carried out and which cannot

---

1   [1952] AC 676.

wait until their arrival at the station; see *R v Khan*[1]. In *Dallison v Caffery*[2], Lord Denning MR gave examples of what would be reasonable, namely taking a theft suspect to his own house to see if any of the stolen property was there, 'else it be removed and valuable evidence lost', or escorting his prisoner to where he says he was in order to confirm or to refute his alibi.

The station to which a detained person must be taken has to be designated by the chief constable under s 35 of PACE 1984, unless it appears to the arresting officer that the detention will last for no more than 6 hours (s 30(3)) or (s 30(5)) if the arresting officer is by himself and cannot obtain assistance and it appears to him that he will not be able to take his prisoner to a designated station without the latter causing injury to himself or some other person. Under s 30(6), a person who is taken to a station which is not a designated one must be transferred to one which is so designated within 6 hours of his arrival at the first station, unless he has been released before then.

10.3   AT THE POLICE STATION

10.3.1   The initial decision to detain

Under PACE 1984, s 36, the chief constable (or in London the commissioner) must appoint sergeants or above as custody officers for all designated police stations (s 36(1) and (2)). The power of appointment can be delegated (s 36(2)(b)). An officer involved in an investigation (other than the drinking and driving procedure under RTA 1988) cannot be the custody officer for a person arrested in connection therewith (s 36(5) and (6)). If no senior officer is readily available, any rank may act as custody officer (s 36(4)). At a station which is not a designated one, any officer can act as a custody officer; even an investigating officer may so act provided that no other policeman is readily available to do so (s 36(7)).

Under PACE 1984, s 37(1), on arrival at a police station, the custody officer must decide if he has sufficient evidence to justify charging the suspect and may detain him until he has done this. If he determines that he does not have sufficient evidence, he must release the prisoner unless he is of the opinion that detention was necessary to secure, or to preserve, or to obtain by questioning, evidence in relation to the offence *for which the suspect had been arrested* (s 37(2)).

In *Wilding v Chief Constable of Lancashire*[3] the Court of Appeal held that the word 'necessary' in s 37(2) was intended by Parliament to be 'interpreted by the ordinary fair-minded English custody sergeant'. Beldam LJ (with whom the other members of the Court agreed) said:

'It seems to me that, therefore, a court, in deciding whether or not a person has been unlawfully detained, should ask itself the question, in circumstances like this,

---

1   [1993] Crim LR 54 (CA).
2   [1965] QB 348.
3   (Unreported) 22 May 1995.

whether the decision of the custody sergeant was unreasonable in the sense that no custody officer, acquainted with the ordinary use of language, could reasonably have reached that decision.'

Although *Wilding* may well have been correctly decided on its facts, it is submitted that the Court's defining of the word 'necessary' by reference to *Wednesbury* principles was totally erroneous. If the statute had said 'if the officer considered detention to be necessary', then the Court's approach could not have been faulted, but Parliament did not do that. It merely used the word 'necessary' and did not go on to leave it to the constable to decide whether that word applied to the situation. Therefore, that word should be given its natural meaning and the police should be under a duty to show that the detention was indeed necessary, ie they had no other option but to keep their prisoner at the station.

In *Clarke v Chief Constable of Merseyside*[1], Sedley LJ said:

> 'The custody officer is not in the position of the arresting officer. He is entitled to assume that the arrest was lawfully effected, though of course he must not shut his eyes to evidence that it was not.'

Thus, the detention remained lawful even though the review officer had testified that he neither knew nor cared what type of drugs Mrs Clarke was suspected of possessing. (If they were only class C, there was no power of arrest.) Therefore, the protection afforded to prisoners by Parliament in 1984 by the appointment of custody and review officers who were independent of the investigation has been considerably weakened by the Court of Appeal 16 years later.

In *Wilding*, above, the plaintiff, in interview, said that she had telephoned the complainant once about some money she owed him and not, as he had originally said, on two occasions to see if he had gone to Ireland. So after they had finished questioning her, the police decided not to make any decision on charging their prisoner until they could speak to the victim of the burglary for his comments on her account of the telephone call. As the police wanted to be in a position to put further matters to the plaintiff based on what the complainant might tell them (ie to obtain evidence by questioning), coupled with the short time involved (20 minutes), the Court of Appeal ruled that it was reasonable to have continued to keep her locked in a cell without charge.

Thus – subject to the time-limits imposed by PACE 1984[2] – it would appear that a person can be kept in custody until the police have sufficient evidence to charge; and, in the interim, they can go about gathering this evidence. This includes:

(1) interviewing all potential witnesses;
(2) then questioning their prisoner about the evidence so obtained;
(3) thereafter making enquiries into the answers he has given; and
(4) where necessary, further interviewing the suspect.

---

1   (Unreported) 5 April 2000.
2   See **10.7** below.

10.4   WRITTEN RECORDS

If the custody officer is of the opinion that detention is necessary, that officer must, as soon as is practicable, make a written record of that fact in the presence of the prisoner who must, at that time, be informed of the grounds for his detention (PACE 1984, s 37(5)), unless (s 37(6)) he is incapable of understanding what is said to him; or is, or is likely to become, violent; or is in need of urgent medical treatment.

10.5   WHEN TO CHARGE – SUFFICIENCY OF THE EVIDENCE

Under PACE 1984, s 37(7), once there is 'sufficient evidence' to charge, then that course of action must be taken or the prisoner must be released without charge. The real significance of charging is that once that event has occurred, a person is, subject to certain exceptions (see below), entitled to be released on bail. Thus, if he is not charged as soon as possible and if, once that has happened, he would be entitled to bail, then the failure to charge will give rise to a liability for the tort of false imprisonment.

Under Code of Practice C, para 11.04, a suspect cannot normally be questioned once the police believe that they have gathered sufficient evidence 'for a prosecution to succeed.' Ever since the Judge's Rules were first formulated, a person cannot normally be interviewed after he has been charged. Thus, the factual situation under s 37(7), which makes it compulsory to charge the detainee, must be the same as that which (by Code C) prevents further questioning. Indeed, all the cases on this topic have been over whether or not the trial judge was right to hold that there had been no breach of para 11.04 of Code C. The attitude of the judiciary about this has changed. At first, the rule was strictly applied. The Court of Appeal in *R v Coleman*[1] decided that no interview should have taken place when the defendant was told by the Fraud Squad:

> 'We consider that there is sufficient evidence to prosecute you for fraudulent trading. However we have not heard your side of the story ... You have not yet had the opportunity to say what you wish about the allegation. Accordingly we propose to interview you and give you that opportunity.'

A similar view was taken in *R v Pointer*[2], where the interviewing officer in cross-examination said that when he had questioned the accused at the station, he believed that he had sufficient evidence to obtain a conviction – namely the testimony of undercover officers to whom the defendant had offered to sell controlled drugs. The facts of *R v Gayle*[3] were more or less identical. In that case, the evidence of the offer to sell had been tape recorded by the CID and,

---

1   Referred to at (1998) 148 NLJ 980.
2   [1997] Crim LR 676.
3   [1999] Crim LR 502.

accordingly, the appellate judges ruled that holding an interview was in breach of Code C. However, later authorities rejected this approach. So in *R v Ioannou*[1] the court stated that:

> '... the interviewing or investigating officer had to be in a position, before he charged, to make an informal decision as to whether or not to charge. He would usually decide that fairness required that any such decision would have to take into account any explanation or information the suspect might volunteer on the topics on which he was questioned. Therefore the suggestion – to take it to its logical conclusion – that the opportunity should not be given to the prospective defendant simply because, absent his comment and explanation, the case seemed overwhelming was nonsense.'

To the same effect is *R v McGuiness*[2]:

> 'Counsel's argument would mean that in every situation where there was a *prima facie* case, the police would be bound to charge and the opportunity would be lost not only for the police to question the suspect but also for the suspect to put forward an explanation which might end the suspicion against him.'

In *Martin (Peter) v Chief Constable of Avon and Somerset Constabulary*[3] the police executed a search warrant at the plaintiff's house for amphetamines, ecstasy tablets and counterfeit currency. None of those things were found, but a small amount of cannabis resin was discovered. The plaintiff confessed to possessing it but stated it was solely for his own use. That was recorded in the arresting officer's notebook and countersigned by the plaintiff. He was arrested, taken to the police station, detained for 4 hours, during which he was interviewed, and a tape recording of the interview was made. The Court of Appeal rejected the argument that:

(a) it was *Wednesbury* unreasonable to have arrested him in order to question him at the station, and

(b) the custody officer was wrong to authorise his detention in order for him to answer questions which would be recorded but should instead have charged him forthwith and then bailed him.

In the words of Otton LJ:

> 'The arresting officer was not exceeding his powers in so acting. He was entitled, out of an abundance of caution, not to rely simply on the informal oral confession but to seek a more formal confession at the police station by means of a tape recorded interview ... But in my view that procedure is not in contravention of section 37 [of PACE 1984]. On the contrary it is in accordance with the purposes of the section because it safeguards and respects the right of a suspect and emphasises the duties of the police.'

However, the reasoning in *R v Pointer*, above, was followed by the Court of Appeal in *R v Dellaway and Moriarty*[4]. In that latter case, the trial judge had held that from the surveillance carried out prior to, and at the time of, the arrest, the

---

1   [1999] Crim LR 586.
2   [1999] Crim LR 319.
3   (Unreported) 29 October 1997.
4   (Unreported) 7 April 2000.

police already had sufficient evidence to prosecute, once they had arrived at the station. Accordingly, they were not entitled to question their suspects, with the result that he directed the jury not to draw any inference from the 'no comment' interviews of certain of the defendants. That ruling was unsuccessfully challenged on appeal by two of their co-accused. Thus, the authorities reveal two contradictory views on when the questioning of suspects must stop. It is submitted that the answer may well be that once there is sufficient evidence to charge, PACE 1984, s 37 and para 11.13 of Code C do not permit any further interviewing, save insofar as is required by the 'anti-verballing' provisions of para 11.13, namely that any conversation with, or comments from, potential defendants before they get to the station must be shown to the latter who must be given the opportunity to make their views thereon known. However, what the correct legal position is will only be discovered once the House of Lords has made an authoritative statement on this topic.

10.6 REVIEWS AND FURTHER DETENTION

Under s 40 of PACE 1984, any detention must be regularly reviewed – by the custody officer if the suspect has been charged and in any other case by an officer not below the rank of inspector who is not connected with the investigation. The first review must be not later than 6 hours after the detention was first authorised and thereafter at intervals not exceeding 9 hours. In *Martin (John) v Chief Constable of Nottinghamshire*[1], it was held that time in transit from one police area to another did not count when calculating the time, at any rate if the prisoner was not interviewed on the journey. A review may be postponed if is not practicable to hold one, for example because the prisoner is being questioned (s 40(4)(b)(i)) or because there is no review officer available (s 40(4)(b)(ii)). If this occurs, a note of it and the reason for it must be made in the inmate's custody record. On the carrying out of the review, the detainee has the right, in person or through his solicitor, to make oral or written representations, unless he is considered by the police to be unfit to do so by reason of his condition or behaviour. In *R v Chief Constable of Kent, ex parte the Police Federation*[2], it was held that a review officer must carry out his duty *in persona* at the location where his prisoner is, and not by means of a video-link. A review officer decides whether or not to order a captive's release in the same way as the custody officer makes that decision; see *Clarke v Chief Constable of Merseyside*[3].

10.7 EXTENDED CUSTODY PERIOD

Under s 41 of PACE 1984, a person who has not been charged within 24 hours of the 'relevant time' (see **10.8** below) must be released either unconditionally

---

1   (Unreported) 29 October 1999.
2   *New Law Digest*, 18 November 1999.
3   (Unreported) 5 April 2000.

or on bail[1]. The only exception is where (s 42(1)) the officer (of the rank of superintendent or above) responsible for the station in which the incarceration takes place, has reasonable grounds for believing that:

(a) detention without charge is necessary to secure, preserve or obtain by questioning, evidence in relation to the offence for which he has been arrested;

(b) the offence is a serious arrestable offence (see Chapter 3); and

(c) the investigation is being conducted with all due diligence.

The prisoner must be given the same opportunity to make representations as he is in the case of a review under s 40 (see s 42(6) *et seq* of PACE 1984). The extensions cannot in total exceed a period of 36 hours after the 'relevant time' (s 42(1)). The extension cannot be granted until after the second review, but must be granted before the expiry of 24 hours after the relevant time (s 42(4) and see *Re an Application for a Warrant of Further Detention*[2]). Thereafter, if no charge has been brought, the police must obtain a warrant of further detention from a magistrates' court after an *inter partes* hearing *in camera*. The court can grant warrants authorising further periods of detentions of up to 36 hours at any one time, but these cannot in total exceed a maximum of 96 hours from the relevant time (see below). If the application is made after the 36 hours, the magistrates have no option but to dismiss it, if it would have been reasonable for the request for more time to have been made within that period; see *R v Slough Justices, ex parte Stirling*[3]. Once the application is lodged in court, a suspect can be kept a prisoner for a further 6 hours after the 36 hours has passed, if the court cannot hear the matter any earlier. Once a warrant is refused, no other application can be made unless supported by evidence which has come to light since the refusal (s 43(17)).

10.8 RELEVANT TIME

'Relevant time' is defined in s 41 of PACE 1984 as starting at whichever is the earlier of:

(1) the prisoner's arrival at the relevant police station,

(2) 24 hours after his arrest, or

(3) if apprehended outside England and Wales, 24 hours after his arrival in one of those countries.

The 'relevant station' is the first station to which the prisoner is taken, unless he was arrested in a police area other than the one in which he was sought and had not been questioned there about the matters for which he had been detained, in which case the relevant station is the first one he is taken to in the area in which he is wanted. In such a case, the 'relevant time' begins with his arrival at the first station in the police area where he is wanted or 24 hours after leaving

---

1   In terrorist cases, a longer time-limit applies (see **10.12**).

2   [1988] Crim LR 296.

3   [1987] Crim LR 576.

the original station in which he was initially detained, whichever is the earlier. If a person in police detention is taken to hospital for medical treatment, the time spent in travelling to or from that place and his sojourn therein it is not to be included in calculating the relevant time, save in respect of such period as was occupied by him being questioned (s 41(6)).

In *Roberts v Chief Constable of Cheshire*[1] the plaintiff's detention had been authorised at the police station at Northwich; but he was then taken to another one in the same county (at Macclesfield) where the custody officer had again authorised his detention. The Court of Appeal held the review time started from when his custody had been authorised at Northwich and the decision of the Macclesfield custody sergeant was a decision to detain under s 37 of the PACE 1984 and not a review under s 40, which was something different.

10.9   RELEASE FROM CUSTODY

10.9.1   No grounds to justify continuance

Under s 34(1) of PACE 1984, a person must be released from police custody once the grounds on which he is being detained cease to exist and there are no other reasons for keeping him incarcerated. (To prevent such a release, s 31 allows him to be arrested for another offence, provided, of course, there exist the requisite grounds for so doing.)

In *Clarke v Chief Constable of North Wales*[2] the plaintiff was sitting in the front seat of a car. Her husband was the driver and in the back was her brother. They were all apprehended when they drove up outside the Cotton Club in Wrexham. The police were acting on information received that they were supplying drugs to one or more of the doormen for distribution to the members and that the illegal substances were being carried both in the wings of their automobile and by the rear seat passenger who would swallow his consignment if intercepted. By the time of the first review:

(1)   no drugs could be found in the car without dismantling it;
(2)   no drugs were discovered near the vehicle; and
(3)   no drugs were found (save for one tablet on the plaintiff's husband) either on any of the occupants of the car after a strip search or at their homes, which had been searched by their local constabulary.

The male passenger had been nearly strangled, thus preventing him from swallowing anything and he had later been formally interviewed, during which he had denied all knowledge of any criminal activity. The Court of Appeal held that the initial suspicion from the data received by the police had not been dispelled and, therefore, they could continue to detain Mrs Clarke for questioning. Why it had not been dispelled was not stated. However, all the information proved false – the car was supposed to be taking drugs to the

---

1   [1999] 1 WLR 662.
2   (Unreported) 5 April 2000.

doormen of a club for resale to its members, yet nothing could be found in it. (It had not been dismantled – but such would have been inconsistent with the information received as the controlled substances were for immediate distribution at the club, therefore they would have had to have been readily accessible without needing to take the vehicle apart.) The alleged carrier (ie the rear occupant) had nothing incriminating on him. If this case was rightly decided, it means that the police can continue to act on information, as if it were reliable, even when everything in it has been found to be totally inaccurate. In argument, Sedley LJ posed the question whether, if the information was very specific but was shown to be wrong about various matters, could one continue to act on it? In addition, would it be otherwise where the information was very general, so that there were few facts against which it could be checked? The answer is surely that the more detailed the information is and the more it is discovered to be false, so the less reasonable it becomes to rely on it. While the vaguer it is, the less reasonable it is to act on it initially, but this will also depend on how trustworthy the source has been in past. Thus, in *Clarke*, once all the details given to the police had been shown to be erroneous (ie there were no drugs in the possession of the people who were supposed to be in the course of actually delivering them to the Cotton Club for sale that night), the author finds it hard to understand how it could be said that the North Wales Constabulary could still have had any reasonable cause to suspect Mrs Clarke of transporting illegal substances to that club.

10.9.2   After charge

Under s 38 of PACE 1984, after charging a person who has been arrested without a warrant for an offence, the custody officer must release him either unconditionally or on bail (s 47) unless one of the conditions set out in s 38(1) applies, namely:

(1)   the prisoner's name and address has not been sufficiently ascertained or the custody officer has reasonable grounds for doubting that the name or address given are in fact genuine; or

(2)   the custody officer has a reasonable belief that:

    (a)   the prisoner will not turn up in court; or

    (b)   his detention is necessary:

        (i)   (in the case of an arrest for an imprisonable offence) to prevent the commission of another offence,

        (ii)   (in the case of an arrest for an non-imprisonable offence) to prevent him causing injury to some other person or loss or damage to property,

        (iii) to prevent him from interfering with the administration of justice or an investigation into one, or more, offences, or

        (iv) for his own protection.

In the case of a juvenile, he can only be detained if (1), above, applies or if the custody officer reasonably believes that it is in the youth's own interest not to be released.

Under s 46 of PACE 1984, once a prisoner has been charged and police bail has been withheld, then he must, at its next sitting, be brought before a magistrates' court for the petty sessional division in which is situated the police station where he was charged (s 46(2)); or (s 46(3)) if an information is to be laid before another magistrates' court, he must be taken to another station which is within that petty sessional division so soon as is practicable and be brought before that magistrates' court as soon as is practicable and, in any event, no later than its next sitting. If the court is not sitting on either the day on which a person was charged (or arrives at the other police station) or the next day, the justices' clerk must be informed and this places him under a mandatory obligation to undertake the necessary arrangements for it to sit on that next day, excluding (s 46(8)) Sundays, Christmas Day and Good Friday. In *R v Teeside Justices, ex parte H (A Minor)*[1], the High Court said that magistrates must be prepared, *during normal courts hours,* to deal with any person who has been charged and refused bail and that some justices should remain at court until that time, even if their lists have finished before then. Also, they cannot have a cut-off point (eg 2 pm) after which they will not deal with prisoners who arrive thereafter. There should also be arrangements for the court to sit on Saturdays if experience shows that there is a demand for this. Failure to do the foregoing could lead to 'the risk of unlawful detentions in breach of s 46 of the Police and Criminal Evidence Act 1984 and s 7 of the Bail Act of 1976'[2].

Once a person has arrived at the court house after being charged, he is no longer in police custody for the purposes of PACE 1984 (see s 118(2)); but remains so at common law until his actual appearance before the justices. (This is because there has not as yet been any judicial authority for his incarceration.) When somebody has actually appeared before magistrates, any liability for the tort of false imprisonment ceases on the part of both the police and anybody else concerned in the arrest. A remand in custody by a court is a judicial act and no action will lie in trespass for that imprisonment[3], even if the actual incarceration occurs in premises under the control of the police in accordance with s 127(7) of the Magistrates' Courts Act 1980; see *Hyland v Chief Constable of Lancashire*[4]. This still applies even if perjured evidence is given to prevent the prisoner's release; see *Amos v Chief Constable of Gwent*[5]. The only remedy would be to sue for maliciously instituting legal proceedings, ie the application for a remand in custody; see *Hyland v Chief Constable of Lancashire*, above.

---

1   (Unreported) 19 October 2000.
2   Ibid, at para 38, per Bell J.
3   It is submitted that an action would lie against the justices under the Human Rights Act 1998 if they exceeded their jurisdiction or acted maliciously – see **17.6.2**.
4   [1996] TLR 60.
5   (Unreported) 5 June 1997.

10.9.3   Unreasonable delay and lack of expedition on the part of the police in charging or releasing

In *Tighe (David) v Chief Constable of Merseyside*[1], the plaintiff had arrived at the police station at 10.35 pm under arrest for attempting to pervert the course of justice. He immediately asked to see a solicitor. His mother was brought to the police station a few minutes later and because of her injuries the custody sergeant telephoned force headquarters for a doctor at 10.50 pm. An hour later, the same constable telephoned for the duty solicitor who called back at 12.09 am. (No reason was given for the delay in contacting this lawyer.) He was not then willing to come to the police station until the next morning. In accordance with the Code of Practice[2], until he arrived the plaintiff could not be interviewed, so he was forced to spend all night in the cells. By 11 pm the arresting officers had written up their note books and at some time between 10 pm and midnight one of their colleagues had obtained a written statement from the 14-year-old complainant. The exact time was not known but, bearing in mind his age, it was more likely to have been earlier than later. It was submitted by the appellant that if the duty solicitor had been called at the same time as the doctor, he might well have been prepared to come to the station there and then, so that the interview could have taken place that night; or any rate the defendant could not prove otherwise. Therefore, the issue of the reasonableness of the length of the incarceration ought to have been left to the jury. The Court of Appeal refused leave to appeal on the grounds that it was solely a matter for the trial judge – the latter having thought that the police had acted reasonably as they had to take statements from witnesses before carrying out an interview. However, the evidence tended to show this had been done by 11 pm, the burden being on the constabulary to establish otherwise. This decision merely goes to show that no longer can the judiciary be relied upon to protect the liberty of the subject. Absolutely no reason was given by the police as to why they did not contact the duty solicitor at the same time as the doctor. For the Court of Appeal to hold that this was acceptable without any explanation is surely contrary to all that for which *Magna Carta* stands.

In *Martin (John) v Chief Constable of Nottinghamshire*[3] the claimant had been arrested at 11.55 am on 4 June and taken to Chippenham police station, where he was collected by the Nottingham police at 11.30 pm and conveyed to that city, arriving at 3 am the next morning. The investigating officer came on duty at 11.30 am and an hour later called the duty solicitor who arrived at 2.00 pm. As soon as the duty solicitor had seen his client in private, the latter was interviewed straightaway from 3.20 to 4.00 pm. He was subsequently released at 7 pm. The duration of the detention was found to be lawful, Otton LJ commenting that no questioning of the prisoner could take place until after the private consultation with his lawyer and that after the interview administrative matters needed to be dealt with, although what these were was not stated in the judgment. Nor was anything said about the duty solicitor not being contacted until 12.30.

---

1   (Unreported) 23 June 1999, CA.
2   Code C, para 11.02, see also para 6.
3   (Unreported) 29 October 1999.

In *Yelin v Chief Constable of the North Yorkshire Constabulary*[1], a driver had been arrested for having taken a positive breath test at the roadside and was then transported to the station. From there, the police did not release him after he had failed to provide a specimen for analysis. Instead, they kept the motorist in custody for over an hour, until they had checked his car to see if they could discover any other offences – which in fact they did, namely one under the Road Vehicles (Construction and Use) Regulations 1986, SI 1986/1078, reg 18 (the handbrake did not work). It was only after this inspection of his vehicle had been carried out, that Mr Yelin was charged and bailed to appear at court. Judge Cracknell held that the above facts did not amount to false imprisonment, but gave no reasons for that decision, which is a little surprising as it is directly contrary to the wording of s 34(1). The grounds for the original detention had ceased to exist as he had refused to blow into the breathalsyer and the custody sergeant had treated that failure as final. Therefore, the police could only have detained him further by arresting him, which they did not do. Nor could they have done so, as there was nothing whatsoever to have made them suspect him of having committed an arrestable offence. (The Chief Constable did not rely on s 10(1) of RTA 1988[2] or on any particular provision of PACE 1984 as a justification for the incarceration.) Also under s 37(7) of PACE 1984, Mr Yelin should have been charged as soon as the police had treated his failure to give a sample as final, in which case he should then have been allowed to go home in accordance with s 38. This submission is supported by *Sanders v DPP*[3] where it was held that s 159 of RTA 1988 made it mandatory for a driver to stop when requested to so by a constable and that a failure to do so was an offence, but that this did not enable the officer to detain the driver or the vehicle (unless one of the general arrest conditions in PACE 1984, s 25 also existed).

10.10 BREACH OF THE RULES LAID DOWN IN PART IV OF PACE 1984

If the custody or the review officer does not follow all the procedures laid down in PACE 1984, Part IV, does that make the detention unlawful? In *London and Clydeside Estates Ltd v Aberdeen District Council*[4] Lord Hailsham LC said:

'When Parliament lays down a statutory requirement for the exercise of a legal authority it expects its authority to be obeyed down to the minutest detail.'

However, over 100 years previously Lord Penzance *in Howard v Boddington*[5] had stated:

---

1   (Unreported) 26 February 1997.
2   In fact, there was no likelihood of Mr Yelin driving with an alcohol level above the prescribed limit because, when released, the police refused to return his car keys – see **10.11**.
3   [1988] Crim LR 605.
4   [1980] 1 WLR 182 at 189.
5   (1877) 2 PD 203 at 211.

'You must look at the subject matter, consider the importance of the provision that has been disregarded, and the relation of that provision to the general object intended to be secured by the Act, and upon a review of the case in that aspect, decide whether the enactment is called imperative or directory.'

That last quotation was applied in *Krohin v DPP*[1] where it was held that a failure of an inspector to make a written record of why he had authorised a search, as required by PACE 1984, s 18(7), did not make those who had obeyed his orders become trespassers. That case was concerned not with the making of a decision, but only with its recording after it had been taken. It is submitted that apart from the keeping of records, all other provisions in PACE 1984 about police detention are mandatory as they are concerned with how long and under what conditions a person can be kept in custody. As these directly affect the right to freedom, any breach of them should surely give rise to an action for false imprisonment.

Thus, in *Roberts v Chief Constable of Cheshire*[2], it was held that failure to hold a review within the time allowed made the continued detention illegal, for which the police would be liable in damages. The Court of Appeal inclined to the view that the custody of the plaintiff would, *ipso facto*, have become lawful again once a review had been held without the need for a re-arrest. (However, on the facts of the case, such a ruling was not necessary.)

Likewise, the same principle will apply when there is a breach of the requirements about locations in which people can be held, as the Act does not sanction detention in stations which are not designated ones. This last proposition is based on *Corbett v Grey*[3], where it was held that a jailer would be liable if he kept an inmate in a part of the prison 'in which by law he could not be confined' – a decision cited to, and not dissented from by, the House of Lords in *Ex parte Hague*[4]. To the same effect *is R v Accrington Youth Court et al, ex parte F*[5], where it was held to be illegal to send those under the age of 21 to a prison for one month before allocating them to a young offenders' institution, because CJA 1982, s 1(1) prohibited the sentencing of people of that age to a term of imprisonment.

In *Mercer v Chief Constable of Lancashire*[6], although not necessary for their decision, the Court of Appeal was clearly of the view that a breach of the procedure for the detention of suspects in police custody was actionable and gave two specific examples of this, ie the incarceration was not in a designated police station or that, although awake, no opportunity was afforded to the prisoner to make representations on the statutory review of his detention.

---

1   (Unreported) 18 March 1996.
2   [1999] 1 WLR 662.
3   (1849) 4 Exch 729 at 737.
4   [1992] 1 AC 58 at 75.
5   [1998] 2 All ER 313.
6   [1991] 1 WLR 367.

10.11 DETENTION OF THOSE ARRESTED UNDER THE RTA 1988

Once arrested, a driver can, of course, be taken to a police station and required, pursuant to RTA 1988, s 7(1) to supply a specimen for analysis. As this is being done to obtain evidence (of the amount of alcohol consumed), it must be a permissible reason for authorising detention under PACE 1984, s 37(2). This request for a sample of breath or body fluid must, it is submitted, be made as soon as is practicable after the arrival at the station. The driver can be kept there until either:

(1) he has given his specimen, or
(2) he has failed to do so and the officer has treated this failure as the end of the procedure under s 7.

Even though under PACE 1984 there are no grounds to justify the motorist's continued incarceration, the police can still keep him locked up for so long as there is any likelihood of him actually driving a mechanically propelled vehicle in a public place while he is either unfit to do so or while his alcohol level is in excess of the statutory limit (see RTA 1988, s 10(1) as amended by RTA 1991, Sch 4, para 43 and *Bourlet v Porter*[1]). If the custody sergeant considers that a motorist's ability to drive is, or may be, impaired through drugs, then a doctor must be consulted before a decision is taken as to whether or not that person is fit to drive; see s 10(3). However, under RTA 1988, s 10(2), a person cannot be detained under the provisions of s 10(1) even though he is still either unfit to drive or his alcohol level is over the prescribed amount, if it appears that there is no likelihood of him driving or attempting to drive while in that condition.

10.12 TERRORISTS

The PT(TP)A 1989, s 14 gives the police extra powers of detention over people arrested under that statute. Instead of having to charge them within 24 hours, or obtain a warrant of further detention, they can hold them initially for 48 hours in the police station – a period which may be extended by the Secretary of State for up to a maximum of 5 days. PT(TP)A 1989 will on a date to be appointed by the Secretary of State[2] be repealed and replaced by the Terrorism Act 2000, Sch 8, which lays down the procedure for holding those arrested under s 41[3] of that statute. Under Sch 8, a constable exercising his powers of arrest under s 41 may take his prisoner to what he considers to be the most appropriate police station (para 1(2)) or to a place designated by the Secretary of State under para 1(1) for the detention of those arrested under s 41 or detained under Sch 5.

---

1 [1973] RTR 293 at 308 F–I per Viscount Dilhorne.
2 Brought into force on 18 February 2001.
3 See **6.7**.

Under para 23, the prisoner may only be incarcerated (at the police station or designated place) if a review officer is satisfied that this is necessary for:

(1) obtaining, or
(2) preserving, evidence relating to the matter for which he was taken into custody, or
(3) while deciding whether to apply to the Secretary of State for the making of a deportation order, or
(4) while the latter is deciding whether or not to make such an order, or
(5) pending a decision on whether to lay charges.

The review officer must be of at least the rank of inspector or in the case of reviews carried out more than 24 hours from the relevant time by a superintendent. By s 41(3), time begins to run from the time of arrest under s 41(4).

Any further extension of the length of the captivity, after 48 hours, can only be granted by a judge or a magistrate (Sch 8, para 29) after a hearing at which the prisoner is entitled to be legally represented (para 33(2)) and the application for which must be made within 48 hours or 6 hours thereafter (para 30(1)) but, in that latter case, only if it was not reasonably practical to have made it within the 48 hours (para 30(2)). Also, in this latter case, the suspect can be detained during this extra 6 hours if the review officer intends to apply for an extension (s 41(5)), and once such an application has been made the detainee can be held until the outcome of that application (s 41(6)). The judiciary can only grant an extension if there are reasonable grounds for believing that this is necessary for: (1) obtaining; or (2) preserving, evidence relating to the matter for which he was taken into custody and the investigation is being conducted expeditiously (Sch 8, para 32).

Schedule 7

A person detained under Sch 7 can be held in custody for a period of 9 hours beginning with the start of his examination.

10.13   LOCATION OF ACTUAL DETENTION

In *Middleweeck v Chief Constable of Merseyside Police*[1] a member of The Law Society had been arrested for theft and placed in the cells. The jury found that, as a solicitor, he should not have been locked up but should have been detained elsewhere, presumably, some place like the interview room where he had been questioned. Accordingly, he recovered £500 in damages. That verdict was set aside by the Court of Appeal on the grounds that no special privileges need be given to a prisoner because of his rank or status and that all those in custody can be kept in a cell.

---

1   [1992] AC 179.

10.14   SERVICEMEN

Under s 202 of AA 1955 and AFA 1955, a soldier or airman respectively who has been charged with, or with a view to being charged with an offence must be kept in a police station for up to 7 days on the written authority of his commanding officer. Similar provisions apply to sailors, see NDA 1957, s 107. Under s 190 of AA 1955 and AFA 1955 the police must detain a serviceman committed to prison by Justices for being absent without leave and keep him in custody until an escort arrives.

10.15   VISITING FORCES

The VFA 1952, s 5 allows the police to keep in custody for up to 3 days a person whom they reasonably believe to be a member of a visiting force with a view to it being determined whether he should be dealt with by courts in the United Kingdom or those of his own country. If within that time he has not been delivered up to his service authority, he must, on its expiry, either be released on bail or brought before a magistrates' court as soon as is practicable. A 'visiting force' is either one listed in s 1(1) or one designated by an Order in Council (s 1(2) as amended by the Armed Forces Act 1996, s 33).

Chapter 11

THE ARMED FORCES

11.1 INTRODUCTION

In order to maintain discipline within their ranks, members of the armed forces have been invested with statutory powers of arrest, detention and imprisonment over their members. In addition, during hostilities or times of civil commotion, soldiers are the ones usually called upon to exercise the common law powers of the citizenry of keeping the peace. Also, ever since the eighteenth century, Parliament has granted them extra powers in order to prevent smuggling. Accordingly, this chapter explores the jurisdiction of members of the armed forces to incarcerate both their comrades in arms and civilians; and if they act in excess of these powers, to what extent, if any, they are protected from actions in trespass.

11.2 POWERS OF DETENTION

11.2.1 The Customs legislation

The CEMA 1979, s 11 imposes a duty upon members of the armed forces to assist in the enforcement of the law relating to customs and excise; and s 138(1) has bestowed upon them the same rights to make an arrest as those granted by that statute to customs officers. If such a power is exercised, then by s 138(4) the arrester must inform an officer of the Customs and Excise thereof at their nearest convenient office. There is no decided case on whether the failure to do so invalidates the arrest, but as it is only a procedural matter, the absence of which will cause no prejudice to the prisoner, the courts are likely to regard s 138(4) as directory only, ie to treat it in the same way as they treated a failure by an inspector to comply with his obligation under s 18(7) of PACE 1984 to record in writing his reasons for authorising a search of premises; see *Krohin v DPP*[1].

Despite the wording of s 11 of CEMA 1979, soldiers, sailors and airmen are not encouraged to make use of the privileges granted to them by s 138, as is made clear in the current *Manual of Military Law*[2]:

> 'The Act is a consolidating statute, embracing many laws which had been passed originally as long ago as the Napoleonic Wars when smuggling was extensive and had to be kept down by army and naval forces in support of the revenue authorities. The powers and duties allotted to the armed forces at that time have been retained, with modifications, as a precaution against any recurrence of the need for military

---

1   (Unreported) 18 March 1996; see also Chapter 10.
2   9th edn, Part 2, s 5 at p 511 (HMSO).

support, but it is most unlikely that, in peace-time particularly, the Commissioners of Customs and Excise would need organised assistance from the forces, nor do they look to individual members for active, unsolicited intervention in customs work ... The normal and proper way of dealing with any breach of the customs laws which might come to notice is by a report to a customs officer or the police.'

Times have changed since that was written in 1968. Nowadays servicemen (at any rate the Royal Marines' special boat squadron) are used to arrest drug smugglers on the High Seas[1]. The use of troops in large-scale operations against drug smugglers now seems commonplace; see *R v Sorrentino*[2].

11.2.2 The Army, Navy and Air Force Acts

11.2.2.1 The Army

Under s 74 of AA 1955 (as amended by NDA 1957, s 136 and Sch 5), a person subject to military law who is found committing, is alleged to have committed or is reasonably suspected of having committed, any offence under that Act can be arrested as set out below. (By s 70, any civil offence is a crime punishable under that Act.)

In accordance with *Wills v Bowley*[3], 'committing' means 'suspected on reasonable grounds of committing'. What is novel is that an arrest need not be made only on reasonable suspicion, rather any soldier may be detained if he is 'alleged to have committed' an offence. There appears to be no judicial decision on its interpretation. Following *Clarke v Chief Constable of North Wales*[4], it could mean that if the person who actually made the apprehension was acting under orders then he would be acting lawfully and any action in trespass would lie, if at all, against the officer who gave the command. Such a meaning would be consistent with the European Court of Human Rights' decision in *Fox v UK*[5] which held it to be a breach of Art 5 of the Convention for domestic law to sanction an arrest merely on suspicion without also imposing any requirement of reasonableness.

An officer can be arrested by a superior rank of the regular military forces, or in the case of a quarrel or disorder, by any such officer. Other ranks may be apprehended by a more senior regular member of the Army. A provost officer or any officer, warrant officer, NCO or rating of any of the armed forces exercising authority under, or on behalf of, a provost officer of the Army, Navy or Air Force may arrest anybody in the Army, save that an officer can only be apprehended on the orders of another officer. A person invested with a power of arrest under this section can exercise it either personally or by giving orders for somebody else to execute it. The order can be oral and no warrant is needed; see *R v Cumings, ex parte Hall*[6]. Section 15 of the Armed Forces Act 1966

---

1   See (1999) *The Guardian*, 5 February at p 4, where two of the apprehended smugglers were serving marines!
2   *New Law Digest*, 14 May 1999.
3   [1983] AC 57 (see Chapter 3).
4   (Unreported) 5 April 2000.
5   (1990) 13 EHRR 157.
6   (1887) 19 QBD 13.

authorises the making of an arrest in like manner as that prescribed in the AA 1955, s 74 if it appears to an officer not below field rank (or equivalent rank in the other two services) that the person's arrest by the civil authorities of a country outside the United Kingdom is imminent or that his apprehension has been requested by such a civil authority. A person detained under s 15 can still be kept in custody notwithstanding that he subsequently has ceased to be subject to military law; see s 15(5).

The procedure for holding soldiers in military custody was held to be a breach of the European Convention on Human Rights in *Jordan v UK*[1], and accordingly, radical changes were made by the Armed Forces Discipline Act 2000, which was passed to bring domestic law in line with the Human Rights Act 1998. Indeed, both statutes were brought into force on the same day, namely 2 October 2000. The AFDA 2000, ss 1–8, repealed AA 1955, s 75 and inserted into that latter statute new sections 75A–75M. These basically bring service law into line with its civilian counterpart regarding the charging and bailing of prisoners. The function of a commanding officer is relegated, in effect, to the performance of the same role as that of a review officer at a police station under PACE 1984, s 40, and a lawyer appointed (by the Judge Advocate-General) to the newly created post of judicial officer performs the duties of a justice of the peace at a remand hearing.

The commanding officer of a soldier who has been arrested and kept in military custody must be notified immediately; and, unless the serviceman is charged in the meantime, he must carry out a review no later than 12 hours after the arrest and, if he authorises custody, he must review the situation after 36 hours. He can only deny the prisoner his freedom for the same reasons as a police custody sergeant can, namely if it is necessary to secure, or to preserve, or to obtain by questioning, evidence in relation to the offence for which the suspect had been arrested. If he wishes to keep his captive in custody without charge for more than 48 hours, he must apply to a judicial officer and, after an *inter partes* hearing (at which the serviceman is entitled to be legally represented), the former may authorise custody for up to a maximum of 96 hours from the time of the apprehension. A person cannot be detained for more than 96 hours without being charged. When that latter event occurs, then, unless the suspect is released, he must be brought before a judicial officer as soon as practicable, who can remand him for up to eight days (or, with his consent, 28 days) at any one time, but only if one of the following conditions apply, namely:

(1) that there are substantial grounds for believing that the prisoner would

    (a) fail to attend his court-martial,
    (b) commit an offence if released,
    (c) interfere with witnesses or otherwise obstruct the course of justice, or

(2) the Judicial Officer is satisfied that it is necessary for the accused's own safety or, if under 17 years old, for his welfare, or

---

1   (2000) TLR, March 17.

(3) further information is required before he can decide on any of the above criteria, or

(4) after charge he deserted or went absent without leave.

A member of the military who has been charged but not kept in custody can be arrested on the orders of his commanding officer if there are substantial grounds for believing that he would:

(1) fail to attend his court-martial,
(2) commit an offence,
(3) injure himself, or
(4) interfere with witnesses or otherwise obstruct the course of justice.

He must be brought before a judicial officer as soon as practicable who in deciding whether or not to order his release, shall apply the same criteria as if the prisoner had been kept in custody after charge.

11.2.2.2   *The Navy and Air Force*

Provisions to the same effect as ss 75–75M of AA 1955 are contained in both the similarly numbered (and amended[1]) section of AFA 1955 and in ss 47A–47N of NDA 1957, which relate to the apprehension of airmen and sailors respectively, both of whom are also subject to the above-mentioned powers of arrest contained in s 15 of the Armed Forces Act 1966. A naval officer of any rank can arrest a brother officer of any other rank, not just in the case of a quarrel or a disturbance as in the other two services, but also where there is a mutiny; see s 45(2)(a) of NDA 1957. Section 70 of AFA and s 42 of NDA 1957 make any civil offence a crime punishable under their respective Acts.

The Royal Air Force has identical Rules of Procedure and Queen's Regulations as the Army has for keeping prisoners in custody.

Under NDA 1957, s 95, a person subject to naval discipline can arrest anybody (which includes a civilian) whom is committing or alleged to have committed (see **11.2.2.1**) or is reasonably suspected of having committed, either while on board a warship or in a Royal Naval establishment outside of the United Kingdom and colonies, an offence contrary to s 93 (spying for an enemy) or s 94 of NDA. (The latter section makes it a crime to endeavour to secude those subject to NDA 1957 from their duty or allegiance to the Her Majesty.)

11.2.2.3   *Serviceman attached to another service*

Under s 208 of AFA 1955, s 113 of NDA 1957 and s 208 of AA 1955, a member of one of the armed forces, while attached to another service, shall also be subject to the laws applicable to that other service.

---

1   Amended by the Armed Forces Discipline Act 2000, ss 1–7. For an account of the old rules, see 'Close Arrest for Military Defendants – Time for Change?' by Judge Advocate Camp [1998] Crim LR 646.

11.2.2.4   *The reserve forces and civilians*

Territorial Army and Royal Auxiliary Air Force officers who are not special members thereof, are, like regular members of the forces, subject to their respective service law at all times. The same applies to other reservists, but only when they are called up, or on duty or undergoing training; see s 205 of AA 1955, s 205 of AFA 1955 and ss 111 and 112 of NDA 1957, as amended by Sch 10 to the Reserve Forces Act 1996. Also subject to the same jurisdiction are United Kingdom civilians employed with the services, either when the latter are on active service or when they are working overseas. The families of servicemen and civilian employees, when living with them abroad, are likewise subject to their respective service law; see s 209 of AA 1955, s 209 of AFA and s 118 of NDA 1957, as amended. The Defence Council has power to place under naval, military or air force law civilian passengers on board naval and military ships and aircraft; see s 208A of AA 1955, s 208A of AFA 1955 and s 117 of NDA 1957.

11.2.2.5   *Visiting forces*

The VFA 1952, s 2 allows the authorities of visiting forces (see Chapter 3) to exercise over their own troops stationed within the United Kingdom such jurisdiction as they are allowed by the laws of their own country. Section 16(2) of the State Immunity Act 1978 precludes that statute from applying to visiting forces. Thus, the common law applies so that anything done by the armed forces of a foreign State when on duty while present in the United Kingdom is covered by the immunity conferred by the doctrine of Act of State with the consequence that it is not justiciable before Her Majesty's courts[1].

11.3   IMMUNITY FROM SUIT

11.3.1   Military discipline

A number of law suits have been brought alleging false imprisonment arising out of the exercise of military discipline by a superior officer. There is conflicting authority as to whether an action can be instigated by a serviceman against his comrade in arms for any tort committed in course of his duty.

11.3.1.1   *Inconclusive House of Lords' cases*

In *Dawkins v Lord Rokeby*[2], an army officer sued a superior for libel. Their Lordships upheld the demurrer, but solely on the basis of the immunity accorded to a witness at a military court of enquiry. Lord Cairns LC[3] expressly asked his fellow peers to base their decision solely on that ground and to make no observations on, or comments about, other matters, and his wishes were followed.

---

1   See *Holland v Lampen-Wolfe* [2000] 1 WLR 1573.
2   (1875) LR 7 HL 744.
3   Ibid, at 754.

In *Fraser v Hamilton*[1] a naval officer sued the Second Sea Lord for maliciously causing him to resign his commission. The Court of Appeal held that no action would lie. The Master of the Rolls (Lord Cozens-Hardy) held that this was because:

(1) a right of redress was given by King's Regulation, ie the right to make a complaint to the Admiralty; and
(2) it was against public policy to allow service discipline to be undermined by such law suits.

Scrutton LJ concurred, but held that it would have been different if there had been an allegation of want of jurisdiction; and that the previous week that Court had allowed a private to sue his colonel for spitting at him because such an activity was not part of a commanding officer's duty. Before an appeal could be heard, the defendant died so that in accordance with the common law the action abated. Accordingly, the plaintiff sued the First Sea Lord for the same cause of action. That claim was also struck out in the lower courts, but this time he was able to appeal to the House of Lords against its dismissal; see *Fraser v Balfour*[2]. Their Lordships expressed no view, stating that they would prefer to reserve their judgment until all the facts were known. The Lord Chancellor (Lord Finlay) recognised:

> 'That question is, therefore, still open, at all events in this House. It involves constitutional questions of the uttermost difficulty and a decision on it should only be given when the facts are before the House in a complete and satisfactory form.'

However, rather than proceeding to trial, the parties preferred to settle the matter out of court, so the Law Lords never had an opportunity to make an authoritative pronouncement. So it will be necessary to look at the rival contentions and see what, if any, conclusions can be drawn from the cases.

11.3.2 Cases favouring immunity

The first relevant lawsuit to come before the Court of Appeal after its creation by the Supreme Court of Judicature Act 1873 was *Marks v Frogley*[3]. On the facts, it was held that the incarceration was lawful, but the lords justices went on to state that even it were otherwise, no action would lie. This was because the Army Act then in force[4] gave a soldier, who thought himself wronged in any matter, a statutory right of complaint, in the first instance to his commanding officer and, if not satisfied with the outcome, then to the general officer commanding him. Smith LJ[5] quoted with approval the words of Lush J in *Dawkins v Lord F Paulet*[6] (a libel action by a lieutenant-colonel in the Coldstream Guards against the general officer commanding his brigade over a report sent by the latter to the adjutant-general):

---

1   (1917) 33 TLR 431.
2   (1918) 34 TLR 502.
3   [1898] 1 QB 888.
4   The same provisions are found today in AA 1955.
5   [1898] 1 QB 888 at 899–900.
6   (1869) LR 5 QB 94 at 121–122.

'Can it be reasonably inferred that any other mode or measure of redress was intended by the Act than that which is specified in this article? It is no argument to say that the remedy is imperfect because no pecuniary compensation is given to the injured party. That defect, if it be one, is a defect in the code itself, which we cannot remedy. The plaintiff has no reason to complain, for he has all which the law military, to which he engaged to submit to when he entered the service, entitles him to have. The same code creates both the right and the remedy, and this court cannot add to the one or to the other.'

Mellor J agreed with Lush J that military matters should be left to the soldiery. Similar sentiments were expressed by Blackburn J and the Court of Exchequer Chamber when the same plaintiff brought another action for defamation, this time against a superior officer who had testified before a military court of enquiry; see *Dawkins v Lord Rokeby (No 2)*[1].

11.3.3   Cases against immunity – the seventeenth and eighteenth centuries

The first case which the author can find on this topic is *Weaver v Ward*[2], where a soldier accidentally shot and wounded a comrade in arms during an exercise. The case was decided upon the normal principles of negligence. Neither the court nor counsel suggested that the fact that both the litigants were servicemen on duty when the alleged tort occurred made any difference to the usual rules to be applied in determining liability. The next relevant recorded case was over 100 years later, namely *Fry v Ogle*[3], where damages were awarded against the president of a court martial for sentencing the plaintiff, a Royal Navy officer, to 15 years' imprisonment, when the maximum sentence was only 2 years. *In argumento* in *Sutton v Johnstone*[4], counsel for the defendant in error cited two cases when damages had been recovered for such a tort. In *Wall v Macnamara*[5], the plaintiff was a captain of the Africa Corps whose initial incarceration by the lieutenant-governor of Senegambia (a military officer) had been lawful but its duration of nine months before trial had been excessive. Lord Mansfield is quoted as summing up to the jury (who subsequently awarded £1,000):

'In trying the legality of acts done by military officers in the exercise of their duty, particularly beyond the seas, where cases may occur without the possibility of proper advice, great latitude ought to be allowed, and they ought not to suffer for a slip of form, if their intention appears by the evidence to have been upright; it is the same as when complaints are brought against inferior civil magistrates, such as justices of the peace for acts done by them in the exercise of their civil duty. There the principal inquiry to be made by a court of justice is how the heart stood? And if there appears to be nothing wrong there, great latitude will be allowed for misapprehension or mistakes. But on the other hand, if the heart is wrong, if cruelty, malice and oppression appear to have occasioned or aggravated the

---

1   (1873) LR 8 QB 255. See **11.3.1**.
2   (1616) Hob 134.
3   *Macarthur on Courts Martial*, 1745 ed at p 268.
4   (1786) 1 TR 493 at 536/7.
5   (1779), cited in (1786) 1 TR 536.

imprisonment or other injury complained of, they shall not cover themselves with the thin veil of legal forms, nor escape, under the justification the most technically regular, from that punishment which is your province and your duty to inflict on so scandalous abuse of public trust.'

In *Swinton v Molley*[1] damages were awarded against the captain of HMS *Trident* for imprisoning the ship's purser for three days before inquiring into the latter's alleged breach of duty, whereas he should have held the inquiry as soon as possible. A contrary view was taken in *Sutton v Johnstone*, above, where the Court of Exchequer Chamber reversed the decision at first instance and held that no action for false imprisonment would lie if the duration of the incarceration had been due to a court martial not having been convened with all due expedition. That decision was upheld in the House of Lords[2], but, according to Lawrence J[3], this was only because the events had occurred overseas during wartime.

11.3.4   The nineteenth century

In *Warden v Bailey*[4], a sergeant sued his adjutant for false imprisonment. At first instance, he was non-suited on the authority of *Sutton v Johnstone*, above. He obtained a rule *nisi* which was made absolute. Sir James Mansfield CJ distinguished *Sutton v Johnstone* as:

'Only a case of imprisonment for disobedience to orders issued in the heat of battle where instant obedience is necessary.'

Lawrence J pointed out *in argumento*[5] that the idea that the Articles of War and the Mutiny Acts gave redress was an illusion because only the Courts of Common Law, and not a court martial, could award damages. However, the Chief Justice made it plain that he totally disapproved of one soldier suing another[6]:

'We, therefore think the rule must be made absolute for a new trial but I express the strongest wish that the case will not again be tried; for all disputes respecting the extent of military discipline are greatly to be deprecated, especially in time of war. They are of the worst consequences and such that no good subject will wish to see discussed in a civil action. They ought only to be the subject of arrangement among military men.'

In *Moore v Bastard*[7], a jury awarded £300 damages to a prosecutor who was illegally arrested on the orders of a president of a court martial. In *Richard Blake's Case*[8] the Court of King's Bench held that they had jurisdiction to grant a writ of *habeas corpus* if a person subject to military law was being illegally

---

1   (1783), cited in (1786) 1 TR 536–7.
2   (1787) 1 Bro PC (2nd ed) 76 at 100.
3   *Warden v Bailey* (1811) 4 Taut 67 at 75.
4   (1811) 4 Taut 67.
5   Ibid, at 78.
6   Ibid, at 89.
7   *Macarthur On Courts Martial*, vol II, 4th edn at p 209.
8   (1814) 2 M & S 428.

detained by the military authorities. In *Allen v Boyd*[1] the plaintiff recovered damages against the governor of a military prison. His incarceration had originally been legitimate, but he had subsequently been moved to a location where he could not lawfully be detained.

It is submitted that the correct view was expressed by Cockburn CJ in his dissenting judgment in *Dawkins v Paulet*[2]:

> 'Men worthy to command would do their duty, as Eyre B expresses it, "fearless of the consequences" and would trust to the firmness of judges, and the honesty and good sense of the juries to protect them in respect of acts done honestly, though possibly erroneously, under a sense of duty.[3] Every day special juries are called upon to decide questions turning on matters of science and professional knowledge, foreign to their ordinary avocations, among others questions of navigation and nautical skill, and their decisions are on the whole satisfactory.'[4]

The Chief Justice also made it clear that, in his opinion, enlistment into the Army did not thereby remove a person's right to institute proceedings in courts of common law or equity[5]:

> '... I cannot bring myself to think that it is essential to the well-being of our military force, that ... [a person] is to be told that the Queen's Courts, in a country whose boast it is that there is no wrong without redress, are shut to a just complaint.... It is undoubtedly true that a man on entering the army or navy subjects himself to military law and whenever that law conflicts with the civil law applicable to the ordinary subject, he must be content to forego the rights which the ordinary law affords. And if, by any provision of the military code, a party subjected to its authority were prohibited from resorting to civil tribunals for the redress of a wrong inflicted under the colour of military authority, there would be an end of the question. But no such prohibition exists; and though the punishment of the wrongdoer may be in some sort a satisfaction to the party injured, it can afford no compensation for the fatal consequences in a professional or pecuniary point of view which may have resulted from the wrong.'

Those sentiments are in line with what Sir James Mansfield CJ said in *Burdett v Abbott*[6]:

> 'A soldier is gifted with all the rights of other citizens and is bound to all the duties of other citizens. It is highly important the mistake should be corrected which supposes that an Englishman, by taking upon himself the additional character of the soldier, puts off any of the rights and duties of an Englishman.'

11.3.5 The twentieth century – pre-Second World War cases

Thus, the predominant view of the judiciary is that there is no immunity from suit. That was also the opinion expressed in the next case on this topic to follow

---

1   (1861) *The Times*, 4 March.
2   (1869) LR 5 QB 94.
3   Ibid, at 108.
4   Ibid, at 109.
5   Ibid, at 108–109 and 109–110.
6   (1812) 4 Taunt 409 at 449.

Fraser v Balfour, namely *Heddon v Evans*[1]. There a former private in the Army Service Corps sued his commanding officer for false imprisonment and libel. McCardie J reviewed the case and, basing his decision on the *dicta* of the Court of Appeal in *Fraser v Hamilton*[2], held that as the law then stood military personnel were liable at common law to actions in trespass if they exceeded their jurisdiction but were immune if they acted within their powers, unless they were motivated by malice[3]:

> 'It was a settled principle of English law that a man who without lawful authority caused another to be arrested, imprisoned or otherwise injured in his person or property was liable to an action for damages. Did that apply to the acts of military tribunals? On principle he could see no good reason for exempting military officials from the operation of law. [See *Dicey's Law of the Constitution*, 8th edn, p 304.] If the acts of military tribunals or officers were unsusceptible of supervision by the civil courts, then the gravest consequences might ensue. It could scarcely be that military men were alone the interpreters on military law. If so, they became above the civil law, and so to hold would be to exclude the Courts from one of their most important and beneficent functions. The military law was a part of the law of the realm. It rested on a statutory basis. A soldier was a person subject to two sets of laws – the military law and the civil law. The liberty of a soldier was not to be infringed save in so far as the infringement was justified either by the law military or the law civil. The question of justification should ultimately be determined by the ordinary courts of law. It was for those courts to determine the extent of the military jurisdiction given to military tribunals and officers by the Acts of Parliament.
>
> . . .
>
> Further, no Army Act or Military Act had contained any provision to the effect that common law relating to false imprisonment or the like suffered by officers or privates should afford no civil remedy if the affair arose in the course of military administration. On the contrary, section 170 of the Army Act pointed in the opposite direction. If the doctrine of compact meant that once a man became a soldier he lost any right whatever to appeal to the civil Courts in respect of any wrongs arising in the course of military discipline, then it went too far. If it meant only that with respect to matters placed within the jurisdiction of military Courts or officers merely exercising powers given to them by the military law, the courts would not interfere, then the doctrine might be sound, subject to a question of whether action would lie for a malicious and groundless abuse of authority causing damage to the soldier or officer complaining. It could not be that no matter how grave and unwarranted was the infringement of a man's person or liberty, no matter how obvious the illegality might be, no matter how contrary to the provisions of the Army Act, no matter how serious or prolonged the physical consequences of the illegality might be, a soldier was wholly devoid of remedy in the civil court.'

---

1   (1919) 35 TLR 642.
2   (1917) 33 TLR 431.
3   (1919) 35 TLR 642 at 643.

11.3.6 Post-Second World War cases and the European Convention on Human Rights

Lord Goddard CJ was also of the view that the civil courts would interfere only if a person's civil rights were violated, but would not intervene in purely military matters. Thus, in *R v Secretary of State for War, ex parte Martyn*[1] he said:

> 'If the court-martial in the present case has not observed the proper rules of procedure, that is a matter for the convening officer and, if necessary, the Judge Advocate General to deal with, but it is not a matter for this court, which can only interfere with military courts and military matters insofar as the civil rights of a soldier or other person with whom they deal may be affected ... The Rules of Procedure are purely a matter of military law and procedure and not one to interfere with which this court has any jurisdiction.'

In that case, the applicant obtained a rule *nisi* for *certiorari* to quash his conviction by a court martial and for *habeas corpus* to secure his release from custody. At his first trial, the judge advocate accepted a special plea that he was not subject to military law. Later a second district court martial was convened at which it was proved that his call-up papers had been posted to his last known address. That made him subject to military law by virtue of s 18 of the National Service (Armed Forces) Act 1939. The grounds of his application for the prerogative writs were that the Rules of Procedure stated that there could only be a retrial if the second court martial was convened immediately after the first one. In his case, it had not happened until a month later. The rule *nisi* was discharged because the court martial had jurisdiction over the applicant and could impose the sentence which it had passed; and the Rules of Procedure were purely military matters and thus not cognisable by the civil courts.

The Lord Chief Justice expressed the same view a few days later in *R v Officer Commanding Depot Battalion, RASC, ex parte Elliot*[2], where he held that gross and oppressive delay in convening a court martial of a soldier under close arrest would result in *habeas corpus* being granted, and in considering whether such had occurred the court would take into account the Rules of Procedure, but their infringement did not automatically mean that the writ would issue. Although that decision was solely concerned with *habeas corpus*, such a remedy could be granted only if the detention was unlawful, in which case an action for trespass would lie. Neither of those last two mentioned cases were cited in the judgment, nor referred to in counsel's argument, in *Cox v Ministry of Defence*[3], although it is inconceivable that they were unknown to the defendant's lawyers. In that case, Judge Hegarty QC found that the written order to detain the plaintiff (pursuant to r 6 of the now repealed Rules of Procedure (Army) 1972) was given 6 days too late; and, accordingly, he awarded damages for that 6 days of false imprisonment. (Rule 6 stated that an accused shall not be held in custody for more than 72 consecutive days before the start of his court martial without a written order to that effect (together with his reasons therefor) by the

---

1   [1949] 1 All ER 242 at 243F.
2   [1949] 1 All ER 373.
3   (Unreported) 21 May 1999.

convening officer. The Queen's Regulations then in force (reg 6.047(c)) prescribed that such a written order shall not be issued without the prior approval of the general officer commanding-in-chief, or equivalent commander.)

Although not mentioned, the rationale of *Cox*, above, must be that by a detention of a member of the armed forces which is not in accordance with the relevant service law (which includes a failure to follow the correct procedure)[1] is a breach of Art 5(1) of the European Convention on Human Rights, which prescribes that 'No one shall be deprived of his liberty save ... in accordance with a procedure prescribed by law'. Since Article 5(1) had in this case been breached, then by Art 5(5) Gunner Cox had (to use the language of the Convention) 'been the victim of ... [a] detention in contravention of the provisions' of Art 5 and, therefore, had 'an enforceable right to compensation'. This decision is in accordance with *Engel v Netherlands*[2], a case brought by a private in the Dutch army. In *Pritchard v MOD*[3], Judge Previte QC held *obiter* that being kept in the forces after the date when one was entitled to be discharged would give rise to an action in tort, namely for false imprisonment, because of the restraints placed on one's freedom of movement by having to undertake military service.

11.4 DECISIONS IN OTHER JURISDICTIONS

In *Wilkes v Dinsman*[4], a marine sued his commanding officer for false imprisonment because the latter had decided to exercise the discretion given to him by military law to keep the plaintiff in the armed forces after the determination of his engagement. The Supreme Court of the United States dismissed the action[5]:

> 'Hence while an officer acts within the limits of that discretion the same law which gave it to him will protect him in the exercise of it. But for acts beyond his jurisdiction or attended by circumstances of excessive severity, arising from ill-will, a depraved disposition, or vindictive feeling, he can claim no exemption, and should be allowed none under colour of his office, however elevated or however humble the victim.'

In *Smith v Lord Advocate*[6], it was held that the Crown was not vicariously liable for torts committed by its servants. While giving judgment, the Lord Justice Clerk (MacDonald) stated[7]:

---

1   No doubt certain rules might be regarded as merely directory but the same principle will apply for ascertaining which of them are, and which are not, mandatory as apply to answering the same question in regard to the procedures laid down in PACE 1984 for the arrest and detention of suspects; see **10.10**.
2   (1976) 1 EHRR 647.
3   (1995) *The Times*, January 27.
4   (1849) 7 How 89.
5   Ibid, at 130.
6   (1897) 25 SC 112.
7   Ibid, at 121.

'It is no doubt true that if the members of a court martial commit illegal and malicious acts, that they may be held liable in damages by a court of law to persons who have suffered from the illegal and malicious conduct.'

In the Antipodes, two cases on this topic occurred (one just before, and the other a short time after, the decision of the House of Lords in *Fraser v Balfour*[1]) and both held that servicemen who acted in excess of their jurisdiction would be liable in damages for any torts they may commit. They were *Lindsay v Lovell*[2], where the court was also of the opinion that acts done maliciously attracted liability, and *Fitzgerald v MacDonald*[3], where some of the judges also expressed that view, on the trial of certain preliminary points, in an action against the members of a court-martial for false imprisonment on the grounds that this tribunal had not been properly constituted. Scout CJ said[4]:

'I am of the opinion that acts done by those in a military capacity may entitle a person to sue them in a civil court. If the law were not so then persons subject to military law would lose all the rights of a civilian and be wholly unprotected by the civil courts.'

11.5   THE DEFENCE OF SUPERIOR ORDERS

As early as the reign of Edward II, the question had arisen as to how far superior orders could be a defence to an action for trespass:

'Evidently the suggestion was made [YB 17 Edw II, p 555, the first unnumbered plea] that it was not good enough for a jailer to plead that the defendant had been ordered into custody by some apparent authority; the authority must actually have been competent. However in 1334 an inconclusive discussion seems to have been dominated by the view that a jailer could plead that the original taking was not to be drawn into new issue. This seems an eminently sensible rule to embrace, but a very interesting case from the regime of Richard II casts some very grave doubt on whether it in fact existed. In it, the defendants pleaded to a writ for imprisonment that the plaintiff had been indicted before of the steward of a hundred jury for theft, that the indictment had been sent to the sheriff, and the sheriff had issued a warrant to them as bailiffs commanding the plaintiff's arrest. On the plaintiff's replication that he was never so indicted, issue was joined. The jury found specially that the steward's clerk had counterfeited an indictment, sealed it, and delivered it to his master; the steward then sent it to the sheriff, who issued a warrant to the defendants, and then arrested the plaintiff in a pursuance of it. The trial court asked the jurors if the defendants knew anything about the clerk's fabrication and they said that they did not. Nevertheless, after an adjournment, judgment was given for the plaintiff. It is possible that judgment was rendered on the narrow ground that, technically, the issue was found for the plaintiff – that is, he was in fact never indicted, just as he claimed. But it is also possible that the judgment is based

---

1   (1918) 34 TLR 502.
2   [1917] VLR 734.
3   [1918] NZLR 769.
4   Ibid, at 785.

on the substantial proposition that the King's ministers, even when commanded to act by warrant act at their peril.'[1]

So far as the criminal law was concerned, by the time of the Restoration it was established that it was no defence to compassing the King's death that one was merely carrying out orders from a superior officer or, indeed, from Parliament itself; see *R v Axtell*[2] and *R v Hacker*[3] (both cases arising out of the execution of Charles I). That principle was followed in the civil courts. In *Annon v Gambier*, cited in *Mostyn v Fabrigas*[4], a sutler had come over to England and had been awarded damages against a Royal Naval Captain who had pulled down his house in Nova Scotia, even though the latter had done so on the express orders of his flag officer. The same stand has been taken by the American courts.

11.5.1   Decisions in the United States

In *Little v Barreme*[5], a United States naval captain was held liable for seizing a neutral ship trading with France. The defendant had been ordered by the President of his country (who was also his commander-in-chief) to capture any vessel trading with France which he suspected to be registered in his own country. That command was illegal as the Act of Congress under which it was given only authorised the taking of ships actually registered in the United States. Marshall CJ said[6]:

> 'I confess the first bias of mind was very strong in favour of the opinion that although the instructions of the executive could not give a right, they might excuse damages ... That implicit obedience to orders which military men usually pay to the orders of their superiors, which indeed is indispensably necessary to every military system appeared to me to strongly imply the principle that those orders, if not to perform a prohibited act, ought to justify the person whose general duty it is to obey them and who is placed by the laws of this country in a situation which generally requires that he should obey them ... But I have been convinced that I was mistaken, and I have receded from this first opinion. I acquiesce in that of my brethren, which is that the instructions cannot change the nature of the transaction or legalise an act which, without those instructions, would have been a plain trespass.'

That decision has been followed in other appeals heard by the United States' Supreme Court; see *Mitchell v Harmony*[7].

---

1   *Select Cases of Trespass from the King's Courts 1307–1399*, vol 1 at p xxxvi, published by the Selden Society 1984.
2   (1660) St Tr (4th edn) 369.
3   (1660) St Tr (4th edn) 382.
4   1 Smith LC 11th edn 591.
5   (1804) 2 Cranch 170.
6   Ibid, at 179.
7   (1851) US 113.

11.5.2   English decisions

The opposite view from that in the United States was taken by Willes J in *Keighly v Bell*[1], where a captain had sued his divisional commander for false imprisonment. The order to arrest him had been ratified by the commander-in-chief. The judge held the detention to have been lawful. He also went on to consider what the legal position would have been if the incarceration had not been justified at law but had been done on the orders of a superior officer:

> 'I believe that the better opinion is, that an officer acting under the orders of his superior not being manifestly illegal – would be justified by his orders.[2]
>
> If it were necessary to state any principle on which it would be competent to decide such a case, it would be that a soldier acting honestly in the discharge of his duty – that is acting in obedience to the orders of his commanding officers – is not liable for what he does unless it be shown that the orders were such as were obviously illegal. He must justify any direct violation of another person by showing not only that he had orders but that the orders were such as he was bound to obey.'[3]

Similar *obiter dicta* were reiterated by Willes J in *Dawkins v Lord Rokeby (No 1)*[4]. The opposite view was taken by Abbott CJ in *Margate Pier Company v Hannon*[5]:

> 'It is obvious that if the act of the justices issuing a warrant be invalid on the grounds of such an objection, all persons who act in the execution of the warrant will act without any authority; a constable who arrests and a gaoler who receives a felon will each be a trespasser ... for acting under an authority, which they reasonably considered themselves to be bound to obey, and the invalidity whereof they are wholly ignorant.'

It is submitted that the above quotation of the Chief Justice of the Court of King's Bench is an accurate statement of the law. If superior orders were a defence, there would have been no need for Parliament to have passed the Constables Protection Act 1750, which gave immunity from suit for acting under a justice's warrant even though the latter was invalid (see **13.6.6**). This is because a person is guilty of trespass even if he does not know that he is committing it, for example *Basely v Clarkson*[6], where the defendant did not realise that he had wandered over his boundary and had mowed some of his neighbour's grass. Can there be any distinction between somebody who mistakenly believes he is on his own land and a soldier who wrongly believes that he is obeying a lawful order?

11.5.3   The twentieth century

In *R v Smith*[7] the Cape of Good Hope Supreme Court acquitted a soldier who had obeyed an order which he had not realised was unlawful.

---

1   (1866) 4 F & F 763.
2   Ibid, at 790.
3   Ibid, at 805.
4   (1886) 4 F & F 806.
5   (1819) 3 B & A 266, 270.
6   (1680) 3 Levinz 37.
7   (1900) 17 *Cape of Good Hope Reports* 561.

Although said in another context, it is submitted that the words of Viscount Cave in *Johnstone v Pedlar*[1] are a correct statement of the law:

> 'When a wrong has been done by the King's officer to a British subject, the person wronged has no legal remedy against the Sovereign, for "the King can do no wrong"; but he may sue the King's officer for the tortious act, and the latter cannot plead the authority of the Sovereign . . .'

Likewise are the words of Lord Goddard CJ in *Brannan v Peek*[2]. In that case, a plain-clothes police officer, in order to secure evidence for a prosecution, had approached the defendant and placed a bet with him in a public place, which was an offence contrary to the Betting Act 1853. His Lordship stated[3]:

> 'I hope the day is far distant when it will become a common practice in this country for police officers to be told to commit an offence themselves for the purpose of giving evidence against someone; if they do commit offences they ought to be convicted and punished, *for the order of their superior would afford no defence.*' (Author's emphasis.)

11.6　*INTER ARMA SILENT LEGES*

Wartime raises many legal problems, two of which are pertinent to this book. First, to what extent do the military forces possess powers – over and above those which can be exercised in peace time – to incarcerate people during hostilities? (Such authority is commonly referred to as 'martial law'.) Secondly, if there is an excess of jurisdiction, will the civil courts give redress at the time or must the litigant wait until the expiration of hostilities?

11.6.1　Martial law

This term has two meanings in English law, which has led to confusion. One meaning is military law, ie the law that governs the discipline of the armed forces. In the twentieth century the courts confined its use to its second meaning, namely actions by members of the armed forces taken against civilians in wartime, although in this case the use of the word 'law' is a misnomer. As Cockburn CJ said in *R v Nelson and Brand*[4]:

> 'Martial law, when applied to civilians, is no law at all but a shadowy uncertain precarious something, depending entirely on the conscious or rather the despotic and arbitrary will of those who administer it.'

The Privy Council in *Tilonko v Attorney-General for Natal*[5] took the same view as the Chief Justice:

> 'Martial law is no law at all.'

1　　[1921] 2 AC 263 at 275.
2　　[1947] 2 All ER 572.
3　　Ibid, at 574.
4　　Forsyth *Leading Cases*, 101 at 110.
5　　[1907] AC 93.

Until the Restoration, there was no standing army in England. Instead, every man of military age was liable to be conscripted in time of war by virtue of the feudal levy and, later on, the Assize of Arms. When an army was raised, the King would make rules for its administration and discipline (called Articles of War[1]) and entrust their enforcement to the Court of the Constable and Marshal – hence the expression 'martial law'. That tribunal gradually encroached upon the common law and began to try civilians in cases of treason and felony. The House of Commons objected to this practice and by 8 Rich 2, c 5 it enacted that this court could not try actions which were cognisable at common law. Despite that and other statutes, the court continued to exceed its criminal jurisdiction of merely trying soldiers in time of war and those serving abroad. The Tudors and early Stuarts issued proclamations of martial law under which the court tried civilians. This was manifestly illegal and had been prohibited by *Magna Carta*, which had laid down that no man could be imprisoned except according to the law. This encroachment on the liberty of the subject finally led Parliament to force Charles I to give the Royal Assent to the Petition of Right in 1627, in which it was declared that martial law had always been illegal, save to the limited extent allowed by the common law in wartime (which nowadays is called military law) and that no unlawful proclamations should be issued in the future. This led to problems as there was now no way of enforcing discipline on the soldiery between the termination of war and the demobilisation of the army. Thus, the Mutiny Acts came to be passed (the first one being in 1689). They put military law on a statutory basis but they did not extend military law to civilians. In *Marais v General Officer Commanding the Lines of Communication*[2] the Privy Council said that the Petition of Right had only forbidden martial law in peacetime. However, no such limitation appears in the statute and, indeed, an attempt by the House of Lords to insert such a provision was rejected by the House of Commons.

Virtually all the cases on martial law have merely confined themselves to holding that any legal redress must wait until the cessation of hostilities rather than making a judgment on the legality of the acts about which complaint had been made. It is submitted that in *Marais* above, (which is in any event a South African decision and not binding on the English courts) the pronouncements on the legality of the imposition of martial law were erroneous and that all that exists in wartime is the common law duty to preserve the peace of the Realm. Similar views that the Privy Council was wrong have been expressed by Maitland in his *Constitutional History of England*[3] and by Holesworth in his *History of English Law*[4]. Dicey discussed French martial law at great length in his *Introduction to the Study of the Law of the Constitution*[5] and concluded:

> 'Martial law is utterly unknown to the [British] constitution.'

---

1   Articles of War were issued under the Royal Prerogative, but the common law only allowed this power of discipline over the army to be exercised during actual hostilities (for a brief history of military law, see *The Manual of Military Law*, ch 2 (HMSO, 1914).
2   [1902] AC 109.
3   At pp 490–491.
4   (Cambridge University Press, 1920), Vol 1 at pp 573–580.
5   (Macmillan) 9th edn, Chapter VIII.

It is submitted that Maitland, Holesworth and Dicey are correct. The normal rules of the common law apply in wartime, namely it is the duty of every citizen to preserve the Queen's Peace. Save where immediate violence was apprehended, it is difficult to see how this would give any justification, even in wartime, for the detention without trial of those lawfully in the United Kingdom. Just because there is a war does not mean that *carte blanche* is given to those who wear the Queen's uniform and that they are immune from the law of tort. In the words of Cockburn CJ in *R v Nelson and Brand*, above:

> 'Martial law is merely the application of the common law principle that life and property may be protected, and crime prevented by the immediate application of any amount of force which under the circumstances may be necessary.'

To the same effect is the Report of the Committee on the Featherstone Riots 1894[1]:

> 'Officers and soldiers are under no special privileges and subject to no special responsibilities as regards the principles of law.'

The latest case to date would appear to be *Burmah Oil Co v Lord Advocate*[2], where the majority of the House of Lords were of the opinion that an otherwise well-founded claim for damages should fail only if it arose out of acts done in the actual course of a battle. That was a claim for compensation for war damage, but there is no reason why immunity from other actions in tort should not also be similarly limited. Indeed, in the debate on the Crown Proceedings Act 1947, Lord Jowitt LC said that it was an open question as to whether or not Lord Raglan and Earl Haig could not have been sued by those under their command for negligence for the way in which they had conducted their respective campaigns!

11.6.2 Acts of State

Immunity attaches to an act of State. However, 'act of State' is very narrowly defined. It is (to quote the Privy Council in *Eshugbayi Eleko v Officer Administering the Government of Nigeria*[3]):

> '… capable of being misunderstood. As applied to an act of the sovereign power directed against another sovereign power or the subjects of another sovereign power not owing temporary allegiance, in pursuance of sovereign rights of waging war or maintaining peace on the high seas or abroad, it may give rise to no legal remedy. But as applied to acts of the executive directed to subjects within the territorial jurisdiction it has no special meaning, and can give no immunity from the jurisdiction of the court to inquire into the legality of the act.'

In *A-G v Nissan* [1970] AC 179, the army had taken over a hotel owned by a Cypriot who was a naturalised British citizen. The building had been used as a headquarters for a 'peace force' sent to prevent hostilities between the local

---

1   C 7234.
2   [1965] AC 75. Insofar as damage to property is concerned, this decision was reversed by the War Damage Act 1965, with retrospective effect, so Burmah Oil Co received nothing.
3   [1931] AC 662 at 671.

Greek and Turkish communities. The House of Lords held that the Crown was liable for any damage caused to the hotel by its armed forces. Their Lordships were of the view that an act of state was not available as a defence to the Crown in an action for trespass (wherever committed) brought against it by citizens of the United Kingdom and Colonies. They left open the question of whether it could be pleaded against others who also owed allegiance to the Crown, for example a British protected person. Such a defence is available to a foreign power if sued in the English courts, see *Holland v Lampen-Wolfe*[1], and **11.3.1**.

11.6.3   When actions can be brought during hostilities

11.6.3.1   Cases arising out of the annexation of India and the Boer War

Elphinstone v Bedreechund[2] was an action brought by a native whose property had been seized when his State was annexed by the British. The Privy Council's advice to the Sovereign was that the civil courts had no jurisdiction over the military during war, 'even if not *flagrante* yet *nondum cessante bello*'. That decision is explicable on grounds of an act of State – that is how it was argued by the Attorney-General and treated by the editor of the *English Reports*, who enumerates for the reader's benefit a list of cases on that topic, not one of which is about martial law.

In *Marais v General Officer Commanding the Lines of Communication and the Attorney-General of the Colony*[3] the Privy Council refused to grant a writ of *habeas corpus*[4]:

> 'The truth is that no doubt has existed that where war *actually* prevails the ordinary courts have no jurisdiction over the actions of the military authorities.
> ... but once let the fact of *actual* war be established and there is an universal consensus of opinion that the civil courts have no jurisdiction to call in question the propriety of the action of military authorities.' (Author's emphasis.)

That was a case during the South African War where a person was arrested and detained in Cape Town without trial by the military authorities because it was suspected that he might aid the enemy. The incarceration took place in an area where actual wartime operations of a violent nature were being conducted against the Boers.

In *Edmonson v Rundle*[5], a sergeant-major sued three officers, including a major-general, for false imprisonment, arising out of an incident during the Boer War which was still continuing when the action came up for trial. Laurence J held that the commands of a military person in authority were not cognisable if arising out of 'a war being waged *at the date of trial*' (author's emphasis).

---

1   [2000] 1 WLR 1573.
2   (1830) 1 Knapp 316.
3   [1902] AC 109.
4   Ibid, at 115.
5   (1903) 19 TLR 356.

11.6.3.2 Irish cases

In *Wolfe Tone*[1] the applicant had tried to stir up a pro-French rebellion in Ireland; for which he had been sentenced to death by a military court. On the day on which his execution was due to take place, Lord Kilwarden (Chief Justice of the Court of King's Bench in Dublin) granted a writ of *habeas corpus,* thus signifying his agreement with counsel's submission[2] that as long as the ordinary courts sat, the military was subject to their jurisdiction. The sentiments expressed in that last sentence were disapproved of by the Privy Council in *Marais,* above. However, a similar test was adopted by the United States Supreme Court in *Ex parte Milligan*[3]:

> 'If, in foreign invasion or civil war, the courts are actually closed and it is impossible to administer criminal justice according to the law, then, in the theatre of active military operations, where war really prevails, there is a necessity to furnish a substitute for the civil authority, thus overthrown, to preserve the safety of the army and society; and as no power is left but the military it is allowed to govern by martial rule until the laws have their free course. As necessity creates the rule so it limits its duration; for, if this government is continued after the courts are re-instated, it is a gross usurpation of power. Martial rule can never exist when the courts are open, and in the proper and unobstructed exercise of their jurisdiction.'

It was only the last sentence which makes that judgment differ from the advice tendered to the King by the Privy Council in *Marais,* that the sittings of the civil courts were evidence, though by no means conclusive, that the location of the incarceration was not in an area of actual military operations.

In the 1920s the Irish judiciary did not follow the views of their former Chief Justice, Lord Kilwarden, and held that during the insurrection which preceded the granting of home rule the courts were impotent in the face of the military; see *R v Major-General Strickland, ex parte Ronayne*[4], *Higgins v Willis*[5], *R v Allen*[6] and *R v Major-General Strickland, ex parte Garde*[7]. O'Connor MR did express some doubts about this principle in *Egan v General Macready*[8], but had clearly overcome them a year later in *R v The Adjutant-General of the Irish Free State et al, ex parte Childers*[9]. These Irish cases covered both applications for writs of *habeas corpus* and suits for damages in tort. The judges did not differentiate between the two types of action and treated the defendants and respondents as if they were diplomats with full immunity under international law (although that analogy was not mentioned).

---

1   (1798) 27 Howell's St Tr 613.
2   Ibid, at 625.
3   (1886) 74 US 1.
4   [1921] 2 IR 333. The respondent was the Military Governor of Cork.
5   [1921] 2 IR 386.
6   [1921] 2 IR 241.
7   [1921] 2 IR 317.
8   [1921] 1 IR 265. The respondent was the General Officer Commanding-In-Chief in C Ireland.
9   [1923] 1 IR 5.

11.6.4   Conclusions

Despite the views of those who sat in his court over 100 years later, it is submitted that Lord Kilwarden was correct. His views are the same as those expressed by Coke CJ[1] and by Sir John Campbell[2] and Sir RM Rolfe[3] (the law officers of the Crown) in 1838 who advised that civilians must be tried by civil courts if they were still open[4]. In *HMS Hydra*[5], Hill J awarded damages against a captain of a destroyer in the First World War for negligent navigation; and a similar action involving *HMS Archer*[6] failed, but only on the merits. Likewise, in the High Court of Australia in *Shaw, Savill and Albion Co Ltd v The Commonwealth*[7], it was held (by a 3:2 majority) that proceedings could be brought during wartime against the Crown for damage caused by the negligent navigation of one of its warships. It was only because the evidence involved military secrets that the action was stayed until the end of hostilities.

11.6.5   After the cessation of hostilities

Once hostilities are over, there has never been any doubt that the legitimacy of wartime acts can be adjudicated upon in the civil courts. In the words of Molony CJ in *R v Major-General Strickland, ex parte Ronayne*[8]:

'When the state of war is over, the acts of the military during the war, unless protected by an act of indemnity, can be challenged before a jury, and in that event, even the King's command would not be an answer, if the jury were satisfied that the acts complained of by the plaintiff were not justified by the circumstances then existing and the necessities of the case.'

The Chief Justice re-iterated those views in *Higgins v Willis*[9]:

'Once martial law ends, the civil courts can inquire into the acts done in time of war.'   .

So in *Burmah Oil Company v Lord Advocate*[10] the House of Lords held that an oil company could recover compensation for its oil tanks which had been destroyed 20 years previously to prevent them falling into enemy hands. However, it is not unknown for a statute to be passed giving *ex post facto* immunity to the military, for example 36 Geo 3 c 26, 38 Geo 3 c 74, 39 Geo 3 c 50, and, more recently, the Indemnity Act 1920 (10 and 11 Geo 5 c 48).

---

1   12 Co Rep 12/3.
2   Afterwards Lord Campbell.
3   Afterwards Lord Cranworth.
4   *Forsyth's Opinion* at p 198.
5   [1918] P 78.
6   [1919] P 1.
7   (1944) 66 CLR 344.
8   [1921] 2 IR 333 at 334.
9   [1921] 2 IR 386 at 387.
10   [1965] AC 75.

11.7 STATUTORY IMMUNITY

By s 142 of AA 1955, s 142 of AFA 1955, s 130A of the Naval Discipline Act 1957 (inserted by the Armed Forces Act 1971, s 71):

> 'No action shall lie in respect of anything done by any person in pursuance of a sentence of imprisonment or detention awarded under this Act if the doing thereof would have been lawful but for a defect in any instrument made for the purposes of that sentence.'

11.8 SUMMARY

Members of the armed forces when carrying out their duties are still liable to pay damages if, without lawful justification, they infringe the freedom of movement of a comrade in arms or of anybody else. If they do exceed their powers, it is no defence that they were acting under orders. It remains for the House of Lords to decide whether they are also liable (as magistrates were at common law) if they exercise their lawful powers maliciously. The fact that the incarceration occurs during wartime will probably not enable a tortfeasor to put off the day of reckoning until the end of hostilities, unless the military situation is such that the civil courts can no longer sit. It must also be remembered that the soldiery, like all citizens, are under a duty to keep the Queen's Peace and this includes detaining those who are a threat to it[1].

---

1   See Chapter 5.

Chapter 12

THE POWERS OF CERTAIN SECTIONS OF THE CITIZENRY TO RESTRAIN THE FREEDOM OF MOVEMENT OF OTHERS

12.1   INTRODUCTION

As well as constables, various other members of the public are allowed to detain people against their will without incurring any criminal or tortious liability in circumstances where the ordinary citizen would be guilty of trespass. The following list does not claim to be exhaustive. It almost certainly omits some private Acts passed in previous centuries that are still extant and relevant to this topic, although these will be very few in number as most local statutes are repealed by the Local Government Act 1972, s 262(9).

12.2   COUNTY COURT BAILIFFS

Section 92 of the County Courts Act 1984 empowers the court bailiff 'to take into custody' and bring before a judge anybody who has rescued, or attempted to rescue, any goods seized in execution under the process of the court.

12.3   OFFICERS OF HER MAJESTY'S CUSTOMS AND EXCISE AND OTHERS AUTHORISED BY THE COMMISSIONERS

Officers of the Customs and Excise are given the same grounds for making an apprehension for an arrestable customs offence as the constabulary possesses, ie they are empowered to arrest all those who they have reasonable grounds to suspect of committing, or of having committed, such a crime, even if in fact it has not been perpetrated. This power is derived as follows:

Customs and Excise Management Act 1979 ('CEMA 1979')

SECTION 138

Crimes under customs and excise Acts
The power of arrest for crimes under the CEMA 1979 is given in s 138(1) of that Act. (A complete list of these offences is set out at **4.2.1**.) This right of apprehension is limited to offences committed within the last 20 years unless (s 138(2)) it was not

CEMA 1979, s 138

practical to make an arrest at the time of the commission of the offence or, if arrested, the person then escaped – in both of these cases the time-limit does not apply. By s 8(2), the Commissioners can authorise any person to carry out the duties of an officer and while so doing, that person has all the powers and privileges of an officer.

Criminal Justice Act 1988

The Criminal Justice Act 1988, s 150 empowers the Treasury to extend the power of officers of Her Majesty's Customs and Excise so that they can grant bail. This section is not yet in force. Once it becomes law, then, by s 151(1), customs officers will be able to arrest those whom they reasonably suspect are not likely to surrender to customs detention, after having been released on bail for possessing a controlled drug or for a drug trafficking offence, other than for assisting somebody else to retain the proceeds of such a crime. By subs (2), their prisoner must, as soon as practical, and in any event within 24 hours (not counting Christmas Day, Good Friday or a Sunday), be brought before a justice of the peace for the petty sessional division in which he was a detainee.

CJA 1988, s 151

Value Added Tax Act 1994 ('VATA 1994')

SECTION 72[1]

VAT offences
The power of arrest for offences contrary to VATA 1994 arises by virtue of s 72(9) of that Act, which also gives the same powers to anybody authorised by the Commissioners of Customs and Excise for that purpose.

VATA 1994, s 72

Finance Act 1994 ('FA 1994')

SCHEDULE 7, PARA 4(6)[1]

Fraud
The power of arrest for offences of fraud contrary to FA 1994 is given pursuant to Sch 7, para 4(6), which also invests the same powers in anybody authorised by the Commissioners of Customs and Excise for that purpose.

FA 1994, Sch 7

---

1   See **4.2.1**.

Finance Act 1996 ('FA 1996')

SCHEDULE 5, PARA 6(1)[1]

Fraud
The power of arrest for offences of fraud contrary to FA 1996 is
enacted in Sch 5, para 6(1), which also gives the same powers to
anybody authorised by the Commissioners of Customs and
Excise for that purpose.

FA 1996, Sch 5

Detention after arrest
Officers of HM Customs and Excise possess the same rights as the
police have to obtain an extension of the custody time-limits for
the suspects they are investigating; see PACE 1984, s 114 and
PACE 1984 (Application to Customs and Excise) Order 1985,
SI 1985/1800 as amended by the following statutory instruments:
1987/439, 1995/3217 and 1996/1860. By implication, the Customs and Excise Officers are no longer subject to the common
law obligation to hand their prisoners over to a constable as soon
as is practicable, but can detain their suspects and question them
for up to 24 hours. However SI 1985/1800 specifically excludes
the Commissioners of Customs and Excise from charging[1] or
granting bail to people. Once charged, only the police have a
power of detention if bail is withheld.

Terrorism Act 2000 (due to come into force in February 2001)
Section 35 and Sch 7 bestow upon customs offices designated for
that purpose by the Secretary of State and Commissioners of
Customs and Excise the same right to detain at harbours and
airports passengers entering and leaving Great Britain as are
given to constables by that Schedule (see **6.7**).

Terrorism Act
2000, s 35,
Sch 7

12.4   HEALTH AUTHORITIES

Mental Health Act 1983 ('MHA 1983')

SECTION 6(2)

Admittance pursuant to necessary procedures
Section 6(2) enacts that if the necessary procedures are followed,
an admittance pursuant thereto 'shall be sufficient authority for
the managers to detain the patient in the hospital in accordance
with the provisions' of that statute. *Re S-C*[2] held this to mean that

MHA 1983,
s 6(2)

---

1   They can, of course, apply to a justice of the peace for a summons.
2   [1996] QB 599.

provided the paperwork appeared to be in order the hospital was protected from an action in tort. In the words of Bingham LJ[1]:

> 'Such a hospital is not at risk of liability for false imprisonment if it turns out that the approved social worker does not meet the definition in s 145(1), or if the recommendations which purport to be signed by registered medical practitioners are in truth not signed by such, although appearing to be so. That is obviously good sense. A mental hospital is not obliged to act like a private detective; it can take documents at face value. Provided they appear to conform with the requirements of the statute, the hospital is entitled to act on them.'

Neil LJ agreed but said[2] that if the original application was in fact defective, s 3 would not prevent a writ of *habeas corpus* being issued. *Re S-C*, above, was approved by the Court of Appeal in *St George's Healthcare NHS Trust v S; R v Collins et al, ex parte S (No 1)*[3].

Section 137 provides that a person required or authorised by the Act to be detained shall be in 'legal custody' while being so detained or while being conveyed to a hospital or a place of safety. MHA 1983, s 137

SECTIONS 2, 3, 11, 26, 29

Detention in hospital for assessment and treatment
Sections 2 and 3 authorise the detention in hospital for assessment and treatment respectively of a person who is certified by two registered medical practitioners as suffering from a mental disorder which warrants his confinement in a hospital and that he needs to be detained in the interests of his own health or safety, or with a view to the protection of another person. Section 1(2) defines 'mental disorder' as: MHA 1983, ss 2 3, 11, 26, 29

> 'Mental illness, arrested or incomplete development of mind, psychopathic disorder and any other disorder or disability of mind and "mentally disordered" shall be construed accordingly.'

In *R v BHB Community Health Care Trust, ex parte B*[4] the Court of Appeal approved the judgment of McCullough J in *R v Hallstrom, ex parte W; R v Gardener, ex parte L*[5] that s 3 only covered those whose mental condition was believed to require a period of in-patient treatment in order to alleviate their illness or to prevent further degeneration. One of the above-mentioned doctors must be approved by the Secretary of State and both must have carried out an examination of the patient either MHA 1983, s 12

---

1   [1996] QB 599 at 605–606.
2   Ibid, at 613.
3   [1998] 3 All ER 673.
4   [1999] 1 FLR 106.
5   [1989] QB 1090.

together or within 5 days of each other; also where practicable one of them must have had previous contact with the person recommended for admittance.

Under s 3, the managers of a hospital may detain a mentally ill patient long-term, but only if there has been a request for admission pursuant to s 11, which requires a recommendation from two doctors. Also the person who appears to the social worker to be the nearest relative must not object to that course of action. (According to *Re D (Mental Health Patient: Habeas Corpus)*[1], the social worker can assume that a person who appears to fulfil this description is that person and is under no duty to make enquiries of him. However, this ratio is hard to reconcile with the *dicta* in the judgment that 'the statute was to be considered strictly since it involved the liberty of the "subject" '.) The nearest relative is defined in s 26(1), in the following order, namely his or her:

(1) spouse,
(2) child,
(3) parent,
(4) grandparent,
(5) grandchild,
(6) uncle or aunt,
(7) nephew or niece.

However, where the patient is ordinarily resident with, or cared for by, a relative, that person is 'his nearest relative' (s 26(4)) and where there are two or more people who fulfil the latter description, the relevant one shall be the oldest (s 26(3)).

Section 29 allows the court to appoint somebody other than a relative to exercise the functions of a relative. The way to overcome the problem of, say, a responsible parent who sees no need for her offspring to be locked up in a mental hospital is to obtain an order under s 29 *ex parte* and without any prior notice being given. Such a procedure was held to be perfectly in order by Hidden J in *R v Uxbridge County Court, ex parte Binns*[2]. The author is of the view that the European Court of Human Rights may well consider such a manoeuvre to be a breach of Article 6, which guarantees a fair hearing with the opportunity to cross-examine witnesses.

SECTION 4

Admission for assessment in cases of emergency
In the case of an emergency, a person – for the same reasons as are applicable to ss 2 and 3 – can be detained in a hospital for 48   MHA 1983, s 4

---

1   [2000] TLR 401.
2   (Unreported) 11 August 2000.

hours on the application of a social worker or his nearest relative and a report by a doctor who, if possible, has had previous acquaintance with him. Further detention requires a report by another doctor which complies with the requirements in s 12.

A patient cannot be detained for more than 6 months without his detention being renewed. Such a renewal by the managers of the hospital can be made only after a report from a medical officer (after examining the patient) that:

MHA 1983, s 20

(1) his mental disorder is of such a nature that it is appropriate to receive him for treatment in a hospital;
(2) either: (a) such treatment is likely to alleviate or to prevent a worsening of the condition; or (b) if discharged, he is unlikely to be able to care for himself or be cared for by others; and
(3) detention is necessary for the safety of the patient or of other people.

In *R v BHB Community Health Care Trust, ex parte B*, above, it was held that a renewal under s 20 could be made, even though at the time the patient had been granted leave of absence under s 17.

In *R v Bournewood Community and Mental Health NHS Trust, ex parte L*[1] the applicant lacked the mental capacity to give his consent. He had been hitting his head and banging it against a wall and was taken to hospital and detained to prevent him causing injury to himself. The House of Lords held that a person could be compulsorily detained in a mental hospital under the common law doctrine of necessity and did not have to be detained solely in accordance with the provisions of MHA 1983. Accordingly, no tort had been committed by the patient's enforced stay in a mental hospital.

In *R v North West London Mental Health NHS Trust, ex parte S*[2], it was held by the Court of Appeal that Part II of MHA 1983 (ss 2–34: dealing with compulsory admission otherwise than in connection with the criminal law) and Part III (ss 35–55: dealing with patients involved in criminal proceedings or under sentence) could co-exist and operate independently of each other. Thus, there was power under s 3 to detain a restricted patient who had been detained without restrictions under s 41 after being convicted at the Old Bailey and who had then been discharged under s 73 but had still remained liable to recall.

In *St George's Healthcare Trust v S; R v Collins, ex parte S*, above, it was held that a patient could not be detained who understood what she was doing, and that applied even when she refused to have an

1   [1999] AC 458.
2   [1998] 2 QB 628.

operation with the result that she endangered her own life and the safety and well-being of her unborn child.

SECTION 72

At the end of six months after his admission, the hospital managers must refer the patient's case to a Mental Health Tribunal who have the power to order his discharge. However, even if such an order is made that does not prevent him being re-admitted and detained under ss 2, 3 or 4, provided that the statutory criteria for such an admission exists, see *R v Tower Hamlets Health Care NHS Trust et al, ex parte Von Brandenburgh Authority*[1] and *R v Managers of South Western Hospital, ex parte M*[2].

MHA 1983, s 72

12.5   IMMIGRATION OFFICERS

Immigration Act 1971 ('IA 1971')

Immigration offences

Section 28A (as inserted by the Immigration and Asylum Act 1999, s 128 on 14 February 2000 by the Immigration and Asylum Act 1999 (Commencement No 2 and Transitional Provisions) Order 2000, SI 2000/168) empowers an immigration officer to arrest without warrant anyone who has, or whom he reasonably suspects to have committed, or to have attempted to commit any offence under the following sections:

IA 1971, ss 24,
24A, 25, 25A,
26, 28B, 28C,
Schs 2, 3
PACE 1984,
s 25

(i)   s 24 (except s 24(1)(d)) – see **6.7.3**;
(ii) s 24A – seeking or obtaining leave to enter, or remaining in, the UK by deception;
(iii) s 25(1), being knowingly concerned in making or carrying out arrangements for anybody to enter the United Kingdom whom he knows or has reasonable cause to believe:
   (a)   to be an illegal immigrant, or
   (b)   to be an asylum seeker, or
   (c)   to be seeking to enter or remain here by deception.
   Under s 25(1A), helping a political refugee is however legal if it is not done for gain or is carried out by an employee of a bona fide organisation whose purpose is to assist refugees;
(iv) s 26(1)(g), obstructing an officer or a person acting in the execution of the Act. However, for this offence, an arrest can only be made if one of the general arrest conditions in PACE, s 25 (see **6.8** above) applies, other than those relating to indecency and obstruction of the highway.

Only in order to make an arrest under s 25(1) can an immigration officer enter premises uninvited (see s 28C) and only

---

1   (Unreported) 26 June 2000 (Burton J).
2   [1993] QB 683 (Laws J).

then if he has reasonable grounds for believing that the person he is seeking is actually there, otherwise for any of the other offences set out above, he needs a warrant from a justice before he can go inside without the occupier's permission (see s 28B).

Paragraph 16(1) of Sch 2 allows an immigration officer to detain a person who has arrived in the United Kingdom in order to examine him under para 2 to decide whether he has a right of entry and if not, whether he should be allowed to remain here. Paragraph 16(2) of the same schedule allows immigration officers to detain, pending his deportation, a person who has been refused entry or who is an illegal immigrant.

Paragraphs 17, 24, 33 of Sch 2 and para 3 of Sch 3 bestow upon immigration officers the same rights of arrest as that given by those sections to a constable; see **6.7.3**.

Asylum and Immigration Appeals Act 1993 ('AIAA 1993')

Fingerprinting
Section 3(5) bestows upon an immigration officer the same power as is given to a constable to apprehend an asylum seeker who fails to attend at the time and date appointed for his fingerprinting under this section. The detained person can be taken to a place where his fingerprints may be conveniently taken and once that has been done, he is entitled to be released. When the Immigration and Asylum Act 1999, Sch 14, paras 99, 100 and 101 are brought into force, this section of AIA 1993 will be repealed and replaced by s 141 of IAA 1999.

AIAA 1993, s 3
IAA 1999,
Sch 14

Immigration and Asylum Act 1999

Breach of bail
Section 50(1) (at time of writing not yet in force) empowers an immigration officer to arrest without warrant anyone whom he reasonably believes to have broken, or is likely to break a condition of bail imposed under s 44 of that Act. The detained person must be brought, within 24 hours, before the person or tribunal before whom, or which, he was under a duty to surrender as a condition of his bail.

IAA 1999, ss 44,
50

SECTION 141
See AIAA 1993, s 3(5) above.

Terrorism Act 2000 (due to come into force in February 2001)
Section 35 and Sch 7 bestow upon immigration officers the same right to detain at harbours and airports passengers entering and

leaving Great Britain as are given to constables by that schedule (see **6.7**).

12.6   INSPECTORS APPOINTED UNDER THE ANIMAL HEALTH ACT 1981 ('AHA 1981')

AHA 1981

SECTION 60(5)

Obstructing officers

Section 60(5) authorises local authorities to appoint inspectors for the execution and enforcement of AHA 1981, but s 51 limits the exercise of their powers to within the territorial boundaries of their employer. The Ministry of Agriculture, Fisheries and Food can also appoint inspectors. Under s 60(5) of AHA 1981, an inspector may arrest without warrant a person who obstructs or impedes him in the execution of either: (1) the Act; (2) an order of the Minister; or (3) a regulation made by a lawful authority. Anybody who assists in such conduct can likewise be apprehended. The inspector must take his prisoner with all practical speed before a justice of the peace and must not, without a warrant, detain him longer than is necessary for that purpose (s 60(6)).

AHA 1981,
s 60(5)

12.7   INSPECTORS OF CANALS

Railway and Canal Traffic Act 1888 ('RCTA 1888')

SECTION 41

Obstruction etc of inspector

Section 41 invests an inspector of canals, when carrying out an inspection, with the same powers as a railway inspector. This includes the latter's power of arrest under s 11 of the Regulation of Railways Act 1871 (RRA 1871) (see below).

RCTA 1888,
s 41

12.8 LANDOWNERS, THEIR SERVANTS AND OWNERS OF SHOOTING RIGHTS

Game Act 1831 ('GA 1831')

SECTION 31

Trespassers in daytime in search of game
Section 31 empowers a landowner, the owner of the rights to   GA 1831, s 31
shoot, their gamekeepers or anyone authorised by them to
require anybody found on their land in daytime in pursuit of
game or woodcocks or snipes or conies to leave and to give his full
name and address. If such a demand is not complied with, the
person making the requirement can arrest the person in default.
The detainee must then be brought before a justice of the peace
within 12 hours of his apprehension or be released from custody.
By s 35, this power of summary arrest can not be exercised
against: (1) those hunting with hounds, or coursing with grey-
hounds, in fresh pursuit of any fox, deer or hare which started on
other land; (2) Royalty; or (3) the lord of the manor or their
gamekeepers.

12.9 LONDON BOROUGHS

London County Council (General Powers) Act 1900 ('LCC(GP)A 1900') (as amended by the Local Goverment Act 1985, Part II)

SECTION 27

Transient offenders against bylaws relating to tunnels
Any officer of a London Borough or the City of London   LCC(GP)A
authorised in writing, or any person called to their assistance,   1900, s 27
may, without a warrant 'seize and detain' and take to a police
station, or bring before a justice of the peace, anybody who is, or
has been, committing any offence against any bylaws relating to a
tunnel, *if* the name and address of the detainee is unknown and
cannot be ascertained.

To exercise this power of arrest the authorised person must
either be in uniform or have with him a written authority which
he must produce on request.

12.10   LOCAL AUTHORITIES

Public Health (Control of Disease) Act 1984 ('PH(CD)A 1984') (as amended by the National Health Service and Community Care Act 1990, s 66, Sch 9, para 26(3) and Sch 10)

SECTION 41

Removal to hospital of inmate of a common lodging house with a notifiable disease

A local authority can order the removal to a hospital (with the consent of the Health Authority for that area) of a person residing in a common lodging house if they are satisfied that he is suffering from a notifiable disease and that there is a serious risk of him spreading his infection to others. A notifiable disease is defined in s 10 as cholera, plague, relapsing fever, smallpox or typhus.

PH(CD)A 1984, ss 10, 41

12.11   OWNERS AND CAPTAINS OF MERCHANT NAVY SHIPS AND AEROPLANES

CEMA 1979

SECTION 138(3)

Arrest of crew member by customs officer

Where an officer of Customs and Excise apprehends, by virtue of the CEMA 1979, a member of the crew of a ship in the employment of Her Majesty, the captain of that vessel, if so requested by the arrester, must keep the detained person on board until he can be brought before a court and shall then deliver him to the proper officer of HM Customs and Excise.

CEMA 1979, s 138(3)

IA 1971

SCHEDULE 2, PARA 8

Persons refused entry to United Kingdom

If a captain of a ship or an aeroplane has brought a person to the United Kingdom who is refused entry, then the captain must, if directed by an immigration officer, remove that person from the United Kingdom by the same vessel or aeroplane on which he arrived. Similar directions may be given to the owners or agents of the boat or aeroplane. In all cases, any such orders must be given within 2 months of the refusal of leave to enter.

IA 1971, Sch 2, para 8

Under para 9, similar directions as those authorised by para 8 can be given in relation to an illegal immigrant who is refused leave to remain in this country.

Under paras 12 and 13, similar directions as those authorised by para 8 can be given in relation to a member of the crew who has overstayed his leave.

SCHEDULE 2, PARA 16(3)

Persons refused permission to land in United Kingdom
A captain of a ship or an aeroplane must, if required to do so by an immigration officer, detain on board a person who has arrived thereon in the United Kingdom and has been refused permission to land.

IA 1971, Sch 2, para 16(3)

SCHEDULE 2, PARA 16(4)

Persons deported from United Kingdom
If so required to do so by an immigration officer, a captain of a ship or an aeroplane must prevent the disembarkation in the United Kingdom of a person who is being deported from this country.

IA 1971, Sch 2, para 16(4)

Prevention of Terrorism (Temporary Provisions) Act 1989 ('PT(TP)A 1989')

SCHEDULE 2, PARA 6(2)(a), (b)

Persons subject to an exclusion order
The Secretary of State may give directions to a captain of a ship or an aeroplane about to leave the relevant territory requiring him to remove a person subject to an exclusion order from that location.

PT(TP)A 1989, Sch 2, para 6(2)(a)

The Secretary of State may give directions to the owners or agents of a boat or aeroplane requiring them to make arrangements for the removal of a person mentioned in s 6(2)(a) in a ship or aeroplane specified in the directions.

PT(TP)A 1989, Sch 2, para 6(2)(b)

SCHEDULE 2, PARA 7(3)

Persons subject to a removal direction
A captain of a ship or aeroplane must, if ordered to do so by an examining officer, prevent a person subject to a removal direction from disembarking prior to his removal and (para 7(4)) the captain may detain him on board in custody to prevent him going ashore.

PT(TP)A 1989, Sch 2, para 7(3)

Merchant Shipping Act 1995 ('MSA 1995')

SECTION 105

Restraint of persons in the interests of safety, etc

Section 105 authorises the master of any ship registered in the United Kingdom to place under restraint anybody on his vessel for so long as it appears to him to be necessary or expedient in the interests of safety, good order or discipline on board ship.

MSA 1995, s 105

12.12 PARENTS AND THOSE *IN LOCO PARENTIS*

Those who are invested with parental responsibility are entitled to confine, within a defined area, those in their custody, provided that they act reasonably. Thus, a teacher can keep a pupil in detention in a classroom after school, as a punishment for bad behaviour. What is reasonable will depend, *inter alia*, on the age of the child.

12.13 PRISON GOVERNORS AND WARDERS

Prisons Act 1952 ('PA 1952')

SECTIONS 12, 43(5)

Confinement of prisoners

A prisoner, whether sentenced to imprisonment, or committed to prison on remand or pending trial, or otherwise, may be lawfully confined in any prison or (s 43(5)) a remand centre, a detention centre or a youth custody centre. Every inmate shall be deemed to be in the legal custody of the governor of the prison (s 13). A prison officer when acting as such has all the powers and privileges of a constable (s 8). However, if he does not set free his detainee on the date when he is due for release or otherwise illegally keeps him in jail, he is likely to become liable in damages. For a full discussion of when and how a warder becomes a trespasser, see Chapter 13.

PA 1952, ss 12, 43(5)

Under s 202 of AA 1955 and AFA 1955, a soldier or airman respectively who has been charged with, or with a view to being charged with, an offence can be kept in civilian prison for up to 7 days on the written authority of his commanding officer. Similar provisions apply to sailors, see NDA 1957, s 107.

AFA 1955, s 202
AA 1955, s 202
NDA 1957, s 107

Under s 190 of AA 1955 and AFA 1955 a prison governor must detain a serviceman committed to prison by justices for being absent without leave and keep him in custody until an escort arrives to take him into military custody.

AA 1955, s 190
AFA 1955, s 190

12.14 THE RAILWAYS AND TRAMWAYS – THOSE ASSOCIATED WITH THEM, INCLUDING INSPECTORS AND EMPLOYEES

Railways Clauses Consolidation Act 1845 ('RCCA 1845')

SECTION 104

Refusing to quit carriage at destination
Section 104 enables the officers and servants of, and anybody acting on behalf of, a railway company to arrest a person who:

RCCA 1845, s 104

(1) is committing,
(2) has committed,
(3) is attempting to commit, or
(4) has attempted to commit,

an offence under s 103, namely knowingly and wilfully refusing or neglecting to quit his carriage when he has arrived at the destination to which he has paid his fare. The apprehended person may be detained until he can conveniently be taken before a justice of the peace or otherwise discharged by due course of law.

Tramways Act 1870

SECTION 52

Arrest for fraud
Enables the officers and servants of the promoters (ie the people who built the tramways; see s 24) or the lessees of a tramway, or anybody called to their assistance, to arrest a person who is committing, or has committed, an offence under s 51, namely avoiding, or attempting to avoid, paying the correct fare for the journey travelled or, having arrived at the destination to which he has paid his fare, knowingly and wilfully refuses to alight from the carriage.

TA 1870, s 52

Regulation of Railways Act 1871 ('RRA 1871')

SECTION 11

Disobedience to or obstruction of inspector or court
Section 11 enables: (1) an inspector of the railways holding an enquiry under that statute; (2) a member of a court holding an investigation under that Act; or (3) anybody called by an such an inspector or member to his assistance, 'to seize and to detain' anybody who prevents or impedes them in the execution of their

RRA 1871, s 11

duty. The person seized may be detained until he can conveniently be taken before a magistrates' court.

Regulation of Railways Act 1889 ('RRA 1889')

SECTION 5

Avoiding payment of fare etc

Section 5 allows an officer of a railway company or railway operator (which includes a ticket inspector; see *Moberley v Allsop*[1]) to detain a person who has either:

(1) failed to produce his ticket,
(2) (having been so requested) failed to deliver up, his ticket showing that he has paid the correct fare, or
(3) failed to pay his correct fare,

RRA 1889, s 5

and that person has refused to give his name and address when requested to do so by any officer or servant of the company. A person who travels 2nd class with a 3rd class ticket has not paid the correct fare; see *Gillingham v Walker*[2]. The detention can last until he can conveniently be brought before a justice or discharged by due course of law. If the correct details are given, then there is no power of detention even though it is on reasonable grounds believed that the information supplied was false; see *Knights v London, Chatham and Dover Railway Co*[3]. This power of arrest also applies to those who fail or refuse to give their details if the railway operator is the London Underground (London Transport Act 1965, s 34(5)). The same extended power applied to British Railways (British Railways Act 1965, s 35(5)) and can be passed on to those franchised to run the old BR services if, pursuant to s 92(1) of the Railways Act 1993, the transfer scheme provided for the transferee to have the benefit of the British Railways Act 1965, s 35(5).

---

1   (1992) 156 JPN 284.
2   (1881) 44 LT 715.
3   (1893) 62 LJQB 378.

12.15   THE SECRETARY OF STATE

London County Council (General Powers) Act 1894 ('LCC(GP)A 1894') (as amended by the Local Government Act 1985, Part II)

SECTION 7 (as amended by the Woolwich Ferry Order 1989, SI 1989/714, regs 3(b) and (c))

Transient offenders against bylaws relating to ferries
Any person authorised by the Secretary of State, or any person called to their assistance, may, without a warrant, 'seize and detain' and take to a police station, or bring before a justice of the peace, anybody who is, or has been, committing any offence against any bylaws of a London Borough or the City of London relating to ferries, *if* the name and address of the detainee is unknown and cannot be ascertained.   LCC(GP)A 1894

To exercise this power of arrest, the authorised person must either be in uniform or have with him a written authority, which must be shown on request.

12.16   SHERIFFS

Sheriffs Act 1887 ('SA 1887')

SECTION 8

Resisting sheriff in execution of writ
Section 8 makes it an offence to resist the sheriff in the execution of a writ (ie any process issued out of a court, see s 38) and authorises the sheriff to arrest, and to commit to prison, any such resister. No time-limit is specified but, as the resistance is also made a crime, presumably the prisoner must be brought from the prison and taken before a justice of the peace as soon as is practicable. The under-sheriff has all the powers of the sheriff (see *Norton v Simmes*[1]) and this still applies on the death or suspension from office of the high sheriff; see s 25 of the 1887 Act.   SA 1887, s 8

---

1   (1614) Hob 12.

12.17   WATER BAILIFFS

Salmon and Freshwater Fisheries Act 1975 ('SFFA 1975')

SECTION 34

Persons fishing illegally at night

Water bailiffs or a person appointed by the Minster of Agricul-   SFFA 1975, s 34
ture, Fisheries and Food, with their assistants, may arrest anybody
who between the first hour after sunset and the beginning of the
last hour before sunrise illegally takes or kills salmon, trout,
freshwater fish or eels or is found on or near any waters with
intent to kill or take illegally any such fish or has in his possession,
for the purposes of the illegal capture of such fish, any
instrument prohibited by s 1, namely: (1) a firearm; (2) an otter
lath or jack, wire or snare; (3) a crossline or setline; (4) a spear,
gaff, stroke-snath or other like instruments; or (5) a light.

12.18   GENERALLY

Although some of the above statutes refer to a person being brought before a
magistrates' court, the judiciary will almost certainly regard that as having been
complied with if the prisoner is handed over to a police officer for onwards
transmission to petty sessions.

Chapter 13

LIABILITY AS A TORTFEASOR

13.1 INTRODUCTION

This chapter considers who can be held liable for an imprisonment contrary to law and who has been granted immunity from their tortious conduct. The Justices of the Peace Act 1997 and the Courts and Legal Services Act 1990 greatly extended the immunity of the judiciary. That was a retrograde step in the protection of the liberty of the subject and fortunately has been put right by the Human Rights Act 1998. The true justice of the case is the view expressed by the Court of Exchequer in *Sutton v Johnstone*[1]:

> 'To situations which require indulgence they will show it; but, be the risk more or less, all men hold their situations in this country upon the terms of submitting to have their conduct examined and measured by that standard which the law has established.'

13.2 COUNSELLING AND PROCURING

Unless granted immunity by statute[2], anybody who is in involved in the commission of the tort can be sued even if they took no part in any overt physical act in the incarceration. In *Barker v Braham and Norwood*[3], a solicitor sued out a writ of *capias ad satisfaciendum* on behalf of his client, ordering the sheriff to arrest the plaintiff for debt. Earl CJ stated[4]:

> 'Now, there being no accessories in trespass, Co Litt. 57, the attorney must either be guilty as a principal or not at all. And it is held, that a trespasser may be, not only he who does the act, but who commands or procures it to be done, Bro *Trespass*, 148, 307; who aids or assists in it, Bro *Trespass*, 232, Salk 409, Pulton, *De Pace*, 22, 4, 49; or assists afterwards, Bro *Trespass*, 113.'

Thus, a person who asks somebody else to carry out an unlawful act would normally be a joint tortfeasor with the actual perpetrator. The problem arises when information is imparted to a police officer and arouses in him a *bona fide* and reasonable suspicion of an arrestable offence, which causes him to apprehend an innocent man. The constable clearly cannot be sued. Is his informant liable? The leading case is *Davidson v Chief Constable of North Wales*[5], where a store detective employed by the second defendant thought that she saw the plaintiff take a cassette and leave the shop without paying for it. So she

---

1 (1786) 1 TR 493 at 504 (per Eyre B, delivering the unanimous opinion of his Brethren).
2 Eg the Constables Protection Act 1750, see **13.6.6**.
3 (1773) 2 Wm Bl 866.
4 Ibid, at p 868.
5 [1994] 2 All ER 597.

called the police and told them what she had observed. They spoke to the plaintiff and as he was unable to produce a receipt, they arrested him. The Court of Appeal held that a person would not be liable for false imprisonment merely by reporting the facts to the police and leaving them to take such action as they thought fit. It would be another matter if she had 'directed, procured or directly requested or encouraged' the police to make an arrest. That case must be now read in the light of the subsequent decision in *Martin v Watson*[1], where the House of Lords held the respondent to be liable in damages for malicious prosecution when her false and malicious accusation led to court proceedings being brought by the police after they had investigated the matter, which included interviewing the appellant. By analogy, the *ratio* of that decision was applied by the Court of Appeal in *Sallows v Griffiths*[2]. There, it was held that where a defendant had knowingly made an untrue and malicious statement to the local constabulary which caused a person to be locked up, he was liable in damages for that detention, where, but for his lies, no action would have been taken by the police. It is for the claimant to prove that that his apprehension was brought about by the malice and falsehoods of the person he has sued for the tort of maliciously procuring his arrest. In *Harris v Dignum*[3], it was held that if the police arrest somebody as a result of an allegation made against him, the complainant is not *ipso facto* liable merely because he signs the charge sheet.

13.3 VICARIOUS LIABILITY

A master is variously liable if his servant, in the course of his employment, falsely imprisons somebody. Thus, the shop owner is liable for the acts of his store detectives see *Timms v John Lewis*[4], where the defendants did not dispute that they were liable on the basis of superior orders if the actions of their employee were tortious. This was no doubt because store detectives are hired to apprehend shoplifters. However, at common law it is not within the normal scope of an employee's duties to execute an arrest unless it is to protect or to obtain the return of his master's property. Thus in *Allen v London & South Western Railway Company*[5] the defendants were not liable for the actions of their booking clerk who, wrongly suspecting the plaintiff of having tried to rob his till, arrested him after the attempt was over. However, the court said that it would be another matter if he was authorised by a byelaw to apprehend fare dodgers. The rationale of this decision is best summed up in the words of Mellor J[6] when he quoted with approval the words of Keating J in *Edwards v North Western Railway Co*[7].

---

1   [1996] AC 74.
2   (Unreported) 25 November 1999.
3   (1859) 1 F & F 688.
4   [1952] AC 676.
5   (1870) LR 6 QB 65.
6   Ibid, at 71.
7   (1870) LR 5 CP 445 at 449.

'There seems no ground for saying that what was done was done in the normal course of business of the company, nor that it was for their benefit, except in so far as it was for the benefit of all The Queen's subjects that a criminal should be convicted. If Holmes acted from a sense of duty which rests on everyone, to give in charge a person whom he thinks is committing a felony, his conduct would in no way be connected with the defendants.'

To the same effect are *Abrahams v Deakin*[1] and *Bank of New South Wales v Owston*[2], where the Privy Council stated that a bank manager did not have any implied authority to arrest the plaintiff for stealing a bill of exchange where the act was passed and the apprehension of the offender was not necessary for the protection of the bank but was made only for the purpose of vindicating the law.

13.4 CHIEF OFFICERS OF POLICE AND POLICE AUTHORITIES

It was held in *Fisher v Oldham Corporation*[3] that a constable held an office under the Crown which he exercised in his own right and therefore his employers (the police authority) were not liable for his actions. That has been altered to some extent by s 88(1) of the Police Act 1996[4] whereby a chief constable for a police area (or in London the Commissioner) is made responsible for the acts done in performance of their duty by the officers of his force to the same extent that he would have been held vicariously liable if he had been their employer. It should be noted that this section does not impose any liability on a head officer of a force not listed in Sch 1 to the Act (for example the Ministry of Defence or the Port of London Police). By s 88(2), a chief officer is entitled to be indemnified out of the police fund against any damages or costs awarded against him by virtue of s 88(1). It should be noted that in *Fisher v Oldham Corporation*, above, McCardie J did cite decisions in which railway companies had been held liable for the torts of their police officers but his Lordship distinguished those authorities on the grounds that they were based on the wording of the private acts which had allowed railway companies to have their own special police forces. The general view is that McCardie J was right and he based his judgment on those of the Supreme Courts of Canada, Australia and South Africa in *McCleave v City of Moncton*[5], *Enever v Rex*[6] and *British South Africa Co v Crickmore*[7]. Parliament clearly thought his view of the law was correct, otherwise it would not have enacted s 88(2) of the Police Act 1966 (see above).

---

1   [1891] AC 521.
2   (1869) 4 App Cas 270.
3   [1930] 2 KB 364.
4   This repealed and re-enacted similar legislation contained in the Police Act 1964.
5   (1902) 32 Can SC 106.
6   (1906) 3 CLR 969.
7   [1921] AD 107.

In *Abrahams v Metropolitan Police Commissioner*[1], two Lord Justices referred to a policeman as being the 'servant of the defendant'. The only issue in that case which had been argued by counsel was estoppel[2]. The pronouncement that Sgt Cook was a servant was part of the ratio explaining why the Commissioner was deemed to have the knowledge of that officer. The authorities referred to in the preceding paragraph must raise considerable doubts about the correctness of the views expressed by the appellate court about the employment status of constables. Further, since the Police Act 1996, s 88 (see above) was not cited, the pronouncement about servants must be regarded as having been uttered *per incuriam.*

13.5 JUDICIAL ACTS

These can be put into three categories:

(1) the people who apply for the order from a judge or magistrate;
(2) those who make the order, ie the judiciary; and
(3) those who execute the orders.

13.5.1 The applicant

In *Roy v Prior*[3], it was held that if somebody, without reasonable cause, maliciously caused a court to arrest somebody, then he could be held liable in damages for the tort of malicious arrest. In that case, a solicitor obtained the arrest of a witness and was sued by the latter who alleged that the warrant had only been obtained by deliberate lies being told to the judge.

13.5.2 The judiciary

The immunity from suit depends on the level of the member of the judiciary sued. Lords of Appeal in Ordinary have the protection of the Petition of Rights 1689, whereby proceedings in Parliament cannot be questioned elsewhere, which means that they cannot be sued for false imprisonment arising out of any judicial act they perform in their office as Law Lords. As to the judges of the superior courts, they are only liable if they exceed their jurisdiction, which includes not complying with a pre-condition to its exercise; see *In re McC (A Minor)*[4]. (In that case, some Northern Irish justices were held liable in damages when they imposed a custodial sentence on a youth. The reason for this was that under their law, they must offer legal aid before imposing custody on somebody who had not previously received such a sentence – which they had not done.)

The common law rules, applicable to judges of inferior courts, made them liable if they acted:

---

1   (2000) *New Law Digest*, December 8.
2   For the facts, see **15.10**, below.
3   [1971] AC 470.
4   [1985] AC 528.

(1) maliciously; see *Morgan v Hughes*[1]; or

(2) without jurisdiction; see *Marshalsea*[2].

Where the excess of jurisdiction occurred because of an error of fact of which the defendant neither knew nor ought to have known, then there is no tortious liability; see *Calder v Halket*[3] and *Palmer v Crone*[4], but it is otherwise if it is due to a mistake of law. In *In re McC (A Minor)*, above, their Lordships' House was divided over whether inferior members of the judiciary were still liable for malicious acts. In view of the wording of s 51 of the Justices of the Peace Act 1997, Parliament clearly thought that liability for such acts still existed. (That makes a magistrate liable in damages 'if, but only if, it is proved that he acted in bad faith'.) The County Courts Act 1984, s 123 remains in force and, by virtue of its provisions, a district judge of that court not only has no immunity but is also liable for the tortious conduct of his bailiffs. In 1990, Parliament extended the immunity of justices of the peace, district judges (magistrates' courts)[5] and their clerks, so that they cannot be sued for anything done while acting or purporting to act judicially except for things done with malice outside their jurisdiction – thus making them even more privileged than High Court judges; see the Justices of the Peace Act 1997, ss 50 and 51 (which re-enacted the Courts and Legal Services Act 1990, s 108). (Those two sections extend to district judges (magistrates' courts) by virtue of ss 13(1) and 19(1), to their clerks by ss 13(3) and 19(3) of the Justices of the Peace Act 1997 and to anybody appointed by a magistrates' court committee to assist a justice's clerk[6].) By s 52, a judge can strike out, with or without an order for costs, an action brought in contravention of s 51.

Article 5(5) of the European Convention on Human Rights states that domestic law shall provide an enforceable right of compensation for those who have been unlawfully incarcerated. Accordingly, s 9(4) of the Human Rights Act 1998 allows a prisoner to recover in Her Majesty's courts such damages as he is entitled to under Art 5(5); but such an award can be made only against the Crown, and only if the Minister responsible for the court concerned (or a person or government department nominated by him) has been made a party to the action. For a full discourse on Art 5, see **17.6** *et seq.* Section 9(3) of the Human Rights Act 1998 provides that no action can be brought under that statute in respect of any judicial act done in good faith save to the extent allowed by s 9(4); and by s 9(5), this immunity applies not only to a member of the judiciary (including a clerk or anybody else entitled to exercise the jurisdiction of the court, whilst so acting) but also extends to a person whilst acting on instructions from the judiciary. However, s 11(b) preserves any other right of legal action a person might have, apart from that given to him by that statute.

---

1   (1788) 2 Term 225.
2   (1613) 10 Co Rep 68b.
3   (1840) 3 Moo PC 28.
4   [1927] 1 KB 804.
5   The new name for stipendiary magistrates, see Access to Justice Act 1999, s 78.
6   Access to Justice Act 1999, s 100.

13.6 COMPLIANCE WITH THE ORDERS MADE, AND THE WARRANTS ISSUED, BY THE JUDICIARY

13.6.1 What are warrants and when can they can be issued?

In *R v Commissioners of Inland Revenue, ex parte Rossminster Ltd*[1], Lord Wilberforce said:

> 'There is no mystery about the word "warrant", it simply means a document issued by a person in authority . . . authorising the doing of an act which would otherwise be illegal.'

Thus, a warrant lawfully issued can authorise the apprehension of the person named in it. Scott LJ in *Leachinsky v Christie*[2] quoted with approval the then current edition of *Halsbury's Laws of England*[3]:

> 'Summons and warrants of arrest are issued by a justice on an information being laid before him.'

Judges and magistrates can also issue warrants, both of committal to prison, for example to enforce a custodial sentence imposed on a convicted criminal, and of arrest to compel appearance before them, for example:

(1) a seek and find order in aid of their wardship jurisdiction; see *In re B (Minors) (Wardship: Power to Detain)*[4] and
(2) the power (granted by s 80(1) of the Supreme Court Act 1981) to arrest a person against whom a voluntary bill is going to be, or has been, preferred.

However, the warrant cannot be executed prior to the actual preferment; see *Brooks v DPP (Jamaica)*[5]. Under s 3 of the Protection From Harassment Act 1997, where the High Court or the county court has granted an injunction to prevent the harassment of the plaintiff then, if the latter considers that the defendant has acted in breach of that order, he can apply to a judge of the court which granted the injunction for the issue of a warrant for the arrest of the person in contempt.

In *R v Scunthorpe Justices, ex parte Parker*[6], it was held that a warrant of commitment could not be issued for failure to pay the costs arising from the obtaining of a liability order for unpaid community charge. Only in respect of the latter could such a warrant be issued. In *R v Doncaster Justices, ex parte Jack*[7], Collins J held that it was unlawful to issue warrants of commitment for non-payment of money in the absence of the defaulter *and* without a proper means enquiry. A warrant of arrest could be used to secure the attendance at such an enquiry of those debtors who would not come to court when summonsed to do so.

---

1   [1980] AC 952 at 1000.
2   [1946] KB 130.
3   Vol 9 at p 77, para 102.
4   [1994] 2 FLR 479.
5   [1994] 1 AC 568 at 582G–583A.
6   (Unreported) 15 December 1998.
7   (1999) 163 JPN 1026.

The Magistrates' Courts (Form) Rules 1981 prescribe the layout of the document to be used for certain types of arrest warrants. Under r 96(2) of the Magistrates' Courts Rules 1981, a warrant of arrest issued by a magistrate must 'name the person to be arrested or otherwise describe the person to be arrested and shall contain a statement of the offence charged in the information or, as the case might be, the ground on which the warrant is issued'. A general warrant (ie without naming the actual individual) is unlawful and not valid; see *Entick v Carrington*[1].

A warrant of arrest remains in force until it is executed or, at any rate, in the case of one issued by a justice of the peace, until it has been withdrawn – which can be done at any time; see Magistrates' Courts Act 1980, s 125(1).

A warrant of committal for contempt of court must set out full details of the contempt so as to enable the contemptor to be in a position to purge his contempt.[2]

Under s 190A of AA 1955 (inserted by AFA 1971, s 44(2)), a commanding officer can issue a warrant authorising the civil police to arrest soldiers under his command suspected of having committed an offence under Part II of AA 1955 and a single warrant may be issued in respect of two or more persons alleged to be guilty of the same crime or of offences of a similar class. When the warrant is executed, the detained person must be handed over to military custody as soon as is practicable. Similar provisions relating to airmen and sailors have been enacted by s 190A of AFA 1955 and s 103 of NDA 1957 respectively.

13.6.2 Where executed

A warrant can be executed only within the territorial jurisdiction of the person who issued it. So in *Syed Mahamad Yusuf-ud-Din v Secretary of State for India*[3] the Privy Council held that the plaintiff had been falsely imprisoned when a warrant issued in British India had been executed, not in that location but in the independent state of Hyderabad. Under the Magistrates' Courts Act 1980, s 2, a justice of the peace can try an indictable or either way offence committed anywhere within England and Wales but, in the case of summary crimes (with a very few exceptions)[4], he can try only those perpetrated either within his commission area or by a person believed to reside therein. The new district judges (magistrates' court) are *ex officio* justices for every part of Britain, south of the Border.

13.6.3 When a wrongly named person is arrested

If somebody other than the man or woman named in the warrant is detained, then the arrester is liable in an action for false imprisonment; see *Walley v*

---

1   (1765) 19 St Tr 1029.
2   *Newman v Modern Bookbinders* [2000] 2 All ER 814.
3   (1903) 19 TLR 496.
4   Eg, if tried together with an indictable offence.

McConnell[1] and *Kelley v Lawrence*[2], where a sheriff was held liable in damages. Blackburn J said *in argumento*[3]:

> 'It is immaterial that the sheriff intended to arrested Ignatius [Kelly], when he in fact arrested Michael [Kelly].'

In *R v Hood*[4], the warrant authorised the apprehension of:

> '[*blank space left for Christian name*] Hood of the hamlet of Berton, in the parish of Fugglestone St Peter in the same county, by whatever name he may be known or called, the son of Samuel Hood.'

There were several people answering that description of Hood, son of Samuel Hood, so the court was unanimously of the opinion that the warrant was bad because it omitted the Christian name; it should have assigned some reason for the omission and have given some distinguishing particulars of the man to be arrested. In other words, a warrant must identify with sufficient particularity the actual person to be detained and not a class of several people, leaving it to the arrester to decide which member thereof was to be apprehended.

13.6.4   Necessity for possession of the warrant

At common law, a person who executed such a warrant had to have it in his possession; see *Codd v Crabb*[5]. By s 125(3) and (4) of the Magistrates' Courts Act 1980 (as amended by PACE 1984, s 33), that requirement does not apply to constables (or (s 125D(2)[6]) any person entitled to execute it) making an arrest on warrant of any of the following categories of people (and this applies even if the document was not issued by a magistrate; see *Magee v Morris*[7]):

(1)   those accused of a criminal offence (including those in breach of a community service order; see *Jones v Kelsey*[8], but not a warrant to compel attendance at a means inquiry for the non-payment of a fine; see *DPP v Peacock*[9]);

(2)   deserters and those who absent themselves without leave from Her Majesty's Armed Forces or from visiting forces;

(3)   those who do not pay their rates or community charge; see the Council Tax (Administration and Enforcement) Regulations 1992, SI 1992/613, reg 48 (5)(b) and (c));

(4)   spouses, where it is necessary for the protection of the parties to a marriage and/or the children of the family, pursuant to the Family Law Act 1996 (which has replaced s 18(4) of the Domestic Proceedings and Magistrates' Courts Act 1978);

---

1   (1849) 13 QB 903.
2   (1864) 3 H & C 1.
3   Ibid, at p 5–6.
4   (1830) 1 Moody 281.
5   (1876) 1 Ex D 352.
6   Section 125D was inserted by the Access to Justice Act 1999, s 96 (at the time of writing, this section had not yet been brought into force).
7   [1954] 1 WLR 806.
8   (1987) 151 JP 429.
9   (1988) TLR, 10 November.

(5) defendants in civil proceedings who do not appear before the justices to answer the complaints laid against them;

(6) those who do not pay monetary sums awarded against them by the justices, for example fine defaulters; and

(7) witness who fail to attend the magistrates' court to testify in criminal proceedings.

In *R v Purdy*[1], it was held that an officer was in possession of the requisite warrant when it was in his police car, which was parked 60 yards away from the scene of the arrest. The Court of Appeal said that the reason for the rule was so that the prisoner could 'buy his freedom', because the actual document would show the amount of the debt for which he was being detained and payment of this sum would procure his release. The court also said that in all of the old cases where the apprehension had been held to be illegal, the warrant was in the possession of somebody other than the arresting officer. Here it was manifestly in that person's possession. The court rejected defence counsel's argument that 'possession' meant 'physically having it on one's person'. However, a warrant was not in the 'possession' of the arrester when it was at the police station half a mile away; see *Small v Kirkpatrick*[2]. The court rejected the argument that as it was addressed to 'all constables', it was in the possession of each of them jointly. The question of whether it would still be in the arresting officer's possession if it was in the latter's personal desk did not arise. That may have been sufficient in view of the comment in *R v Purdy*, above, about the fact that the authorities from the nineteenth century were about warrants which were in the possession of somebody other than he who had executed the apprehension. However, as the rationale is that a person must know the amount by which he can 'buy' his freedom as stated on the warrant, that document must clearly be near at hand, and not miles away, so that the necessary information can be readily obtained and told to the prisoner.

13.6.5 Obeying the terms of the warrant

No liability can attach to a person who acts in accordance with a warrant 'good on its face'; see *R v Governor of Brockhill Prison, ex parte Evans (No 2)*[3]. Thus, in the case of a warrant that discloses nothing which might impugn its validity, a jailer can rely upon it as a defence if sued; see *Henderson v Preston*[4] and *Greaves v Keene*[5]. It would be otherwise if its invalidity was apparent by reading it, for example if a justice were to issue a warrant of commitment in excess of his jurisdiction, such as for a period of confinement in excess of the statutory maximum for the crime for which the prisoner had been convicted[6]. A good example of this is *R v Accrington Youth Court, ex parte F*[7], where the High Court held that a warrant of commitment for a sentence of imprisonment on a person

---

1   [1975] QB 288.

2   (1978) 66 Crim App R 186.

3   [1999] QB 1043 at 1056C/D.

4   (1888) 21 QBD 362.

5   (1879) 4 Ex D 73.

6   See the Constables Protection Act 1750 at **13.6.6**.

7   [1998] 2 All ER 313.

aged under 21 was a nullity and 'bears the brand of invalidity on its forehead'. (This is because CJA 1982, s 1(1) prevents a person of that age being sentenced to imprisonment.) The warrant also said that the Governor was to receive F into his custody and 'keep the accused for the said period'. The omission of any mention of remission also made the warrant bad on its face.

However, that was an application for habeas corpus. In *R v Bow Street Justices, ex parte McDonald*[1], it was held that, even though the warrant was bad on its face, those who executed it did not incur any tortious liability by acting in obedience to it. In that case, some employees of Westminster City Council, in ignorance of the invalidity of the warrant, had seized the respondent's guitar in Leicester Square. The magistrate had issued a warrant under the London Government Act 1963, s 42(2) but that statute did not authorise the taking of goods in an unenclosed open space. That case appears to be the first one where a warrant protected a person who executed it, even though it was invalid on its face, although that would only be apparent to somebody who had an intimate knowledge of the law. If that case was rightly decided, then there would have been no need for the Constables Protection Act 1750[2]. The common law gives immunity from suit to those who executed warrants which were regular on their face. If that exemption from tortious liability applied to all warrants, then there would have been no need to have given extra statutory immunity to policemen when obeying the terms of a warrant, when the reading of them (with sufficient legal knowledge) would have shown them to be invalid. Accordingly, it is submitted that *R v Bow Street Justices, ex parte McDonald* was wrongly decided. The House of Lords did not consider this point in *R v Governor of Brockhill Prison, ex parte Evans (No 2)*[3]. There, the warrant of committal showed that the prisoner had been sentenced to two years' imprisonment. It was up to the gaoler to release her when that sentence had been served. By the Criminal Justice Act 1967, s 67 (as amended by s 49(2) of the Police and Criminal Evidence Act 1984 and by s 130 of the Criminal Justice Act 1988), the time spent in custody from the date of the arrest automatically counted towards the length of the incarceration to be served[4]. Because this had not been done in her case, Miss Evans was held entitled to recover damages for false imprisonment from her warder. Abbott CJ was of the view that no protection was given by an invalid warrant – see the quotation at **11.5.2** above. To the same effects is *Comyn's Digest*[5] and *Shergold v Holloway*.[6]

However, in that case, Lord Hobhouse in his speech made this comment[7]:

---

1   [1998] EHLR 216.
2   See **13.6.6**.
3   [2000] 3 WLR 843.
4   In *Burgess v Governor of Maidstone Prison* [2000] All ER (D) 1688, the plaintiff had daily to surrender to his bail an hour before his trial began and was not released until half an hour after its finish. The Court of Appeal held that his was not 'custody' within the meaning of that word in CJA 1967, s 67 and therefore did not count towards the time which he had to serve in prison under his sentence.
5   Imprisonment, 4, 8, 9.
6   (1735) 2 Str 1002.
7   [2000] 3 WLR 843.

'The critical importance of the warrant and what detention it actually commands and authorises applies both ways as illustrated by the judgment in *Demer v Cook*.[1] Alverstone CJ contrasted two situations. One was where the gaoler receives a prisoner under a warrant which is correct in form in which case no action will lie against him if it should turn out that the warrant was improperly issued or the court had no jurisdiction to issue it. The other was where the warrant had on its face expired or the gaoler has received the prisoner without any warrant, in which case the action will lie. The warrant and nothing else is the protection to the gaoler and he is not entitled to question it or go behind it.'

In *Greaves v Keen*[2] a solicitor was kept in prison for over a year for not paying over the sum of £100. That was a contempt of court but under the Debtor's Act 1869, s 4, the maximum length of the incarceration that could be imposed for keeping the money in disobedience to a court order was 12 months. The warrant of committal merely said he was to be locked up for contempt and did not specify the reasons. As any other contempt carried unlimited imprisonment, the warrant disclosed no defect so that no action lay by the prisoner against his warder.

In *Olotu v Home Office and the Crown Prosecution Service*[3], the plaintiff was committed in custody by the justices for trial to the Crown Court and held there for two months after the time-limit for so doing had expired. The warrant of commitment commanded the prison governor:

'[To] keep the accused until the accused is delivered in due course of law. The custody time-limit which applies to these proceeding is due to expire on 15 August 1994.'

It was common ground that 'delivered in due course of law' meant being taken to the Crown Court. Under the Prosecution of Offenders (Custody Time Limits) Regulations 1987 as amended, the Crown Prosecution Service had to notify the Crown Court five days before the expiry of the time-limit, and, if they wanted bail conditions imposed, inform the prisoner accordingly. Also they had to bring the detainee before the Crown Court two days before the time-limit expired, so that the Crown Court could fulfil its statutory duty of granting bail in accordance with the Bail Act 1976. The Crown Prosecution Service did not comply with these obligations and instead did nothing. The Court of Appeal held that a prison governor who obeyed a warrant of commitment which was valid on its face could not be sued for false imprisonment. In that case, after 112 days the plaintiff's right was not to be released by the prison authorities but merely to be granted bail by the Crown Court; and, until that happened, she was in the custody of the Crown Court and the governor was under a duty to keep her incarcerated. As for the Crown Prosecution Service, as a matter of public policy their failure to act could not give rise to any liability. From October 2000, a prisoner detained in the same circumstances as Mr Olotu almost certainly has a right of action for damages by virtue of the Human Rights Act 1998, s 7(1); see Chapter 17. The European

---

1   (1903) LT 629.
2   (1879) 4 Ex D 73.
3   [1997] 1 WLR 328.

Convention on Human Rights will certainly regard as unlawful the keeping of a prisoner in captivity after the period laid down in the 1987 Regulations has expired, unless this extra detention has been authorised by a judicial authority.

If the detention is by a judicial authority within his jurisdiction (ie an order which he has power to make), then no action will lie in trespass against anybody, no matter how it was brought about – whether by perjury or through malice. A High Court judge has unlimited jurisdiction. In *Vickerstaff v Edbro Ltd*[1], Potter LJ stated:

> 'Suffice it to say that the order for imprisonment was regularly made before a judge for proved disobedience to an extant order of the court. As such, it cannot be the subject of an action of false imprisonment according to our law.'

In *Clarke v Chief Constable of Northamptonshire*[2], the plaintiff was arrested by the police on 10 April under a warrant of commitment for nine days for non-payment of a fine. A constable took him to a prison on the 13 April but the warrant was endorsed with that date as the one on which he had been apprehended. Therefore, he was detained until the 22 April, when he should have been released on 19 April. The Court of Appeal was of the opinion that the prison authorities accordingly were liable for false imprisonment, although this was said *obiter* in a judgment upholding a finding of negligence against the defendant for having informed the prison authorities of the wrong date on which the plaintiff had first been taken into custody.

There is also statutory immunity in certain cases when dealing with military, naval or airforce prisoners (see **11.6**).

In *R v Marylebone Magistrates' Court, ex parte Amdrell (t/a Get Stuffed)*[3], Rose LJ and Bell J were not enamoured by the fact that in certain high profile cases the police alerted the press to the fact that a warrant was going to be executed, which, of course, assured the attendance of the newspaper reporters at the arrest. Nevertheless, such a practice did not give rise to any illegality *actus legis nemini facit injuria* (see *Barker v Leister*[4]).

13.6.6   Backing of warrants

A warrant of arrest for an indictable offence issued by an Irish, Scottish or Channel Island magistrate or judge can be executed here if 'backed', ie if, but only if, the back of the warrant is signed to that effect by a justice of the peace, see the Indictable Offences Act 1848, ss 13 and 32. This requirement must be strictly complied with, see *R v Metropolitan Police Commissioner, ex parte Melia*[5] where it was held that pinning a signed form to the back was not sufficient.

---

1   (Unreported) 7 April 1997.
2   (1999) 149 NLJ 899.
3   96 (24) LSG 38.
4   (1859) 7 CB (NS) 190, per Byles J.
5   [1957] 3 All ER 440.

13.6.7   Constables Protection Act 1750

Under s 5 of the Constables Protection Act 1750, no legal action can be brought against any constable, headborough or other officer (for example a jailer; see *Butts v Norman*[1]) or any person acting by his order and in his aid for anything done pursuant to a warrant issued by a justice of the peace (including a district judge (magistrate's court)), unless a written and signed demand by the proposed plaintiff or his agent has been made to the proposed defendant at his place of abode to see the warrant and take a copy thereof and that demand has not been complied with within 6 days of its making. (A request for a copy specifying a shorter time is valid, save that the time specified is void; see *Collins v Ross*[2].) If the requirement is complied with and a writ issued, then judgment must be entered for the defendant, notwithstanding any want of jurisdiction by the said justice, but only for anything done which was expressly or impliedly authorised by the warrant. The Act gives no protection to, for example, the unauthorised execution of a warrant outside the jurisdiction; see *Milton v Green*[3]. A person can take the benefit of the Act even if the demand for the warrant is met outside the 6 days allowed by the statute, provided it is complied with prior to the writ being issued; see *Jones v Vaughn*[4]. It should be noted that the protection given applies only where the warrant has been issued by a justice of the peace or district judge (magistrates' court) and not anybody else, for example judges of the superior courts; see *Gladwell v Blake*[5].

The Act does not absolve liability for a wrongful execution of the warrant. In *Horsfield v Brown*[6] the plaintiff was arrested by a policeman who did not have the warrant in his possession. He was taken to the station and detained until the next day when (as the warrant ordered) he was brought before the court. The warrant was invalid, because it did not state that if he discharged the sum owing under a maintenance order, he should be released. McNaughton J held that there should be an award of damages for the initial arrest because of the incorrect mode of execution (ie the arrester did not have the warrant with him) but none for the detention at the police station (where the warrant was located). This was because the enforced stay at the station was just what the warrant had ordered, so that s 5 applied, even though the warrant was bad on its face at it did not state that that the prisoner had to be set free if he paid the money – which was, in fact, tendered to the police both by his father and his solicitor.

Nor does the Act offer any protection if somebody other than the person named in the warrant is detained. See *Hoye v Bush*[7], where Richard Hoye was arrested (as the magistrate intended) instead of John Hoye, the name on the warrant.

---

1   (1819) Gow 97.
2   (1839) 5 M & W 194.
3   (1804) 5 East 233.
4   (1804) 5 East 445.
5   (1834) 1 Cr M & R 636.
6   [1932] 1 KB 355.
7   (1840) 1 Man & G 775.

13.6.8 Ministerial officers

A person who works in a merely ministerial capacity to the judiciary is not liable in tort just because he signs or draws up an unlawful warrant issued by a member of the judiciary. Such people include county court clerks (see *Dews v Riley*[1]) and clerks of the peace (see *Demer v Cook*[2]) It is otherwise if he takes part in its execution.

13.6.9 University policemen

Constables who are appointed by the chancellor or vice-chancellor or the pro- or deputy vice-chancellors of Oxford or Cambridge and who are members of one of those universities cannot claim any of the privileges attaching to such membership if sued for any act done in the execution of their office (see the University Act 1825, s 1).

13.6.10 County court bailiffs and those assisting them

Under s 123 of the County Courts Act 1984, a district judge is made liable for the acts of his county court bailiffs to the same extent as a sheriff is for his officers, (see below). The bailiffs (and those acting by their order and in aid of them) when acting in obedience to a district judge's warrant are given (by s 126) the same immunity as policemen have under the Constables Protection Act 1750, ie no action can be instituted against them unless a written and signed document has been left at their office, requesting an inspection of, and a copy of, the warrant; and that request was not complied with within 6 days of its making. Also, s 126(3) specifically states that this immunity from suit applies not only to a defect of jurisdiction in the district judge, but also to 'any other irregularity in the warrant'.

13.6.11 Sheriffs

Under s 15 of the Sheriffs Act 1887 ('SA 1887'), any person unlawfully imprisoned by a sheriff or any of his officers acting in the course of their duty is given a statutory right to sue the sheriff for damages for his incarceration. This applies even if the tort is committed contrary to the sheriff's express orders (see *Scarfe v Hallifax*[3]), but he is not liable if his officer was not purporting to act under his authority, for example *Smith v Pritchard*[4], where the High Bailiff of a county court was held not liable for the trespass of his bailiff when the latter made the arrest, not by virtue of his warrant, but under an assertion of a statutory power given to an individual officer.

As to the limitation period, see **15.2**.

---

1   (1851) 11 CB 434.
2   (1903) LT 629.
3   (1840) 7 M and W 288.
4   (1849) 8 CB 565.

13.6.12   Diplomats and members of international organisations

Various statutes have been passed to grant the above-mentioned people and their households diplomatic immunity for all torts committed in the United Kingdom.

Chapter 14

REMEDIES FOR FALSE IMPRISONMENT

14.1 INTRODUCTION

The are two remedies for false imprisonment. The first is a writ of *habeas corpus* to secure the release of somebody who is being unlawfully detained. In addition, such a person can seek to recover damages in an action for trespass. In *Dumbell v Roberts*[1], Scott LJ said:

> '... the double-sided interest of the public in the liberty of the individual as well as the detection of crime. For that reason, just as it is of importance that nobody should be arrested by the police except on grounds which in the particular circumstances of the arrest really justify the entertainment of a reasonable suspicion, so also it is the public interest that sufficient damages should follow in such a case in order to give reality to the protection afforded by law. Personal freedom depends upon the enforcement of personal rights; and the primary personal right, apart from *habeas corpus*, is the common law right of action for damages for trespass to the person, which is called "false imprisonment" just because it is for a trespass which has involved interference with personal freedom. By the common law there is no fixed measure of damages for such an interference when unjustifiable because the damages are at large, and in so far as they represent the disapproval of the law – historically of a jury – for improper interference with personal freedom they may be "punitive" or "exemplary", given by way of punishment of the defendant or as a deterrent example, and they are not limited to compensation for the plaintiff's loss.'

14.2 *HABEAS CORPUS*

This is a speedy remedy to enable a prisoner to obtain his release. If it is shown that a person is being incarcerated without justification, the High Court will issue a writ of *habeas corpus ad subjiciendum*, ordering the body of the prisoner to be brought before it. It will then decide whether or not to order his release. The writ was described by Blackstone[2] as follows:

> 'The great and efficacious writ in all manner of illegal confinements is that of *habeas corpus ad subjiciendum*, directed to the person detaining another, and commanding him to produce to the court the body of the prisoner with the day and cause of his caption and detention ...'

The *Manual of Military Law*[3] describes the writ thus:

> 'Any person who is detained in what he conceives to be illegal custody by order of a court martial or other military authority can apply for a writ of *habeas corpus ad*

---

1   [1944] 1 All ER 326 at 329.
2   14th edn, vol 3 at p 131.
3   9th edn, vol 2, Part IVA at p 413.

subjiciendum. The writ is the most celebrated in English law, being the constitutional remedy for a person wrongfully deprived of his liberty. It is addressed to
the person who detains another in custody and commands him to produce and
"have the body" of the prisoner before the court to "undergo and receive" whatever
the court considers proper. It issues out of the Divisional Court[1] of the Queen's
Bench of the High Court of Justice and into all parts of the Queen's Dominion
except that, by the Habeas Corpus Act 1860, s 1, "No writ of habeas corpus shall
issue out of England by authority of any judge or court of justice therein, into any
colony or foreign dominion of the Crown where Her Majesty has a lawfully
established court of justice having authority to issue the said writ and to ensure the
due execution thereof".

   The person to whom it is addressed must make a "return" to the writ stating why
he holds the prisoner in custody; and upon consideration of such return the
prisoner is either discharged or if the return shows sufficient cause for the
detention in custody, is remanded to custody or is admitted to bail.'

However, the court is concerned only with whether there exists jurisdiction for
the detention. If such exists, the writ will not be issued; there will be no inquiry
into how that jurisdiction was exercised, for example the sufficiency of the
evidence. A more liberal approach may well be called for by HRA 1998, see
17.5. On the other hand, a writ will lie if an inferior court did not have power to
try the offence or to impose the sentence which it did. In *R v Suddis*[2], Grose J
said[3]:

   'It is enough that we find such a sentence pronounced by a court of competent
   jurisdiction to inquire into the offence and with power to inflict such a sentence; as
   to the rest we must presume *omnia rite acta.*'

The writ can be applied for by a friend of the prisoner; see *Re Ning Yi-Ching*[4], but
the application must usually be made by counsel; see *Re Green*[5]. Prior to 1960, if
the application was refused by one judge, it could be made to another. Now a
second application can be made only if fresh evidence is adduced (see the
Administration of Justice Act 1960, s 14(2)), which the applicant could not
reasonably have been expected to have put forward at the original hearing (see
Re Tarling[6]).

14.3   DAMAGES

A person who has had his liberty unlawfully interfered with is presumed to have
suffered harm and is entitled to recover damages. They are four types of
damages:

(1) general or basic;
(2) aggravated;

---

1   Under s 65(1)(a) of the Access to Justice Act 1999, these applications can be heard by a
     single judge, see *Trew v Chase Farm Hospital* (unreported) 17 May 2000.
2   (1801) 1 East 306.
3   Ibid, at 315.
4   (1939) 56 TLR 3.
5   (1941) 57 TLR 533.
6   [1979] 1 All ER 981.

(3) exemplary or punitive; and

(4) special.

In *Thompson v Metropolitan Police Commissioner*[1], Lord Woolf MR said that a jury should be instructed to make a separate award for each category.

14.3.1   General damages

14.3.1.1   *Definition*

General or (to quote Lord Woolf MR in *Thompson v Metropolitan Police Commissioner*, above) basic damages are intended to compensate the claimant, so far as money can do. In *R v Governor of Brockhill Prison, ex parte Evans (No 2)*[2], Lord Woolf MR said:

> '... there can be two elements to an award of [basic] damages for false imprisonment; the first being compensation for loss of liberty and the second being the damage to reputation, humiliation, shock, injury to feeling and so on which can result from the loss of liberty.'

If a jury were to consider the amount of the basic award to be inadequate, they may be able to give in addition aggravated and/or exemplary damages, topics dealt with in **14.3.2** and **14.3.3** respectively.

14.3.1.2   *Court of Appeal guidelines on quantum*

Section 8(2) of the Courts and Legal Services Act 1990 for the first time allowed an appellate court to substitute its own award for that of 12 good men and true when it allowed an appeal of quantum. Previously, unless both litigants consented, it had no discretion but to order a re-trial. Consequently, there was no 'tariff', nor any judicial pronouncement by a higher court on the appropriate level of damages. That has now changed with the landmark decision of *Thompson v Metropolitan Police Commissioner*, above, when the Court of Appeal laid down guidance for those juries whose task it was to award damages against their tortious captors.

In *Thompson v Metropolitan Police Commissioner*, above, the Master of the Rolls was of the opinion[3] that the first hour should attract general damages of £500 with an increase as the duration of the incarceration increased, but of smaller proportions, reaching £3,000 for somebody who had been locked up for 24 hours. Thereafter, the daily rate would be on a progressively reducing scale.

In *Gerald v Metropolitan Police Commissioner*[4], Auld LJ said:

> 'The *Thompson* guidelines as to amount are not a rigid code and are not to be applied in a mechanistic manner; they do no more than provide for jury directions as to normal brackets for basic damages and maxima for aggravated and exemplary damages.'

---

1   [1998] QB 498 at 516D.

2   [1999] QB 1043 at 1060A.

3   [1998] QB 498 at 515, para 5.

4   (1998) TLR, 26 June.

That statement was approved in *Sutton v Metropolitan Police Commissioner*[1], where the Court of Appeal refused to interfere when the trial judge summed up that the figure of £500 per hour for basic damages was a 'starting point … [from which] they could go up or down'.

These views of the judiciary on fair compensation should be compared to those of 12 citizens chosen at random. They made an award of £1,500 basic damages to a prisoner who was in lawful custody but had been handcuffed, without reasonable cause, on his journey from the police station to the court cells. At the cells his hands had been freed, but later on he was again restrained in a similar fashion while he was being taken to the dock; see *Laine v Chief Constable of Cambridge*[2].

In *Ex parte Evans (No 2)*, above, the Court of Appeal was of the view that for detentions exceeding a certain (unspecified) period a global approach should be taken. In the words of Lord Woolf MR[3]:

> 'We recognise that it is possible to work out a daily, weekly or monthly figure from this amount for the approximate 2 months' extra imprisonment of this case but we discourage such an exercise. No two cases are the same. The shorter the period, the larger can be the *pro rata* rate. The longer the period, the lower the *pro rata* rate.'

14.3.1.3 Applying the guidelines – arrests lasting no more than a day

In *Clark v Chief Constable of Cleveland*[4], the appeal court refused to interfere with an award of £750 for unlawful incarceration and £150 for the slight injuries received in the course of the arrest. Roch LJ stated:

> 'The award of £750 for wrongful arrest and false imprisonment in arresting and detaining him was, although at the bottom of the bracket of permissible awards, adequate compensation for a person who had been arrested without the use of unreasonable force and detained for a little under 5 hours, when for at least 2 hours of that period he had been asleep and for approximately half of that period he was being interviewed.'

The author would merely comment:

(1) why should the jury have awarded damages for assault if no unreasonable force had been used; and

(2) surely being subjected to hostile questioning is an aggravating and not a mitigating factor.

In *Barnet and Wilkinson v Chief Constable of West Yorkshire*[5], the plaintiffs had been lawfully apprehended on suspicion of being in possession of prohibited drugs. After 6 hours at the police station, the police realised that they had no case against them. Instead of releasing them, they were rearrested for conspiracy to cause a public nuisance. The trial judge held that there were no grounds to justify that second incarceration. Thus, Barnet was unlawfully detained for 11

---

1   (Unreported) 29 July 1998.
2   (Unreported) 14 October 1999.
3   [1999] QB 1043 at 1060F/G.
4   (1999) 96 (21) LSG 28.
5   (Unreported) 24 April 1998.

hours and 15 minutes and Wilkinson for 12 hours and 30 minutes. The Court of Appeal increased the jury's award from £200 each to £600 for Barnett and £400 for his co-plaintiff. The distinction was because the former was in effect of good character while the latter had previous experience of prisons (including an 8-year sentence) and was well used to being arrested, with seven convictions. The Court recognised that damages for this tort are 'front loaded', so here there could be no claim for the initial shock of being apprehended and locked up in a cell. Also the false imprisonment occurred mainly at night which was occupied by sleep, (which it will be remembered was described by Oscar Wilde in *The Ballad of Reading Gaol* as the 'prisoner's friend'). In *Gerald v Metropolitan Police Commissioner*[1], the Court of Appeal assessed the basic damages for 2 hours and 45 minutes of false imprisonment at £1,500. The plaintiff was a man of good character (ie had no previous experience of being detained). An element of the damages was the public nature of the arrest, ie in front of his friends, and the fact that he was in pain throughout his detention. (The Court of Appeal assessed the damages for his assault at £8,000 in accordance with the guidance issued by the Judicial Studies' Board.)

In *Roberts v Chief Constable of Cheshire*[2], the plaintiff had been lawfully arrested but the police reviewed his custody too late. For that illegal detention, the trial judge had awarded £500 damages. Although there was no appeal on quantum, Clarke LJ stated:

> 'I would only add this. A sum of £500 is substantially more than I would have awarded to compensate the respondent for false imprisonment for a period of 2 hours 20 minutes during which he was asleep, especially in circumstances that if a review had been carried out at 5.25 am, his detention would have been lawful.'

However, the last two lines of the above quotation must be read in the context of his Lordship's earlier rejection of the defendant's argument that because the plaintiff would have been lawfully detained if a review had been carried out, and as there was no allegation of *mala fides*, the plaintiff was entitled only to receive nominal damages.

In *Samuels v Commissioner of Police*[3] the appellate court reversed the trial judge's ruling on liability and then assessed the damages for about 3 hours and 30 minutes' incarceration at £1,000. The plaintiff had been arrested and handcuffed in his front garden, but this had been witnessed only by his mother and had not been seen by any of his neighbours. In *Cumber v Chief Constable of Hampshire Constabulary*[4], the Court of Appeal awarded a 16-year-old girl of good character £350 for just under 4 hours and 30 minutes of unlawful detention by the local constabulary. In *Goswell v Metropolitian Police Commissioner*[5] and *Frewin v Metropolitan Police Commissioner*[6], both plaintiffs had both been detained for 20 minutes before being told why they had been apprehended. The Court of

---

1   (1998) TLR, 26 June.
2   [1999] 1 WLR 662.
3   (Unreported) 3 March 1999.
4   [1995] LS Gaz 39.
5   (Unreported) 7 April 1998.
6   (Unreported) 1990 (Popplewell J).

Appeal awarded the first plaintiff £100, whilst, eight years earlier, a jury had given Mr Fruween £1,000. In the latter case, after his captivity had become lawful, he had to spend another 14 hours at the station before being released without charge.

14.3.1.4 *Juries*

However, it must be remembered that juries do not award large amounts of money if they consider the matter to be trivial. They are not overpowered by the thought that they have to give enormous sums to every victim of some tortious act. In *Clarke v Chief Constable of West Midlands*[1], the Court of Appeal refused a motorist leave to appeal against an award of £1, with no order as to costs. He had been asked to undergo a breath test and had been required to wait at the scene in the back of a locked police car until the equipment arrived, which in fact showed his alcohol level to be below the prescribed limit. He had parked his car on an open space with grass in order to exercise his dog. Police officers present took the erroneous view that he was under the influence of drink and 'over the permissible limit'. The basis on which liability was established is not revealed in the report, presumably it was that the facts did not give rise to a reasonable suspicion of having consumed alcohol and (to quote Butler-Sloss LJ) he had been held against his will. Most likely he had been threatened with arrest for failing to take the test if he were to try to leave before being breathalysed. Henry LJ said:

> 'It is clear from the orders that they had made [as to damages and costs] both the jury and the Judge indicated that in their view it was a storm in a tea cup. They were there, they heard the evidence; they were entitled to take that view. Any appeal is doomed to failure given the primacy of the jury in our system.'

In *Kay and Helm v James and Peacock*[2], a jury awarded 10p each to two buskers who had been wrongly arrested under the London Transport by-laws on a stationary tube train at St James Park and had been detained in a room at that underground station for about 30 minutes during which time they had engaged in a friendly discussion with British Transport police officers, the main topic being the railway by-laws. The award was made on the basis of the judge's summing up that the jury could award nominal damages if they thought that the plaintiffs had brought their incarceration upon themselves. In *Holden v Chief Constable of Lancashire*[3], a similar mistake in the judge's address to the jury led to an award of £5. There the plaintiff went with some friends to Blackpool. They were acting highly suspiciously which resulted in their arrest and detention for 20 minutes. The plaintiff had a criminal record and had twice before sued for false imprisonment, which latter fact led Judge Morris-Jones QC to invite the jury to consider whether on the night in question he and his companions were 'trailing their coats'. (In both those cases, the judge had of course misdirected the jury[4] and new trials were ordered on appeal, but the actions were then settled out of court.)

---

1   (Unreported) 18 December 1998.
2   (Unreported) 21 April 1989.
3   [1987] QB 380.
4   See **14.7**.

Although due to the same error in the summings up, these cases clearly indicate that juries award large sums only when they think that they are deserved and not where the plaintiff's own conduct has contributed to his unlawful confinement or where the incident giving rise to the liability was trivial.

14.3.1.5 Present-day awards compared with those awarded pre the Thompson case

Anybody who believes in the liberty of the individual can only wish that Pratt CJ was still on the Bench. In *Huckle v Money*[1], he would have awarded £20 basic damages to a journeyman printer earning a guinea a week who had been kept in custody under an illegal general warrant by the Secretary of State for about 6 hours. The defendant had 'very civilly and well treated him', feeding him with beefsteak and beer. A guinea in those days was far more than the average weekly wage, which is now about £400. To apply the same multiplier to today's average earnings, he recovered the equivalent of about £7,000, ie about £1,000 an hour, or well over double what today's judges would have given him. All the above damages were calculated on the basis of what sum would represent fair compensation for the injury suffered. A similar 'damages/duration ratio' (allowing for inflation) received the approval of Purchas LJ in *Castorina v Chief Constable of Surrey*[2] where he could see nothing wrong with an award of £4,500 (ie about a £1,000 per hour of incarceration) in a case where there were no aggravating features. As the judgment on liability was reversed, no comment whatsoever was made about the quantum by the other two members of the tribunal (Woolf LJ and The Rt Hon Sir Frederick Lawton).

In *Kuchenmeister v Home Office*[3] (for the facts see **2.1**), Barry J said[4]:

'No pecuniary damage has been suffered but the very precious right of liberty – which is a right available to everyone who can for the time being be regarded as a subject by local allegiance to Her Majesty – is one which must be protected. I think that a fair figure which will vindicate the plaintiff's rights without amounting to a vindictive award would be £150. I should have felt fully entitled to increase that amount to a very great extent if there had been any suggestion here that the plaintiff was being ill treated by any of the immigration officials but I am quite satisfied that they all genuinely considered that they were doing the best possible thing in difficult circumstances, and in my judgment no blame of any kind rests upon them.'

That sum of £150 in today's money would be about £2,000. At first sight, this is in line with the view of the present Court of Appeal for that length of incarceration but Mr Kuchenmeister's detention was 11 hours in the transit lounge at Heathrow Airport at night-time, a far more welcoming place than a police cell, especially when, in the latter case, the inmate has almost nearly always already suffered the indignity of having been arrested for a crime he did not commit.

---

1   (1763) 2 Wil 205.
2   (1988) NLJ (R)180.
3   [1958] 1 QB 496.
4   Ibid, at 513.

14.3.1.6   The guidelines – incarcerations lasting more than 24 hours

In *Ex parte Evans (No 2)*, above, the respondent had miscalculated the applicant's date of release from her 2-year prison sentence and had kept her incarcerated for 59 days longer than he ought to have done. At first instance, Collins J was of the opinion that the correct amount of damages was £2,000 (which is the equivalent of £33 per day). The appeal court took a more generous view and assessed them at £5,000, ie a figure of just under £100 per day. That relatively low amount was justified on the basis that the claim was for not having been released 2 months earlier, as she should have been, after she had served over a year in prison. Thus, at the time of the commission of the tort, the plaintiff was totally accustomed to her loss of liberty and suffered none of the trauma normally felt by a prisoner when he or she is initially locked up in a cell. Accordingly, the length of her lawful sentence was a relevant consideration, as was the fact that she was prepared to risk losing her remission by committing disciplinary offences. The House of Lords[1] declined to interfere with the award. That case must be contrasted with *Lunt v Liverpool City Justices*[2], where the turning of the key for the first time in the cell door was the reason why, on appeal, the damages for 42 days' false imprisonment were increased from £13,500 to £25,000. In that case, the plaintiff was a man of good character and none of his detention was justified. In the words of Bingham LJ, such an experience in those circumstances was 'horrific'. In *Perks et al v UK*[3], the European Court of Human Rights awarded £5,500 plus costs for 6 days' unlawful incarceration in a prison to which the applicant had been confined for non-payment of the community charge.

14.3.2   Aggravated damages

14.3.2.1   Definition

In *Gerald v Commissioner of Police*[4], Lord Woolf gave his views on the role of aggravated damages:

> 'Guideline (no 8) in *Thompson* is that the role of aggravated damages, where appropriate, is to compensate for additional harm other than physical or mental injury resulting from the manner of the wrong, whatever its nature. That included humiliation or affront to dignity but was not confined to those features.
>
>   Trauma falling short of physical or mental injury seems to fall conveniently and more appropriately into [this] category.'

At first sight, he appears to be advocating exactly the same criteria for deciding on whether or not to make an award of aggravated damages as he had done when laying down the matters to be taken into account when quantifying the amount of basic damages. (The latter having been done only 9 days earlier in *Ex parte Evans*; see above). However, these apparently contradictory statements must be read in the context of the facts of the cases in which they were made. Compensation for the humiliation caused by being imprisoned as a result of a

---

1   [2000] 3 WLR 843.
2   (Unreported) 5 March 1991.
3   (1999) 30 EHRR 33.
4   10 June 1998, very briefly reported in (1998) TLR, 26 June. For the facts, see **14.3.3.2**.

bona fide mistake should be part of the basic damages, but it would be otherwise if a police officer taunted his prisoner with racial insults. The extra suffering caused by this needless humiliation would aggravate the damages entitling the jury to make an extra award. This is because aggravated damages are to compensate for the additional harm suffered by a claimant when the defendant deliberately inflicts extra suffering when he commits his tort, over and above what is strictly necessary to achieve his objective. The following definition is given by the editor of *Halsbury's Laws*[1]:

> 'In the first and strict sense of the word the defendant's motives, conduct or manner of inflicting the injury may have aggravated the plaintiff's damages by injuring his proper feelings of dignity and pride.'

14.3.2.2   The conduct of the defence in court

In *Gerald v Metropolitan Police Commissioner*, above, the Court of Appeal held it not to be an aggravating factor that, despite the acquittal at the Crown Court, the defendant had relied upon his officers' truthfulness and sought their vindication in the civil proceedings. That was contrary to a long line of cases which have held that the jury can take into account the whole of the conduct of the tortfeasor up to the date of the trial, including his manner of conducting the latter, for example *Cassell and Co Ltd v Broome*[2]. In view of the pronouncements in the latter case in the House of Lords, the dicta in *Gerald* must be regarded as erroneous.

14.3.2.3   Quantum

In *Thompson v Metropolitan Police Commissioner*, Lord Woolf MR pronounced[3]:

> '(10) We consider that where it is appropriate to award aggravated damages the figure is unlikely to be less than a £1,000. We do not think it is possible to indicate a precise arithmetical relationship between basic damages and aggravated damages because the circumstances will vary from case to case. In the ordinary way, however, we do not expect the aggravated damages to be as much as twice the basic damages except perhaps where, on the particular facts, the basic damages are modest.
>
> (11) It should be strongly emphasised to the jury that the total figure for basic and aggravated damages should not exceed what they consider is fair compensation for the injury which the plaintiff has suffered. It should also be explained that if aggravated damages are awarded such damages, though compensatory are not intended as a punishment, will in fact contain a penal element as far as the defendant is concerned.'

In *Sallows v Griffiths*[4] the Court of Appeal upheld the award, by the judge at first instance, of £10,000 basic and aggravated damages for 4 hours' false imprisonment. A director had told the police malicious falsehoods about his fellow director, which led to the latter's arrest. The basis of the award was:

---

1   4th edn, vol 12, para 1186.

2   [1972] AC 1027, per Lord Hailsham LC (at 1071), per Lord Reid (at 1085) and per Lord Diplock (at 1125).

3   [1998] QB 498 at 516.

4   (Unreported) 25 November 1999.

(1) £4,000 for injury to his feelings, including the anxiety he felt during the 6 months the charges were hanging over him before they were discontinued;
(2) £5,000 to compensate him for his inability to obtain employment during that period; and
(3) £1,000 aggravated damages.

The Court of Appeal appears to have overlooked the fact that the claimant only lost his freedom for 4 hours. Compensation for any injury which had not been caused by that time was not recoverable in his action for trespass but flowed from his prosecution; and could only be recovered, if at all, in an action for malicious prosecution.

14.3.3   Exemplary damages

14.3.3.1   Their purpose and scope

In *Rookes v Barnard*[1] the House of Lords (per Lord Devlin) adopted the view of Professor Harry Street and held[2] that where a holder of an office under the Crown (which includes a constable) was guilty of 'oppressive, arbitrary or unconstitutional conduct', then exemplary damages may be awarded by a jury to act as a deterrent and to mark their disapproval of what has occurred if, but only if, the basic and aggravated damages were not sufficient for this purpose. In *Holden v Chief Constable of Lancashire*[3], the Court of Appeal held that the use of the word 'or' by Lord Devlin was disjunctive, so that any of the three types of conduct individually could attract an award of exemplary damages; and (following Pratt CJ in *Huckle v Money*[4]) that an arrest was contrary to *Magna Carta* and, therefore, unconstitutional. That decision is binding on the Court of Appeal; see *Young v Bristol Aeroplane Company*[5]. However, in *Sutton v Metropolitan Police Commissioner*[6], Kennedy LJ said *obiter*:

> 'With all due deference to the approach adopted by Purchas LJ [in *Holden*], I doubt if Lord Devlin intended his words to be construed disjunctively as though they formed part of a statute ...'

That was not how Lord Diplock understood the *dicta* of Lord Devlin, according to what he said in *Cassell and Co Ltd v Broome*[7] about when exemplary damages can be awarded:

> 'The first category comprised cases of abuse of an official position of authority ... It would not appear that the actual conduct of the defendant himself need justify an award of aggravated damages. In *Huckle v Money* (1763) 2 Wils 205 [for the facts see below] the defendant appears to have treated the plaintiff with courtesy and consideration. The servant was the whipping-boy for the political head of the government. Nor need he have known that his act was wrongful. Money, a mere

---

1   [1964] AC 1129.
2   Ibid, at 1226.
3   [1987] QB 380.
4   (1763) 2 Wil 205.
5   [1944] KB 718.
6   (Unreported) 29 July 1998.
7   [1972] AC 1027 at 1128 G/H.

subordinate official, can hardly have been expected to know that general warrants issued by the Secretary of State were illegal.'

In view of the above quotation from the speech of Lord Diplock, it is submitted that Lord Devlin's words were correctly interpreted by Arnold P and Purchas LJ. Indeed, one is tempted to ask why would Lord Devlin use the word 'or' as conjunctive, rather than the word 'and'. However, clearly the views of these Law Lords and Family Division judges are not regarded as binding by those who sit in the Queen's Bench Division. In *Marsorella v Chief Constable of Hampshire*[1], there had been reasonable suspicion justifying the apprehension of the claimant, but it was alleged that he was not told why he was being locked up and that his 4 hours' detention was too long. Exemplary damages were sought, *inter alia*, because in his interview the police had misrepresented to the claimant the evidence of a witness and had falsely asserted that a footprint found at the *locus in quo* matched the pattern on his footwear. Schiemann LJ upheld the striking out of the claim for exemplary damages with the simple comment:

'In my judgment, the pleaded case goes nowhere near to justifying such a claim.'

However, no decision of the supreme appellate court was cited. What is rather surprising is that the family judge sitting with him concurred (without giving any reasons), rather than upholding the decision of a former President of his division. The correct view is surely the advice of the Privy Council in *Hussien v Chong Fook Kam*[2]:

'The court is not in this category of case confined to awarding compensation for loss of liberty and for such physical and mental distress as it thinks may have been caused. It is also proper for it to mark any departure from constitutional practice, even if only a slight one, by exemplary damages: but these do not have to be large ... The Board approves also of what was said on this topic by Scott LJ in *Dumbell v Roberts* [1944] 1 All ER 326. In particular, the Lord Justice said, at p 329:

"The more high-handed and less reasonable the detention is, the higher may be the damages; and, conversely, the more nearly reasonably the defendant may have acted and the nearer he may have to justification on reasonable grounds for the suspicion on which he arrested, the smaller will be the proper assessment." '

In that case, two of the defendants were police officers directly concerned in the arrest while the third was the Government of Malaya. The Privy Council said:

'Nothing turned on the separate responsibility of any of the appellants, and the action can be described as one brought against the police.'

Those sentiments are, it is submitted, preferable to those expressed by the court in *Thompson*, above (which did not have the benefit of either *Hussien* or *Dumbell* being cited to it)[3]:

'... it is more difficult to justify an award [of exemplary damages] where the defendant and the person responsible for meeting any award is not the wrongdoer, but his "employer". While it is possible that a chief constable could bear a

---

1 (Unreported) 29 June 1999.
2 [1970] AC 942 at 950.
3 [1998] QB 498 at 512H per Lord Woolf MR.

responsibility for what has happened due to his failure to exercise proper control, the instances when this is alleged to have occurred should not be frequent.'

Is not an excellent way of stopping people being wrongly locked up by the police to make the latter pay through their pockets for such torts? In *Thompson*, above, Lord Woolf MR did also say[1]:

'... (c) that an award of exemplary damages is in effect a windfall for the plaintiff and, where damages will be payable out of police funds, the sum awarded may not be available to be expended by the police in a way which would benefit the public (this guidance would not be appropriate if the claim were to be met by insurers); ...

As punishment is the primary object in this class of case it is more difficult to tie the amount of exemplary damages to the award of compensatory damages, including aggravated[2]. ...

... the sum awarded by way of exemplary damages should be sufficient to mark the jury's disapproval of the arbitrary behaviour but should be no more than is required for this purpose.'[3]

It is surely worth a high price and is not a misuse of public money to ensure that innocent people are not incarcerated for no good reason. Indeed, bearing in mind the way most judges assess damages, one who did not know better might think that the money came out of their own pockets.

It is submitted that until the members of the House of Lords rule that their noble and learned friends misunderstood the law in the two cases mentioned above, the position is that it is entirely up to '12 good men (and women) and true' to decide whether or not such an award is to be made, after taking into account the conduct of the parties and the claimant's antecedents. They have an unfettered discretion whenever the paying party is a police officer. This seems to have been grudgingly recognised by the judges in *Gerald*, above, where they approved of the views expressed by Simon Brown LJ in *Goswell v Commissioner of Police*[4]:

'Exemplary damages here present particular difficulties. It is the appellant Commissioner who will pay the damages out of police funds, yet it is for the gross misconduct of his junior officer that he is to be punished.' [It is submitted that the deletion of the word 'gross' would give a more accurate statement of the law.]

... it seems to me that what the court (generally the jury but now us) is required to do is to mark its disapproval of the oppressive or arbitrary conduct in question, tempering its outrage, of course, with the thought that the exemplary damages constitute a windfall for the plaintiff and a depletion of police funds to the possible disadvantage of the general public.'

14.3.3.2 *Judicial awards*
The Master of Rolls in *Thompson*, above, also considered the quantum of exemplary damages[5]:

1　　[1998] QB 498 at 517A/B.
2　　Ibid, at 518A.
3　　Ibid, at 517B.
4　　(Unreported) 7 April 1998.
5　　[1998] QB 498 at 517.

'(13) Where exemplary damages are appropriate they are unlikely to be less than £5,000. Otherwise the case is probably not one which justifies an award of exemplary damages at all. In this class of action the conduct must be particularly deserving of condemnation for an award of as much as £25,000 to be justified and the figure of £50,000 should be regarded as the absolute maximum, involving directly officers of at least the rank of superintendent.'

In *Sutton v Metropolitan Police Commissioner*, above, the trial judge wrongly failed to leave the question of exemplary damages to the jury. The Court of Appeal held that as the damages awarded were less than £5,000, the 'case is probably not one which justifies exemplary damages'. So the Court of Appeal upheld the jury's award. In that case, the first plaintiff's incarceration had been about 3 hours and the jury had found that the police had acted in good faith. So, on the facts of that case, the jury probably would not have awarded exemplary damages, even if that option had been left to them. It is submitted that a day's incarceration is another matter. Basic damages would be only £3,000 (ie £2,000 less than £5,000), but it is submitted that false imprisonments of 24 hours must be discouraged and that a jury would be perfectly entitled to give exemplary damages if they thought that such an award might act as a deterrent and thus help to prevent such illegal incarcerations in the future. The Court of Appeal did hold that the trial judge had been wrong to tell the jury not to award exemplary damages for the assault to the third plaintiff, but in view of the amount they actually awarded (£1,000 compensatory and £2,250 aggravated damages), that appeal was also dismissed for the same reasons.

In *Hsu v Metropolitan Police Commissioner*[1], two constables had unlawfully broken into the plaintiff's residence, wrongly arrested him, subjected him to racial abuse and assaulted him so that 3 years later he was still suffering from some symptoms of post-traumatic stress disorder. The appellate court refused to interfere with the award, in total, of £20,000 basic and aggravated damages. (In the author's experience, juries have always regarded trespass in a person's home as far more serious than a wrongful arrest.) However, the lords justices also reduced the £200,000 exemplary damages to £15,000, because the whole incident had only lasted a few hours and aggravated damages had been recovered. One might not agree with the amount, but can it really be said that the jury's award was unreasonable bearing in mind that it was intended to act as a deterrent and to mark its disapproval? The adequacy of that sum can be judged by the fact that the usual order is for the losing side to pay the costs of the appeal. If such an order was made (and presumably it was), then it will have, most likely, resulted in the plaintiff being not even a penny better off as a result of winning his law suit. This assertion is not fanciful. In *Williamson v Metropolitan Police Commissioner*[2], one side claimed £30,000 for their costs of, and incidental to, a 3-day hearing in the county court over what a statement in open court should contain.

---

1   [1998] QB 498.
2   [1997] CL 4857.

In *Goswell v Metropolitan Police Commissioner*[1], the police were investigating a stolen car and spoke to the plaintiff. He began shouting and swearing at them, so he was handcuffed with his wrists behind his back. During that arrest, an officer struck a blow to his head, causing him to bleed profusely. He was taken into custody and later convicted of threatening behaviour. Liability was admitted, the defendant accepting that excessive force had been used, but denying that the blow had been struck after the handcuffing of Mr Goswell. Disciplinary action was taken against the officer responsible for the injury and he was dismissed, but later reinstated after a Home Office tribunal was unable to determine whether the assault took place before or after the plaintiff had been handcuffed. The appeal court reduced the damages from £12,000 to £100 for the 20 minutes he was illegally detained until given the reason for his arrest[2]. The compensation for the assault was reduced from £120,000 to £32,500 and the exemplary damages from £170,000 to £15,000. Simon Brown LJ said that the defendant's failure to offer any apology, coupled with the officer's reinstatement, severely aggravated the plaintiff's sense of hurt and probably went some way to explaining the jury's evident sense of outrage. His Lordship explained his approach to exemplary damages:

> 'The other conceptual difficulty in all these cases is in deciding what sum in addition to the compensatory damages is required to punish the Commissioner for the officer's misconduct. After all, the same blow struck in the same circumstances might have caused much greater injury or it might have caused no substantial injury at all. There is a large element of chance as to how punitive the requirement to pay compensatory damages would itself be. Here the appellant is to pay a total of £32,500 for PC Trigg's assault even before the question of exemplary damages arises. By what touchstone should one judge that to be a sufficient or insufficient sum to punish him? The problem becomes the greater, moreover, once one recognises the inevitable overlap between aggravated and exemplary damages in the first place: it is the very fact that injuries are inflicted by someone abusing his position of power which makes them the more painful to bear and at the same time exposes the tortfeasor to liability for an exemplary damages' award. Here, as indicated, in deciding the figure for aggravated damages, I have already sought to reflect the circumstances of the assault including the fact that the officer was behaving in a high-handed, insulting and oppressive manner at the time.
>
> Given that the conduct here was a single blow by a single junior officer whom the Commissioner then sought to discipline, I would award £15,000 under this head. This is not to minimise the seriousness of the case but rather to seek to give it its appropriate place in the overall spectrum of police behaviour. In such cases, the court should temper their outrage with concern for police funds.'

In *Gerald*, above, the damages of £125,000 (£25,000 basic plus £100,000 exemplary) were reduced on appeal to £50,000. The plaintiff was a man of good character who sued for false imprisonment, assault and malicious prosecution. He was arrested by the police after complaints about drug dealings. No illegal substances were found on him, but he suffered two black eyes, a bleeding lip and nose, cuts to his wrist and a broken bone in his foot. All four officers

---

1   (Unreported) 7 April 1998.
2   See *Fruween v Metropolitan Police Commissioner* (unreported) 1990 (see **14.3.1.3**) where, 8 years previously, a jury had awarded 10 times as much for a similar incarceration.

involved concocted a story to conceal that one or more of them had battered the plaintiff and had charged him with police assault, but no disciplinary proceedings were taken against any of them. The Court said 'while we have no doubt that there should be exemplary damages (a marking of disapproval) it should be modest'. It was originally reported as a news item in *The Times*[1] and on the same page was a report of the case of *R v Taylor*, where a police officer had been acquitted by a jury of assault. He had twice squirted CS gas into the face of an old-age pensioner who had parked on a double yellow line. He had then arrested him and held him in custody for 9 hours. Judge Rodway QC told the jury after they had delivered their verdict:

> 'I think that you will reflect that if other old age pensioners are gassed or assaulted by the police they will indeed have this case in mind.'

It is submitted that the police will also have in mind the decision in *Gerald*, above.

14.3.3.3 Juries

Generally speaking, the 'generosity' of the judiciary towards those who claim compensation for a few hours spent in police cells is out of step with those members of the public who are chosen at random to try these law suits. The former clearly do not travel to work on the Clapham omnibus. To be fair to the judges, very often, until recently, a jury made just one award which could well have included an element of exemplary damages but the total was far out of line with those cases where quantum was decided by judges. So for example, £12,000 was awarded in *Reynolds v Commissioner of Police*[2] for 14 hours in police custody and £4,250 in *Hurlings v Chief Constable of Merseyside*[3] for 4 hours and 30 minutes in the cells (plus £5,500 for the broken nose he had received in the course of his arrest). In *Withnall v Chief Constable of Lancashire*[4], the plaintiff went voluntarily to the station where he was asked to wait in a room until the inspector could see him. While waiting, he wished to go to the toilet but discovered the door was locked, the total length of time in which he was trapped in the room being about 30 minutes. While so confined, the police had 'borrowed' his keys out of his overcoat pocket, which was hanging up in the corridor and had used them to gain entry to his house which they searched. No damage was caused and the premises were left as they had been found. The jury awarded:

(1) £1,500 for the 30 minutes' false imprisonment which according to *Whitaker's Almanac* is now (2000) worth about double; and

(2) an additional £5,000 for the trespass to his land.

The trial judge would have given a grand total of £1,000, while over lunch at St George's Hall, the local circuit judges decided that a fair figure was £3,500, which is the same amount in today's figures as had been awarded 50 years previously by a Manchester jury for an incarceration of the same length. That

---

1   10 June 1998.
2   [1982] Crim LR 600.
3   [1984] CLY 1019.
4   (Unreported) 21 July 1982, Balcombe J sitting at St George's Hall, Liverpool.

was in the case of *Horsfield v Brown*[1], where McNaughton J[2] had stated that 'the circumstances of the case well warranted the substantial damages as the jury awarded'. There the plaintiff's arrest for non-payment of maintenance was unlawful, but no damages could be awarded for his incarceration at the police station because of the Constables Protection Act 1750. For that initial detention of approximately 30 minutes before he arrived at the station (which was unlawful because the arrester did not have the warrant with him), he recovered £175. The judiciary are under no illusions that they are out of touch. In *Holden v Chief Constable of Lancashire*, above, when asked why he was insisting on a re-trial on quantum, the plaintiff (through his counsel) replied that it was because:

> 'A jury would be far more generous than Your Lordships would ever be!'

To which Arnold P retorted, before he went on to order a new trial:

> 'You have given a very good reason.'

14.3.4   Special damages

These are to reimburse money actually spent as a result of the commission of the tort and which debts would not otherwise have been incurred. In *Boyce v Bayliffe*[3], the plaintiff had been a passenger on board ship and had been placed in irons by the captain when they were about to be attacked by an enemy warship. Once the danger was over, he was released. At the next port, he left the boat although it had not yet reached the destination to which he had booked his ticket and took another vessel to get there at a cost of £80. In his action for false imprisonment, Lord Ellenborough CJ ruled the £80 to be irrecoverable, because the plaintiff had not been forced to redeem himself from any great peril.

14.3.5   Loss of earnings

Normally, if as a direct result of a tort a claimant is unable to work, he will be able to claim, as compensation, any loss of earnings. Supposing that somebody was wrongly arrested and taken to a police station where he was required to provide a specimen of breath but refused to do so; or he did give a sample which, on analysis, showed his alcohol level to have exceeded the prescribed limit. He is then prosecuted and disqualified from driving and this causes him to lose his job. Could he recover, as damages, the loss of wages which, but for his unlawful arrest, he would have continued to receive? There is no case on this issue. However it is a fairly 'safe bet' to conclude that the judiciary would hold the damage too remote; the cause of the loss would not be the wrongful incarceration, but the deliberate disobedience of the provisions of RTA 1988.

---

1   [1932] 1 KB 355.
2   Ibid, at 364.
3   (1807) 1 Camp 58.

14.4   AN OVERVIEW OF THE LEVEL OF DAMAGES RECOVERED

In the author's view, the general level of damages awarded by judges as compensation for short periods in police custody can best be summed up in the description of general warrants given by Pratt CJ in *Huckle v Money*, above: 'a daring attack on the liberty of the subject'; and the Chief Justice did not consider in any way excessive the damages of £300 for 6 hours' loss of liberty during which time the prisoner was properly treated and supplied with beefsteak for his food and ale for his thirst. That sum was nearly 300 times the plaintiff's weekly salary or using the same multiplier to the current average wage, it is the equivalent of at least £100,000 today. Those are the figures that the Court of Appeal should be thinking about in these types of cases. Mackinnon J did so in *Treadaway v Chief Constable of the West Midlands*[1], where he found as a fact that the plaintiff had been seriously assaulted by four junior police officers in order to try to obtain a confession. His Lordship awarded £40,000 exemplary damages in addition to £7,500 aggravated damages and £2,500 basic damages. Also not all juries are influenced by the views held by lords justices. In *Randles v Chief Constable of Merseyside*[2], a Liverpool jury awarded £40,000 for post-traumatic stress, £3,500 for the physical injuries, £100,000 aggravated and £300,000 exemplary damages. The plaintiff had been attacked by two constables who had ordered him to move his taxi while he waited to collect a fare-paying passenger. He had been kneed in his testicles and shoulder-charged so that he fell through an open police van door. One officer had come down on his back with both knees and punched him around the head. Having then been turned on his back, his throat was squeezed and a policeman had sat with his knees on his chest. He suffered such severe injuries that he had to give up work. He had moved out of his home into a nearby flat where his wife visited him daily. He also still suffered from fits eight years after the incident, which he attributed solely to the assault. In *Godsell v Chief Constable of the Greater Manchester Police*[3], the plaintiff at first instance recovered £4,000 for assault, £5,700 for malicious prosecution and £25,000 exemplary damages. She had been taken to the police station after her boyfriend had been arrested for shoplifting. When she protested her innocence, she was hit on the jaw, was told to 'shut up' and was called 'a bitch'. She was held in custody for 36 hours in the same cell as two drug-addicted prostitutes. Her ordeal caused her sleepless nights and she became irritable with her children. She was diagnosed as suffering from post-traumatic stress disorder. For longer incarcerations, the Court of Appeal is more generous and makes a just award, as illustrated by the case of *Lunt*[4], where, in 1991, it gave £25,000 for 42 days' false imprisonment, which, in the author's view, is very fair compensation.

---

1   (1994) TLR, 25 October.
2   (1998) *The Times*, March.
3   (1998) *Daily Mail*, 8 February.
4   For the facts, see **14.3.1.6**.

14.5   SETTLEMENTS

It is interesting to look how this new power of the Court of Appeal to interfere with an assessment of damages made by a jury has influenced settlements. (Over a 2-year period to June 1998, on 8 occasions the Court of Appeal reduced a jury's award for trespass and malicious prosecution [1].) Between the trial at first instance and the hearing of the appeal in *Goswell*[2], the police offered to settle for £50,000, but the plaintiff held out for £130,000 [3]. Two instances of out of court settlements were reported in *The Times*[4]. Without any admission of liability, the Metropolitan Police paid Mr Harrison £27,500 and Miss Bruno-Gilbert £35,000. They had alleged that when they went to complain to the police station about a violent arrest which they happened to witness, they were detained, assaulted and maliciously prosecuted respectively for police obstruction, and (Miss Bruno-Gilbert) assault. On the same day, the West Midlands police paid Mr Lewis £200,000 compensation for having had a confession beaten out of him, as a result of which he had spent 5 years in prison for a crime he did not commit.

14.6   THE LAW COMMISSION

The Law Commission, in its report *Aggravated, Exemplary and Restitutionary Damages*[5] recommended the keeping of exemplary damages but that their award should only be by a judge alone, even if the rest of the action was tried by a jury. One can only hope that this report ends up like most of their others, with the government taking no action, otherwise it will be the most serious interference with civil liberties. It raises the question of what will occur if the judge takes a different view of the evidence before him. This will lead to all cases where exemplary damages are claimed being triable only in the non-jury list. That is totally unacceptable in a democratic society because in the United Kingdom the judiciary often take the opposite view of police evidence from that of a jury composed of people travelling on the Clapham omnibus. (This is borne out by the facts found by some of the juries in the actions already referred to in this chapter compared with the views expressed in *Clarke v Chief Constable of North Wales*[6], see Chapter 15.)

14.7   THE CLAIMANT'S CONDUCT

At common law, a claimant's conduct might deprive him of his right to sue (for example, contributory negligence) but, if it did not do so, then it played no part

---

1   (1998) *The Times*, 10 June.
2   (Unreported) 7 April 1998.
3   (1998) *The Guardian*, 8 April. For the facts, see **14.3.3.2**. The Court of Appeal reduced the damages to £47,600.
4   20 January 1998.
5   (1997) No 247.
6   (Unreported) 5 April 2000.

in the assessment of compensatory damages, save where, after the commission of the tort, the victim had failed to take reasonable steps to mitigate his loss. (Parliament has only intervened in actions for negligence, so that nowadays a contributory fault no longer deprives an injured person of all of his compensation.) Thus, the fact that the actions of a claimant may have contributed to his loss of freedom is not a relevant consideration when assessing basic damages; see *Holden v Chief Constable of Lancashire*[1], and *Kay and Helm v James and Peacock*[2]. (The only judicial disagreement with this proposition comes in the dissenting judgment of Henry LJ in *Clark v Chief Constable of Cleveland*[3]). According to *R v Governor of HM Prison Brockhill, ex parte Evans (No 2)*[4], above, when assessing damages for not being released from goal on the due date, a relevant consideration is the fact that the prisoner was prepared to risk losing her remission by committing disciplinary offences.

On the other hand, it is an important factor in assessing aggravated or exemplary damages; see *Bishop v Metropolitan Police Commissioner*[5]. In *Treadaway v Chief Constable of the West Midlands*[6], the plaintiff had been seriously assaulted while being interviewed about a robbery, for which offence he was subsequently sentenced to 15 years' imprisonment. At the criminal trial, no *voir dire* had been held to determine whether his confession had been improperly obtained. McKinnon J said that the medical evidence supported the claim and no explanation had been offered by the defendant for how the plaintiff sustained his injuries at the police station. His Lordship went on to state:

> 'The court should not reduce the exemplary damages because of the sort of man the plaintiff was with serious convictions.
>
> That was because the plaintiff, with all his faults, had been placed in a position where he was a entitled to expect that he would be given the protection of the law.'

14.8 NOMINAL DAMAGES

The damages for being unknowingly incarcerated will usually, if not always, be nominal. So, in *R v Bournewood Community and Mental Health NHS Trust, ex parte L*[7], the Court of Appeal granted a writ of *habeas corpus* and awarded £1 to a person who was illegally detained for a number of days in a mental hospital, the correct procedure under MHA 1983 not having been followed. The applicant (suing by his next friend) was incapable of understanding that the hospital would have prevented him from leaving if he had attempted to do so. (The House of Lords upheld the Court of Appeal on liability, but made no comment on the question of quantum.) Likewise, in *Roberts v Chief Constable of Cheshire*[8], Clarke LJ stated:

---

1   [1987] QB 380.
2   (Unreported) 21 April 1999.
3   (1999) 96 (21) LSG 38.
4   [1999] QB 1043.
5   (1989) 133 SJ 1626.
6   (1994) TLR, 25 October.
7   [1999] AC 457.
8   [1999] 1 WLR 662.

'A person who was falsely imprisoned but who was unaware of it and who *suffered no harm* would be entitled to only nominal damages.' (Author's emphasis.)

14.9 DETENTION ONLY BECOMES UNLAWFUL BECAUSE OF A *BONA FIDE* ERROR ON THE PART OF THE JAILER

The fact that a plaintiff could have been lawfully imprisoned does not reduce his damages to a nominal sum; see *Roberts v Chief Constable of Cheshire*, above.

14.10 THE SUMMING UP TO THE JURY

In *Scotland v Metropolitan Police Commissioner*[1], the Court of Appeal was of the view that judges could give guidance to the jury about the appropriate level of damages and that there should be a discussion between the judge and counsel about that matter in the absence of the jury. A judge could remind the members of the latter body of the value of money and tell them to ask themselves what could be bought with the sum which they proposed to award. That decision was approved in *Thompson v Metropolitan Police Commissioner*, above.

14.11 DATE FOR ASSESSMENT OF, AND INTEREST ON, DAMAGES

Holtham v Metropolitan Police Commissioner[2] followed the decision in *Saunders v Edwards*[3] (a case of deceit) and held that interest was not payable on damages relating to non-economic loss but only on special damages. This was because a jury, when deciding on the amount of general damages, had to do so on the basis that the incarceration had occurred on the very date on which they were making their award and that they should not make any deduction for the fact that inflation had increased the quantum to more than it would otherwise have been if the damages had been assessed on the date when the tort had been committed. That case was not cited in *Samuels v Metropolitan Police*, above, which must, accordingly, be regarded as having been decided *per incuriam*. (There, the Court of Appeal, after itself assessing the damages, awarded thereon interest at judgment debt rate from the date of the commission of the tort.) However, in *Cunningham v Essex County Council*[4], this principle of not giving interest was followed by Eady J in a libel action.

---

1   (1996) TLR, 30 January.
2   (1987) TLR, 28 November.
3   [1987] 2 All ER 651.
4   (Unreported) 26 June 2000.

14.12 CONCLUSIONS AND FUTURE DEVELOPMENTS

Section 8 of the Courts and Legal Services Act 1990 has enabled the Court of Appeal for the first time to lay down and to enforce a tariff for the amount of damages to be awarded to those who have been falsely imprisoned. These start with basic damages of about £500 for the first hour rising on a reducing scale to £3,000 for 24 hours. After a longer period (as yet not specified by the judiciary) a global rather than an incremental approach should be adopted. For 42 days' unlawful incarceration, the appellate court increased the award in *Lunt*[1] to £42,000. The damages are 'front loaded' to take into account the initial shock of being locked up for the first time in a cell. If the tortfeasor deliberately makes the plaintiff's suffering worse, for example by making the arrest in front of his friends, there being racial insults or due to the way in which the defence at trial is conducted etc, then an additional sum can be awarded as aggravated damages but normally it should not exceed twice the basic amount. Also, exemplary damages can be awarded when the tortfeasors are officers or servants of the Crown but only if the jury does not consider the basic and aggravated sums to be sufficient to mark its disapproval, to act as a deterrent and, where the actual arrester himself is sued, to punish the latter. Exemplary damages should range from £5,000 to £25,000; and could reach up to £50,000, but only in respect of the direct conduct of an officer not below the rank of superintendent. A factor to be taken into account when calculating the quantum of exemplary damages is that where the constabulary was uninsured, it was being deprived of funds which might well be better and more usefully employed in policing. False imprisonment may not be the only tort committed; it is often accompanied by an assault. The compensation for the latter is calculated in accordance with the guidelines for the assessment of damages in personal injury cases issued from time to time by the Judicial Studies Board.

Under Art 5(5) of the European Convention on Human Rights, a person is entitled to compensation if he is falsely imprisoned. The court at Strasbourg has yet to rule on whether the level of damages laid down in *Thompson*, above, is sufficient to comply with that treaty obligation. There appears to be only one reported case where damages for non-pecuniary loss were avoided against the Crown for false imprisonment, namely £5,500 for a 6-day incarceration; see *Perks v UK*[2]. In *Steel et al v United Kingdom*[3], two of the applicants had been arrested outside the Queen Elizabeth Conference Centre in Westminster for handing out leaflets, and holding up banners, protesting against arms sales. As there was no reason to apprehend a breach of the peace, the European Court of Human Rights held the arrest to be illegal, but as that was actionable under English law, the court gave no damages for that tort, but did award £500 for breach of the right to free expression under Art 10. Those sums in the above two cases were decided upon without the benefit of any domestic judicial pronouncement as to what the level should be in the United Kingdom. Thus, there could be no 'margin of appreciation' to be considered. Provided the sum

---

1   (Unreported) 5 March 1991.
2   (1999) 30 EHRR 33.
3   (1998) 28 EHRR 603.

awarded by an English court was not so small as to be totally disproportionate to the injury suffered, the Court at Strasbourg is unlikely to interfere.

Finally, the author can do no more than quote with approval what Lord Hobhouse said in *R v Governor of Brockhill Prison, ex parte Evans (No 2)*[1]:

'In the present case, the State (through the legislature) has defined the power of detention; the State (through the executive) has detained the plaintiff in excess of that power; it creates no injustice that the State should compensate the plaintiff. It certainly does not make it just for the State to fail to compensate the plaintiff that one or more emanations of the State have misunderstood the legislation. Under the Convention, the State is already under an obligation to compensate; when the Human Rights Act 1998 comes into force it will also be under a domestic law obligation to do so.'

---

1   [2000] 3 WLR 843 at 867A–B.

Chapter 15

CIVIL ACTIONS FOR FALSE IMPRISONMENT

15.1   PRE-ACTION DISCOVERY

In *Tooms v Metropolitan Police Commissioner*[1], an information had been laid against the applicant charging him with conspiracy. Three months later, the charges were dropped. The applicant sought pre-action discovery (pursuant to CPR, r 31.16) to find out if he could bring a case against the police for false imprisonment. Sullivan J granted the application stating that 'if there is a sensible reason for the arrest and prosecution it is clearly desirable that that is flushed out at the earliest possible opportunity, so the action is stopped in its tracks'. By analogy, the same must apply to an action for false imprisonment. Of course, certain documents might be protected by public interest immunity, see below.

This chapter considers the special rules of practice and procedure which govern legal proceedings for false imprisonment. They are not necessarily unique to this tort, but are not normally of relevance to other litigation tried by a judge alone. They are set out in the chronological order in which they will be encountered by the claimant once he has instituted proceedings. (Legal aid is considered separately in Chapter 17.)

15.2   LIMITATION

In *Padmore v Commissioner of Police*[2], the Court of Appeal held that the limitation period for actions of false imprisonment was 6 years. Time starts running when the prisoner is released on bail and not at the later date when the warrant (or conviction) is set aside; see *Syed Mahamad Yusuf-ud-Din v Secretary of State for India*[3]. In *Fitzgerald v MacDonald*[4], the New Zealand Court of Appeal held that as false imprisonment was 'a continuing wrong', the limitation period ran from the date of release. In *Laine v Chief Constable of Cambridge*[5] the claimant had been arrested on Friday afternoon and had not been taken before the justices until the following Monday. He alleged that the length of his incarceration was too long, ie *Wednesbury* unreasonable. The appellate tribunal ruled that the following amendment was statute-barred, ie an averment that a local magistrates' court had in fact sat on the Saturday, before whom the claimant should have been brought. This was because, previously, the claimant had been complaining about the 'speed with which the police dealt with him'; whereas

---

1   (Unreported) 15 November 2000.
2   (Unreported) 17 December 1996.
3   (1903) 19 TLR 496 (PC).
4   [1918] NZLR 769.
5   (Unreported) 14 October 1999.

the alleged failure to produce him at the Saturday court was a fresh allegation based on different facts.

There is a two-year limitation period for suing a sheriff, one of his officers or a bailiff who does not release from captivity a prisoner who is bailable and for whom sufficient security has been offered: see Sheriffs Act 1887, s 29(7). The same limitation period also applies to anybody who procures that tort. A much shorter limitation period applies for breaches of the European Convention on Human Rights; see Chapter 17.

15.3   FOREIGN CLAIMANTS

In *R v Immigration Officer, ex parte Quaquah*[1] the applicant was an illegal immigrant. He was also suing the Home Office and Group 4 Security for malicious prosecution. Turner J held that in ordering the applicant's deportation the respondent had failed to take into account that under Art 6 of the European Convention on Human Rights everybody was entitled to a fair hearing to determine their civil rights. Here the law suit was not merely a claim for damages for an infringement of a private right. The applicant was seeking to assert a human right by bringing proceedings for damages arising out of a trial in which he had been acquitted. If he was deported, he would not be able to prosecute his claim effectively. Accordingly, an order of *certiorari* was made. Logically, the same principles must also apply to an alien who was suing for false imprisonment, at any rate where the defendant was a public body, for example the police. In *R v Home Secretary, ex parte Quaquah (No 2)*[2], the High Court held that it was unreasonable not to grant the applicant limited leave to remain until his case was over. The Home Secretary had revoked the deportation order but would not do anything further because if he gave him permission to stay in this country, then Mr Quaquah would be entitled to the same social security entitlements as citizens of this country were.

15.4   THE PLEADINGS

15.4.1   Generally

The usual rule is that a litigant must plead every fact on which he relies. Thus, all that needs to be averred by a claimant was that he has been imprisoned, because the law assumes all incarcerations to be unlawful until proved otherwise[3]; whereas for a defence of confession and avoidance, it was necesssary to aver all the facts relied upon to sustain the plea of justification. In *Mercer v Chief Constable of Lancashire*[4], Lord Donaldson MR said that at the summons for directions, the District Judges should:

---

1   (Unreported) 15 December 1999.
2   (Unreported) 1 September 2000.
3   See **15.10.1**.
4   [1991] 1 WLR 367.

(1) force a plaintiff to state the reasons which made his detention unlawful, for example that he was not held in a designated police station; and

(2) order him to be debarred from raising at the trial any new reasons which cast doubt on the legality of the restraint on his liberty and which had not been disclosed in advance to the defendant.

A specimen particulars of claim is included in Appendix 2.

15.4.2 Damages

Under the old rules, in the High Court exemplary damages had to be specifically pleaded together with a statement of why they were being claimed; see RSC Ord 18, r 8(3), and the same applied in the county court, with the insertion in 1989 of a new r 1B in CCR Ord 6 (thus reversing Lord Denning's judgment in *Drane v Evangelou*[1]).

The Civil Procedure Rules 1998 (CPR 1998) have not in any way altered these requirements; see CPR 1998, r 16.4(1)(c), which makes it mandatory for a litigant who is asking for aggravated or exemplary damages to aver that fact in the particulars of claim together with the grounds on which they are sought.

15.5 SUMMARY JUDGMENT

For the first time, the CPR 1998 allow a party to seek summary judgment in a false imprisonment action and, indeed, in all those matters where an automatic right to jury trial still remains. In *Conlon v Chief Constable of Northumbria*[2], the Court of Appeal set aside a summary judgment in favour of the defendant, saying[3] that:

> '... it would be exceptional for a court to deal summarily with a claim for false imprisonment ...'

In *Safeway v Tate*[4] (a libel action), Otton and Mantell LJJ and Sir Robert Waterhouse emphasised the importance of jury trial and held that in those cases where the litigants were entitled, as of right, to that mode of trial, then if any issue of disputed fact arose, that was the province of the jury and must be left to them, and a judge could not award summary judgment. In that case, Blofeld J had held that no jury could find otherwise than that the words were defamatory. As this was a question of fact for that latter tribunal, the appeal against his decision was allowed and a jury trial ordered. The extra costs that would be incurred were not a relevant factor to be taken into account. In *Marsorella v Chief Constable of Hampshire*[5], the appellate tribunal upheld the striking out of that part of a claim which averred that there were no reasonable grounds to suspect the claimant of an arrestable offence and where the witness

---

1   [1978] 2 All ER 437.
2   (Unreported) 2 March 2000.
3   Ibid, per Judge LJ, para 18.
4   (2001) *The Times*, January 25, CA.
5   (Unreported) 29 June 1999.

statement of the arrester – which was not challenged – showed that there had been reasonable cause. Presumably, if, in that case, the only cause of action alleged was the lack of reasonable suspicion (which is a question of law for the judge), then no doubt summary judgment for the defendant could have been awarded. It is submitted that summary judgment cannot be awarded whenever there is a dispute of fact, even if one party's account of the matter appears to be unbelievable, as that would be usurping the role of the jury as the finder of fact.

15.6   DISCLOSURE

The normal rules for the disclosure of documents apply, namely that such is only to be ordered if it be necessary to dispose fairly of the cause or matter or to save costs, the burden being on those who wish to inspect them to establish these matters; see *Ventouris v Mountain*[1]. The usual exception to this is documents brought into existence for the litigation (for example Counsel's opinion). Thus, advice sought by a litigant from his legal advisers is privileged from discovery. Does this apply to communications between the police and the Director of Public Prosecutions? Although the latter office was established in 1879, it was not until well over 100 years later that this issue came before the courts in *Goodridge v Hampshire Constabulary*[2], where Moore-Brick J held that advice given by the Director of Public Prosecutions to the police and *vice versa* where the latter was investigating crime was not the normal type of advice tendered by a solicitor to his client but was given under a statutory duty (now s 3 of the Prosecution of Offences Act 1985) and that, therefore, such was not covered by the normal solicitor–client privilege.

15.6.1   Public interest immunity

The unusual feature in cases brought against the police is that some of the relevant documents will be protected by public interest immunity, for example the names of informers. In 1997, all police forces and the Director of Public Prosecutions agreed a series of forms which they would use to communicate with each other and to keep a record of the progress of the investigation. They are numbered MG 1–20 and were considered in *Kelley v Metropolitan Police Commissioner*[3], where the Court of Appeal held that forms MG 3A, 6, 6A, 6D, 6E

---

1   [1991] 1 WLR 607 at 623B, per Parker LJ.
2   [1999] 1 All ER 896.
3   (Unreported) 22 July 1997.

and 20 belonged to a class which was entitled to public interest immunity[1]. The Court went on to state that an assistant commissioner should first decide whether disclosure would cause real damage to the public interest, and if it did not, then immunity should not be claimed. If it did cause harm to the public good, then, in the words of Kennedy LJ:

> '... [I would hold] that the forms belong to a class which attracts Public Interest Immunity, it would still be open to the plaintiffs to satisfy the [trial] judge that, on the facts of the case, the public interest in disclosure of the contents of the form or forms, or some part thereof, outweighs the public interest in preserving the confidentiality of the form or forms [see *Taylor's Case* at 465H[2]]. In reality that is something which can only be evaluated by examining the forms and the judge will be able to evaluate if need be if he comes to the conclusion that he must examine the forms for the purpose of the freshhold test.'

It is difficult to elaborate on this and every case will turn on its own special facts as to whether the defendant's documents are likely to contain anything relevant to the issues involved. In the above cited case, two constables alleged that they saw two men acting suspiciously near a van and they recognised them. One of these was the plaintiff. The policeman saw by the side of the van a box on the ground. On becoming aware of the officers' approach, the plaintiff picked up the box, which was later found and contained a mobile telephone, and ran off. The police obtained a report stating that there were fingerprints on the box belonging to the other man but not the plaintiff. Thereafter, the latter was arrested for theft, indicted in the Crown Court, but subsequently prosecuting counsel offered no evidence. The result was an action for malicious prosecution and false imprisonment, in the course of which the plaintiff wanted to know when the police had obtained the results of the fingerprint tests and when they had informed the Crown Prosecution Service of them. The Court of Appeal held that the MG forms might indeed be relevant to those issues and ordered the lower court to look at them to see if there was anything in those documents which ought, in the interests of justice, to be disclosed.

---

1   A description of the forms (taken from the judgment of Kennedy LJ) is set out below. Their use to a plaintiff in a claim for false imprisonment will be very limited and they will only really become of relevance in malicious prosecution actions:
     Form 3A is headed 'Confidential Information Form' (it is only used for juvenile offenders).
     Form 6 has various headings and informs the prosecutor of all relevant background information.
     Form 6A is a continuation form for form 6.
     Form 6C is what the police think should be disclosed, but the DPP may disagree.
     Form 6D lists what the police think is sensitive material and should for that reason not be made available to the accused.
     Form 6E is headed 'Disclosure Officer's Report' and sets out his views on what should or should not be disclosed to the defence.
     Form 9 is headed 'Confidential Witness List'. It sets out the names, addresses, occupations and dates of birth of the prosecution witnesses.
     No description was given of form 20, whose relevance was described as minimal.
2   *Taylor v Anderton* [1995] 1 WLR 447.

In *R v Chief Constable of the West Midlands, ex parte Wiley*[1], the House of Lords held that statements made for the purposes of an inquiry into a complaint by a member of the public against the police were not a class of documents covered by public interest immunity. *Taylor,* above, held that the report of the investigating officer need not be disclosed because it only contained his views and was not first-hand evidence of what had occurred. In *Evans v Chief Constable of Surrey*[2], Wood J refused to order disclosure of the report sent by the police to the Director of Public Prosecutions because it would be of no assistance to the plaintiff. This was because the burden of proof was on the defendant to justify the incarceration and the primary evidence of this was contained in the witness statements taken during the course of the investigation; and, as malice was not alleged, the motives of the police for arresting were irrelevant. In other words, the case turned on what facts the police could prove were known to them and this depended on what information they were given by other people and not on what they told the Director of Public Prosecutions.

In *R v Metropolitan Police Commissioner, ex parte Hart-Leverton,*[3] the High Court ruled that although documents were privileged from disclosure because of public interest immunity, there was no rule of law preventing the person who lawfully possessed them from showing them to his legal advisers and the latter using them as they considered expedient, so long as that was consistent with the immunity attaching to them, for example to decide upon questions to be asked in cross-examination.

Lamothe v Metropolitan Police Commissioner[4], was an action for trespass arising out of a search by the police for a murderer. The Court of Appeal set aside a circuit judge's *ex parte* ruling that the claimants could not ask questions of any constable about their belief that their suspect was at the premises which they had entered in order to effect an arrest pursuant to PACE 1984, s 17 (see **9.2**). Bingham LJ held that this was in reality an application not to disclose documents on the grounds of public interest immunity and, as such, had to be heard *inter partes*. If any of the application was granted, then the trial should take place before another judge who could not be influenced by what he had read and which he had held need not be given in evidence. (That would nowadays no longer be possible in view of the decision of the European Court of Human Rights in *Rowe & Davies v UK*[5].) Also, it is submitted that public interest immunity is a shield, not a sword. It permits one party not to have to give discovery of written evidence favourable to himself. It surely does not allow assertions of fact to be made to the jury and then prevent cross-examination thereon. To give an example, public interest immunity could prevent the police from having to give any evidence at all of a letter which they had acquired by surreptitious means. What it would not authorise is the production of that letter but it would stop all questioning about it, for example on its authenticity. To deny that right of cross-examination can either be called 'a breach of a

1   [1995] 1 AC 274.
2   [1988] QB 588.
3   [1990] COD 240.
4   (Unreported) 25 October 1999.
5   (2000) TLR, 1 March.

fundamental right or simply a denial of a fundamental right'. That quotation of Watkins LJ in *Young v Flint*[1] has now been given statutory recognition in HRA 1998 as Art 6(3) of the European Convention on Human Rights states:

> 'Everybody charged with a criminal offence has the following minimum rights:
> ...
> (d) to examine or have examined witnesses against him ...'

Although it refers to criminal trials, it has been held that the same applies to cases about 'the determination of one's civil rights', which of course clearly embrace actions for false imprisonment as the privilege not to be 'deprived of one's liberty, contrary to law' is a civil right protected by the Convention, see *R v Immigration Officer, ex parte Quaquah*[2].

15.6.2 Informers

Often the only ground of an arrester's suspicion is 'information received'. The Court of Appeal has taken a very strict line and has given complete exemption to the police from having to disclose any details whatsoever which might lead to the identification of an informant. The reason for this is that information would dry up if those who supplied it thought that there was any possibility of their names becoming known. In *Powell v Chief Constable of Cheshire*[3], the claimant was certain that he knew the identity of the informer and wished to ask the officer who had apprehended him to confirm this and then demonstrate that it was not reasonable to have relied upon what that person might say. The trial judge ruled that the witness would have to answer those questions, but to provide as much anonymity as possible, he ordered the trial to be by judge alone and to be held *in camera*. The Court of Appeal held that even this compromise was not sufficient protection for those who did not wish their assistance in helping crimes to be solved to become public knowledge. That decision and its rationale was expressly approved in *Whitewash v Chief Constable of Somerset and Devon*[4] In that case, the facts were that Constable Olds had testified to having received information from a reliable source. The Court of Appeal was also of the view that his identity was of no relevance. That, it is submitted, would depend on who he is. He might be known as somebody upon whom it would not be reasonable to rely; see the quotation in Chapter 8 from the judgment of Watson B in *Hogg v Ward*[5]. The Court of Appeal recognised (para 22) that it will be simply a matter of whether or not the jury believes the witness when he says that the facts he was told about came from a reliable source. Questions will be limited to whether this person had assisted the police in the past and how reliable he had proved on previous occasions. However, without knowing anything else about the informer, it will not be an easy task for the claimant to challenge the honesty of the police officer's assertions about this matter. In other words, *salus populi, suprema lex*, ie the right of the individual

---

1   [1987] RTR 300 at 305D.
2   (Unreported) 15 December 1999.
3   (Unreported) 16 December 1999.
4   (Unreported) 31 March 2000.
5   (1858) 4 H and N 417 at p 423.

to obtain redress for the loss of his liberty must take second place to not in any way discouraging from coming forward those who know of matters that might interest the police. How far this complies with Art 5(5) of the European Convention on Human Rights (the right to compensation for an unlawful incarceration) is discussed in Chapter 17.

15.7 SETTLEMENTS – STATEMENTS IN OPEN COURT

Schedule 1 to the CPR as originally promulgated contains some of the old RSC, including Ord 82, r 5 which enacted that if a claimant accepted a payment into court in, *inter alia*, a false imprisonment action he could make a statement in open court, subject to the judge's approval. By virtue of s 76 of the County Courts Act 1984 this same right also applied in that tribunal; see *Williamson v Metropolitan Police Commissioner*[1] where the Court of Appeal assumed, without argument to the contrary, that such a right existed in the county court. However, in February 2000, the Civil Procedure (Amendment) Rules 2000, SI 2000/221, came into force, which repealed the old RSC Ord 82 and replaced it with CPR Part 51. However, it applies only to defamation actions and makes no mention of 'statements in open court'. At the same time, a new Practice Direction 53 (Defamation Claims) for libel and slander cases was issued which dealt with, *inter alia*, statements in open court, for example that the judge must agree to its contents in advance. However, a Practice Direction can never bestow upon a court additional jurisdiction; it can merely prescribe how procedural matters should be dealt with by that tribunal. Thus statements in open court are no longer possible in false imprisonment actions.

The judiciary naturally reserves to themselves the discretion to refuse to allow a statement to be made, for example where only nominal damages have been accepted, so that there has been no vindication of the claimant (as happened in *Church of Scientology of California v North News Ltd*[2]). In *Williamson v Metropolitan Police Commissioner*, above, it was held that any such statement should not be defamatory of people who were not parties to the action, for example the policemen who were accused of being the actual tortfeasors, if they were not also sued as joint defendants. Judge LJ said:

> 'The approval of the judge of a statement to be made under Ord 82, r 5 is a not a matter of form but of substance. He must first decide whether it is appropriate to permit a statement to be made, and if so whether the statement should be made in the terms proposed.'

---

1   (Unreported) 23 July 1997.
2   (1973) 117 SJ 566.

15.8 WANT OF PROSECUTION AND DISOBEDIENCE TO COURT ORDERS

All civil actions are liable to be struck out for want of prosecution if the claimant does not proceed with all due expedition or disobeys time-limits laid down by a judge or set out in CPR 1998. However, in *Smith et al v Chief Constable of Kent*[1], the Court of Appeal stated that in claims for trespass against the police a judge can take into account the fact that there was a public interest in having the case heard in open court, especially where the fault lay with the solicitors rather than with the litigant himself. In the words of Roch LJ:

> 'If the police have made wrongful arrests, unlawfully imprisoned people or maliciously prosecuted these plaintiffs, then these matters should be exposed in open court.'

Thus, the Court of Appeal upheld Judge Coombs who had refused to dismiss the action on those very grounds despite non-compliance with numerous consent orders and who had also stated that if the defendant had been a private citizen he would have reached the opposite conclusion. There the delay was on the part of the defence. In theory, similar principles should apply whenever the police seek to have an action dismissed because of the failure by the claimant to have prosecuted it expeditiously. However, that is not the case, at least according to *Rose and Hamil v Commissioner of Police*[2] where the Court of Appeal upheld the striking out of very serious allegations against the police because the plaintiff's solicitors did not issue a summons for directions until almost 3 years after they ought to have done, in accordance with the Rules of Court. No explanation for the delay was proffered and the court held that the question of whether a fair trial could still take place was irrelevant. Whether *Smith et al v Chief Constable of Kent*, above, was cited in *Rose and Hamil* is not known. Such an uneven approach is clearly contrary to Art 6 of the European Convention on Human Rights, as such cases involve a person's civil rights. Those lawsuits require a 'fair hearing', ie that the same principles are applied to both parties. Due to the importance of allegations of impropriety by the police being investigated properly, it is submitted that the best approach was that adopted in *Smith*, above, and that this should be applied equally to alleged abuses of process by the citizenry through non-compliance with court orders as it is to such conduct by the constabulary when defending this type of litigation.

In *Padmore v Metropolitan Police Commissioner*[3], the Court of Appeal dismissed the plaintiff's action for false imprisonment, assault and malicious prosecution when the cause of action had arisen 7 years before the defendant had issued his strike out summons. The Court of Appeal said that it was not a case which could be decided on contemporaneous documents, thus not accepting the plaintiff's argument that no prejudice would occur by the passage of time as the officers still had their notebooks and there was the transcript of his trial and re-trial.

---

1   (Unreported) 26 January 1998.
2   (Unreported) 15 December 1998.
3   (Unreported) 17 December 1996.

However, this was a case where there was a very clear conflict of evidence, with the accuracy of the notebooks being challenged. What clinched the matter was that by accident the plaintiff's solicitors told the defendant that the case was no longer being pursued which was passed on to the police witnesses. In addition, Waller LJ also said:

> 'In my view, a jury, despite proper directions, would be less able to give proper allowance for memories dimming than a judge alone.'

15.9   MODE OF TRIAL

15.9.1   The importance of jury trials

Section 69(1)(b) of the Supreme Court Act 1981 and s 66(3)(b) of the County Courts Act 1984 are in identical terms and bestow on any party an almost automatic right to a trial by jury. The reason for this was clearly stated by Hobhouse LJ in *Ward v Chief Constable of West Midlands Police*[1]:

> 'Trials such as this are conducted with the assistance of the jury because of the nature of the allegations made and the issues raised and the desirability in the interests of justice not only being done but being seen to be done of having a jury to decide disputed issues of facts.'

In *Darragh v Chief Constable of Thames Valley Police*[2], Sir Patrick Russell stated:

> 'There is no doubt whatever that some of the issues in this case would be best tried by a jury, for example, allegations of police brutality and, generally, of police misconduct. Those issues are eminently suitable for the decision of a jury and are frequently within the province of the jury, not only in a civil court but more particularly in the criminal courts.'

In *Thompson v Commissioner of Police for the Metropolis*[3], Lord Woolf MR expressed similar views:

> '... there are arguments which can be advanced to justify the retention of the use of juries in this area of litigation. Very difficult issues of credibility will often have to be resolved. It is desirable for these to be determined by the plaintiff's fellow citizens rather than judges, who like the police are concerned in maintaining law and order. Similarly the jury because of their composition, are a body which is peculiarly suited to make the final assessment of damages, including deciding whether aggravated or exemplary damages are called for in this area of litigation and for the jury to have these important tasks is an important safeguard of the liberty of the individual citizen.'

It should not be thought that all juries are anti-police while judges are pro-constabulary. In *Tighe (Mary) v Chief Constable of Merseyside*[4], the claimant testified that she had been told that she was being arrested only for obstructing

---

1   Reported only very briefly at (1997) TLR, December 15.
2   (1998) 95 (43) LSG 32.
3   [1998] QB 498 at 513.
4   (Unreported) 2 March 2000.

the police and that is what the notebooks of each of the three officers present recorded. Yet, in the witness box, those same policemen swore that she had been apprehended on suspicion of perverting the course of justice but could offer no rational explanation as to why they had not recorded detaining Mrs Tighe for the far more serious of her two alleged transgressions of the law. The jury found for the defendant. In the case of professional judges, the more serious the allegations are, the more difficult the judiciary find it to believe that police officers could be guilty of such conduct. Thus, the trial judge said in *Clarke v Chief Constable of North Wales*[1]:

> 'In over 30 years of being in a position to observe the North Wales police force I have never heard allegations remotely like this before. They bespeak not just an odd rogue officer but an entire culture of wicked disregard for the rights of detained persons, bad officering, no discipline and not a single voice raised in protest. It is a startling picture and on the face of it difficult to believe; but I approach it with a completely open mind.'

That led to Sedley LJ commenting:

> 'Shorn of its final disclaimer, it belongs not in a judgment but in a speech for the defence; and the final disclaimer serves only to underscore its infelicity.'[2]

To be fair to the trial judge, even when (in the author's view) he has arrived at the correct decision, the lords justices still disagreed with his rulings. Thus, in *Roberts v Chief Constable of Cheshire*[3], the judge's proper award of damages in an action for false imprisonment was considered by the appellate tribunal to be over generous and his very sensible compromise in another such action to protect the identity of an informant similarly did not meet with the approval of that court; see *Powell v Chief Constable of Cheshire*, above.

15.9.2   THE MAKING OF THE APPLICATION FOR TRIAL BY JURY

Under the old RSC (for example CCR Ord 13, r 10(2)) an automatic right to a trial by one's peers applied only if the application for a jury was made at the summons for directions. If made afterwards, the mode of trial was at the discretion of the court, but if the judiciary follow the decision of Owen J in *Cooper v Chief Constable of South Yorkshire*[4], there will be a jury. That is because 'misconduct by the police is a matter of public concern and it was for that reason that Parliament directed them to be tried by jury'[5]. In *Testill v Chief Constable of Essex*[6], it was held that a district judge was entitled to refuse an application for a jury trial after the summons for directions because of the delay it would cause in bringing the matter on for trial. (The cause of action had arisen 4 years earlier.)

---

1   (Unreported) 5 April 2000, para 11.
2   (Unreported) 5 April 2000, at para 12.
3   [1999] 1 WLR 662.
4   [1989] 1 WLR 333.
5   Ibid at 340F/G.
6   (Unreported) 5 March 1999 (CA).

To the same effect is *Oliver v Calderdale Borough Council*[1] (a malicious prosecution action), Buxton LJ is reported to have said:

> 'The instant application was wholly out of time and unreasonable. It could not possibly be right where a non-jury trial was fixed for the end of June to come along and make application [in the preceding April] for a jury trial.'

Under r 10 of the Civil Procedure (Amendment) (No 4) Rules 2000[2] which came into force on 2 October 2000, an application for a jury trial must be made within 28 days of the service of the defence. A court can always extend the time. When a late application is made, it is submitted that the true test should be whether or not it was still possible to obtain a jury without having to vacate the trial date. That would no doubt depend on its venue, whether it was a county court that did not normally have juries and has to make special arrangements for their attendance or a combined courts centre, where there was always plenty of spare good men (and women) and true hanging around waiting (whether eagerly or reluctantly) to administer justice.

15.9.3 Where a court need not order trial by jury

Any 'spurning of jurors' can best be described as 'an unforgivable offence in the eyes of any true blooded Englishman' to quote the *dicta* of Lord Donaldson MR in *The Goring*[3], when describing the removal of the right to trial by jury in the admiralty court. Accordingly, the only exception to this automatic right is (in the words of the relevant statutes)[4] where 'the court is of the opinion that the trial requires any prolonged examination of documents or accounts or any scientific or local investigation which cannot conveniently be made with a jury'.

In *Harmsworth v London Transport*[5], it was held that Judge Deborah Rowlands was wrong to refuse a jury trial because the costs outweighed the damages and she was not entitled to form the view that the claim was suspect. The plaintiff was seeking £50 for having been unlawfully detained by a ticket collector at the barriers of Paddington underground station. The issue was whether or not he had supplied his name and address. *Hill v Chief Constable of South Yorkshire*[6], held that a judge could look at the facts to see if the claim for false imprisonment was a sham to enable a jury to be empanelled, but if they did disclose such an issue, the judge could not investigate the merits of the averments. In that case, the plaintiff was held to be entitled to insist on his claim being tried by his peers when he had alleged:

(1) an assault; and

(2) being detained for too long.

The basis of the latter pleading was that he had not been charged as soon as there was sufficient evidence to do so as required by PACE 1984, and that this dilatoriness in charging had delayed the grant of bail to him. Accordingly, the

---

1   (1999) TLR, July 7.
2   SI 2000/2092. See CPR 1998, r 26.11.
3   [1987] QB 687 at p 701.
4   Supreme Court Act 1981, s 69(1) and County Courts Act 1984, s 66(3).
5   (1979) 123 Sol Jo 825.
6   [1980] 1 All ER 1046.

ratio of that case is that provided the facts relied on amount in law to a claim for false imprisonment, then the veracity of those facts must be decided by a jury.

In *Rothermere v The Times*[1], (a libel action), it was held that the reference to an examination of documents meant the amount actually to be considered by the jury and not the number in the parties' lists. In *Goldsmith v Pressdram Ltd*[2], the Court of Appeal said that whether or not one of the exceptions to the automatic right to jury trial existed is a question of fact. If it did exist, the judge has a discretion whether or not to order that mode of trial. In another defamation case, *Beta Construction Ltd v Channel Four TV*[3], the Court of Appeal refused a trial by one's peers as the issues involved extremely detailed and complex documents about asbestos and its removal from buildings. Stuart-Smith LJ held that there were four main areas within which the administration of justice might be rendered less convenient if the trial took place with a tribunal of fact consisting of 12 members of the public chosen by lot:

(1) the physical problems of handling large and bulky bundles of documents within the confines of a jury box, particularly if there was a need to cross-refer to documents in different bundles or to consider two or more at the same time;

(2) jury trials took longer than those tried by a judge alone – if the prolongation was substantial because of the number and complexity of documents, the administration of justice was likely to be affected;

(3) if litigation costs were substantially increased by the extra cost of a jury trial, justice might be denied – costs might also be increased by the extra expense incurred in having to copy extra documents for the use of a dozen additional people; and

(4) the risk that the jury might not sufficiently understand the issues in the documents or accounts to resolve them correctly (a judge might make the same mistake, but that would become apparent from his judgment and could then be put right on appeal; but this would not be so in the case of a jury) – the risk is enhanced when the average juror could not be expected to be familiar with the type of documents which were going to be placed before him.

Thus, in *Dodd v The Chief Constable of Cheshire and the Chief Constable of Devon and Cornwall*[4]. the Court of Appeal refused a jury trial although the number of documents was not that great, but their complexity was such that the estimated length of the trial was 4 weeks with a jury and 1 week by a judge alone.

In *Oliver v Calderdale Borough Council*, above, the Court of Appeal held that the conditions for a non-jury trial were made out where there was a dispute about the claimant's psychological state. It was not convenient for those sorts of medical questions to be investigated before a jury.

---

1   [1973] 1 All ER 1013.
2   [1987] 3 All ER 485.
3   [1990] 1 WLR 1042.
4   (Unreported) 22 October 1997.

Where a claim is made to dispense with a jury on the basis that the case involves scientific or local investigation which cannot conveniently be done with a body of 12 people, the experience of Cockburn CJ will be of great value in determining the validity of such a contention [1]:

> 'Every day special juries are called upon to decide questions turning on matters of science and professional knowledge, foreign to their ordinary avocations, among others, questions of navigation and nautical skills, and their decisions are on the whole satisfactory.'

However, in *Darragh v Chief Constable of Thames Valley Police* [2] (where neither party wanted a split trial), the Court of Appeal was of the view that the words 'scientific investigation' should not be given a limited meaning and included medical investigations. Accordingly, the Court upheld an order for a non-jury trial because the issue of damages was not free from difficulty and involved extensive medical reports. It is submitted that the view of Cockburn CJ is far more likely to be right as, unlike a modern judge, he will have had great experience of civil jury trials.

15.9.4   Split trials

If a scientific investigation is needed only for quantum then, in keeping with the intention of Parliament, there should be a split trial with liability being decided by 'twelve good men [and women] and true'. That is how road traffic accident cases are tried in Eire. To be fair to the lords justices in *Darragh*, above, Potter LJ agreed with Sir Patrick Russell who would have looked most favourably at an application for a split trial, ie liability determined by a jury, and quantum by judge alone:

> '... allegations of police brutality and, generally, of police misconduct ... are eminently suitable for the decision of a jury ... On the other hand, the question of damages in this case is not free from difficulty. There are very extensive medical reports and extensive conflicts of medical opinion as to the sequelae consequent upon the alleged police malpractice to which I have referred ... one has in the case the conflict between, first, the issue of liability which, as I have indicated, I would be inclined to the view should be tried by a jury and, secondly, the question of damages which, in my view, should definitely be tried by a judge.
>
> Is there any solution to this conflict? Neither counsel for the appellant nor counsel for the defendant is in favour of a split trial though that was debated during the course of the hearing.'

Indeed, s 69(4) of the Supreme Court Act 1981 expressly recognised split trails with different modes. In *Coenen v Payne* [3] (a running down case), Lord Denning MR said:

> 'In future the courts should be more ready to grant separate trials than they used to do.'

---

1   *Dawkins v Lord F Paulet* (1869) LR 5 QB 94 at 109.
2   (1998) TLR, October 20.
3   [1974] 1 WLR 984 at 988F.

Nowadays, r 3.1(2)(i) of CPR 1998 gives the court a specific power to 'direct a separate trial of any issue'. In *Conlon v Chief Constable of Northumbria*, above, the claimant alleged that he had been unlawfully incarcerated and beaten up in a police van. The defendant wanted trial by judge alone because the medical evidence was not straightforward. A split trial was ordered, with Judge LJ saying[1]:

> 'It therefore follows that there is no sufficient basis demonstrated for depriving the claimant of that which the section says on the face of it he is entitled to in a case of false imprisonment.'

The court also said that if it was relevant to an issue regarding liability, then such evidence could be adduced before the jury. Also the judge should at the first trial ask the jury to make a finding on any disputed issue of fact which he considered relevant to quantum and was suitable for determination by that tribunal.

In *Marks v Chief Constable of Greater Manchester*[2] (a malicious prosecution case), the Court of Appeal upheld the refusal by Hodgson J to grant the defendant's application for a split trial as the matter was within the discretion of the trial judge and there were no grounds for interfering. The plaintiff had been acquitted of obstructing the police. The judgment of the Recorder of Manchester accused the police of lying. The plaintiff wanted to claim exemplary damages because of the conduct of the Chief Constable in defending the action when the testimony he relied upon had already been disbelieved by the Recorder. The defendant said that such evidence would prejudice their defence on quantum. The Court of Appeal said the trial judge could give to the jury a very clear direction as to the limited use that it could make of the remarks of the Recorder.

In *Burke v Metropolitan Police Commissioner*[3], the Court of Appeal held that any appeal over whether or not there should be a split trial (which in that case had been ordered) must be made before the hearing of the case. In the words of Simon Brown LJ:

> 'The one thing that could not possibly be appropriate was to wait and see whether the plaintiff succeeded on liability before the jury and then, having failed, seek to appeal.'

15.9.5 Number of jurors

In *Hamilton v Fayed*[4], Morland J held that a judge had an unfettered discretion to allow a jury to continue with less than 12 members even if one of the litigants objected.

---

1   (Unreported) 2 March 2000 at para 20.
2   (1991) 156 LGR 990.
3   (Unreported) 12 January 1999.
4   (Unreported) 20 December 1999.

15.10   EVIDENCE

15.10.1   The burden of proof

In any action for trespass, it is for the claimant to prove, on a balance of probabilities, that the act complained of as constituting the tort actually occurred. If that is done, then it is up to the defendant (if it be part of his case) to establish to a similar standard that what he did was done under a lawful authority (for example a valid warrant); see *Dallison v Caffery*[1]. The arrester must also justify the continuance of his custody by showing that it was reasonable[2]. To the same effect are the words of Hawkins J in *Hicks v Faulkner*[3] and approved by Roch LJ in *R v Governor of Brockhill Prison, ex parte Evans (No 2)*[4]:

> '... that in false imprisonment the onus lies upon the defendant to plead and prove affirmatively the existence of reasonable cause as his justification ....'

That view was held up on appeal. Lord Steyn said:

> 'It is common ground that the tort of false imprisonment involves the infliction of bodily restraint which is not expressly or impliedly authorised by the law. The plaintiff does not have to prove fault on the part of the defendant. It is a tort of strict liability.'[5]

15.10.2   Estoppel and the findings in a previous trial

Often an action of trespass has been preceded by a criminal trial arising out of a police investigation, one of the steps of which has been an arrest; and it is that apprehension which has led to the Chief Constable being sued. The legal consequences that flow from an acquittal or a conviction differ.

In *Hunter v Chief Constable of the West Midlands*[6], the House of Lords held that a statement of claim should be struck out if it amounted to a collateral attack on a final decision of a court of competent jurisdiction in which the party making the attack had a full opportunity of testing the decision. In *Stopford v Chief Constable of Dorset*[7], Stuart-Smith LJ held that 'collateral attack' meant that a second tribunal was being invited to reach a decision which was inconsistent with that of a previous one. Thus, a plaintiff cannot deny the guilt of an offence for which he had been convicted. However, having committed a crime does not automatically equate with having been lawfully arrested for it, as was made clear in *Hill v Chief Constable of South Yorkshire*[8] where it was held that a guilty plea was no proof of a legal apprehension. The plaintiff had been convicted upon his own confession of having being drunk and disorderly and had then sued in the

---

1   [1965] 1 QB 348 at 365F (per Lord Denning MR) and p 370G (per Diplock LJ).
2   Ibid at 371A.
3   (1881) 8 QBD 167 at 170.
4   [1999] QB 1043 at 1066.
5   [2000] 3 WLR 843 at 847H.
6   [1982] AC 529 at 541B.
7   (Unreported) 6 October 1988.
8   [1990] 1 All ER 1046.

county court, alleging that he had never been told the reason for his arrest and had been detained for too long in police custody, without being charged as soon as possible. The Court of Appeal held that the county court judge had been wrong to strike out the claim for false imprisonment. Purchas LJ said[1]:

> 'The fact that the person arrested is in fact guilty, as subsequent events establish, would only be relevant if the arrest was challenged as being made without reasonable grounds for believing that an offence had been committed. It cannot, in my judgment, logically affect other requirements provided by statute for the protection of the individual without whose observance Parliament has specifically provided the arrest or the detention shall be "unlawful".
>
> ... The established fact of the arrested person's criminality merely touches upon the obviousness of the grounds for the arrest and, therefore, is specifically excluded by the terms of the Act as a reason for establishing the lawfulness of either the arrest or the detention.'

As the standard of proof is different, an acquittal does give rise to an estoppel against an arrester; see *Hunter v Chief Constable of the West Midlands*, above, and *Stanley v Benning*[2].

What is the position if at the end of the prosecution case, the judge rules the arrest illegal? The answer will depend on which standard of proof was applied in reaching that decision. In the words of Stuart-Smith LJ in *Stopford*, above:

> 'It seems to me that the court should only strike out a defence [of lawful arrest] if we are satisfied that the very question was decided against a party[3] seeking to set up the case either on a similar standard of proof or on a more stringent one.'

In that case, the original ruling on the lawfulness of the arrest was made by the Crown Court sitting on appeal. In upholding the submission of no case to answer, the recorder had uttered comments about the impression formed by the Bench on the real motives of the arrester, which of course were being judged against him on the criminal standard of proof. So the Court of Appeal refused to strike out the defence of lawful justification. From their judgment, it is clear that the two lords justices would have reached a different conclusion if the recorder had made his ruling on the basis that every word of the prosecution evidence was true. That case does not appear to have been cited in *Nawrot v Chief Constable of Hampshire*[4]. In that case, the High Court had quashed the plaintiff's conviction for police assault[5]. This was because the offence for which he had been apprehended was not an arrestable offence, so his incarceration could be justified only if the arrester had acted in order to prevent a breach of the peace. However, the justices in their case stated said that: 'PC Robertson did not at this stage apprehend a breach of the peace'. This

---

1   Ibid, at 1053.
2   (Unreported) 4 July 1998 (CA) per Schiemann LJ.
3   The judgments in *Stopford* do not say who the prosecutor was. In view of this comment, it was presumably the Chief Constable. The date of the offence is not given, but as the Crown Court appeal was in August 1986, the information may well have been laid before the Crown Prosecution Service was set up. The CPS did not take over prosecutions commenced before they existed.
4   *The Independent*, 7 January 1992.
5   [1988] Crim LR 107.

meant, of course, that the arrest was unlawful, thus PC Robertson was not acting in the execution of his duty, so no offence could be committed under s 51(1) of the Police Act 1964. The plaintiff then sued for false imprisonment and sought to strike out, on two grounds, the defence of 'lawful arrest'.

The first ground argued was issue estoppel. The High Court held that such could arise (if at all) only where the parties in both actions were the same but here the defendant had not been a party to the criminal case, which had been litigated by the Director of Public Prosecutions. The Court had grave doubts as to whether it could ever be relied upon except where to litigate would amount to an abuse of process. That could not arise in the present case because the justices did not set out the facts on which they had reached their decision about there being no apprehended breach of the peace. They may merely have decided that this issue of fact had not been proved to the standard required in a criminal case, whereas in a civil suit the burden is less onerous. Also the defendant had not been a party to the previous action and had had no control over how it was conducted; there might be other witnesses that he would wish to call who did not give evidence in the criminal trial. In addition, it would be unjust in an action for exemplary damages to prevent the defendant putting forward his account of what had happened. Finally, the Court was of the view that all *Hunter*, above, did was to give the defendant in a civil action a shield; it did not put a sword into the plaintiff's hands to be used to obtain compensation.

Thus, there is a conflict between *Stopford*, above, and *Nawrot*, above, although it is more theoretical than real. The difference between those appeals would only arise in a case where there was no conflict of evidence because the burden of proof required to establish facts in a criminal court is higher than in a civil action. Thus, the principle of *Hunter*, above, against a defendant in a civil action could apply to a ruling of law only on the basis that all the prosecution evidence was true. Also, where the civil defendant was not the prosecutor, there must be no additional evidence produced at the hearing of the false imprisonment case which had not been before the criminal tribunal. Thus, the question is whether, in those limited circumstances, a person is prevented from being able to challenge the prior ruling of another court as to the legal position arising from the same facts as those being litigated in a subsequent action.

According to *Nathaniel v Metropolitan Police Commissioner*[1], the answer would depend on whether the legal ruling had been given by a court of first instance or on appeal. In that case, the plaintiff had provided a specimen for a DNA test during an inquiry into an allegation of rape. However, contrary to the express provisions of PACE 1984, s 64, the sample was not destroyed after the latter's acquittal but was later adduced before a jury in another rape case which resulted in his conviction at first instance. The Court of Appeal[2] subsequently quashed the verdict on the grounds that the trial judge had erred in law in not exercising his powers under PACE 1984, s 78 to exclude the results of the DNA test for breach of s 64. In the ensuing civil action, the defendant submitted that

---

1   *New Law Digest*, 20 February 1998.
2   [1995] 2 Cr App R 565.

there had been no breach of statutory duty by him. Eady J held that as the Commissioner had not been a party to the proceedings which had resulted in the quashing of the conviction, no estoppel arose, and it was not an abuse of process to put forward the argument which he did. However, Eady J went on to say that he was bound by the decision of the Court of Appeal to hold that there had been a breach of s 64; but in his judgment that did not give rise to an action in tort. If he had found for the plaintiff, then the Commissioner could have appealed to the House of Lords, which, of course, would not have been bound by the *ratio* of the Court of Appeal (Criminal Division). The latest case to date appears to be *McCauley v Vine*[1], where the Court of Appeal held that there was no attack being made on a decision of a court of competent jurisdiction by a *defendant* in a civil case disputing his conviction in a criminal court. (That was a running down case where the defendant challenged the correctness of his conviction for careless driving.)

For an issue of estoppel to arise, both actions must have been between the same litigants. Since the setting up of the Crown Prosecution Service, the police are no longer a party to the criminal trial. Probably the only time when an estoppel could arise would be where Customs officers had arrested and prosecuted somebody under the Customs legislation, as in that case the Crown would have been the prosecutor and subsequently the defendant in the false imprisonment action. In *Hunter*, above, the arising of an issue estoppel from a criminal trial was recognised by all three lords justices who heard the first appeal and by Lord Diplock. (The view expressed in *Nawrot*, above, that even in those limited circumstances there could not be any estoppel was, of course, *obiter* as the parties to the later action were not the same as those in the earlier case.)

To sum up, the law would appear to be that a tortfeasor who is sued can dispute any findings made in a criminal trial, unless either:

(1) he had been the prosecutor; or
(2) the Court of Appeal had given a ruling upon the issue, when the evidence was the same as that in the civil case,

and in both (1) and (2) the standard of proof in the criminal case applied in reaching the decision of fact had been the same as in the civil case.

15.10.3 Police cautions

In *Abraham v Metropolitan Police Commissioner*[2], the plaintiff, having been arrested for a public order offence, had accepted a police caution. She then sued for false imprisonment in relation to her apprehension. The Court of Appeal set aside the striking out of the claim. It held that a formal caution was not the same as finding of fact by, or a judgment of, a court of law, so that the principles laid down by the House of Lords in *Hunter v Chief Constable of the West Midlands*[3], had no relevance. It was as a condition of being cautioned, rather

---

1   [2000] RTR 70.
2   (2000) *New Law Digest*, 8 December.
3   [1982] AC 529.

than prosecuted, that the appellant had to admit her guilt. However, this could not give rise to any estoppel. To quote from the report:

> 'The claimant, a person of good character, had been brought to the police station on a false pretext. She would have been anxious about her two children from whom perforce she had been separated on arrest. Her admission had been to an account of events, which both she and the arresting officer knew to be false. Her admission had been contributed to, if not caused, by the wrongful arrest and the false recounting of events by the arresting officer, who had been throughout the defendant's servant.'

Thus, this case sensibly recognises that some people will say anything to get out of a police station and therefore they are allowed thereafter to contradict their false confessions.

It is submitted that on those grounds the case was rightly decided. It was argued by counsel solely on the basis of estoppel. The other ground on which the decision was reached, namely the imputed knowledge of an employer, must be regarded as being *per incuriam* in view of s 88 of the Police Act 1996 which was not cited in the judgment or by counsel (see **13.4**, above).

15.11   THE TRIAL – JUDGE AND JURY, THEIR RESPECTIVE ROLES

Normally, issues of law are for the judge and questions of fact are for the jury:

> 'It is necessary to define the role of the jury in civil cases where the jury will not simply be asked to give a "general" verdict but a "special" verdict consisting of answers to a series of questions. The fundamental principle is that the jury makes specific findings on the various issues raised in the case. Thus the jury is presented with a "questionnaire" to answer which deals with disputed issues of fact. The jury make their findings of fact. The jury's findings then provide the judge with material so that he can give a ruling. In principle this means that the judge rather than the jury makes the final decision on liability.'[1]

However, it is for the judge to rule on whether an arrester's suspicion was reasonable; see *Ward v Chief Constable of the West Midlands*, above. A possible reason for this was given by Diplock LJ in *Dallison v Caffery*[2]:

> 'It may be that this rule reflects the judicial distrust of Jacobinism among juries at the formative period of this branch of English law; but it can at least be rationalised on the grounds that a judge, by reason of his office and his experience, is better qualified than a juryman to determine what conduct is reasonable or unreasonable in furtherance of the administration of justice. In those days, however, the jury was the only tribunal which at common law was competent to determine disputed issues of fact.'

---

1   *Ward v Chief Constable of the West Midlands* (1997) TLR, December 15.
2   [1965] 1 QB 348 at 372A.

Thus, it is only necessary to leave to the jury questions of disputed fact where the resolution of that dispute is necessary before the judge will be in a position to make his ruling; see Diplock LJ in *Dallison v Caffery*[1].

However, the jury has the final say over whether or not the length of the incarceration was reasonable in all the circumstances. In *John Lewis & Co Ltd v Tims*[2], Lord Porter said:

'... there may be cases in which it could be contended that, though a reasonable amount of detention was justified, the actual detention was unduly long. In such a case it would be the duty of the judge to determine whether there was or was not evidence from which it could be deduced that the detention was unduly long, and, if he held that there was, to leave the question to the jury whether in fact it was longer than was justified.'

The above quotation was cited with approval by Beldam LJ in *Foulkes v Chief Constable of Merseyside*[3]. Likewise, in the case where *mala fides* is alleged, where any question of whether the police acted from malice should be left to the jury only if there is sufficient evidence to raise this issue.

However, subject to the exceptions set out above, it is solely for the jury to decide if the actions of the police were reasonable; see *Pollard v Chief Constable of West Yorkshire*[4] where the Court of Appeal held that it was for the jury to decide if it had been reasonable for the local constabulary to have used a dog when making an arrest. (The plaintiff, having been bitten by the dog, had sued, *inter alia*, for assault.)

15.12   THE SUMMING UP

In *Sutton v Metropolitan Police Commissioner*[5], Kennedy LJ said:

'But the case [*Ward v Chief Constable of West Midlands*, above], is not to be taken as authority for the proposition advanced by [the appellants' counsel], namely that in every case of this kind it is necessary to instruct the jury as to the legal ingredients of false imprisonment and malicious prosecution. As in any other jury trial, the jury needs be told as much – and no more – of the law as they need to know to play their part in the trial process.'

15.13   COSTS

Where a jury disagrees and no settlement is reached, the usual order for costs is that the costs of the first trial is to abide the results of the new trial; ie the winner

---

1   Ibid, at 372.
2   [1952] AC 676 at 682.
3   [1998] 3 All ER 705 at 711h/j.
4   [1999] PIQR P219.
5   (Unreported) 29 July 1998.

of the second trial also gets his costs of the first hearing, see *Camiller v Metropolitan Police Commissioner*[1].

In *Heaven v Chief Constable of West Midlands*[2], the plaintiff sued for false imprisonment and malicious prosecution. As he only succeeded on the first issue, the Recorder awarded him two-thirds of his costs. The Court of Appeal ordered[3] that he receive his entire costs, on the standard basis, as 'all the issues arose out of the same series of facts and could not be appropriately segregated'.

15.14   APPEALS

15.14.1   Leave

From 26 April 1999, leave has been needed before an appeal can be made to the Court of Appeal in any action for trespass; see CPR 1998, r 52.3(1)(a) (as amended by SI 2000/221). This has brought High Court cases into line with those in the county court. The latter were governed by the County Court (Appeals) Order 1991, art 2(1) which stipulated that leave was required where the amount claimed either did not exceed £5,000 or was not quantifiable. In *Deflorimonte v Metropolitan Police Commissioner*[4], the Court of Appeal held that damages in actions for false imprisonment were at large and within the province of the jury. Therefore, they were not quantifiable, so that in all such cases leave to appeal was necessary.

15.14.2   On fact

In *Castorina v Chief Constable of Surrey*[5], Woolf LJ was of the view that the issue of the reasonableness of the suspicion held by the arrester was a question of fact for the judge, and therefore an appellate tribunal could interfere only if there had been a misdirection of law or the decision was clearly wrong. It is submitted that the better view was that expressed in the same case by Sir Frederick Lawton that they could substitute their own views for that of the trial judge where the primary facts were not in dispute. That is in line with RSC 1965, Ord 59, r 10(3) that the Court of Appeal can draw its own inferences from the primary facts as found by the judge.

On 3 May 2000, r 52.11(1) of CPR 1998, was brought into force (SI 2000/221). Under that rule, every appeal will be limited to a review, unless the court considers it to be in the interests of justice to hold a rehearing. This raises an interesting question which was previously only of academic interest, namely whether the issue of reasonableness is a question of law or of fact. It is submitted that the *obiter dicta* of Woolf J in *Castorina*, above, were erroneous. *Ad questionem*

---

1   (1999) TLR, June 8.
2   (Unreported) 27 July 2000.
3   Ibid, at para 22.
4   (Unreported) 18 August 1998.
5   (1988) NLJ (R) 180.

facti non respondent judices, ad questionem juris non respondent juratores[1]. Or to quote more modern authority, in *British Launderers Association v Hendon Rating Authority*[2] Denning LJ pronounced:

> 'If, and in so far ... as the correct conclusion to be drawn from primary facts requires, for its correctness, determination by a trained lawyer ... the conclusion is a conclusion of law.'

As (to repeat the words of Diplock LJ *in Dallison v Caffery*[3]) 'a judge, by reason of his office and his experience, is better placed that a juryman to determine what conduct is reasonable', then that issue is a question of law which means that an appeal court is able to substitute its own views for that of the trial judge. However, the power of an appellate court to interfere with any fact found by a jury is strictly limited. To quote from the headnote in the report of *Mechanical and General Inventions Co Ltd et al v Austin et al*[4]:

> 'When it is decided that a case is to be tried by a jury, that tribunal is the only judge of the facts, and no appellate tribunal can substitute its finding for that of the jury. The appellate court has a revising function to see, first, whether there is any evidence in support of the issue found by the jury; and secondly whether the verdict can stand as being one which reasonable men might have come to.'

15.14.3 On quantum

Prior to the Courts and Legal Services Act 1990, all an appellate tribunal could do if an appeal on quantum succeeded was to order a retrial. The principle to be applied was that laid down in *Landell v Landell*[5]:

> 'It is clear, in order to warrant the application of the term "excessive" [to the award], the damages must be held to exceed, not what the court might think enough, but even that latitude, which, in a question of amount so very vague, any set of reasonable men could be permitted to indulge. The excess must be such as to raise ... the moral conviction that the jury, whether from wrong intention or incapacity or some mistake, have committed gross injustice ...'

Unfortunately, by s 8(2) of the Courts and Legal Services Act 1990, the Court of Appeal was given power to substitute its own figure instead of, as previously, ordering a new trial. However, by RSC Ord 59, r 11(4), this new power could only be excercised where the sum awarded by a jury was 'excessive or inadequate'. As this was the same test used by courts when previously deciding whether a new trial on damages should be ordered, then in theory Parliament did alter the basis on which an appeal should be allowed. However, this has not proved to be the case and the threshold for intervention has been lowered, as was expressly recognised in *Clark v Chief Constable of Cleveland*[6], where Roch LJ said that the Court of Appeal:

---

1   Co Litt 295.
2   [1949] 1 KB 434 at 472.
3   [1965] 1 QB 348 at 372A.
4   [1935] AC 346 at 347.
5   (1841) 3 D 819 at 825. This *dictum* was approved by the House of Lords in *Girvan v Inverness Farmers' Dairy* 1998 SC (HL) 1.
6   (1999) TLR, May 13 (Henry LJ dissenting).

'... had to use its judgment to decide whether the award the jury had made was, in the circumstances of the case before it, disproportionate.

In cases of false imprisonment and malicious prosecution there would be an equal concern to see that the compensation for tortious interference with individual liberty was adequate and consistent as there would be to see that damages did not go beyond compensation and become enrichment.'

Peter Gibson LJ, after acknowledging the supremacy of the jury, went on to say:

'But if the award when considered against the facts is seen to be substantially out of line with the guidelines, then in my judgment the appellate court can and should interfere.'

There, a jury's award of £500 for having been maliciously prosecuted was increased to £2,000, because that was the minimum figure suggested in the guidelines laid down in *Thompson v Metropolitan Police Commissioner*[1]. The majority was of the view that because the period between the institution and the conclusion of the criminal proceedings was nearly 1 year, the quantum would in usual circumstances have been increased by about £4,000 in accordance with the guidelines, but that increase was counterbalanced by the fact that the plaintiff had been cautioned in the past for theft and that he:

'might well have appeared to the jury from the evidence of his interview on the night of his arrest as a person who would suffer less distress from a prosecution hanging over him that the average person and again that is a depreciatory factor to be taken in account'[2].

The CPR 1998 r 52.10(3) (as amended by SI 2000/221) gives the Court of Appeal a power to vary an award of damages made by a jury. It does not (as the old RSC did) limit that power to where the amount was 'excessive or inadequate'. However, as its powers are now usually limited to a review (see r 52.11(1)), this presumably means that the threshold for intervention has not in fact altered. In *Thompson*[3], the jury had awarded £51,000 and the appellate tribunal considered the correct figure to be £45,000. Lord Woolf MR stated:

'This is marginally less than the total award of the jury but when considering whether to allow the appeal we are concerned with the totality of the award. We will not allow the Commissioners' appeal as the jury retain a margin of appreciation so this court will not intervene unless the difference as to amount is greater than this error.'

In other words, an appellate tribunal will not interfere with an award within about 15% of the *Thompson* guidelines.

1   [1998] QB 498.
2   In *Clark v Chief Constable of Cleveland* (1999) TLR, May 13, per Peter Gibson LJ.
3   Ibid, at 519C/D.

Chapter 16

THE CRIMINAL LAW

16.1 INTRODUCTION

False imprisonment was a common law misdemeanour until the latter was abolished in 1967 when the crime became an arrestable offence. In addition, an illegal arrest gives the judge a discretion under PACE 1984, s 78 to exclude any evidence in a criminal prosecution which flowed from it.

16.2 THE CRIME OF FALSE IMPRISONMENT

The *actus reus* of false imprisonment was defined by the Court of Appeal in *R v Rahman*[1] as:

> 'The unlawful and intentional or reckless restraint of a victim's movement.'

The above quotation was approved in *R v James*[2]. That case also discussed the requisite *mens rea* and held that it was necessary to prove in relation to the act causing the restriction that it was not accidental but that the accused had intended by his actions to restrain or had been 'reckless' within the definition ascribed to this word in *R v Cunningham*[3], namely he had foreseen the possibility of the victim being falsely imprisoned and had gone ahead with his plans, taking the risk that it might occur. In *R v James*, above, it was also ruled that it was a crime of basic intent. To the same effect on this latter point is *R v Hitchins*[4], in which it was held that self-induced intoxication was no defence to the charge. (There the defendant, after having taken various drugs, had attacked one girl and taken another as a hostage.)

Unlike the civil courts, the person in the dock must be judged on the facts as he honestly believed them to be; see *R v Williams*[5] (an assault case). This consideration is very important as the defence is almost invariably 'a lawful arrest'. A citizen may apprehend anybody whom, on reasonable grounds, he suspects to be guilty of an arrestable offence, provided that such has actually been perpetrated (see PACE 1984, s 24(5)). Thus, an honest belief that the crime has been committed is sufficient to overcome the second hurdle. What is undecided is whether it was sufficient for the accused to have had an honest belief that his prisoner was guilty or whether the facts honestly believed to exist by the arrester must have amounted as a matter of law to a reasonable suspicion.

---

1   (1985) 81 Cr App R 349 at 353.
2   [1997] TLR 493.
3   [1957] 2 QB 396.
4   [1988] Crim LR 379.
5   [1987] 3 All ER 411.

It is submitted that, by applying strict legal principles[1], the answer is the latter, in accordance with the maxim '*ignorantia facti excusat, ignorantia juris non excusat*' (see *Mildmay*[2]). Although this does not happen at present, should it become fashionable for those who have been falsely imprisoned not only to sue the chief constable for damages but also to lay information against those officers who had actually imposed the restraint on their freedom of movement, then the judiciary, as a matter of policy, may well hold that an honest belief in guilt was, *ipso facto* sufficient to merit an acquittal irrespective of the legal position – in order that the fear of a subsequent prosecution does not deter the police and their fellow citizens from carrying out their moral or legal duty of catching suspected criminals.

16.3 ATTEMPTS

An attempt to commit false imprisonment is an offence contrary to s 1 of the Criminal Attempts Act 1981. To be guilty, a person must have done an act which (to use the language of that statute) 'is more than merely preparatory to the commission of the [substantive] offence'. In *R v Geddes*[3], the defendant entered a school but was seen by a teacher and departed from the premises. In a cubicle in the school lavatory, he left a cider can. His rucksack was found in the bushes and contained a large kitchen knife, some lengths of masking tape and a rope. The Crown alleged that these items were to catch and to restrain a boy entering the cubicle. The Court of Appeal quashed the conviction, stating:

> 'It was an accurate paraphrase of the statutory test to ask whether the available evidence, if accepted, showed that the defendant had done an act [which] showed that he had actually tried to commit the offence in question or whether he had only got ready or put himself into a position or equipped himself to do so.'

The Court of Appeal said that Geddes had only done those latter things, since he had never had any contact or communication with any of the pupils. Thus, it would seem that, as a matter of law, no attempt will have taken place until a person actually sees his victim and then does something, the object of which is to detain the victim.

16.4 PACE 1984

Section 78 of PACE 1984 enacts:

> '(1) In any proceedings the court may refuse to allow evidence on which the prosecution proposes to rely to be given if it appears to the court that, having regard to all the circumstances, *including the circumstances in which the evidence was obtained,* the admission of the evidence would have such an adverse effect on the fairness of the proceedings that the court ought not to admit it.

---

1   See *R v Lee* [2000] Crim LR 991.
2   (1584) 1 Co Rep 175a at 177b.
3   [1996] Crim LR 894.

(2) Nothing in this section shall prejudice any rule of law requiring a Court to exclude evidence.' (Author's emphasis.)

Thus, when the Crown wishes to tender illegally obtained evidence, judges and magistrates have to perform a balancing act, as was recognised by Lord Elwyn-Jones in *Fox v Chief Constable of Gwent*[1], where he quoted with approval the words of the Lord Justice-General in *Lawrie v Muir*[2]:

'From the standpoint of principle it seems to me that the law must strive to reconcile two highly important interests which are liable to come into conflict: (a) the interest of the citizen to be protected from illegal or irregular invasions of his liberties by the authorities, and (b) the interest of the State to secure that evidence bearing on the commission of crime and necessary to enable justice to be done shall not be withheld from courts of law on any merely formal or technical ground. Neither of these objects can be insisted upon to the uttermost. The protection of the citizen is primarily protection for the innocent citizen against unwarranted, wrongful and perhaps high-handed interference, and the common sanction is an action of damages. The protection is not intended as a protection of the guilty citizen against the efforts of the public prosecutor to vindicate the law. On the other hand, the interest of the State cannot be magnified to the point of causing all the safeguards for the protection of the citizen to vanish, and of offering a positive inducement to the authorities to proceed by irregular methods. Irregularities require to be excused, and the infringements of the formalities of the law in relation to these matters are not likely to be condoned. Whether any given irregularity ought to be excused depends on the nature of the irregularity and the circumstances under which it was committed. In particular the case may bring into play the discretionary principle of fairness to the accused ...'

In theory, any evidence obtained by the commission of the tort of false imprisonment could be excluded by the judiciary using their powers under s 78 of PACE 1984. In practice, this has been confined to preventing the Director of Public Prosecutions adducing evidence, in drinking and driving cases, of the requirement for, and the results of an analysis of, a sample of blood, breath or urine. This is because, but for the illegal arrest, the defendant would never have been at the police station and, without his presence at that location, the constabulary would never have been in a position to demand that he supply a specimen for analysis.

Earlier cases suggested that this discretionary power under s 78 arose only in cases of *mala fides*. In *R v Samuels*[3], the Court of Appeal held that it was not so limited. Hence the decision in *DPP v Godwin*[4] where the High Court upheld the acquittal of the defendant for driving with excess alcohol as he had been illegally arrested. At the roadside, he had been asked by a constable if he had been drinking, to which he replied in the negative. Despite that denial, the officer still asked him to take a breath test and when this was refused, the motorist was arrested. No evidence was given as to why a test had been requested. Accordingly, the justices held that this requirement was illegal and

---

1   [1986] AC 281 at 293.
2   (1950) JC 19 at 26–27.
3   [1988] QB 615.
4   [1991] RTR 303.

the constable had no power to arrest for non-compliance therewith, and for that reason refused to allow the Intoximeter printout to be produced to the court, notwithstanding that the accused had clearly been lying when denying that he had been drinking, as the analysis of his breath revealed an alcoholic level in excess of twice the legal limit. That ruling was upheld on appeal to the High Court. Bingham LJ stated that the illegal arrest gave the magistrates the discretion under s 78 to exclude evidence of the breath analysis and that, whichever way that discretion was exercised, it could not be challenged in a higher court. Indeed, his Lordship stated that some might consider the defendant fortunate. However, he also went on to say[1]:

'The justices were entitled to conclude that the substantial breach by the constable of the protection afforded to members of the public by s 6 was denied to the defendant, that as a result the prosecutor obtained evidence which he would not otherwise have obtained, and that as a result the defendant was prejudiced in a significant manner in resisting the charge against him.'

Those sentiments did not find universal favour with other judges. In *DPP v Kay*[2], Roch LJ said:

'If the officers at the roadside and at the police station or hospital are conducting in good faith a genuine inquiry into whether an offence under s 3(a), 4, or 5 of the Act has been committed, magistrates should be slow to exclude evidence of the taking of the specimen of breath, blood or urine because of a technical shortcoming in the procedure carried out at the roadside. The magistrates must weigh the defect in the roadside procedure and consider its effect on the evidence of the police officer who has taken the specimen of breath, blood or urine by following the correct procedures at the police station or hospital. It is only if the admission of the second officer's evidence in the light of what had gone wrong at the roadside would have such an adverse effect on the fairness of proceedings that the court ought not to admit it that the second officer's evidence may be excluded. The magistrates must have in mind when weighing the failure to follow the correct procedure at the roadside and its effect on the fairness of proceedings that Parliament enacted the provisions in the 1988 Act in their present form precisely to avoid motorists who were over the permitted limit escaping responsibility on technicalities. The dangers created to innocent persons by those who drive with an excess of alcohol in their blood were well established and well known to Parliament when Parliament changed the wording of these provisions in 1981.'

It is true that the legislature did reduce the protection given to the motorist, but of far more relevance, it did not abolish these safeguards altogether. If Parliament had wanted to make anything which occurred prior to the arrival at the police station incapable of affording a defence, then RTA 1988 could have easily said this. Thus, the opinion expressed by Bingham LJ is much preferable. After he became Lord Chief Justice, he expressed similar views in *DPP v MacPhail*[3]. There the justices had excluded evidence of the analysis by the Intoximeter, because of the *mala fides* of the arresting officer. He had administered a screening breath test within 20 minutes of the driver's last

---

1   [1991] RTR 303 at 308H/J.
2   [1999] RTR 109.
3   (Unreported) 8 July 1997.

drink, in the full knowledge that this should not be done. The DPP argued that it was unfair to the prosecution not to allow her to adduce evidence of the Intoximeter reading at the station because the reliability of that testimony was unaffected by what had happened at the roadside (ie the illegal arrest). Lord Bingham CJ said *in argumento* that there would be 'no incentive to the police' and it would 'drive a coach and horses through the statutory provisions' if justices had no power to exclude evidence of what had occurred at the station 'no matter how unfairly and oppressively the police had acted to get the defendant there'. The President of the Queen's Bench Division also said that where the admission of evidence 'was very damaging [to the defence], that was precisely where the justices had to look at it very carefully' when considering whether to admit it.

It is submitted that *MacPhail* above, sets out the correct approach. There would have been no point in the legislature (when amending RTA 1972) still to have imposed some limitations (though much less than before) on the powers of the constabulary to require a roadside breath test, if Parliament had wanted to give the police *carte blanche* in the matter. As it chose not to do that, then much more preferable are the earlier views expressed in 1991 by Roch J (as he then was) than those proffered by him in 1998. In *Renshaw v DPP*[1], he was fully in agreement with the judgment delivered by Watkins LJ who said:

> '... but where there has been a denial of something which Parliament says shall be provided by the police ... then the courts must take account of it.'

The fact that the failure to observe the safeguards given to a motorist happens to be due to ignorance of the law is irrelevant. *Ignorantia facti excusat, ignorantia juris non exusat*' (see *Mildmay*[2]). It is submitted that the best view is that taken by Lord Griffiths in *Lam Chi-ming v The Queen*[3]:

> 'It is better by far to allow a few guilty men to escape conviction than to compromise the standards of a free society.'

In *Braham v DPP*[4], it was held that an application for the court to exercise its discretionary powers under s 78 cannot be made for the first time on an appeal. That issue must be raised in the lower court. (Despite what the judgments say in that case, the point was indeed taken at first instance but the junior counsel who had appeared below had been replaced by a Queen's Counsel for the appeal, so the High Court was not informed that the matter had indeed been argued before the justices.)

---

1   [1991] RTR 186 at 191.
2   (1584) 1 Co Rep 175a at 177b.
3   [1991] 2 AC 212 at 222.
4   [1994] RTR 30.

16.5 SENTENCING

False imprisonment being a common law crime, the maximum penalty is life imprisonment and an unlimited fine. In *R v Liverpool Youth Court, ex parte C*[1], it was held that the justices had power to commit a juvenile for trial at the Crown Court under s 24 of the Magistrates' Courts Act 1980 on a charge of false imprisonment.

As the circumstances in which it can be committed vary so much, no tariff has been laid down by the Court of Appeal. This was recognised by Lord Lane CJ in *R v Spence and Thomas*[2]:

> 'It seems to this court that, as with many crimes so with kidnapping, there is a wider possible variation in seriousness between one instance of the crime and another. At the top of the scale of course, comes the carefully planned abduction where the victim is used as a hostage or where ransom money is demanded. Such offences will seldom be met with less than 8 years' imprisonment or thereabouts. Where violence or firearms are used, or there are other exacerbating features such as detention of the victim over a long period of time, there a proper sentence will be very much longer than that. At the other end of the scale are those offences which can perhaps scarcely be passed as kidnapping at all. They are often arise as a sequel of family tiffs or lovers' disputes, and seldom require more than 18 months' imprisonment, and sometimes a great deal less.'

Those *dicta* were not cited in *R v Winters*[3], where on the facts of that particular case, Hutchinson J said:

> 'But they are serious charges, are they not, kidnapping and false imprisonment?'

Often during his loss of his liberty the victim will be threatened or assaulted. It is the seriousness of that conduct coupled with the duration of the incarceration which determines the sentence. Also to include such a count in an indictment allows the court to increase the maximum sentence which could otherwise have been awarded. In *R v Willoughby*[4], a sentence of life imprisonment for false imprisonment and 10 years for indecent assault (the maximum) was upheld on appeal. The defendant argued that the incarceration lasted 20 minutes and was incidental to the assault, so a life sentence was not appropriate. He argued that it should not be used to enable a custodial period to be imposed in excess of the maximum for the assault. The Court of Appeal rejected that argument. It said that the reason for restricting the victim's free movement was solely to enable the attack to take place. With due respect to the court, assaults, other than a single blow, often involve preventing the victim from running away, so that this element (the crime of false imprisonment) in effect increases the maximum sentence beyond that laid down and intended by Parliament.

A few examples of the sentences passed are set out below. However, as the Court of Appeal has frequently stressed, the facts of the appeals vary so widely

---

1   *New Law Digest*, 7 May 1998.
2   (1983) 5 Cr App R(S) 413.
3   (Unreported) 1 December 1997.
4   [1999] Crim LR 244.

that each individual case must be considered on its own merits and often little assistance is derived from other appellate decisions. Also, merely because the punishment is upheld does not mean that the appellate tribunal did not think that it was in fact too lenient. Thus, in *R v Prince*[1], the Court of Appeal said that the sentence was entirely deserved and not a day too long, when upholding the appellant's sentence of 4 years' imprisonment. The facts were as follows. A gas fitter had attended the defendant's home and concluded that all that was required was to change the programmer on the heating system. The defendant was of a rather different opinion and said that a new pump and valve were needed. The gas fitter disagreed. The defendant lost his temper and was joined by a second man. They threatened to beat up the complainant if he did not do the work required and the defendant picked up a large kitchen knife and started to stab the worktop with it and then held it against his victim's stomach saying that if he did not do as he was told, he would be killed. The fitter was detained there for 3 hours and 30 minutes until he had completed the work demanded of him. He then departed from the premises in a state of shock, and was off work for 6 months.

In *R v Ahmed*[2], the Court of Appeal upheld a 4-year sentence after a trial. The defendant had invited the complainant back to his flat where they spent the first 3 hours in civilised conversation. When the complainant stood up to leave, he was prevented from so doing by threats of violence that so frightened him that he jumped out of a first floor window, seriously injuring himself. In *R v Targett and Watkins*[3], the appellants entered a public toilet, produced a knife, said they had a gun and threatened to shoot the complainant if he did not give them his wallet. They then forced him to go to a cash machine with them and draw out money (£40) and give it to them. The Court of Appeal upheld concurrent prison sentences of 6 years for robbery and 4 years for the false imprisonment lasting at most 20 minutes, but did state that they were 'at the top of the bracket'. The Court took into account the guilty pleas, but also referred to the bad record of the appellants and the increasing frequency with which offences of that type were being committed.

In *R v Berry et al*[4], a woman had been kidnapped from her home, blindfolded, gagged and assaulted. She was held captive for over 24 hours. The Court of Appeal reduced the sentence on the ringleader to one of 12 years' imprisonment and on his accomplices to 9 and 8 years respectively. In *R v Peumans and Doucet*[5], the appellants had pleaded guilty to kidnapping a debtor to enforce payment of the debt. A custodial sentence of 4 years was considered to be appropriate. In *R v Lowe and Adair*[6], the defendants were convicted after a 5-day trial. They had visited the victim's house and taken him in the middle of the night to Lowe's bungalow. It was made plain to him that his kidnappers wanted money. He was told to sleep on the couch during the night. Adair (who was on

---

1   (Unreported) 16 February 1998.
2   (Unreported) 8 December 1998.
3   (Unreported) 2 February 1999.
4   (1984) 6 Cr App R (S) 350.
5   (1990) Cr App R (S) 303.
6   (Unreported) 2 October 1998.

bail for other offences) threatened to break his legs if he did not get any cash for them in the morning and assaulted him, but was restrained by Lowe. The next day, they all walked 2 miles to the bank where they tried to get their victim to use his debit card, but he foiled their attempts by using the wrong PIN number. They got no money, so they released him. The Court of Appeal reduced the 6-year sentences to 5 years for Adair and 4 years for Lowe; the difference being that the former had been on bail while the latter had restrained his confederate from assaulting the complainant.

In *R v Arif*[1], the defendant, a man of good character, pleaded guilty to falsely imprisoning his wife on a number of days in the matrimonial home. The Court of Appeal halved the sentence to 1 year's imprisonment as 'appropriate for the number of isolated days of restraint on her freedom to leave the house'. In the words of the Court:

> 'It seems clear from the wife's statement, despite her use of the phrase that she was kept "a prisoner in her own house", that there were few, if any, occasions when she was locked in and at all restrained in a physical sense, as opposed to being thoroughly dominated into subjection within a narrow family circle by a husband who appears to have been obsessively jealous and possessive.'

In *R v Laing*[2], it was held that an aggravating feature which could be taken into account when sentencing was if the victim had suffered any harm in trying to escape. However, this did not apply if, in relation to those injuries, there had been a separate count of causing grievous bodily harm and the jury had acquitted on that charge.

Hopefully, the facts of the above decisions have given the reader some insight into the appropriate punishment for this crime. However, a word of warning: each offence must be considered in the context of its own factual matrix and no two cases are ever the same. Hence, no guidelines or tariff have been laid down by the judges. In the words of the Court of Appeal in *R v Norman*[3]:

> 'We have given anxious consideration to all the circumstances of this case, and have taken into account a number of decided cases, which have been drawn to our attention and helpfully summarised by learned counsel. But each case is different and it is not difficult to draw distinctions between the facts of each of these cases and those in the present case.'

---

1   (Unreported) 26 November 1998.
2   (Unreported) 17 June 1997.
3   (Unreported) 15 June 2000.

Chapter 17

HUMAN RIGHTS

17.1 INTRODUCTION

On 2 October 2000, the Human Rights Act 1998 (HRA 1998) incorporated into English law the European Convention on Human Rights. By s 7(1)(b) of HRA 1998, the Convention applies to actions by or against a public body, for example the police; but (s 22(4)) it is not retrospective, save where the proceedings are brought by a public body. It does not extinguish any right possessed prior to its enactment; see s 11. Its importance for those who are incarcerated is that they will have the protection of Art 5 of the Convention. This provides as follows:

'(1) Everyone has the right to liberty and security of person. No one shall be deprived of his liberty save in the following cases and in accordance with a procedure prescribed by law:

(a) the lawful detention of a person after conviction by a competent court;
(b) the lawful arrest or detention of a person for non-compliance with the lawful order of a court or in order to secure the fulfilment of any obligation prescribed by law;
(c) the lawful arrest or detention of a person effected for the purpose of bringing him before the competent legal authority on reasonable suspicion of having committed an offence or when it is considered reasonably necessary to prevent his committing an offence or fleeing when he has done so;
(d) the detention of a minor by lawful order for the purpose of educational supervision or his lawful detention for the purpose of bringing him before the competent legal authority;
(e) the lawful detention of persons for the prevention of the spreading of infectious diseases, of persons of unsound mind, alcoholics[1], or drug addicts or vagrants;
(f) the lawful arrest or detention of a person to prevent his effecting an unauthorised entry into the country or of a person against whom action is being taken with a view to deportation or extradition.

(2) Everyone who is arrested shall be informed promptly, in a language which he understands, of the reason for his arrest and of any charge against him.

(3) Everyone arrested or detained in accordance with the provisions of paragraph 1(c) of this Article shall be brought promptly before a judge or other officer authorised by law to exercise judicial power and shall be entitled to trial within a reasonable time or to release pending trial. Release may be conditioned by guarantees to appear for trial.

---

1   This includes those whose behaviour under the influence of that liquor poses a threat to public order or themselves. See *Litwa v Poland* (2000) *Legal Action Group Bulletin*, July, p 19.

(4) Everyone who is deprived of his liberty by arrest or detention shall be entitled to take proceedings by which the lawfulness of his detention shall be decided speedily by a court and his release ordered if the detention is not lawful.

(5) Everyone who has been the victim of arrest or detention in contravention of the provisions of this Article shall have an enforceable right to compensation.'

The rationale behind this Article was explained in *Fox et al v UK*[1]:

'The court has already recognised the need, inherent in the Convention system, for a proper balance between the defence of the institutions of democracy in the common interest and the protection of individual rights.'

In *R v Governor of Brockhill Prison, ex parte Evans (No 2)*[2] the United Kingdom judiciary took the opportunity of pronouncing their view on Article 5. Lord Hope said[3]:

'The jurisprudence of the European Court of Human Rights indicates that there are various aspects to Article 5(1) which must be satisfied in order to show that the detention is lawful for the purposes of that Article. The first question is whether the detention is lawful under domestic law. Any detention which is unlawful in domestic law will automatically be unlawful under Article 5(1). It will thus give rise to an enforceable right to compensation under Article 5(5), the provisions of which are not discretionary but mandatory. The second question is whether, assuming that the detention is lawful under domestic law, it nevertheless complies with the general requirements of the Convention. These are based upon the principle that any restriction on human rights and fundamental freedoms must be prescribed by law: see Articles 8 to 11 of the Convention. They include the requirements that the domestic law must be sufficiently accessible to the individual and that it must be sufficiently precise to enable the individual to foresee the consequences of the restriction: *Sunday Times v United Kingdom* (1979) 2 EHRR 245 and *Zamir v United Kingdom* (1983) 40 D & R 42, paras 90–91. The third question is whether, again assuming that the detention is lawful under domestic law, it is nevertheless open to criticism on the ground that it is arbitrary because, for example, it was resorted to in bad faith or was not proportionate; *Engel v The Netherlands (No 1)* (1976) 1 EHRR 647, para 58 and *Tsirlis and Kouloumpas v Greece* (1997) 25 EHRR 198, para 56.

In the present case the governor's decision not to release the applicant until the date which he had calculated as being her release date under the current Home Office guidelines cannot be said to have been arbitrary. ... The crucial point is whether the applicant's detention after 17 September 1996 which was held by the Divisional Court to be unlawful was nevertheless to be regarded as lawful under domestic law for the purposes of the Convention. If it was, paragraph (a) of Article 5(1) would apply. If it was not, it would follow that there was a contravention of Article 5(1), with the inevitable result that there was enforceable right to compensation under Article 5(5).

... It had been recognised by the Strasbourg Court in *Benham v United Kingdom* (1996) 22 EHRR 293 that the mere fact that the order was set aside on appeal did

---

1   (1990) 13 EHRR 157, para 28.
2   [2000] 3 WLR 843. For the facts, see **3.16.5**.
3   Ibid at 857 et seq.

not in itself affect the lawfulness of the detention; see also *Tsirlis and Kouloumpas v Greece* (1997) 25 EHRR 198, para 56. ...

For the reasons which I gave when I was dealing with the issue of justification I am not persuaded that these arguments would support the submission that the • continued detention of the applicant after 17 September 1996 was lawful within the meaning of Article 5(1) of the Convention. As I have said, it is sufficient to show that there was a contravention of that Article to demonstrate that the detention was unlawful under domestic law. The question whether detention is or is not lawful under domestic law for the purposes of the Convention is a matter which the jurisprudence of the Strasbourg Court has left for decision by the domestic courts. The Divisional Court held that the applicant was entitled to release on 17 September 1996. It must follow that under domestic law her continued detention after that date was unlawful. This would indicate that there was a contravention of Article 5(1). The consequence of the Divisional Court's order under domestic law is that the governor is liable to the applicant for damages under the tort of false imprisonment. The conclusion that the applicant has an enforceable claim for damages is consistent with Article 5(5) of the Convention.'

Lord Hobhouse held a similar opinion:[1]

'The basic distinction between an ex facie invalid order and an order *prima facie* valid but which is liable to be set aside is also to be found in the case-law of the European Court of Human Rights as illustrated by *Benham v United Kingdom*, 22 EHRR 293. The Human Rights Commission had categorised the relevant order as coming into the former category and therefore held that there had been a breach of Article 5; the court disagreed, categorising the order for detention as prima facie valid, and held that there had been no breach of that article. The commission and the court applied the same criteria in considering whether the detention had been lawful under the domestic law. Paragraph 42 of the judgment relied on by the Solicitor-General does not support his argument:

"A period of detention will in principle be lawful if it is carried out pursuant to a court order. A subsequent finding that the court erred under domestic law in making the order will not necessarily retrospectively affect the validity of the intervening period of detention. For this reason the Strasbourg organs have consistently refused to uphold applications from persons convicted of criminal offences who complain that their convictions or sentences were found by the appellate courts to have been based on errors of fact or law."

In the present case there was an order; it was never set aside nor did it have to be. The illegality arose because it did not authorise the detention which took place. The order was not obeyed.

Article 5 of the Convention is inconsistent with the Solicitor-General's arguments and corresponds to the existing English law. It is therefore highly persuasive against accepting the Solicitor-General's arguments or introducing the new rule he contends for into English law. The elements to be found in Article 5(1)(a) are, first, an affirmation of the basic right not to be deprived of one's personal liberty (Lord Atkin), secondly, the recognition of the legal significance of a conviction by a *competent* court (*In re McC (A Minor)* [1985] AC 528), thirdly, the recognition that lawful detention may consequently be ordered and, fourthly, that legal procedures must be followed: *Demer v Cook*, 88 LT 629. Article 5(4) is a requirement that there be a specific remedy for unlawful detention as afforded by habeas corpus. Article

---

1   [2000] 3 WLR 843 at 886–7.

5(5) further requires the payment of compensation for unlawful detention as does English law (Lord Atkin).

The Solicitor-General sought to reconcile his argument with Article 5. But it did not assist him on the facts of the present case to argue that the detention was "lawful at the time" or to rely on paragraph 42 of *Benham's* case 22 EHRR 293. He also submitted that the European Court of Human rights may take a different view to domestic law as to what is "lawful", but this argument failed to recognise that the European Court of Human Rights cumulatively applies a *double* test. For detention to be lawful under Article 5, it must be *both* lawful under the domestic law and the domestic law must (substantively and procedurally) be in compliance with the requirements of the Convention: *Benham v United Kingdom* and *Tsliris and Kouloumpas v Greece*, 25 EHRR 198. If it fails either test, it is unlawful for the purposes of Article 5 and 5(5) applies. Here the detention failed the domestic law test (*Evans (No 1)*) and, like English law, Article 5(5) requires compensation to be paid. Section 9 of the Human Rights Act 1998 reinforces the same conclusions.'

17.2   ARTICLE 5(1)

In *Guzzardi v Italy*[1], the Court explained what right that Article was designed to protect:

'92. The Court recalls that in proclaiming the "right to liberty", paragraph 1 of Article 5 (art 5–1) is contemplating the physical liberty of the person; its aim is to ensure that no one should be dispossessed of this liberty in an arbitrary fashion. As was pointed out by those appearing before the Court, the paragraph is not concerned with mere restrictions on liberty of movement; such restrictions are governed by Article 2 of Protocol No 4 ... "deprived of his liberty" within the meaning of Article 5 (art 5), the starting point must be his concrete situation and account must be taken of a whole range of criteria such as the type, duration, effects and manner of implementation of the measure in question ...

93. The difference between deprivation of and restriction upon liberty is nonetheless merely one of degree or intensity, and not one of nature or substance. Although the process of classification into one or other of these categories sometimes proves to be no easy task in that some borderline cases are a matter of pure opinion ...'

In that case, the applicant was confined to about one and a half square miles on an island which was around 20 square miles in total. The hamlet where he resided with his son and wife consisted of mainly dilapidated buildings, and also a police station, chapel and school. The only other people living there were mostly those in a similar predicament to himself and policemen. He had to be inside his dwelling every night between 10 pm and 7 am. He also had to report to the authorities twice a day and inform them of whom he was telephoning whenever he used that contraption. The facts led the Court to state[2]:

'It is admittedly not possible to speak of "deprivation of liberty" on the strength of any one of these factors taken individually, but cumulatively and in combination they certainly raise an issue of categorisation from the viewpoint of Article 5 (art 5).

---

1   (1980) 3 EHRR 333.
2   Ibid, at para 95.

In certain respects the treatment complained of resembles detention in an "open prison" or committal to a disciplinary unit ...

The Court considers on balance that the present case is to be regarded as one involving deprivation of liberty.'

That decision must be contrasted with *Engel v Netherlands*[1] where it was said that the Dutch equivalent of being 'confined to barracks' was not 'detention' within the meaning of the Convention, even though it consisted of the soldiers not being allowed out of camp. Nor could they use the recreational facilities therein, such as the NAAFI. However, their daily routine was not much different from that of any other of their comrades, or in the words of the Court[2], they 'remained within the ordinary framework of army life'. Accordingly, the restraint placed on their freedom of movement was not such as to amount to a breach of Article 5.

Thus, for a breach of Article 5, there must be confinement within a given area with defined boundaries on all sides and in which major restrictions are placed on the inmate's normal course of living. A soldier lives in barracks, then keeping him in there without the recreation facilities does not involve much difference from his usual lifestyle that such is acceptable under the Convention. However, being kept on a small part of an island with virtually no opportunity of mixing with people other than those also banished there and the police, together with no confidential communications with those living elsewhere is another matter. That involves an unacceptable interruption of a person's accepted way of life to such an extent that it is forbidden by the Convention, unless one of the other exceptions in subparas (a)–(f) applies.

The ECHR in *Engel v Netherlands*[3] and in *Ireland v UK*[4] held that the words 'save in the following cases' in Article 5(1) were all inclusive and that the Convention did not therefore allow incarceration on any other grounds than those set out in that Article, which will therefore now be considered in detail. It should also be noted that, under HRA 1998, ss 14 *et seq*, the Government has made a reservation in relation to terrorism in Northern Ireland. This allows it to relax the criteria for incarceration laid down in Article 5. In *Ireland v UK*[5], the European Court held that the situation in the Six Counties justified the making of such a derogation but it had to be reasonable in relation to the danger faced and that the Court, and not the Crown, was the final arbitrator on this question of proportionality. In that decision, it held that the power to arrest solely in order to interrogate was lawful on the special factual matrix of that case.

17.2.1 Subparagraphs (a) to (f) – compatibility with domestic law

In *Winterwerp v The Netherlands*[6], the European Court of Human Rights ruled that it was for domestic law to lay down when a person could be arrested and

1   (1976) 1 EHRR 647.
2   Ibid, at para 61.
3   Ibid, at para 57.
4   (1978) 2 EHRR 25 at para 194.
5   Ibid.
6   (1979–80) 2 EHRR 387.

detained, but that law must be in conformity with the Convention, which is designed to prevent arbitrariness. English law clearly lays down when a person can be arrested, so that in this respect it clearly complies with the Convention.

In *Steel et al v UK*[1], it was held lawful to detain a person who had refused to be bound over, because the court had taken that course of action in order to secure compliance with one of its orders, which is permitted by para 1(b). For the same reason, a poll-tax payer who defaulted on a liability order could lawfully be incarcerated; see *Benham v UK*[2].

There has been some jurisprudence on para (1)(c). In *Fox et al v UK*, above, the European Court of Human Rights stated that a power of arrest may be exercised (at the very least) only on 'reasonable suspicion', which is indeed the minimum requirement of the common law and of all statutory provisions providing for an arrest. The European definition of those words is the same as given to them by the English judiciary; see *Fox*[3]:

> '... [h]aving a "reasonable suspicion" presupposes the existence of facts or information which would satisfy an objective observer that the person concerned may have committed the offence.'

In *Brogan v UK*[4], it was held that para (1)(c) also included apprehending somebody in order to interrogate him with a view to bringing him before a court if the suspicion turned out to be well founded. In *W v Switzerland*[5], the Court of Human Rights held that to justify withholding bail pending trial there must be specific indications of a genuine requirement of public interest (notwithstanding the presumption of innocence) which outweigh the rule in respect of individual liberty. This must be more than just the length of captivity likely to be imposed on a conviction and must also take into account the accused's previous record and lifestyle, his links with the community in which he will be tried and his international contacts. Whereas it might be justifiable to keep a suspect in custody initially to prevent his hindering the investigation, the more the inquiry progresses, the less this reason will apply for keeping him under lock and key.

In *Weeks v UK*[6], the Court held that if a decision to recall a prisoner on licence to gaol was based on grounds which were inconsistent with the objectives of the sentencing court, then the captivity was unlawful.

In *Re K*[7] the Court of Appeal held that a secure accommodation order under the Children Act 1989, s 25, was 'a depreciation of liberty' within Article 5 but was justified under subpara 1(d) if it was made in order to facilitate 'educational

---

1   (1998) TLR, October 1.
2   (1996) 22 EHRR 293.
3   (1990) 13 EHRR 157, para 32.
4   (1988) 11 EHRR 117, para 53.
5   Case no A254, 23 January 1993.
6   (1987) 10 EHRR 293.
7   [2000] All ER (D) 1834.

supervision' – a word which 'should not be equated rigidly with notions of classroom teaching but, particularly in a care context, should embrace many aspects of the exercise by the local authority of parental rights for the benefit and protection of the child concerned'.

17.3 ARTICLE 5(2)

The provisions of Art 5(2) have been enacted into domestic law by s 28 of PACE 1984, which in fact only codified the common law. Indeed, in this regard, the domestic law was far ahead of the Convention, as the latter has given a much more liberal meaning to the word 'promptly', see *Wilson v Chief Constable of Lancashire*[1].

17.4 ARTICLE 5(3)

Article 5(3) does not conflict with English law. Before the abolition of the Commission, the body had held that any complaint of undue delay in being taken before a judge or magistrate was 'manifestly ill-founded', if the duration complained of was less than 4 days, which is considerably longer than the times laid down by PACE 1984. As to the length that a person can be remanded in custody for his trial, this will depend on the circumstances of the case and its complexity; see *Chahal v UK*[2] where the test of 'due diligence' was applied in determining whether or not there had been a breach of Art 5(3). The custody time-limits prescribed by the Home Secretary almost certainly do comply with the Convention. The one exception is PT(TP)A 1989, s 14(5) whereby a person arrested under that statute can be detained for up to 5 days before being taken before a court. In respect of this power, the present government has notified a Reservation to the Council of Europe under Art 15 – in other words, this detention for the 5 days is not a breach of the Convention[3].

17.5 ARTICLE 5(4)

Whether the writ of *habeas corpus* complies with the requirement of a speedy court hearing to decide upon the lawfulness of the detention all depends on how far the judges hearing the application will go behind the return to the writ; see *Ireland v UK*[4]. It is submitted that if a court uses its powers under s 3 of the Habeas Corpus Act 1830 to the full and with no artificial restrictions placed

---

1   (Unreported) 23 November 2000, para 27.
2   (1996) 23 EHRR 413.
3   The PT(TP)A 1989 was repealed by s 125 of and Sch 16 to the Terrorism Act 2000 when the latter was brought into force on 18 February 2001. Under Sch 8 to that statute, the maximum length of detention without judicial intervention cannot exceed two days or 54 hours but in the latter case only if it had not been practical to have made the application within 48 hours (see **10.12**).
4   Case no A25, 18 January 1978.

upon them, then the writ is a sufficient remedy. Under s 3, a court can go behind the reasons on the writ and enquire into the truth of the facts stated thereon; see *In re Iqbal*[1], and indeed it is under a duty do so in order to comply with the Convention; see HRA 1998, s 6(1). Where inquiring into the legitimacy of a captivity, traditionally the High Court merely looked to see if the facts found by the inferior body gave it jurisdiction to detain the applicant. The High Court did not itself sit as an appeal tribunal from those facts. So far as the latter were found by judicial intervention, the remedy of *habeas corpus* will satisfy Article 5(4). (Being wrongly incarcerated following a conviction because a jury has made an erroneous finding of fact is not a violation of the defendant's rights under the Convention.) However, subject to a short period around the initial detention (see **17.4**), any continued incarceration must be authorised by a judicial authority, see *X v UK*[2]. To comply with the Convention, the Crown has introduced that element into review procedures. So, instead of the Home Secretary deciding when a patient from a mental hospital could be released (as he did in *X v UK*, above), nowadays that decision is taken by a mental health tribunal chaired by a circuit judge. Likewise, the release of murderers serving life sentences is now up to the Lord Chief Justice and not the Home Secretary. *X v UK*, above, held that the writ of *habeas corpus* did not comply with Article 5(4) because the High Court would not go behind the facts found by a non-judicial body. As the High Court must give effect to the Convention, it must interpret s 3 of the Habeas Corpus Act 1830 as giving it the freedom to inquire and to make its own findings of fact where detention has been authorised by a non-judicial authority. This will be more theoretical than real as Parliament has now involved the members of the judiciary in making the decision on whether or not to impose restraints on a person's freedom of movement. For example, a soldier could, until 2 October 2000, have been held in military custody for a long period, pending the date of his court-martial, solely on the orders of his colonel or a more senior army officer. Nowadays, that can only be done on the authorisation of a Judge-Advocate, see **11.2.2.1**.

Also the periodical investigations by a judicial authority of the detention must be 'speedily' carried out. Thus a period of two years between reviews by the Parole Board was held to be a breach of Art 5(4), see *Oldham v UK*[3]. Likewise, 15 months was 'not speedy' enough for holding reviews of the confinement of patients in mental hospitals, see *Herzcegfalvy v UK*[4].

17.6   ARTICLE 5(5)

17.6.1   The common law prior to October 2000

The species of the tort of trespass known as 'false imprisonment' complies with the requirements of Art 5(5) so long as a writ for that action is available to a

---

1   [1979] 1 All ER 685n.
2   (1981) 4 EHRR 188.
3   (2000) TLR, October 24.
4   24 September 1992 (Series A No 244).

person who has been illegally incarcerated. However, prior to the incorporation of the European Convention on Human Rights, a prisoner had very little redress if the cause of his captivity was an unlawful act by a member of the judiciary. Basically, no action would lie so long as the latter acted within their jurisdiction and possibly in the case of an inferior judge so long as he had not acted maliciously. (The liability of the judiciary under domestic law is set out in Chapter 13.)

This immunity is clearly a contravention of Art 5(5). This violation has now been put right by s 9(3) of HRA 1998, which gives a person who has been unlawfully detained a statutory right to sue for damages for his incarceration when it has been caused by a judicial act, provided (s 9(4)) and (5)) he also joins as a defendant the Minister responsible for the court concerned or a person or governmental department nominated by him.

17.6.2 The common law from October 2000

From 2 October 2000, when declaring what is the common law, the courts must make it fully compatible with the Convention. This is because, under s 6(3)(a) of HRA 1998, they are a 'public authority' and, therefore, by s 6(1), it is unlawful for them to act in a way which is 'incompatible with a Convention Right'. Accordingly, it is submitted that s 6(1) has revived the common law. As there is no rational reason for distinguishing the liability of the judiciary solely on the basis of the tribunal in which they administer justice, then (in order to comply with the Convention) it must be the common law rules which give the greater protection to the wronged citizen which should prevail and have universal application. There can be no logical explanation for exempting from tortious liability only judges who sit in the superior courts (as opposed to those who sit in other tribunals) if they should deliberately act contrary to their oath – especially as on one day they may sit as (an inferior) county court district judge and on the next day as a (superior) Crown Court recorder.

The rationale of why allegations of malice cannot be made against judges was stated in the Court of Common Pleas in Dublin in *Taaffe v Downes*[1]. (There the Lord Chief Justice of Ireland had been sued for false imprisonment by the plaintiff who had been arrested upon a warrant issued by that judge.) According to Mayne J:

> 'The constitutional idea of a Judge is "*dignity*", for the sake of the King and people ... Liability to every man's actions, for every judicial act a Judge is called upon to do, is the degradation of the judge; and cannot be the object of any true patriot or honest subject. It is to render Judges slaves in every Court that holds plea, to every Sheriff, Juror, Attorney and Plaintiff. If you once break down the barrier of their dignity, and subject them to an action, you let in upon judicial authority a wide wasting and harassing persecution, and establish its weakness in a degrading responsibility.'[2]

---

1   (1813) 3 Moo PC 36.
2   Ibid, at 40.

Fox J was of the same view:

> 'It is necessary to free and impartial administration of justice, that the persons administering it should be uninfluenced by fear and unbiased in hope. Judges have not been invested with this privilege for their own protection merely; it is calculated for the benefit of the people by ensuring a calm, steady and impartial administration of justice; it is a principle coeval with the law of the land, and the dispensation of justice; and is founded on the very frame of the constitution; it is to be met with in the earliest books of law; and continued down to the present time, without one authority or *dictum* to the contrary, that I have been able to find.'[1]

Lord Denning MR in *Sirros v Moore*[2] expressed similar sentiments to those of his Irish brethren quoted above; but a different view was taken by Cockburn CJ in his dissenting judgment in *Dawkins v Lord F Paulet*[3]:

> 'Men worthy to command would do their duty, as Eyre B expresses it, "fearless of the consequences", and would trust to the firmness of the judges, and the honesty and good sense of the juries to protect them in respect of acts honestly, though, possibly erroneously, done under a sense of duty".'

> 'At all events trial by jury in matters of wrong between man and man is an essential part of our judicial system.'[4]

Although that was an action by a commanding officer of a battalion against his brigade commander for libel, the Chief Justice was firmly of the view that army officers would not be deterred from doing what they believed to be right merely by the thought that if they got it wrong, it could land them in court. The author can see no reason why the judiciary would not likewise be undeterred from doing their duty by threats of litigation.

To comply with the Convention the common law must also allow damages to be recovered for an action done in excess of jurisdiction, irrespective of the reason for this lack of authority. This is because any incarceration done without the necessary authority is clearly unlawful and likewise, acts done with malice by the superior as well as the inferior judiciary, for such acts are outside their jurisdiction as their only power is to act impartially with no improper motive.

Accordingly, it is submitted that from October 2000 a prisoner can, by virtue of s 7(1)(b) of HRA 1998, rely on Art 5. The result of this is that a claimant will be entitled to recover damages at common law from anybody (except a paid or lay magistrate acting *bona fides*[5] and Law Lords[6]) who, while purporting to act in a judicial capacity, has unlawfully incarcerated him. Under the now repealed provisions of the Summary Jurisdiction Act 1848 and the Justice of the Peace Act 1979, s 45(3) no action could be brought before the order of imprisonment was set aside. It would no doubt be open and in conformity with the Convention to extend the common law to include such a requirement, just as in a malicious

---

1   (1813) 3 Moo PC 36, at 48.
2   [1975] QB 118 at 136.
3   (1869) LR 5 QB at p 108.
4   Ibid at 109.
5   See Justice of the Peace Act 1997, ss 50 and 51. This is one of the statutory provisions about which a court could make a declaration of incompatibility under HRA 1998, s 4.
6   Petition of Right 1689, s 1, Article IX.

prosecution case, the conviction must be quashed before proceedings can be instituted seeking redress for that tort; see *Dunlop v Customs and Excise Commissioners*[1].

17.6.3 The right to institute legal proceedings under the HRA 1998

In the case of justices of the peace and district judges (magistrates' court), their statutory immunity from suit will remain for non-malicious acts, save when sued under s 7(1)(a) of HRA 1998, which states:

> '7(1) A person who claims that a public authority has acted (or proposes to act) in a way which is made unlawful under section 6(1) [ie acting contrary to the Convention] may –
>
> (a) bring proceedings against the authority under this Act in the appropriate court or tribunal.'

The cause of action given by s 7(1)(a) can be brought in the County or High Court and will almost certainly be classified as 'a breach of statutory duty'. This will have three important consequences. First, exemplary damages cannot be awarded, at any rate if *AB v South West Water Services Ltd*[2] was decided correctly. Whether or not that was so is now before the House of Lords in another case. Secondly, there is no automatic right to jury trial. So far as liability is concerned, a jury would very often be irrelevant because whether 'a court had exceeded its jurisdiction' would usually be a pure question of law with a consensus by the litigants about what had happened – although occasionally there might be disputed factual issues. However, when it comes to assessing damages, judges are usually far less generous that the average 12 good men (and women) and true. Finally, the limitation period for bringing an action under HRA 1998 is 1 year, although the court can extend this period if it thinks it is 'equitable' to do so 'having regard to all the circumstances'; see s 7(5).

17.6.4 The Law Lords

Although the Law Lords are a public authority when acting judicially (see s 6(3)(a) and (4) of HRA 1998), they would still have the total immunity granted to them by the Petition of Right 1689, so that no action against them could even be bought under s 7(1) of HRA 1998. This is because that Act does not overrule a previous statute which is incompatible with it; see s 4. It is for Parliament to remove this incompatibility, should it choose to do so (s 10 of HRA 1998).

17.6.5 Bringing a claim under the HRA 1998

Under the Civil Procedure (Amendment) Rules 2000, r 8 and CPR Practice Direction 16, para 16, a party seeking to rely on the Human Rights Convention must, in his statement of case, give full particulars of that allegation. If damages are sought in relation to a judicial act or if a declaration of incompatibility is

---

1   (1998) 95 (17) LSG 31.
2   [1993] QB 507.

sought, then the proceedings must be served on the Crown. In the case of a judicial act the Lord Chancellor must be joined as a party unless it relates to a court martial, in which case the Secretary of State for Defence must be joined. Their address for service in both cases is the Treasury Solicitor (see CPR PD 19).

17.7 INFORMERS

As has already been mentioned in Chapter 15, often the only ground of an arrester's suspicion is 'information received'. The Court of Appeal has taken a very strict line on how far this can be explored by claimants seeking redress for their loss of liberty. The European Court of Human Rights in *Fox et al v UK*[1] specifically recognised this right to withhold relevant evidence which might lead to the identification of an informant. Thus, it would appear that the restrictions which the English judiciary have placed on the questions that can be asked in a civil case about those who assist the police do not offend against Art 5(5).

17.8 PUBLIC FUNDING

The right under Art 5(5) would be illusory if the costs of bringing the action made it impossible to commence legal proceedings. One of the categories for which a contract can be granted by the Legal Services Commission to solicitors is for 'actions against the police', which, of course, includes any allegation of false imprisonment. Such will also amount to an infringement of the Convention on Human Rights, namely of Art 5. This gives the claimant special status. Under a Direction of the Lord Chancellor, he or she is to have priority when it comes to funding. Further, the Commission is prepared to grant financial assistance if it is a 'borderline case', ie where the chances of success are only 50/50 or even a little less; see s 8 of the Legal Services Commission *Funding Code* (2000). It is submitted that the fact that the costs might be more than the amount to be recovered is not a relevant consideration. In *Steel et al v UK*[2], the Court of Human Rights merely awarded £500 damages for non-pecuniary loss suffered by being denied the right to free speech, and £20,000 costs. It that case, legal aid had been granted. Indeed, the old Human Rights' Commission seems never to have applied the 'cost/benefit' rule, so it is hard to see how the Legal Services Commission would be able to justify such a practice in these cases. Indeed, as Art 5(5) guarantees 'an enforceable right to compensation', it is submitted that legal aid cannot be denied to an applicant who fulfils the financial criteria and whose chances of success are at least 'borderline' (see above). A refusal would be to deny him his right to claim compensation and, therefore, would amount to a breach of the Convention (see *Faulkner v UK*[3] and *G v UK*[4]). This is because the Legal Services Commission is a public body, and

---

1   (1990) 13 EHRR 157, para 34.
2   (1998) 28 EHRR 603.
3   (2000) TLR, January 11.
4   (2000) TLR, November 1.

under s6 of HRA 1998, it is unlawful for them to act in a way which is 'incompatible with a Convention Right'; and if they did so, they could be sued under s7(1)(b). This would probably still apply even if the likely damages would be nominal because of the shortness of the duration of the captivity; the reason being that often the Court of Human Rights holds that a 'finding of a violation' is sufficient vindication for the infringement of a person's Convention rights.

17.9 DAMAGES

The only case the author can find is *Perks v UK*[1], details of which are given at **14.3.1.6**.

---

1 (1999) 30 EHRR 33.

Chapter 18

CONCLUSION

18.1   POWERS OF APPREHENSION

Englishmen have always valued their liberty and freedom[1]. For the safety of society, such rights cannot be absolute. Those who offend against the law in appropriate cases have to be incarcerated, as a deterrent to others, for the protection of society and as retribution. Legislation has permitted the apprehension by members of the public of those amongst them who have offended against the law. In addition, extra powers have been granted to the police and others, such as customs and excise officers. The present legislation generally allows people to be apprehended without a warrant only for crimes which are either serious (ie their maximum sentence is 5 or more years' imprisonment for a first offender), where an arrest is needed to prevent either violence or disorder, or where it will be virtually impossible to trace a culprit if he is able to leave the scene, for example, the Theft Act 1978.

18.2   IMPRISONMENT TO ENFORCE PAYMENT OF DEBTS

Imprisonment can also be used to enforce the payment of debts, although nowadays it is limited to spouses who fail to honour their financial obligations to their estranged family and those who fail to pay their rates and taxes to central and local government. As Megarry J said in *Felton v Callis*[2]:

> '1968 is not 1868 or 1768; and today the more powerful processes of the law are less readily available than they once were to compel honesty in the discharge of civil obligations.'

To which Wilson J in *B v B*[3] added:

> 'For "1968" read "1997".'

18.3   THE BALANCE BETWEEN AUTHORITY AND FREEDOM

This book has attempted to set out the circumstances which enable people to be deprived of their liberty and the remedies available where that has been done contrary to law. Whether the right balance has been struck between authority and freedom is a matter for politicians not lawyers – save to this extent, that any interference with the freedom of movement of an individual must now comply with the European Convention on Human Rights and whether or not it does so will ultimately be decided by the judges at Strasbourg.

---

1   See *Magna Carta* 1215.
2   [1969] 1 QB 200 at 214.
3   [1998] 1 WLR 329 at 336.

Appendix 1
ARRESTABLE OFFENCES

Set out below is a list of all arrestable offences. Unless otherwise stated, they are arrestable by virtue of s 24(1)(b) of PACE 1984, ie a crime for which a first offender can be sentenced to 5 years' imprisonment. The list may well not be exhaustive, as there could be the odd offence which the author has failed to locate. In addition, certain statutes give a power of arrest, without a warrant, for crimes which do not come within the statutory definition of 'an arrestable offence' (for example RTA 1988, which authorises the incarceration of those who fail to take a breath test); and these are not included in the list. This is because the circumstances under which such an arrest can be made may not be the same as for an arrestable offence, for example the power to apprehend may solely be exercised by a constable or upon a reasonable belief (rather than mere suspicion) of the detained person's guilt. Full details of these other powers of summary arrest will be found in the appropriate place in this book.

The following list is to some extent based on the Table of Offences in Part V of the Legal Aid in Criminal and Care Proceedings (Costs) (Amendment) (No 2) Regulations 1996, SI 1996/2655, although that statutory instrument classifies indictable offences by the amount of fees allowable to counsel acting under a legal aid certificate in the Crown Court. The author of this book has reclassified them as follows.

OFFENCES INVOLVING DAMAGE TO PROPERTY

Arson	Criminal Damage Act 1971, s 3(1)
Criminal Damage	Criminal Damage Act 1971, s 1
Destroying ships	Aviation and Maritime Security Act 1990, s 11
Endangering the safety of aerodromes	Aviation and Maritime Security Act 1990, s 1
Other acts endangering safe navigation	Aviation and Maritime Security Act 1990, s 12
Making threats	Aviation and Maritime Security Act 1990, s 13
Exhibiting false signals etc	Malicious Damage Act 1860
Making threats to destroy property	Criminal Damage Act 1971, s 2
Offences against the safety of ships and fixed platforms	Aviation and Maritime Security Act 1990, ss 9, 10 11 and 12
Placing wood etc on a railway, taking up rails etc with intent to obstruct an engine etc	Malicious Damage Act 1861, s 35
Possessing anything with intent to destroy or damage property	Criminal Damage Act 1971, s 3

OFFENCES OF DISHONESTY

Abstraction of electricity	Theft Act 1968, s 13
Blackmail	Theft Act 1968, s 21
Burglary	Theft Act 1968, s 10
Copying a false instrument with intent	Forgery and Counterfeiting Act 1981, s 2
Control or custody of a false instrument	Forgery and Counterfeiting Act 1981, s 5(1) and (3), but not contrary to subss (2) and (4) which are not arrestable offences
Control and custody of counterfeiting materials	Forgery and Counterfeiting Act 1981, s 17
Counterfeiting of marks and dyes	Hallmarking Act 1973, s 6
Counterfeiting of notes and coins	Forgery and Counterfeiting Act 1981, s 14
Destruction of registers of births etc	Forgery Act 1861, s 36
Evasion of liability by deception	Theft Act 1978, s 2
False accounting	Theft Act 1968, s 17
Forgery	Forgery and Counterfeiting Act 1981, s 1
Fraudulent use of telecommunications system	Telecommunication Act 1984, s 42(1)(b)
Going equipped for stealing (arrestable by virtue of PACE 1984, s 24(2))	Theft Act 1968, s 25(1)
Handling stolen goods	Theft Act 1968, s 22
Making false entries in copies of registers	Forgery Act 1861, s 37
Making, or having custody or control, of counterfeit notes or coins	Forgery and Counterfeiting Act 1981, s 16
Misleading statements and practices	Financial Services and Markets Act 2000, s 397
Money laundering	Criminal Justice Act 1988, s 93A
Obliterating marks on Her Majesty's property with intent to concealment	Public Stores Act 1875, s 5
Obtaining by deception	Theft Act 1968, s 15
Obtaining pecuniary advantage by deception	Theft Act 1968, s 16
Obtaining services by deception	Theft Act, 1978, s 1
Offences in relation to dyes and stamps	Stamp Duty Management Act 1891, s 13
Passing counterfeit notes and coins	Forgery and Counterfeiting Act 1981, s 15
Possession and supply of anything for fraudulent purpose in connection with use of telecommunication system	Telecommunication Act 1984, s 42A
Procuring execution of valuable security by deception	Theft Act 1988, s 20(2)
Removal of articles from places open to the public	Theft Act 1968, s 11
Suppression of documents	Theft Act 1988, s 20(1)
Theft	Theft Act 1968, s 1

Unauthorised use of a trade mark	Trade Marks Act 1994, s 92
Using a copy of a false instrument	Forgery and Counterfeiting Act 1981, s 4
Using a false instrument	Forgery and Counterfeiting Act 1981, s 3

DRUG OFFENCES (INCLUDING ALCOHOL-RELATED OFFENCES) OTHER THAN THOSE INVOLVING MOTOR VEHICLES

Activity relating to opium	Misuse of Drugs Act 1971, s 9
Cultivation of a cannabis plant	Misuse of Drugs Act 1971, s 6
Drug trafficking offences at sea	Criminal Justice (International Co-operation) Act 1990, s 18
Manufacture and supply of scheduled substances	Criminal Justice (International Co-operation) Act 1998, s 12
Occupier knowingly permitting drug offences etc	Misuse of Drugs Act 1971, s 8
Offences in relation to proceeds of drug trafficking	Drug Trafficking Act 1994, ss 49, 50 and 51
Offences in relation to a money laundering investigation	Drug Trafficking Act 1994, ss 52 and 53
Possession of a class A or B drug	Misuse of Drugs Act 1971, s 5
Possession of a controlled drug, with intent to supply	Misuse of Drugs Act 1971, s 4
Practitioner contravening drug supply regulations	Misuse of Drugs Act 1971, ss 12 and 13
Producing or supplying a controlled drug	Misuse of Drugs Act 1971, s 4
Use of ships for illicit traffic in drugs	Criminal Justice (International Co-operation) Act 1998, s 19

HOMICIDE, OFFENCES INVOLVING A FATALITY (OTHER THAN THOSE ARISING OUT OF ROAD TRAFFIC ACCIDENTS) AND RELATED OFFENCES

Aiding and abetting suicide	Suicide Act 1961, s 2
Attempting to cause an explosion, making or keeping explosives	Explosive Substances Act 1883, s 3
Causing an explosion likely to endanger life	Explosive Substances Act 1883, s 2
Child destruction	Infant Life (Preservation) Act 1929, s 1
Infanticide	Infant Life (Preservation) Act 1929, s 1
Manslaughter	common law
Murder (arrestable by virtue of PACE 1984, s 24(1)(a))	common law
Soliciting to murder	Offences Against the Person Act 1861, s 4

War crimes   War Crimes Act 1991, s 1

OFFENCES INVOLVING INSOLVENCY AND COMPANIES

Bankrupt concealing, destroying etc books, papers or records or making false entries in them	Insolvency Act 1986, s 355
Bankrupt disposing of property obtained on credit and not paid for	Insolvency Act 1986, s 359
Bankrupt failing to deliver books, papers and records to the official receiver or trustee	Insolvency Act 1986, s 355
Bankrupt failing to deliver property to, or concealing property from, the official receiver or trustee	Insolvency Act 1986, s 354
Bankrupt failing to disclose property or disposals to official receiver or trustee	Insolvency Act 1986, s 353
Bankrupt making a false statement, or failing to inform a trustee, where false debt is proved	Insolvency Act 1986, s 356
Bankrupt making material omission in a statement relating to his affairs	Insolvency Act 1986, s 356
Bankrupt removing property which he is required to deliver to the official receiver or trustee	Insolvency Act 1986, s 354
Being a party to carrying on a company's business with intent to defraud creditors, or for any fraudulent purpose	Companies Act 1985, s 458
Destroying or mutilating company documents; falsifying such documents or making false entries; parting with such documents or altering them or making omissions	Companies Act 1985, s 450
False representation or fraud for the purpose of obtaining creditor's consent to an agreement in connection with winding up	Insolvency Act 1986, s 211
False statements by company directors	Theft Act 1968, s 19
Fraud etc in anticipation of winding up	Insolvency Act 1986, s 206
Fraud or privity to fraud etc during a winding up	Insolvency Act 1986, s 206
Insider dealing	Criminal Justice Act 1993, s 52
Knowingly taking in pawn or pledge, or otherwise receiving the same recklessly	Insolvency Act 1986, s 206
Obtaining property in respect of which money is owed by a bankrupt	Insolvency Act 1986, s 359
Officer of a company making a material omission from a statement relating to company's affairs	Insolvency Act 1986, s 210
Officer of a company misconducting himself in course of winding up	Insolvency Act 1986, s 208

Officer of a company or contributor destroying, falsifying etc company's books	Insolvency Act 1986, s 209

IMMIGRATION OFFENCES

Assisting illegal entry or harbouring persons	Immigration Act 1971, s 25

OFFENCES INVOLVING MOTOR VEHICLES

Aggravated vehicle taking resulting in death	Theft Act 1968, s 12
Death by careless driving whilst under the influence of drink or drugs	Road Traffic Act 1988, s 3A
Causing danger to road users	Road Traffic Act 1988, s 22A
Death by dangerous driving	Road Traffic Act 1988, s 1
Taking a motor car without authority (arrestable by virtue of PACE 1984, s 24(2))	Theft Act 1968, s 12(1)
Touting for car hire services (arrestable by virtue of PACE 1984, s 24(2))	Criminal Justice and Public Order Act 1994, s 167

SEXUAL OFFENCES AND OFFENCES AGAINST CHILDREN AND PUBLIC DECENCY

Acts outraging public decency	common law
Abduction of woman by force	Sexual Offences Act 1956, s 17
Administering drugs to obtain intercourse	Sexual Offences Act 1956, s 4
A man living on the earnings of prostitution	Sexual Offences Act 1956, s 30
A woman exercising control over prostitutes	Sexual Offences Act 1956, s 31
Buggery of a person under the age of 16 or of an animal	Sexual Offences Act 1956, s 12
Buggery of a person under the age of 18 by a male of 21 years or older	Sexual Offences Act 1956, s 12
Causing prostitution of women (arrestable by virtue of PACE 1984, s 24(2))	Sexual Offences Act 1956, s 22
Child abduction by a connected person	Child Abduction Act, 1984, s 1

Child abduction by another person	Child Abduction Act 1984, s 2
Cruelty to persons under the age of 16	Children and Young Persons Act 1933, s 1
Gross indecency between a man aged 21 or older with a male under the age of 18, or attempting to procure such an act of gross indecency	Sexual Offences Act 1956, s 13
Incest	Sexual Offences Act 1956, ss 10 and 11
Indecent assault on a female	Sexual Offences Act 1956, s 14
Indecent assault on a man	Sexual Offences Act 1956, s 15
Keeping a disorderly house	common law
Living on the earnings of male prostitution	Sexual Offences Act 1956, s 5
Permitting girl under the age of 13 to use premises for sexual intercourse	Sexual Offences Act 1956, s 25
Procurement of a defective	Sexual Offences Act 1956, s 9
Procuring of girl under the age of 21 to have unlawful sexual intercourse (arrestable by virtue of PACE 1984, s 24(2))	Sexual Offences Act 1956, s 23
Rape	Sexual Offences Act 1956, s 1
Sexual intercourse with a defective	Sexual Offences Act 1956, s 7
Sexual intercourse with girl under the age of 13	Sexual Offences Act 1956, s 5
Sexual intercourse with girl under the age of 16	Sexual Offences Act 1956, s 6
Taking, possessing for gain etc of indecent photographs of children (arrestable by virtue of PACE 1984, s 24(2))	Protection of Children Act 1978, s 1

TREASON AND SIMILAR OFFENCES INCLUDING TERRORISM

All offences (arrestable by virtue of PACE 1984, s 24(2))	Official Secrets Act 1920 and 1989, save under s 8(1), (4) and (5) of the 1989 Act
Assisting another to retain the proceeds of terrorist activities	Northern Ireland (Emergency Provisions) Act 1989, s 53
Assisting in the retention or control of terrorists bonds	Prevention of Terrorism (Temporary Provisions) Act 1989, s 11
Bomb hoax	Criminal Law Act 1977, s 51
Endeavouring to seduce sailors from their allegiance to Her Majesty	Naval Discipline Act 1957, s 95
Failure to disclose information about terrorism	Prevention of Terrorism (Temporary Provisions) Act 1989, s 18
Frustrating investigation of terrorist activities	Prevention of Terrorism (Temporary Provisions) Act 1989, s 17

(1) Membership of,	Prevention of Terrorism (Temporary
(2) soliciting or inviting support for, or	Provisions) Act 1989, s 2
(3) organising a meeting of three or	
more people for,	
a proscribed organisation	
Mutiny	common law
Offences involving contributions to	Prevention of Terrorism (Temporary
prescribed organisations	Provisions) Act 1989, s 10
Offences involving money or property to	Prevention of Terrorism (Temporary
be used for terrorism	Provisions) Act 1989, s 9
Offences in respect of exclusion orders	Prevention of Terrorism (Temporary
	Provisions) Act 1989, s 8
Possession of articles for terrorist	Prevention of Terrorism (Temporary
purposes	Provisions) Act 1989, s 16
Spying for the enemy	Naval Discipline Act 1957, s 94
Treason	common law
(arrestable by virtue of PACE 1984,	
s 24(1)(a))	
Unlawful drilling	Unlawful Drilling Act 1819, s 1
Unlawful collection of information for	Prevention of Terrorism (Temporary
terrorist purposes	Provisions) Act 1989, s 16
The following terrorism offences	Terrorism Act 2000 (not yet in force at
	time of writing – due to be brought into
	force by February 2001)
Membership of a proscribed organisation	Terrorism Act 2000, s 11
Inviting or canvassing support for a	Terrorism Act 2000, s 12
proscribed organisation	
Involved in fundraising to support	Terrorism Act 2000, s 15
terrorism	
Possessing property or money to be used	Terrorism Act 2000, s 16
for the purposes of terrorism	
Fundraising for the purposes of	Terrorism Act 2000, s 17
terrorism	
Money laundering for the purposes of	Terrorism Act 2000, s 18
terrorism	
Failure to disclose to the police the	Terrorism Act 2000, s 19
names of those who have committed an	
offence contrary to any of the above	
sections of the Terrorism Act 2000	
Weapon training	Terrorism Act 2000, s 54
Directing a terrorist organisation	Terrorism Act 2000, s 56

OFFENCES INVOLVING ACTUAL OR THREATENED PERSONAL INJURY OR FIREARMS OFFENCES

Abandonment of children under 2 years	Offences Against the Person Act 1861,
of age	s 27

Acquisition by, or supply, of a firearm by a person denied them	Firearms Act 1968, s 21
Administering chloroform, laudanum etc to commit or to assist in the commission of an indictable offence	Offences Against the Person Act 1861, s 22
Administering poisons etc so as to endanger life	Offences Against the Person Act 1861, s 23
Assaulting a prison officer whilst possessing a firearm	Criminal Justice Act 1991, s 90
Assault occasioning actual bodily harm	Offences Against the Person Act 1861, s 47
Assaults on officers saving wrecks	Offences Against the Person Act 1861, s 37
Assault with intent to rob	Theft Act 1968, s 8
Attempting to choke, suffocate, strangle etc	Offences Against the Person Act 1861, s 21
Blackmail	Theft Act 1968, s 21
Carrying an offensive weapon (arrestable by virtue of PACE 1984, s 24(2))	Prevention of Crimes Act 1953, s 1
Carrying a loaded firearm in a public place	Firearms Act 1968, s 19
Causing bodily injury by explosives	Offences Against the Person Act 1861, s 28
Causing miscarriage by poison instrument	Offences Against the Person Act 1861, s 58
Channel Tunnel (seizing or exercising control of)	Channel Tunnel Act (Security) Order 1994, SI 1994/570
Circumcision of females	Circumcision Act 1985, s 1
Contamination of goods, with intent	Public Order Act 1986, s 38
Dealing in firearms	Firearms Act 1968, s 3
Endangering the safety of railway passengers	Offences Against the Person Act 1861, ss 32 and 33
Failing to keep a dog under proper control resulting in injury	Dangerous Dogs Act 1991, s 3
Failure to comply with a certificate when transferring a firearm	FA 1968, s 42
False imprisonment	common law
Football match offences arrestable by virtue of PACE 1984, s 24(2)	Football (Offences) Act 1991, Football Spectators Act 1989 and the Public Order Act 1986
Grievous bodily harm or wounding	Offences Against the Person Act 1861, s 20
Harassment (arrestable by virtue of PACE 1984, s 24(2))	Prevention of Harassment Act 1997, s 2 and Crime and Disorder Act 1988, s 32
Having an article with a point or blade in a public place (arrestable by virtue of PACE 1984, s 24(2))	Criminal Justice Act 1988, s 139
Having an article with a point or blade on school premises (arrestable by virtue of PACE 1984, s 24(2))	Criminal Justice Act 1988, s 139(A)

Hijacking	Aviation Security Act 1983, s 1 and Aviation and Maritime Security Act 1990, s 9
Hostage taking	Taking of Hostages Act 1980, s 1
Impeding persons endeavouring to escape wrecks	Offences Against the Person Act 1861, s 17
Kidnapping	common law
Landmines, use of	Landmines Act 1998, s 2
Making gunpowder to commit offences	Offences Against the Person Act 1861, s 64
Making or possessing explosives in suspicious circumstances	Explosive Substances Act 1880, s 4
Making threats to kill	Offences Against the Person Act 1861, s 16
Neglecting to provide food for or assaulting servants etc	Offences Against the Person Act 1861, s 26
Offences against international protection of nuclear material	Nuclear Material (Offences) Act 1983, s 2
Piracy when accompanied by violence (arrestable by virtue of PACE 1984, s 24(1)(a))	Piracy Act 1837, s 2
Placing explosives with intent to cause bodily injury	Offences Against the Person Act 1861, s 30
Possession, acquisition of certain prohibited weapons	Firearms Act 1968, s 5
Possession of a firearm without certificate	Firearms Act 1968, s 1
Possession of a shotgun without a certificate	Firearms Act 1968, s 2
Possession of firearms by a person convicted of crime	Firearms Act 1968, s 21
Possession of firearms with criminal intent	Firearms Act 1968, s 18
Possession of firearms with intent to endanger life	Firearms Act 1968, s 16
Riot	Public Order Act 1986, s 12
Robbery	Theft Act 1968, s 8
Setting spring guns with intent to inflict grievous bodily harm	Offences Against the Person Act 1861, s 31
Shortening of a shotgun or possession of a shortened shotgun	Firearms Act 1968, s 4
Supplying instrument etc to cause miscarriage	Offences Against the Person Act 1861, s 59
Torture	Criminal Justice Act 1988, s 134
Trespassing with a firearm	Firearms Act 1968, s 20
Use of firearms to resist arrest	Firearms Act 1968, s 17
Using explosives or corrosives with intent to cause grievous bodily harm	Offences Against the Person Act 1861, s 29
Violent disorder	Public Order Act 1986, s 2
Wounding or grievous bodily harm with intent to cause grievous bodily harm etc	Offences Against the Person Act 1861, s 18

OFFENCES AGAINST PUBLIC JUSTICE AND CORRUPTION

Assisting an offender of a crime punishable with 10 years' imprisonment	Criminal Law Act 1967, s 4
Assisting prisoner to escape	Prison Act 1952, s 39
Breach of prison	common law
Corruption in public office	Public Bodies Corrupt Practices Act 1889, s 1
Corrupt transactions with agents	Prevention of Corruption Act 1906, s 1
Disobeying an order by a constable to remove an item which is intended to conceal one's identity (arrestable by virtue of PACE 1984, s 24(2))	amended Criminal Justice and Public Order Act 1994, s 60(8)(b)
Embracery	common law
Escaping from lawful custody	common law
Fabricating evidence with intent to mislead a tribunal	common law
False evidence before the European Court	European Communities Act 1972, s 11
Harming, threatening to harm a witness or juror	Criminal Justice and Public Order Act 1994, s 51
Intimidating a witness or juror	Criminal Justice and Public Order Act 1994, s 51
Perjury	Perjury Act 1911, s 1
Permitting an escape	common law
Personating for the purposes of bail etc	Forgery Act 1861, s 34
Personation of jurors	common law
Perverting the course of justice	common law
Prison mutiny	Prison Security Act 1992, s 1
Rescue	common law
Tipping-off	Regulation of Investigatory Powers Act 2000, s 54
Unlawful disclosure	Regulation of Investigatory Powers Act 2000, s 49

OFFENCES AGAINST PUBLIC MORALITY

Blasphemy	common law
Conspiracy to corrupt public morals	common law
Libel	common law
Publishing material intended or likely to stir up racial hatred (arrestable by virtue of PACE 1984, s 24(2))	Public Order Act 1986, s 19
Publishing obscene matters (arrestable by virtue of PACE 1984, s 24(2))	Obscene Publications Act 1959, s 2

REVENUE OFFENCES

Any customs and excise offence (arrestable by virtue of PACE 1984, s 24[2](a))	Customs and Excise Management Act 1979
Fraudulent evasion of insurance premium tax (arrestable by virtue of PACE 1984, s 24(2)(a))	Finance Act 1994, Sch 7, para 9
Fraudulent evasion of land fill tax (arrestable by virtue of PACE 1984, s 24(2)(a))	Finance Act 1996, Sch 5, para 15
Fraudulent evasion of value added tax (arrestable by virtue of PACE 1984, s 24(2)(a))	Value Added Tax Act 1994, s 79
Non-payment etc of duty on alcohol (arrestable by virtue of PACE 1984, s 24(2)(a))	Alcoholic Liquor Act 1979, s 17
Unlawfully distilling etc spirits (arrestable by virtue of PACE 1984, s 24(2)(a))	Alcoholic Liquor Act 1979, s 25

Appendix 2

CLAIM FORM

IN THE BLANKSHIRE COUNTY COURT
BETWEEN

JOHN DOE

Plaintiff

-and-

THE CHIEF CONSTABLE OF BLANKSHIRE

Defendants

PARTICULARS OF CLAIM

1. The Defendant is the Chief Officer of Police for the Blankshire Constabulary. All the police officers hereinafter referred to were at all material times constables in the aforesaid police force acting in that capacity.

2. At about 7 o'clock in the evening of the 10th day of January 2000 at his residence in Main Street, in Blanktown in the County of Blankshire, the Claimant was wrongfully arrested by police officers and taken in handcuffs to Scotland Yard Police Station where he was unlawfully detained against his will until about 2 o'clock in afternoon of the following day.

3. The said arrest was illegal as hereinafter set out
   PARTICULARS
   (i) The Claimant was arrested for the offence of ....
       The arresting officers did not have any reasonable suspicion of the Claimant having committed that or any other arrestable offence; or
   (ii) The Claimant was arrested for the offence of ....
        That offence carries no power of summary arrest. Even if the arresting officers did have any reasonable suspicion that the Claimant had committed the said offence, none of the general arrest conditions applied to the circumstances of the arrest; or
   (iii) The Claimant was not told the reason for his arrest; and [IF APPROPRIATE] in any event, the arresting officers did not have any reasonable suspicion of the Claimant having committed any offence and/or [IF APPROPRIATE] none of the general arrest conditions applied to the circumstances of the arrest;
   (iv) [IF APPROPRIATE] The Claimant was arrested on premises were he was lawfully entitled to be; but the arresting officers were trespassers.

4. The said arrest was witnessed by John Smith a neighbour of the Claimant.

5. If, which is denied, there was a lawful arrest, the duration of the Plaintiff's imprisonment was unreasonable and lasted too long.

6. Further during his incarceration the Claimant had to undergo the indignity of being questioned and fingerprinted by police officers.

7. [IF APPROPRIATE] During the course of his arrest, the Claimant was assaulted.
PARTICULARS
The Claimant's arms were seized and he was placed in a grip known as 'a half Nelson'. He was then carried in to a police van by 4 officers.

8. The Claimant's detention was a breach of Article 5 of the European Convention, AS HEREINAFTER SET OUT:
PARTICULARS
As hereinbefore set out, the Claimant was deprived of his libery contrary to domestic law.

9. The false imprisonment of the Claimant caused him injury and damage. He suffered humiliation, upset, anger, hurt feeling and embarrassment. The Claimant's suffering was made worse by the fact that he had no idea when he was going to be released and by the fact that a neighbour had seen him taken away in handcuffs. Further the assault caused injury to his arm and caused pain and suffering.
PARTICULARS OF SPECIAL DAMAGE
Cost of new suit £1,000
(During the course of his arrest the Claimant's Savile Row suit was damaged beyond repair.)

10. As the aforementioned torts consisted of arbitrary, oppressive and unconstitutional behaviour by officers of the Crown, the Claimant is entitled to and does seek exemplary damages.

AND THE CLAIMANT CLAIMS DAMAGES.

Statement of Truth etc.

INDEX

References are to paragraph numbers and Appendices.